Bribery and Corruption Casebook

Bribery and Corruption Casebook

THE VIEW FROM UNDER THE TABLE

Edited by

Joseph T. Wells
Laura Hymes

John Wiley & Sons, Inc.

Published by John Wiley & Sons, Inc., Hoboken, New Jersey.
Published simultaneously in Canada.

For general information on our other products and services or for technical support, please contact our Customer Care Department within the United States at (800) 762-2974, outside the United States at (317) 572-3993 or fax (317) 572-4002.

Wiley also publishes its books in a variety of electronic formats. Some content that appears in print may not be available in electronic books. For more information about Wiley products, visit our web site at www.wiley.com.

Library of Congress Cataloging-in-Publication Data:

ISBN 978-1-118-24878-2 (book); 978-1-118-28263-2 (ebk); 978-1-118-28339-4 (ebk); 978-1-118-28710-1 (ebk)

Printed in the United States of America.

10 9 8 7 6 5 4 3 2 1

To Kathleen Hymes, a shining example of honesty in sharp contrast to the corrupt individuals in these pages

Contents

Preface   **xi**

Chapter 1   The Hot-Tub Highwaymen   1
                  Ted Wendling

Chapter 2   Trouble Brewing   13
                  Jay Dawdy and Angela Clancy

Chapter 3   In the State's Interest   23
                  Gary Graff

Chapter 4   Odd Bedfellows   35
                  Jon Cohen

Chapter 5   When Bribery Becomes a Way of Doing Business   43
                  Amine Antari

Chapter 6   Kickbacks for Comic Books   53
                  Rafael A. Garcia

Chapter 7   Interrupted Production   65
                  Carl Knudson

Chapter 8   High-Plains Grifter   75
                  Carolyn Conn, Katie Houston, and Brandon Tanous

Chapter 9   Getting a Free Ride   85
                  William J. Kirby

Chapter 10   Conflicting Interests, Conflicting Cultures   95
Douglas M. Watson

Chapter 11   But We Thought He Was *Saving* Us Millions   107
Gary E. Gaugler

Chapter 12   The Construction of a Fraud   115
Lorna Leung

Chapter 13   The Summer Bribe   123
Mark Dron

Chapter 14   Brazen Bank Manager   133
Antonio Ivan S. Aguirre

Chapter 15   In Bed with the Tax Man   141
Hanif Habib

Chapter 16   High-Rise Rollers   149
Richard F. Woodford, Jr.

Chapter 17   Decorum Across the International Date Line   159
Jim Pelczar

Chapter 18   The Kickback Mine   169
J. Aaron Christopher

Chapter 19   A Sweet Deal   177
Jason Petrusic

Chapter 20   Da' Money   187
Michael Carr

Chapter 21   The Seemingly Upstanding Citizen   199
Austine S. M. Adache

Chapter 22   Big Dangers from a Small Vendor   209
Kimiharu Chatani

Chapter 23 A Drop in the Ocean 217
Ludmila Grechanik

Chapter 24 The Professor and the Deputy 225
Paul Keyton

Chapter 25 Calling for Kickbacks 235
Anil Kumar

Chapter 26 Going Green in Mexico 245
Ronald L. Durkin

Chapter 27 A Wolf in Sheep's Clothing 253
Daniel Nita

Chapter 28 Dances with Fraud 261
Hank J. Brightman

Chapter 29 The Corrupt Public Servant 271
Sandeep Mehra

Chapter 30 Romance, Jewels and Kickbacks:
All in a Day's Work 279
Dennis Thomas

Chapter 31 Power Corrupts and Absolute Power Corrupts
Absolutely 287
Jim Cali

Chapter 32 For Love or Money? 299
John R. Holley

Chapter 33 Ethical Governance: A Mandate for
Outsourcing 309
Jyoti Khetarpal

Chapter 34 Friends and Lovers in High Places 319
Rick Hoye

Chapter 35 Kickbacks on Demand 329
Philip Levi

Chapter 36   High-Flying Ambition   341
                   Manjit Chodha

Chapter 37   The Cleaner Who Swept His Way to the Top   347
                   Shane Ringin

Chapter 38   Sorry, This Fraud Has Been Disconnected   357
                   Meric Bloch

Chapter 39   Bid Rigging and Kickbacks under the Bridge   369
                   Edward J. Gaio

Index   **377**

Preface

Corruption is not a new development for humankind. As long as there have been recorded accounts of human history, there have been stories of deceptive self-dealing and betrayal for personal gain. We need to look no further than the Roman Empire for countless examples of corruption, bribery, political dishonesty and discarded alliances. The civilization that helped establish a blueprint for modern democratic governments also created a model for just about every corruption scheme imaginable.

Take the account of Emperor Nero's rise to power as an example. He gained the title of emperor amid rumors that his mother, Agrippina, poisoned her own husband and Nero's stepfather, then-emperor Claudius, so her son could ascend to the throne. Nero was still a teenager at the time, and Agrippina believed she would be able to direct the course of the empire by manipulating her son. However, when Nero began asserting his own power and eschewing his mother's influence, Agrippina turned her hopes to her stepson Britannicus. As the birth son of Claudius (although he was younger than Nero), Britannicus could challenge Nero for the throne — a threat the emperor took seriously.

As the story goes, Nero first poisoned the 15-year-old Britannicus to assert himself as Rome's rightful leader and then arranged for his mother to be killed. After these shocking crimes, he embarked on a spree of executions to eliminate senate members he did not trust and anyone else he considered a political threat. And there we have the framework for a leader to corruptly consolidate and establish his power.

Modern corruption has become slightly more subtle and, luckily, we see fewer outright assassinations these days, but that comfort does nothing to reduce the damage that this fraud still causes. *Black's Law Dictionary* defines *corruption* as "depravity, perversion, or taint; an impairment of integrity, virtue, or moral principle; esp., the impairment of a public official's duties by bribery." Corruption can include conflicts of interest, bribery, economic extortion and illegal gratuities. It is everywhere — an insidious, communicative disease that plagues private industry, public service and the political process. It destroys trust, bottom lines, careers and even lives. As the cases in this collection demonstrate, no one is immune to corruption. Try as we might to implement controls and procedures to prevent ourselves and our employers or businesses from becoming victims, cunning criminals make it their goal to circumvent our hurdles in pursuit of their own self-interest.

Most people have heard of Rod Blagojevich. You might think of President Barack Obama when you hear his name, or you might simply picture that trademark Blago hair. Either way, in the past few years he has become a poster boy for corruption. In 2008, when then-Senator Obama was elected to the presidency, he left a vacant U.S. Senate seat up for grabs in Illinois. As governor of Illinois, Rod Blagojevich had the authority to appoint someone to fill the vacant senate seat, but he abused his gubernatorial power and solicited bribes and other favors from parties who had an interest in the seat. As part of the investigation into Blagojevich's suspected corruption, the FBI wiretapped his phone. Perhaps the most infamous sound bite to come from those recordings was the one where he described his position as "f___ing golden" and said he wouldn't give the appointment away "for f___ing nothing." The recorded evidence turned out to be the most damning against Blagojevich, and he was eventually found guilty of 17 out of 20 criminal charges, including bribery and attempted extortion. He was sentenced to 14 years in prison.

Corruption is not confined to the political circus. Public and private companies often suffer losses, both financial and reputational, from the corrupt actions of owners, executives and staff members. The primary anti-corruption legislation in the United States is the Foreign Corrupt Practices Act (FCPA), a law that Congress enacted in 1977. The FCPA makes it illegal for U.S. companies or individuals acting anywhere in the world to directly or indirectly offer or pay anything of value to foreign officials to obtain or retain business. In addition to U.S. citizens and enterprises, the FCPA also applies to foreign companies that have securities registered in the United States or file reports with the Securities and Exchange Commission, and to foreign individuals and companies that take any action to promote a corrupt payment while in the United States.

Remember the Siemens bribery scandal in 2008? The German engineering firm was undergoing scrutiny in the United States and Europe based on claims that staff and managers paid bribes to foreign officials in various countries to secure lucrative contracts. The amounts were staggering; for example, according to a *Frontline* article called "At Siemens, Bribery Was Just a Line Item," one single accounting employee at Siemens claimed to oversee an annual "bribery budget" of $40 to $50 million. That is just one staff member at a company that employed thousands. The company faced FCPA charges in the United States and eventually reached a settlement agreement that included paying $800 million in fines. At the same time Siemens settled another case, this one in Europe, for hundreds of millions of dollars as well. In total, Siemens paid $1.6 billion to settle corruption charges around the world.

In 2010, news emerged of another multimillion-dollar international corruption scheme. Six oil and gas companies (Transocean Inc., Tidewater Marine International Inc., Pride International Inc., Noble Corporation, Shell Nigeria Exploration and Production and Global Santa Fe Corporation) and one shipping company (Panalpina) were accused of bribing officials in various countries for the ability to import equipment into the countries without paying the necessary taxes and fees. This case was also settled and the companies collectively agreed to pay $236 million in fines.

According to the ACFE's 2010 *Report to the Nations on Occupational Fraud and Abuse*, corruption cases accounted for 32.8 percent fraud cases during the reporting period, and the median loss per case was $250,000. To prevent and detect corruption schemes, it helps to be aware of the common red flags associated with such frauds. In 45.6 percent of corruption cases in the *Report to the Nations*, the perpetrators displayed unusually close ties with a vendor or customer. The second most common behavioral red flag was living beyond their means, as seen in 42 percent of cases. Clearly, corruption is a costly fraud, and knowing what warning signs to watch for might help business owners prevent future cases.

In this book, you will read corruption cases from around the globe, large and small, punished and unpunished. We have changed the names of people, places and companies to maintain the anonymity of those involved, but the facts of the cases are genuine. These are real corruption cases, investigated by members of the ACFE. All profits from this book will be donated to the ACFE Scholarship Foundation in the hope that future fraud fighters will receive the education they need to carry the torch into the next generation.

Publishing a book is a collaborative effort, and this one was no exception. The members of the ACFE who submitted case studies to this project deserve the lion's share of recognition for all their hard work. It was a pleasure collaborating with these professionals who are out in trenches every day. Without their efforts, this book would not be in your hands right now. In addition, we would like to thank ACFE editors Laura Telford and Diane Calmes for providing invaluable editing assistance. Stacey Rivera and Natasha Andrews-Noel at John Wiley & Sons are consummate professionals and made the sometimes-tumultuous publishing process run seamlessly.

Bribery and corruption are among the oldest and most primitive fraud schemes that humans commit. People have been acting corruptly for centuries, and they don't appear to be slowing down. "It's just the cost of doing business in foreign countries." This weak excuse is commonly offered by corporate officers facing charges of violating the FPCA. However, committing fraud should never be a cost of doing business. The greater awareness we, as a community, can bring to this issue, the greater our power will be to combat it. Whether you are a practitioner, educator or simply a concerned citizen, we hope this book will motivate you to continue the fight.

Dr. Joseph T. Wells, CFE, CPA
Laura Hymes, CFE
Austin, Texas
April 2012

The Hot-Tub Highwaymen

TED WENDLING

As companions, William Lassiter and Larry Evans appeared to be an unlikely pair. An urbane, college-educated entrepreneur, Lassiter had carved out a lucrative niche in the domestic snow-removal market by patenting a durable, carbide snowplow blade guard that extended the blade's cutting edge, thereby increasing its life span. In contrast, Evans was a high-school dropout, a crude, overweight, uncultured laborer who liked to hunt and fish. Evans' grooming habits included a weekly toilette that he conducted in the privacy of his dingy office at the Ohio Department of Transportation (ODOT) in which he would cut his fingernails and toenails, leaving the yellowed clippings strewn under his desk.

Dissimilar as Lassiter and Evans were, fortune had cast them into an economic symbiosis that made them fast friends: Evans, the equipment superintendent at ODOT's Cleveland district office, awarded millions of dollars in business to the Lassiter Blade Company. In turn, Lassiter treated Evans to all-expenses-paid trips to Las Vegas and spent thousands of dollars on fishing excursions aboard "Captain Larry's" private Lake Erie charter fishing boat, the *Walleye Warrior*.

As the men bobbed together in Lassiter's hot tub on a warm summer night, surrounded by other ODOT vendors and dancers from Lips & Sips, a Cleveland strip club, they toasted to their mutual success. Lassiter's summertime soirees, dubbed "Fat Man Soup" parties by some of the dancers, were blue-collar bacchanalias that included other people who were feeding off of ODOT's largesse: Craig Horford, a germaphobic information technology whiz whose climate-control company had a lock on all of the ODOT district office's HVAC work; Dennis Pfister, the ODOT facilities manager who managed Horford's contract and worked down the hall from Evans; and Jennifer Moore, a young Lips & Sips dancer who had clawed her way into Pfister's wallet by duping him into believing that he had sired her four-year-old daughter. As Pfister often boasted to his ODOT colleagues, not bad for a 63-year-old.

Missing on this evening was Fred Waxman, another ODOT vendor who had helped furnish an apartment for Moore and had picked up bar tabs for Pfister all over northeast Ohio in exchange for hundreds of thousands of dollars in unbid ODOT garage-door contracts. Waxman had been invited but had been unable to attend. Also missing was Evans' top purchasing official, Rick Rogers, who was working his own side deals with the Lassiter Blade Company and some of Evans' other vendors.

"Where's Dennis?" Lassiter asked Evans.

"I think he's in the house with Ruby," Evans responded. Lassiter, a divorced father who had left his wife for a stripper and now shared custody of their two daughters, had learned long ago that Evans and Pfister were a matched pair. But as fond as he was of Evans, he considered Pfister to be untrustworthy and a lecherous boor. Lassiter stalked into the house, quickly found the missing couple and escorted them outside. Sliding back into the hot tub, Lassiter hissed into Evans' ear: "They were in my daughter's bedroom!"

Building an Empire

District 12 of the ODOT is headquartered in the Cleveland suburb of Garfield Heights. One of 12 ODOT district offices that operated as virtual fiefdoms, it spanned three counties, employed nearly 500 people and had an annual budget of $50 million.

Two of the district's largest divisions are Facilities and Equipment. They were headed, respectively, by Dennis Pfister and Larry Evans. Together, the men oversaw an empire that included the maintenance and repair of all buildings and structures as well as the purchase and maintenance of all trucks, snowplows, garage equipment and supplies, ranging from chain saws and weed-eaters to light bulbs and bug spray.

Pfister, Evans and their subordinates worked in a warren of offices down the hill from the district headquarters, where the white-collar bureaucrats were ensconced. The men's mandate was simple: plow the roads in the winter and cut the grass and remove the roadkill from the highways in the summer. If you could accomplish that agenda, you could have the distinction of winning a rare public-sector award for organizational excellence from the Ohio Partnership for Excellence, which ODOT District 12 did, twice. But unfortunately for the taxpayers, you could also have carte blanche to commandeer ODOT's entire purchasing and procurement apparatus for personal gain.

Thus it was that vendors who wanted maintenance contracts from ODOT were told by Pfister to pony up: out-of-state hunting trips, vacation junkets, bar tabs and cash — lots of it. Down the hall, vendors who sought ODOT equipment contracts were told by Evans that Lake Erie walleye and perch charter bookings aboard the *Walleye Warrior* — at $300 to $500 a day and up to $1,000 a day for "executive charters" that included strippers — were going fast.

Pfister's and Evans' various business enterprises were aided by the fact that ODOT empowered the two men with direct-purchasing authority, which allowed them to choose the companies from which they sought competitive bids. ODOT's regulations regarding obtaining items that were not on contract were simple: purchases up to $1,000 required one quote, purchases up to $2,500 required two quotes, and purchases above $2,500 required three. ODOT also treated subsidiary companies as unrelated enterprises as long as they had unique tax identification numbers. Thus, three companies could share the same business address and the same corporate officers and still bid against one another as long as they had separate tax ID numbers.

This unusual practice gave Pfister and Evans wiggle room when dealing with the State Controlling Board's mandate that Ohio agencies could spend no more than $50,000 per vendor per fiscal year for supplies and services that were not covered by existing contracts. The purpose of the $50,000 cap was to enable as many small businesses as possible to compete for State of Ohio business. Under ODOT's tax ID policy, circumventing the cap was easy: as soon as Company A hit the $50,000 ceiling, subsidiary Company B would take over. For purposes of meeting the three-quote regulation, ODOT even accepted throw-away quotes from ineligible companies that had already reached the $50,000 cap.

As part of its fiscal oversight of its 12 districts, ODOT headquarters seemingly went to great lengths to track the vast quantity of supplies and equipment that the districts purchased by requiring that all purchases be entered into one of two computerized inventory-tracking systems. There was only one problem: ODOT had no method of ensuring that the products it was buying were actually entered into the two systems.

Swimming Trips

I was a newly hired deputy inspector general (IG) in the Ohio Inspector General's Office in Columbus when my boss, Inspector General Tom Charles, forwarded me a two-sentence, typewritten allegation that had arrived in the mail: "Check into ODOT Boat Days. Fred Waxman has been taking Dennis Pfistler [*sic*] and other ODOT vendors fishing on Lake Erie." The note was unsigned.

Waxman owned Erie Overhead Doors, a state vendor. Pfister was his ODOT contract manager. If true, the trips constituted a potential misdemeanor ethics violation. After reviewing Waxman's contract with ODOT and examining numerous invoices from Erie Overhead Doors, I asked ODOT's accounting administrator to have one of her auditors review the previous year's purchases from Waxman's company. The audit identified $84,000 in questioned costs, including inflated labor rates that Pfister had approved.

Using the IG's administrative subpoena authority, I summoned Waxman to Columbus for an interview. Based on several earlier phone conversations, I was unsurprised when he denied virtually every allegation. Sure, he said, he had sold garage doors, at fair-market value, to Pfister and a couple of other ODOT employees. But he had not overcharged ODOT a nickel, and he had never taken Pfister fishing. Instead, Waxman claimed, he, Pfister and some other men had taken Waxman's 36-foot Tiara yacht out on Lake Erie and had gone swimming.

"You're lying, Fred," I told him. "Grown men don't go swimming together in Lake Erie."

"Ted, I swear, I'm telling the truth," he insisted. "There wasn't a rod on that boat."

In the following weeks, I continued to hound Waxman, telling him that I was writing my report and that it would include a criminal referral to a county prosecutor. One day, he phoned me, clearly frantic. "I'm a wreck," he said. "I've lost weight and my wife doesn't understand what's wrong with me. I want to cooperate, but I want amnesty." I told him I would talk to my boss and the prosecutor but couldn't promise him anything.

"Okay," he said, "tell them this: I was paying Pfister. You can also tell them that I was telling you the truth. They *were* swimming trips, but there were strippers on the boat."

Waxman's admissions made it clear that what was going on at ODOT District 12 involved more than mere ethics violations. In addition to Pfister and the strippers, other participants in Waxman's "ODOT Boat Days" excursions were Evans, the ODOT equipment superintendent, and several other vendors over whom either Pfister or Evans had contract authority. It appeared that the investigation would require more resources. Given the fact that the matter now involved criminal allegations of bribery and contract steering, the IG also requested the assistance of the Ohio State Highway Patrol, which has jurisdiction over crimes that occur on state property. Unlike the deputies in the Inspector General's Office, Highway Patrol investigators also have arrest powers and the ability to conduct search warrants.

In the following months, our office issued dozens of administrative subpoenas to ODOT vendors, banking institutions and other businesses, focusing on the vendors that had done the most business with Pfister's and Evans' divisions during the previous decade. As we pored through the boxes of records generated by the subpoenas, an interlocking web of schemes began to take shape, including what appeared to be the centerpiece of the conspiracy: almost all of Evans' *Walleye Warrior* customers were ODOT vendors over whom either he or Pfister had contract authority. Illustrating Evans' complete disregard to the impropriety of this mutual back-scratching arrangement was an entry on one of his calendars, noting that he was scheduled to attend mandatory state ethics training on a Wednesday morning. Later that day, along with five other days that week, Evans had booked fishing trips with ODOT vendors on the *Walleye Warrior*.

The searches also generated more evidence of improper gratuities and relationships: "kill-it-and-grill-it" hunting trips to game ranches in Texas to shoot wild boar and blackbuck, an exotic species of antelope imported from India, followed by cross-border visits to a Mexican brothel; a trip to Seward, Alaska, to participate in a salmon fishing tournament; hotel accommodations and meals in Las Vegas; bar tabs at Lips & Sips and other strip clubs throughout northeast Ohio; and golf outings at a private country club that featured strippers in various stages of undress frolicking with drunken ODOT vendors on the front nine.

The subpoenas were followed by the execution of search warrants by the Highway Patrol and our office at Pfister's and Evans' homes, as well as the homes or businesses of six ODOT vendors. Evidence seized during those searches included numerous computers and hard drives, hundreds of floppy discs and CDs and tens of thousands of pages of paper records. As teams of investigators fanned out at the spacious offices of the Lassiter Blade Company, Lassiter gathered his employees in a conference room to express his outrage and demand an apology. "Larry Evans is a dear friend of mine," he thundered. "He is a great hunter; I love to hunt. He is a great fisherman; I love to fish. I have done nothing wrong." Among the investigators, Lassiter would come to be known as "the strippers and hams guy" due to his infatuation with strippers and his habit of sending $50 gift certificates for HoneyBaked Hams to his ODOT contract managers at Christmas.

At Evans' home, investigators found thousands of dollars' worth of stolen ODOT tools and equipment, ranging from chain saws, to Weed Eaters, to welders. The search of Pfister's home also turned up stolen ODOT equipment as well as a Ruger semiautomatic pistol with an illegal, handmade silencer.

Stored in the attic of Pfister's garage was the blueprint to his scheming — a banker's box filled with color-coded envelopes containing doctored ODOT quotes. The box was a virtual encyclopedia of fraud that included fictitious company letterheads, forged signatures of real and fictitious vendors and cut-and-paste competitive quotes that Pfister had meticulously altered by applying tiny dots of ink to the overlaid quotes to match the paper stock.

More Tips, Lips & Sips

Weeks of time-consuming work followed as my colleagues and I sifted through thousands of phony quotes and the huge trove of evidence seized during the searches. Providing me with what I call my Ahab moment (and fueling my obsessive hunt for Pfister) during these periods of drudgery were the words that Pfister had uttered to a cooperating bartender whom the Highway Patrol had secretly wired. Speaking into a microphone that had been inserted between the bartender's surgically enhanced breasts, Pfister counseled her to lie under oath, telling her that the Inspector General's Office was all bark and no bite. "All they can do is write a report," he told her. I taped those words to my office door.

As investigators zeroed in on several bid-rigging schemes that were being carried out by Pfister and Evans, an anonymous call came in about Rick Rogers, Evans' top purchasing guy. "Check out RIP Cleanout Specialists, Rick's private company," the caller said.

RIP was a home-foreclosure business. A check of ODOT records showed that the company had done more than $43,000 in work directly for ODOT and that Rogers had brazenly used his home address to invoice ODOT. On top of that, he had been billing ODOT for work that his company had not performed.

During an interview of Rogers, one of my incredulous colleagues asked him how he justified using RIP to buy cell-phone cases at a big-box discount store and then reselling them to ODOT at a 150 percent markup. "I run a small business," Rogers answered without a trace of sarcasm. "I'm in business to make money."

As the investigation demonstrated, he made plenty of it — lodgings at the Marriott for his wedding anniversary; contributions to a men's hockey league that he managed; donations to his daughter's gymnastics meet; and more than $25,000 in gifts and gratuities for rigging bids on the sale of $1.4 million in trucks and truck parts, including a membership to a private golf club. Among the phony truck-parts quotes that sailed past ODOT auditors were 20 quotes in which Rogers had transposed two letters in the company president's last name.

"I don't know how that happened," he said.

Court Date

Eighteen months after the anonymous letter about Waxman and Pfister first landed on my desk, Deputy IGs Jim Canepa, Don Petit and I forwarded a nearly 500-count criminal referral to Paul Soucie, head of the Economic Crime Unit at the Cuyahoga County Prosecutor's Office in Cleveland. The referral documented nearly $11 million in improper or questionable payments that had been made to ODOT vendors as a result of bid rigging or fraud or of the improper relationships that existed among vendors and ODOT purchasers. Our investigation also documented nearly $400,000 in gratuities and other improper payments that had been made to Pfister, Evans and Rogers by dozens of ODOT vendors. The payments included $227,000 that ODOT vendors had put into Evans' pocket by chartering fishing trips with the *Walleye Warrior*.

Including exhibits and nearly 150 witness statements, our criminal referral filled 10 banker's boxes. Soucie also asked us to design a pyramid chart that ranked our targets based on the level of their criminality. The pyramid included the names of 33 ODOT employees and vendors. Pfister topped the chart.

The prosecutor then scheduled 30-minute "groveling sessions" with the targets' attorneys. The format for these sessions was the same: I would present a brief case synopsis and Soucie would follow by giving the attorney a glimpse of an eye-popping electronic adaptation of the referral. This was designed by a Highway Patrol colleague, and it hyperlinked every exhibit and witness statement to each defendant. Soucie would then end the session by presenting the state's offer. The attorneys could take it or leave it and roll the dice at trial.

Pfister's attorney, puffed up with feigned indignation and a five-figure retainer, was the last in the door.

"Congratulations," Soucie told him as the lawyer took a seat. "Your guy won the lottery. He's the worst of the worst."

Tactically, the prosecutor elected to first handle the cases of nine middle-tier defendants who had fully cooperated and had agreed to plead guilty to low-level felony charges. Under normal circumstances, the defendants, who included three ODOT officials and six vendors, likely faced fines, restitution and probation. However, by the bad luck of the draw, the nine defendants drew Judge Kathleen Sutula, an imperious jurist who had earned a reputation as the toughest of the 34 judges on the Cuyahoga County bench. Again and again, the judge harangued the ODOT employees and vendors for consorting with strippers and contributing to the "culture of corruption" that permeated state and local government in northeast Ohio.

"Let me guess: I'll bet when you were out on the boat with the strippers, you told your wife that you didn't even want to go but that it was business, right?" she mocked one of the defendants.

"Yes, your honor. That's correct," the defendant answered sheepishly.

"I feel sorry for your wife," the judge retorted.

With the exception of one vendor who had endured a double lung transplant and consequently was homebound and tethered to a respirator, the judge sentenced all of the defendants to six months in prison. Most of them, protesting that they were deeply sorry and that the sentence was unduly harsh, were frog-marched out of the courtroom in handcuffs. Nor was I spared her honor's wrath. As I nervously recounted the state's case against one of the defendants, the judge's officious bailiff sidled up behind me, pulled my hands out of my pockets and ordered me to stand up straight at the lectern. For a moment, I considered the possibility that I might be headed for a stint in the Big House too.

As the first defendants — one by one — agreed to pleas and signaled their intent to cooperate with the state, my colleagues and I began to hear that Pfister was coming unglued. On the day that a 71-year-old vendor named James Wright was seated outside Judge Sutula's courtroom, preparing to plead guilty to charges that he had paid Pfister more than $34,000 in cash bribes that he had handed to Pfister on the ODOT loading dock, Wright's cell phone lit up with a call from an unknown number.

"If you value your health and your family, you'll take the Fifth," the caller said, referring to the Fifth Amendment right that protects citizens from self-incrimination.

Wright was stunned. The voice at the other end was unmistakably Pfister's. A few weeks earlier, a mysterious fire in Wright's garage had sent him and his wife fleeing to a nearby motel. In turn, a contractor who had been hired to renovate the garage had noticed that a silver Chrysler Town and Country minivan had been circling the block. He copied down the license plate number. It came back to Pfister.

My Highway Patrol colleagues traced the phone number from the call received by Wright to a gas station located about five miles from Pfister's home. On the other side of the street sat Lips & Sips. A review of the station's surveillance cameras confirmed that Pfister had made the call. The video clearly showed Pfister walking up to a cashier, handing her a dollar bill and receiving four quarters in change. The cameras then followed Pfister back to his silver van, where he drove up to an outdoor pay phone and made the fateful call to Wright at 8:57 a.m. — the exact moment that Wright's phone lit up in the courthouse.

Going Back for Seconds

Armed with this evidence, the prosecutor obtained a warrant to conduct a second search of Pfister's home. This one, however, would be different. At Soucie's request, the judge had signed a no-knock warrant, giving officers the authority to forcibly enter Pfister's residence.

At dusk on a warm fall evening, ten members of the Highway Patrol's Special Response Team, traveling in an armored vehicle dubbed "The Bear," rumbled through Pfister's neighborhood in the bucolic suburb of Chagrin Falls. They were followed by an entourage of troopers and one deputy inspector general — me. As the Bear stopped in front of Pfister's home, the ten SRT members rushed the front door. One jolt with a battering ram tore the door from its hinges. Within seconds, Pfister, who was watching TV with his wife, was in handcuffs and under arrest for witness intimidation.

Pfister's dumbfounded neighbors watched the spectacle from their porches as my colleagues and I entered the house to search for evidence. Hanging on a coat hook near the kitchen was the jacket that Pfister had been wearing when he made the call from the pay phone. On the floorboard of the minivan, I found the hunting cap he wore that morning.

The second wave of indictments charged Pfister, Evans and Rogers, along with five vendors, with participating in an elaborate bid-rigging and kickback scheme that spanned more than a decade and cost the state millions of dollars. Pfister was indicted on 26 counts, including racketeering, bribery, theft in office, tampering with records and obstruction of justice. A second indictment charged Pfister with two additional counts of witness intimidation.

In all, 18 people were convicted, including six ODOT officials and 12 vendors. Of that group, 13 went to prison for sentences ranging from six months to seven years — Pfister's term of incarceration. The defendants also were ordered to pay a total of more than $600,000 in restitution to ODOT.

Fittingly, Pfister was sent to prison on my last day at the Inspector General's Office. I began my new job as chief of investigations at the Ohio Bureau of Motor Vehicles two weeks later.

Lessons Learned

Over the nearly three-year period that this case took to investigate and prosecute, my colleagues and I learned a great deal about how a byzantine network of laws and purchasing regulations can be circumvented by employees who are intent on stealing from the public.

In particular, I learned how to recognize some of the telltale signs of bid tampering: altered company letterheads and signatures, fictitious company names and principals, and fax headers showing that three ostensibly "competitive" quotes had been transmitted in sequence from the same fax machine. Unfortunately, although many of the quotes submitted to ODOT were clearly phony, the fraud was not discovered by ODOT auditors who were preoccupied with simply ensuring that the requisite number of quotes had been obtained.

Many state agencies in Ohio have regulations pertaining to secondary employment, requiring employees to request permission to operate private companies or work in the private sector. These policies ensure that state employees' private business interests do not conflict with their public duties. ODOT, however, had no such requirement, which allowed Rogers and other employees to operate companies with impunity that enriched themselves at the taxpayers' expense. The employees contended, falsely, that they were actually saving the taxpayers money. That is almost never true, and our investigation proved that it certainly wasn't in this case.

By closely examining bidding patterns and noticing that Pfister, Evans and other ODOT purchasers often obtained competitive quotes from the same firms, we also identified a practice in which the winning bidder would subcontract a portion of the work to one or both of the losing bidders.

This was another method of circumventing the controlling board's $50,000 cap, one that had been perfected by the Lassiter Blade Company and other ODOT vendors. It worked like this: after reaching the $50,000 ceiling on non-contract purchases, William Lassiter would contact two business colleagues

(continued)

(continued)

and induce them to submit quotes to ODOT. When one of Lassiter's colleagues won the bid, Lassiter would receive a subcontract from the winning bidder in exchange for a nominal finder's fee. After receiving payment from ODOT, the winning bidder would forward the majority of the money to Lassiter, keeping only the finder's fee.

Invariably, Lassiter and the other vendors also argued that they were only trying to save the taxpayers money. That proved to be patently untrue, particularly when you consider that Lassiter and the other vendors who utilized this method of bid fraud were factoring the kickback they paid to the winning bidder into the price for the job.

Recommendations to Prevent Future Occurrences

As a result of this investigation, the director of ODOT ordered more than 1,200 purchasing employees and their supervisors to undergo retraining on the ethical principles of purchasing, contract administration and the use of agency credit cards. These seminars, which occurred over a period of several months and included a representative from the Inspector General's Office, addressed numerous weaknesses that our office identified in ODOT's purchasing regulations.

Segregation of Duties

For years, ODOT had given Pfister, Evans and other ODOT purchasers unilateral authority to initiate and approve requisitions, order products and sign documents attesting that the items had been received. By allowing the same employee to authorize a purchase and also verify delivery, ODOT left itself vulnerable to employee theft of tools, equipment and supplies. After Evans, Pfister and Rogers were sent to prison, ODOT managers conducted an inventory check and discovered marine filters, motor oil suitable for boat motors and 55-gallon drums of heavy duty boat-cleaning solvent sitting on the warehouse's shelves. Needless to say, ODOT's fleet does not include a single boat. Evans had bought the products with a department credit card for the *Walleye Warrior*.

Credit Card Policies

ODOT issued credit cards to most of its purchasers to enable employees to make necessary emergency purchases of up to $1,000. However, ODOT's policy did not require the card holder to be solely responsible for the card's use, permitting supervisors to authorize purchases on their subordinates' credit cards. This practice allowed Rick Rogers to charge thousands of dollars for work that was not completed on his employees' credit cards. We recommended that such purchases be prohibited unless the supervisor's request has been documented by the card holder, including the supervisor's name and location of the delivery.

Require Signed Quotes

Although confessions and handwriting analyses confirmed that signatures had been forged on numerous quotes, the practice of allowing vendors to submit unsigned quotes made it easier to commit fraud. Again and again, we found that Pfister had typed up a phony losing quote on authentic blank company letterhead and included it in his bid package, allowing him to steer the purchase to a favored vendor. The "losing" vendors never knew the difference.

Prohibit Quotes from Related Parties

As explained earlier, ODOT policies permitted related companies to submit competitive quotes against one another as long as the firms had unique tax identification numbers. This policy spawned a practice in which ODOT purchasers would call an official at one company and ask for three "competitive" quotes — one from the official's company and two from subsidiary firms. Over and over, we noticed that the fax headers on these quotes showed that they had been sent from the same fax machine on the same day and at the same time. This practice became so ingrained at ODOT that it was even utilized by ODOT purchasers who had no criminal intent but were simply lazy. After all, calling three people and getting three quotes is a lot more work than calling one person and getting three quotes.

Policy changes and ethics seminars alone will never deter employees and vendors who are committed to gaming the system. But creating an environment in which ethical principles and ethical behavior are emphasized, as well as closing glaring loopholes in the purchasing procedures of large and complex state agencies, can go a long way toward deterring the rampant corruption that permeated ODOT District 12 for more than a decade.

About the Author

Ted Wendling is chief of investigations at the Ohio Bureau of Motor Vehicles in Columbus. Prior to working as a deputy inspector general in the Ohio Inspector General's Office, he had a 28-year career as an investigative reporter and editor at the *Cleveland Plain Dealer* and the *Columbus Dispatch.*

2

Trouble Brewing

JAY DAWDY AND ANGELA CLANCY

For the past few years, Billy Hays, the president of Brew Corp., a regional coffee roaster, had noticed a decrease in profit margins that was troubling. The company's revenues were consistently up, but margins kept shrinking. Hays knew that smaller profits meant less money in his pocket, and he didn't like that. He wanted answers quickly. He pressed his longtime and trusted CFO, Sandy Dawson, to check it out. Then she had her best accountant, Luke Smith, analyze the problem.

Smith and Dawson met with Hays and gave him the news. Smith provided a very plausible explanation for the shrinking margins. It was simple; there had been a steady increase over the past several years in both repair costs and information technology (IT) expenses. Smith and Dawson explained to Hays that these increases were due to Brew Corp.'s outdated coffee-processing equipment and recent attempts to upgrade their old technology; they hadn't invested in new plant equipment in many years. Also, their computer systems were dated and required more IT support than ever before.

Hays was embarrassed when he heard these explanations because he knew that Brew Corp.'s equipment was outdated. He had denied several requests to buy new plant and computer equipment in recent years. So, it seemed that Hays was the one causing the problem. He simply didn't want to bite the bullet and spend the money to upgrade. He was nearing retirement, so the last thing he wanted to spend money on was new tools that he didn't understand anyway. Instead, Hays wanted to squeeze as much money out of the company as he could before he retired.

The explanation Hays received from Dawson and Smith seemed plausible, but Hays was paranoid. He couldn't believe they had to spend that much on parts and repairs or that IT expenses had gone up so significantly. He also wondered whether Dawson really knew what was going on inside the financials of the company. He kept asking himself, "Did she work with Luke

Smith and really drill down and get to the bottom of this problem?" He had his doubts. In recent years, Dawson had become increasingly hands off and unconcerned with details. She simply wasn't working as hard as she used to. But Hays kept telling himself that Luke Smith had performed the analysis, so it was probably spot on. Smith was simply the best accountant Hays had ever met. Any time Brew Corp. had a tough financial problem or when Hays had questioned Smith in the past, Smith had always come up with the right answer. Hays thought to himself, "Smith is good. Damn good. Maybe he is too good?"

People at Brew Corp. referred to Luke Smith by his nickname, Cool, which was short for Cool Hand Luke, inspired by the movie character played by Paul Newman. Smith was cool under pressure, smart as a whip and had done some great analysis for Hays in the past. But that little voice inside Hays' head just wouldn't shut up. So he asked lots of questions and tried to understand their explanations and challenge their analysis. He also looked for any hints that they were lying. After that meeting, he thought they were a little nervous, but seemed pretty certain of what was going on and provided the right answers. But Hays still thought he was missing something.

A Little Paranoia Isn't Such a Bad Thing

Brew Corp. had been defrauded before. It never ceased to amaze Hays how crooked some of his employees were. Over the years, he'd witnessed plant employees steal coffee beans, delivery drivers pocket cash payments and others steal computers. One employee even tried to steal a 16-wheeler delivery truck.

As a result, Hays had taken significant steps to control fraud. This made him a darn good client for my firm, Gryphon Strategies. Hays believed in the investigative process. He liked catching the bad guys and making an example out of them. After some incidents of theft a few years ago, Hays invested in a state-of-the-art surveillance system that we installed. There were cameras everywhere — in the plant, in the executive offices and on the delivery trucks themselves. They could be accessed and viewed over the Internet; my firm did periodic security monitoring of the video feeds as part of an ongoing retainer relationship we had with Brew Corp. Cameras were activated by sensors, and certain cameras were set up so that if motion was detected during suspicious times, an e-mail would be triggered and we could investigate possible incidents. The cameras worked well and had acted as a great preventive control for thefts in the plant facility over the years. They were also a great investigative tool — as they demonstrated in this case.

Sunday at 1:00 a.m., shortly after Hays had been stewing over the decreasing margins at Brew Corp., the cameras were activated in the corporate offices and we received an e-mail alert. This had happened before when office workers had gone in late to catch up on work, but never at 1:00 a.m.

on a Sunday. We watched the video and checked the key code access system to see who was there and what they were doing in the office at that hour. It was clear from the tape and access code that Cool Hand Luke had come into the office and stayed for two hours, leaving at 3:00 a.m. We called Hays on Monday morning to discuss the incident.

Hays was very surprised, indicating that Cool never worked on the weekends. Hays said, "Cool is so damned smart, he gets his work done by noon each day! What the heck was he doing here on Sunday at 1:00 a.m.?!" Hays also found the timing interesting because he'd "just chewed out Cool on Friday over some profitability stuff." Hays asked us to determine whether Cool was up to no good. He explained that Brew Corp.'s repair and IT expenses were up significantly, profitability was down and he wasn't very satisfied with Cool or Sandy Dawson's explanations the Friday before. "They gave me all the right answers, but it just doesn't sit well with me. Look into Dawson too while you're at it," Hays said before he hung up the phone.

Investigating Accountants and Beyond

Since we would be investigating the company's accountants and examining the books and records, I knew I'd need help from a forensic accountant who could also perform data analysis. I called Angela Clancy from RGL Forensics. After hearing a little about the case, Angela said she had some great technology that she'd used previously and she couldn't wait to get started.

Among the first things we did was download Brew Corp.'s general ledger to examine Cool and Dawson's accounting entries, look for abnormal activity and perform other data analysis. We also immediately obtained a mirror image of their computer hard drives, including all of their e-mails, and exported those into a program that would help us visually chart them, examine e-mail trends and look for improper activity.

Cool logged into the accounting system shortly after arriving in the office at 1:00 a.m. We identified a number of entries that he made, mostly related to the approval and payment to suppliers. However, there were two invoices processed for a company named Exile Industries that supplied manufacturing parts for repairs. I remembered Hays mentioning that Brew Corp.'s repair costs seemed "out of whack" to him, so we made a note of these entries for additional analysis. Also, since Exile was the only parts supplier Cool accessed that night, I said to Angela, "Let's keep an eye out for anything else involving these guys." I also mentioned that we might want to perform a background investigation on Exile and some of the other vendors.

Angela's data analytics and e-mail analysis was quite interesting. The software she used allowed her to map trends in e-mail traffic of who e-mailed whom and in what volume. Although Dawson and Cool e-mailed each other quite a bit, which was to be expected, we also identified a very high traffic between Cool and another employee, engineer Jane Brown. There wasn't any real business reason for so many e-mails between Brown and Cool, so we drilled a little deeper. Upon first glance, a few of the e-mails between Cool and Brown seemed overly friendly and indeed flirtatious, so we decided to download Brown's e-mails as well. At the time, we didn't know if this was just an office romance or something more sinister. I remember asking Angela, "Who is this Jane Brown and what is her connection to Cool?" Through the computer forensics, we also captured and later analyzed instant messages between Cool and Brown that would provide insights later in the investigation.

We found an interesting trend between both Cool and Brown's e-mail traffic that did not show up for Dawson's e-mails. Independently, both Cool and Brown had a high volume of communications with the address ghostrider@gmail.com. The owner of the account wasn't obvious from the e-mails we viewed, and checks with Gmail returned no registration information; however, there were a few references in the e-mails to "Wild Bill" and "WB." We looked at some of these e-mails a little closer, and they seemed to be written in a sort of vague code. They appeared to be related to invoices that were being submitted and processed. We also saw references to both "WB" and "Wild Bill" in instant messages between Cool and Brown that mentioned some in-person meetings. Angela turned to me and said, "We gotta figure out who Wild Bill is!"

We wanted to examine the e-mails from Cool, Brown and ghostrider in more detail and run some keyword searches on their e-mails at some point. But in the meantime, we started conducting preliminary background investigations of Exile Industries as well as a few of the other vendors that Cool had accessed that Sunday morning. Most of the vendors checked out, but Exile grabbed our attention right away.

We ran all the standard checks on Exile through a variety of public records databases — corporate records, civil litigation, criminal records, bankruptcy filings, a variety of financial searches, derogatory media, and so on — and got immediate results. It turned out that Exile had declared Chapter 7 bankruptcy three years ago, had liquidated and gone out of business. Now the big question was: why were they still being paid by Brew Corp., and why was Cool processing their invoices at 1:00 a.m. on a Sunday? We were obviously on to something with Exile and we needed to dig deeper, so we pulled hard copy records for the company, including the corporate records and the bankruptcy paperwork, and determined that the owner of Exile was a guy by the name of William Panetta. Angela made the connection right away: "Wild Bill?!"

We conducted a similar background investigation of Panetta and found that, while he had severe financial problems around the time of the Exile bankruptcy, he seemed to have bounced back quite nicely in the past few years. Before the bankruptcy, Panetta was a financial wreck. Litigation checks showed that he'd been sued by numerous parties for nonpayment of debts resulting in a variety of liens and judgments. But Department of Motor Vehicle registration searches showed that, in the past year, Panetta had purchased a Mercedes SL550 Roadster and paid cash. "Damn, that's a nice car," I said to Angela, "After his company went bankrupt, where did he get a hundred grand for a Mercedes roadster?"

The data analytics had focused our direction — we knew about the connections among Cool, Brown and Wild Bill. Without these tools, we would have spent days going through general ledger accounts and e-mails and we would have missed some of the macro-trends as well as the details. Then some background investigation had helped take us to the next step by revealing that Exile had gone bankrupt and by connecting Exile and Wild Bill to a real person, William Panetta. Things were moving along well, but now we needed to look further into the details.

We started running analyses of all vendor invoices, particularly parts suppliers, to see how many suspicious payments there were. We were checking for things like out-of-sequence invoice numbers, excessive purchases and other trends that might represent questionable activity. Most of the purchasing activity seemed normal, aside from the purchases from Exile. (Those purchases had increased over the years, even after the company had gone bankrupt three years ago.) We examined the purchasing from Exile over the past five years in detail and saw that almost all of these purchases had been authorized by one person, Jane Brown.

Given these findings, as well as Cool's and Brown's connection to Panetta, we knew we had to focus the investigation on the three individuals and Exile. At this point we had circumstantial evidence that Cool, Brown and Panetta were very likely involved in a fraudulent purchasing and billing scheme. Now we needed to start talking to people and developing information regarding our three primary suspects. But first we wanted to gather some additional intelligence from other witnesses.

Since Brown had approved all of the purchases from the bankrupt Exile, we wondered why the normal receiving procedures at Brew Corp. did not flag these phantom purchases. We started our interviews with Brian Jones, the head of the receiving department. Jones and his employees indicated that instead of the parts from Exile coming through receiving, as was the normal process, Jane Brown would notify them that she had received the parts directly. She also provided them with related FedEx documentation, which they subsequently entered into their receiving log. Brown had explained to Jones that she did this because the replacement parts could be used for immediate equipment repairs so as not to affect Brew Corp.'s processing capacity. This explanation seemed plausible at the time, and, since Brown was providing the FedEx receipts as documentation, no one challenged her. None of the employees in the receiving department wanted to be responsible for a delay or shut down in production, so they didn't raise any questions.

We also interviewed some lower-level employees, including repair and plant personnel, who indicated they had no knowledge of using parts from Exile for repairs in the past few years. When we asked about Brown, they shared some scuttlebutt that she and Cool were involved romantically.

After receiving the explanation regarding the FedEx documentation, Angela asked for a database of the receiving log activity. The receiving department also provided us with the original FedEx documents that Brown had given to them as proof of delivery, which looked just like all the other FedEx receipts. Angela then exported the delivery data to the FedEx website, ran a comparison and bingo — all the deliveries that were supposed to have been received after the Exile bankruptcy returned "Not Found" in the FedEx system.

The Jig Is Up

Armed with all of this evidence, we were confident that we could prove there was a fraud, but we were hoping to get a confession from one or all of the parties involved to seal the deal. We also wanted their help in recovering some of the funds, if possible. Our analysis showed that purchases from Exile exceeded $6 million in five years, including close to $4 million since Exile went bankrupt. When we presented these findings to Hays, he was apoplectic, insisting that we "lock those crooks up and find that money!"

As the investigation unfolded, we collected other damning information proving that Cool and Brown had conspired with Panetta over a five-year period to engage in a kickback scheme initially and then, after Exile's bankruptcy, in an outright fictitious vendor scheme.

We started by interviewing Panetta, since we felt he was the weak link of the three. After many denials, when confronted with overwhelming evidence and our explanation that we were really after Brown and Cool, Panetta confessed.

He described how the scheme worked and, as we suspected, pinned responsibility on Brown and Cool. He said his business with Brew Corp. was legitimate in the beginning but, after a few years, Brown, who had been ordering most of the parts from him, presented an opportunity for a kickback. She'd send more work his way if he kicked back 20 percent to her, and he could even raise his prices by 20 percent to offset the kickback. So that's exactly what he did. Panetta went along with the scheme because he had recently divorced and needed the money from his continued business with Brew Corp.

Then, when his company went bankrupt three years ago, Brown said she could continue to feed him some additional cash if they kept the scheme up and Panetta didn't have to do a damn thing — except operate as a front company and bill Brew Corp. as directed by Brown. After the bankruptcy,

Panetta received 30 percent of the invoice totals for continuing the illusion and kicked the rest back to Cool and Brown. Panetta wondered how Brown could get away with it but later came to understand that she was in bed with Cool (both literally and figuratively), and they were working the scheme together. Cool was covering for them on the financial end and Brown was the front person for dealing with Wild Bill.

Armed with Panetta's confession, we tried to get Cool and Brown to confess as well, but word of the investigation spread quickly inside the company and they were well prepared for our interviews. They denied everything and lawyered up immediately. Their attorney was sharp and wanted to work out a settlement where his clients would provide information in return for a plea bargain and a "good word" with law enforcement. Hays would have none of it. "Screw their deal," he said. "Let's prosecute them and find that money!"

Show Me the Money

We handed the case over to law enforcement wrapped up in a bow. The culprits were charged criminally, prosecuted, received felony fraud convictions and served time in prison but refused to cooperate in recovering the stolen funds. And unfortunately, local law enforcement didn't have much interest or capability when it came to recovering Hays' money. He hired a lawyer and they obtained a civil judgment against Cool and Brown for more than $3 million. Of course, Cool and Brown didn't pay, saying all the money was gone. But Hays wasn't buying it and neither were we. Now I said to Angela, "We have to find that money!!"

Before confronting Cool and Brown, we had put them under surveillance and picked up intelligence that would help in the asset recovery process. It showed them going into a few select banks and also revealed that they traveled frequently to the island of Tortola. With that intelligence, the attorneys on the case subpoenaed bank records for both subjects. We received a significant number of statements from four different banks where they had accounts. Instead of plowing through them manually and trying to figure out where the tainted funds had flowed, we used Angela's expertise to scan in the statements into a data analytics program.

We were able to track the flow of money from the fraud and isolate the remaining bank balances in the United States. These funds were subsequently seized by counsel. We were also on the lookout for any payments or transfers that appeared to be asset purchases, such as cars, real estate, jewelry or other assets that we could track down and recover. In addition to finding a number of other bank accounts, for which statements were also subpoenaed, we found specific payments that we wanted to investigate further.

One of those was to a marina in Southampton, New York, that Angela thought could be for watercraft mooring costs. We ran searches of boat registrations under both Cool and Brown but came up with zilch. We also looked for corporate entities in the United States that Cool might have set up and registered a boat under, but again we came up empty. So we took a ride out to the marina in Southampton armed with photos of Cool and Brown and started asking questions.

We found a helpful harbormaster who recognized their pictures and told us Cool and Brown had moored a boat in the Hamptons for a few months, but then "they took off and moved it down south somewhere warm . . . to one of them islands." He thought it was somewhere in the Caribbean. And, after some prompting, he remembered the name of the boat: "*Giovanna*, a beautiful 50-footer." Angela pointed out that *Giovanna* was Italian for Jane, as in Jane Brown.

Our surveillance showed the couple traveling to Tortola, so we embarked on some investigation in the islands. I wish I could say that we took a trip to the beach and enjoyed a few piña coladas, but instead I contacted a local investigator who had done great work for me in the past. The investigator canvassed the marinas in Tortola and, after a few weeks, he found *Giovanna* sitting pretty in the bay. Once we uncovered the boat, we found that it was registered under a local corporate name that Brown had established in Tortola. Once we knew that, we subpoenaed more bank accounts in Tortola. Angela worked her magic, and we found some $900,000 sitting in an account under the corporation that Brown had established, Giovanna Enterprises.

Between *Giovanna*, which was assessed at just shy of $1 million, the $900,000 we found in the Tortola bank and the other accounts we traced in the United States totaling $750,000, we ended up recovering more than $2.6 million of the $3.2 million that Cool and Brown had taken. Together with some recovery from Panetta, Hays ended up getting back close to $3 million of the total loss of $4.4 million. Not a bad return on Hays' investigative cost, but of course he was still angry that we didn't find it all.

Lessons Learned

This case taught me the importance of collaboration and teamwork. I decided to bring Angela into the project because I knew her skills in data analysis would be immensely helpful to the case. Fraud examiners should be aware of their strengths and weakness and try to establish a network of experts who can complement their skills.

This case was also a testament to the importance of perseverance in investigations. If we had wrapped up the case after Hays received a favorable civil judgment, he probably would never have collected a dime from Cool or Brown. Our job didn't end when we were able to prove the fraud; we needed to keep looking to recover Hays' stolen assets.

Recommendations to Prevent Future Occurrences

It is important to maintain a level of skepticism in business dealings, even with valued employees. Cool was a trusted accountant at Brew Corp. who used his position to defraud the company. He had the ability to doctor the records to cover his scheme because he was the only one who maintained the financials. Hays has since implemented a tougher anti-fraud policy that includes separation of duties in the accounting department and the shipping and receiving department. We also recommended he purchase data analysis software to run period checks for suspicious patterns.

About the Authors

Jay Dawdy, CFE, CMA, is the president of Gryphon Strategies. He has more than 20 years of finance, accounting and investigative experience and concentrates on solving complex, high-dollar financial fraud cases internationally. Jay is a frequent instructor and speaker on financial fraud investigation and prevention.

Angela Clancy, CA, is a senior manager with PPB Advisory. She has more than eight years' experience working in the United States and Australia, including extensive experience within the fraud and litigation arena. Throughout her career she has utilized electronic data analysis to accomplish accounting investigations.

CHAPTER 3

In the State's Interest

GARY GRAFF

Glenn Brooks, fresh out of college in the early 1980s, was looking for the fast track to success. He had an abundance of clever business schemes but was short on the money and connections to put them in motion. As luck would have it, he happened to reside in the district of long-standing State Senator Carl Sampson, and the senator was in possession of the very things Glenn lacked: power, influence and wealth. Glenn Brooks called on the senator, seeking financial backing for one of his promising ventures. Senator Sampson was impressed with the young man's bold approach and decided to provide the funding and clout Brooks sought. Glenn Brooks' business skills and Senator Sampson's political influence gave rise to a formidable partnership, one that would create numerous successful corporate enterprises throughout the state.

After Glenn's initial contact with the senator, he went on to marry, become a father and get involved in community affairs. He was elected to the school board and became a member of Rotary. Courting public loyalty and affection, Brooks hosted yearly Christmas parties for his entire town, and every summer he treated more than 40 of his employees and their spouses to weeklong trips to various vacation spots.

Senator Sampson's state roots ran deep. Born into a large farming family, his adult life took him away from his family's poorly producing plot of land. After serving in the military, he completed law school and quickly proved to be an articulate and charismatic speaker. At the age of 22 he ran for the state senate and became one of the youngest people ever elected to state office. With his wife, Ethel, at his side, he rose to power quickly, securing influential senate positions that he would hold for decades. In the 1960s and 1970s, there were allegations of corruption, but three separate federal indictments of Sampson over two decades all resulted in acquittals. It appeared that Senator Sampson was untouchable, due in part to his impenetrable circle, held together by loyalty and fear. Sampson opened his law office on Saturdays to provide free legal advice, endearing himself to many. With calculated forethought, he took special care to help those he knew would someday reciprocate; conversely, those who opposed him paid the price of political defeat or were ostracized from the business community. Sampson's influence was usually exercised behind the scenes, earning him the nickname "Prince of Darkness." Sampson became a multimillionaire, owning a law firm with three branches in the state, a number of newspapers and radio stations, numerous businesses and substantial real estate. This combination of wealth and legislative seniority made Sampson the state's most powerful senator.

Sampson resided in Waynesboro, a small city of 20,000 people. He and his brother Richard owned much of the prime real estate in town and had substantial influence over business development. For example, when a local philanthropist offered to donate land on which to build a new school, the city council instead voted to purchase land from Senator Sampson. New roads and highways always seemed to be routed past land owned by the Sampsons, thereby increasing the value of the property.

Mark Manford obtained power through the senator's influence. With Sampson's help, he rose from poor, working-class roots to a seat in the state House of Representatives, eventually becoming the Appropriations Committee chairman. Many regarded Manford to be Senator Sampson's puppet in the state house. Sadly, he also developed a gambling problem, which placed stress on his financial position and opened him to corruption.

Representative Ron Endler, a close friend of Manford's, was chairman of the House Natural Resources Committee, through which most state funding was allocated. Well known as a ladies' man, his charming demeanor made him well suited for politics. Endler had a master's degree in school administration and was married with two children in college.

Less than Arm's Length?

The setting for the crime was two pronged: Brooks' and Sampson's business network and the state legislature.

Brooks' network of businesses was complicated. In addition to Brooks Enterprises, consisting of 13 title and abstract companies co-owned with Senator Sampson, he owned a food processing plant (in which Senator Sampson was a silent partner) and a gaming machine manufacturing enterprise, National Entertainment. National Entertainment leased gaming machines to casinos. Brooks also incorporated a number of shell corporations that were used to insulate certain financial transactions.

The state legislature appropriated state funds through legislation. The Appropriations Committee drafted the bills that allocated the money. These bills, after being passed by both houses, were signed into law by the governor. Much of the funds were distributed through the Department of Commerce, which further allocated them through regional agencies known as councils of government (COGs). The COGs then contracted with and allocated the funds to the receiving entities.

The "Hip Pocket" Concept

Waynesboro was the largest community in a 6,000-square-mile territory covered by two local FBI agents, Jim Pearson and me.

I was aware through the local newspaper that Brooks had received $450,000 in state funds to build a food processing plant, Quality Foods Unlimited. The money had been allocated through a local business development group, the Waynesboro Foundation, one of whose board members was Sampson's brother Richard. Rumors abounded that Brooks was misappropriating the money. Finally, when an informant alleged that Brooks was purchasing old, worn-out equipment for next to nothing but representing it to the state granting agency as new equipment at an inflated purchase price, I decided to open an investigation. First I subpoenaed Quality Foods Unlimited's financial records to determine how grant funds were being spent. I received a small package of records from Brooks through his attorney. Sometimes I learn more from what I don't get from a subpoena than from what I do get.

In this case, I received everything except what I needed. There were no supporting documents for the invoices submitted to the state. I didn't believe this was an oversight. Interestingly, there was one supporting invoice inadvertently stuck to the back of an unrelated document. It noted that $219,000 had been provided by the food processing plant to Burton Farm Supply Company to purchase grain storage bins and a food mixer. There was a phone number for Burton Supply on the invoice. I called the number and Ed Burton answered. I identified myself and asked Ed if he was the owner of Burton Farm Supply. He hesitantly said yes. I asked him where his business was located. "I operate it part time out of my house. My full-time job is a traveling salesman." I asked him about the specific invoice, and he didn't remember it. I asked him the amount of Burton Farm Supply's annual sales. "About $450,000." Yet he didn't remember a large invoice for half of that, I thought. Upon pressing him for more details, I learned that his only sales for the year had been to Quality Foods and that he had set up Burton Farm Supply as a conduit for the purchase of equipment at the request of his longtime friend Glenn Brooks. Burton simply served as a broker, and all the invoices had been prepared by Brooks. Burton did not know if they were accurate because he hadn't seen them.

My conversation with Burton raised my suspicions. I decided to visit the COG through which the $450,000 in state funds to Quality Foods had been provided to obtain a copy of the invoices submitted by Brooks for the expense of state funds. The COG fiscal officer, Ingred Greenspan, had all of the invoices, most of which were from Burton Farm Supply. When I completed my review of the file for the $450,000 grant, I asked her if there were any other state funds that had been allocated to Quality Foods. She responded, "Oh, yes," and brought out a box of records. I spent the rest of the day reviewing state grants. I discovered that Brooks' businesses had received $3.2 million in state funds, most of which had passed through a nonprofit organization, the Rural Progress Foundation. The $3.2 million accounted for half of all the special project money for the entire state for that fiscal year. Some of the Burton Farm Supply invoices used to obtain the funds were partially duplicitous from grant to grant. When I asked Greenspan how the Rural Progress Foundation received so much money, she said that each year when the state funding came in, she received a phone call from the House fiscal analyst, Steve Sellors, telling her how much of the money was allocated to Representatives Manford and Endler. During the course of the year, Sellors would call her and tell her where Manford or Endler wanted money sent. She then prepared contracts for those entities and sent them the money. For the two fiscal years in question, Sellors had instructed her to send almost all Manford's and Endler's special project money to the Rural Progress Foundation, with further allocation to Quality Foods Unlimited.

Assessing a case's potential comes with experience. Early in my career, I learned from a senior agent what he called the "hip pocket" concept: before devoting months or years to a complex white-collar investigation, the investigator should have sufficient evidence in his or her hip pocket that will result in at least some sort of prosecution that will make a relevant difference in the community. Up until the time I visited the COG to review supporting invoices, I was conducting a limited assessment to determine if criminal violations might have occurred. Once I found the duplicitous and inflated invoices, I had found my "hip pocket" violation. However, upon discovering that half of the state's special project money for one fiscal year went to Brooks' businesses, I realized I had discovered something much more involved than just false or inflated invoices. I was ready to commit the time and resources for a full, long-term investigation.

Italian Food and Interviews

Developing a public corruption case through historical evidence requires corroborated documentary and witness evidence. To determine how Brooks manipulated $3.2 million out of the legislature, I needed to thoroughly examine the money trail and determine why money was provided to Brooks. I also needed to develop a few cooperative witnesses along the way. During the next two years, records filling 40 file cabinets were obtained from more than 250 entities including banks, individuals and government agencies. Brooks had more than 20 businesses with multiple bank accounts through which monies were exchanged. I also had to learn the legislative appropriations process and how state grant money was processed. Armed with this knowledge, my partner and I could conduct more effective interviews of those involved in the distribution of the funds in question.

Records from the COG provided a snapshot of the $3.2 million and were good starting points to trace the money in both directions. About 80 percent of the money was provided to the nonprofit Rural Progress Foundation and half of that was then allocated to Brooks' plant, Quality Foods Unlimited. Bank records showed that the other half went to Brooks' gaming machine company, National Entertainment. Interestingly, there were no supporting invoices at the COG indicating that any state funds had gone to National Entertainment. I thought perhaps a review of the Rural Progress Foundation records would provide an explanation.

I contacted the president of Rural Progress Foundation, Janet McClain, an outgoing, overworked mother of two, who was a vice president at a local bank. She seemed nervous yet agreed to meet in a week with all the records from the foundation. She arrived with two boxes of records as scheduled. I started the interview with open-ended questions and let McClain explain the origins and purpose of Rural Progress Foundation. A couple years earlier, Brooks, a longtime friend from high school, informed her that he was forming a nonprofit foundation to assist rural businesses. He wanted her to be president of the board. It seemed a worthwhile endeavor, and McClain felt honored to be asked to participate. Several other friends agreed to serve on the board, including a feed store owner, a rancher and a probation officer. Brooks served as an unofficial advisor to the board and arranged for the group to receive state funding. To facilitate obtaining state money, Brooks had McClain file for nonprofit status with the state and file as a 501(c)(3) with the Internal Revenue Service. Foundation board meetings were held once a month at a local Italian restaurant, where Brooks treated board members to a feast as they discussed ways to help the rural business community. However, during the meetings, very little of substance was actually accomplished.

As my partner and I reviewed the foundation documents with McClain, I noticed there were minutes kept for all the foundation meetings.

"Who kept the minutes?"

"Brooks."

"But I thought he was not a member of the board?"

"He wasn't. He offered to keep the minutes as a favor to the board." The minutes showed that through an 18-month period, the board had voted to provide funding to Brooks' food processing plant and gaming machine company.

"Was the board aware that more than $2.5 million went to Brooks?"

"Not exactly. We discussed funding Quality Foods, but no dollar amounts were mentioned."

"But the minutes state specific amounts and that the board voted to fund National Entertainment."

"That didn't happen." McClain's voice began to shake. I stared at McClain, awaiting further explanation. "I told him I couldn't lie." She began to cry. "Last week, when I told Brooks that I was required to bring you all the foundation records, he told me to bring them over to his house first. A few nights ago, he and I reviewed the records as well as the minutes of the foundation meetings that he had saved on his computer. He changed the minutes to reflect that the board had voted for all this funding."

"What happened to the old minutes?"

"He told me to destroy any hard copies and that he would take care of the electronic copies. I told him I didn't feel comfortable with all this, and he said that the issue of the minutes probably would never come up."

I thought to myself that Brooks had conspired to obstruct justice, another criminal violation for my hip pocket. This case was getting much stronger.

McClain was not a criminal. She had allowed herself to be manipulated. Even though McClain kept the books and was aware that the money went to Brooks, he had convinced her that his companies were creating jobs that benefited the community. I told her she was standing on very thin ice and that the decisions she made over the next hours, days and weeks could determine whether she kept her job or went to jail. Fortunately for her and her family, she made the right choice. We prepared a signed statement to lock in her version of events. Her statements were later corroborated by the other foundation board members and by some of the original foundation meeting minutes later recovered from the deleted files on Brooks' computer.

Brooks had used this nonprofit foundation as a cover and conduit to obtain his state funds and conceal the fact that more than a million of the $3.2 million had gone to his gambling machine business. I still didn't know how he obtained the money from the state, other than that it was money allocated by Representatives Manford and Endler.

To learn how the money was allocated, I worked backward from the COG records and determined that the funds had come from the Department of Commerce (DOC). From DOC, I learned which specific bills had allocated the funds for disbursement. I figured out that although the bills had different sponsors, they had all been drafted by House fiscal analyst, Steve Sellors, the same person who had instructed the COG fiscal officer, Greenspan, to send Representative Manford's and Endler's special project money to the Rural Progress Foundation. I needed to interview this guy.

After several attempts to schedule a meeting, Sellors finally showed up with his attorney. He appeared to be a very slippery fellow. He had worked directly for Appropriations Committee chairman Mark Manford, and Natural Resources Committee chairman Ron Endler. Although no longer employed by the House, Sellors remained politically involved and was still very loyal to both men. Although cautious and reluctant to cooperate, Sellors clarified elements of the appropriations process. He seemed a little more comfortable as long as I avoided specific questions about Manford and Endler.

I learned from Sellors that these two committee chairmen controlled how funds were allocated, and Sellors drafted legislation based on their guidance. Both committees had perfunctory meetings to discuss funding projects, but the committee chairmen made the final decisions. No minutes or other records were kept of the process. Funds sent to nonprofit organizations such as the Rural Progress Foundation were known as special project funds. Such funds were usually distributed through the Department of Commerce to regional COGs, where they were "parked" for later distribution at the legislators' discretion. Most legislators were oblivious to the fact that these funds existed, as the monies were concealed in the legislation as part of funding for nonobjectionable items, such as rural fire departments. Bills were purposely brought to the floor at the last minute so legislators would not have time to read them or question certain allocations. Sellors admitted that for the two fiscal years in question, Manford and Endler concealed more than $2 million by legislative sleight-of-hand, which they parked in their COG to distribute later to their constituents. Sellors also conceded that he sent most of this money to the Rural Progress Foundation, but he was adamant that all of this was perfectly legal and the process was simply "how things are done at the state house."

When I left the interview with Sellors, my head was spinning. It was a lot of information to absorb. It was clear that Representatives Manford and Endler had sent most of their special project money to the Rural Progress Foundation and ultimately to Brooks. The obvious question that remained was Why? I suspected a reciprocal relationship among Brooks and the representatives. The challenge was to prove it.

A review of bank accounts of Brooks' various businesses revealed that almost $200,000 in "consulting fees" had been paid to Representative Manford. This included $122,000 paid by American Waste Disposal for Manford to promote a waste disposal project that never materialized. American Waste Disposal became Brooks' shell company, used to funnel kickbacks to Manford. Another $70,000 in promotional charges had been paid by National Entertainment to Manford. Clearly, it was a conflict of interest if not a quid pro quo for Manford to be paid by Brooks, to whose businesses he was directing state funds. At this point, the evidence of corruption was mounting, but the prosecution team felt we needed to develop one of the key players as a witness to tie it all together.

To develop more evidence and place pressure on Brooks to cooperate, we executed simultaneous search warrants on his residence and several of his businesses, including Quality Foods Unlimited and National Entertainment. It was time well spent. At National Entertainment, we found records indicating they received almost $100,000 in cash "off the books" from a casino to lease gaming machines. There were also records of cash disbursements to Manford, Endler and a third state representative, Jim Hunter. The pressure from the search warrant was ultimately too much for National

Entertainment's operations manager Keith Starkey, who decided to get on the right side and cooperate. He had maintained the records for the cash intake from the casino. At Brooks' instruction, he prepared envelopes of cash for Representatives Manford, Endler and Hunter. Each envelope contained 10 percent of the profits from the gaming machines placed at the casino. When the representatives came to town, Brooks treated them to lunch at one of the local Italian restaurants, where he slipped them the cash.

Even with the evidence obtained from the search warrants, Brooks resisted cooperating. At this point, it was the government's position that any plea agreement with Brooks must include jail time. I decided to make a pitch to Representative Mark Manford to cooperate, as the evidence against him had become substantial. I knew that Manford often came home for the weekends while the legislature was in session. He lived with his wife on a modest 40-acre ranch about four miles outside of town. On Saturday morning, I drove out to his place and couldn't help but notice that the newly improved road surface from town ended a few hundred yards past Manford's driveway. From the road, I could barely see his car parked in front of the house. Thinking nothing ventured, nothing gained, I drove down the long driveway to his residence.

I knocked on the door and Manford answered. A half-lit cigar dangled from his lip.

"Morning, Mr. Manford. I'm Gary Graff with the FBI."

"I've heard of you. . . . How can I help you?" The newspapers had been tracking the investigation, and Manford was well aware he had a problem.

"Mark, you're in a bit of trouble. I felt you deserved to know what's going on. You don't need to answer any questions if you don't want to, but I really think it would be a good idea if you at least listened to what I have to say. Do you have a few minutes to chat?" Manford looked at me for a moment and took a puff of his cigar.

"Sounds okay. Come on in and have a cup of coffee."

Manford introduced me to his wife, and he and I sat down at his kitchen table. We talked for about an hour. I laid out selective evidence and explained that in conspiracies, the first person to cooperate usually received the best deal. I said it wouldn't be painless, but early cooperation on his part might avoid disaster. I could sense that the investigation was weighing heavily on him and that he wanted to come to terms with it. However, he wasn't quite ready. Our meeting ended on friendly terms, and I felt I had at least planted a seed.

Apparently Brooks heard about my meeting with Manford. Soon thereafter, he entered a plea agreement with the U.S. Attorney's office, perhaps in hopes that he could get a better deal. My initial debriefing of Brooks took 12 hours as he detailed his knowledge of criminal activity throughout the state. He explained how his long-term business relationship with Senator Sampson had consumed his moral compass in political corruption.

Sampson was benevolent and charming with his friends and ruthless with his enemies. When Brooks and Sampson started Quality Foods Unlimited, Sampson wanted Brooks to access special project money, but Sampson didn't want to be directly involved because of my ongoing investigation of him regarding federal election violations. He introduced Brooks to Representative Manford, recently elected Appropriations Committee chairman. Sampson explained to Brooks that any state monies brought by Manford would require a 10 percent kickback and that "Manford will try to get more than 10 percent from you, but don't give it to him. Ten percent is what it is, what it always has been and is all he should get." To obtain the initial $450,000 for Quality Foods, Brooks negotiated the kickback with Manford, but the payment was made by Sampson and carried on his books as a "loan" to Manford, which provided Sampson cover should the payment ever be questioned.

Brooks continued to develop his relationship with Manford and was introduced to other representatives, including Endler and Hunter. Brooks visited the capitol at least once or twice a week and took all three representatives to lunch. They were interested in providing more state funds to Brooks but advised him to set up a nonprofit recipient to provide cover.

Brooks then set up the Rural Progress Foundation, keeping his name off the charter and other foundation records. All three representatives had their special project money parked at a COG, where the directors were political appointees, so they never questioned what the representatives did with the money. Manford started sending his funds to the Rural Progress Foundation in amounts ranging from $100,000 to $350,000 at a time. In return, Brooks paid Manford as a consultant to two of his businesses. Endler and Hunter were wary of the paper trail that consultant payments cause and insisted on a different arrangement. Since one of the casinos serviced by National Entertainment paid in cash, all three representatives agreed to receive, in cash, 10 percent of the gross profits from that casino.

Brooks' cooperation moved the investigation forward quickly. Manford finally felt enough heat and came in to plea. The focus of the investigation turned to Sampson and his brother Richard, who were both directly involved in appropriating the initial $450,000 of state funds to Quality Foods. Search warrants were executed on Sampson's office as well as the office of his accountant.

The Outcome of the Investigation

Pursuant to his plea agreement, Brooks gave substantial assistance to my investigation. His information led to other investigations regarding corrupt activities in state government, resulting in other high-profile prosecutions and convictions. His efforts reduced his federal prison sentence to two years. Manford's guilty plea resulted in a two-year sentence; he had gambled away his $300,000 in kickbacks, and his home was in foreclosure. Sampson and his brother Richard were indicted by a federal grand jury on conspiracy charges regarding the $450,000 appropriation and kickback. The lead Assistant United States Attorney who prosecuted the case was a former rugby player who was not afraid to take a difficult, complex case to court. However, Sampson, still on probation from his conviction on federal election fraud charges, convinced the court he was mentally incompetent to stand trial. Richard went to trial and was convicted, but he passed away from natural causes before he was sentenced. Representative Endler was indicted for the cash kickbacks from National Entertainment but was eventually acquitted after two trials. With Endler's acquittal, the U.S. Attorney decided not to pursue charges against Hunter. Following the investigation, the governor and state legislature closed loopholes regarding special project monies in the appropriations process.

Lessons Learned

Public corruption cases were my most challenging and time-consuming investigations. Sixty- or seventy-hour workweeks were my norm. Defendants often have the power and influence to affect the process and may accuse the prosecution team of political motivations. Quid pro quo is especially tough to prove in cases based solely on historical evidence. Kickbacks may be often disguised as consulting fees, loans, attorney's fees or retainers and are difficult to prove without corroboration from multiple witnesses or tape-recorded contemporaneous conversations. In this case, I believed it was important to develop witnesses to corroborate the documentary evidence. Poor witness performance, a biased jury member or errant court rulings regarding evidence or witness testimony can weaken even the strongest case. Take the time to fully develop all of the available evidence. One method of obtaining valuable evidence is through search warrants.

During the course of my investigation, 12 search warrants were served, resulting in the collection of valuable documentary and computer evidence. Search warrants are also a valuable tool because they place pressure on the target and his associates. The search of National Entertainment resulted in the cooperation of its operations manager. Additionally, a search warrant's supporting affidavit, when released to the public, presents a rare opportunity for the prosecution to state its case. A thorough, detailed affidavit can exhibit the strength of the case and help persuade suspects and potential witnesses who are wavering to cooperate.

Once a subject agrees to cooperate, plea agreements shouldn't be finalized until the individual is on record under oath with the full truth about his or her criminal activity and that of others. Developing the complete facts about all these activities may take weeks or even months, as the subject passes through various emotions and stages of denial, blame, finger-pointing and, finally, full acceptance and cooperation. The prosecution team must patiently work through this process if they want to have a defendant who will later be a good witness. In this investigation, Representative Manford accepted full responsibility for his conduct. However, he finalized his plea agreement without completely detailing the criminal activities of his close friends Endler and Hunter. Manford remained loyal to his friends, assumed all the blame and became a pitiful defense witness at Endler's trial.

Recommendations to Prevent Future Occurrences

Politicians love to bring money back to their districts to demonstrate that they are helping the community. Such funding may open the door for corruption as those who are politically connected receive the funds, usually for a price. This was clearly the case in my investigation. Such funding should either be eliminated or distributed under strict controls.

With rare exception, all legislative meetings and subcommittee meetings should be recorded and open to the public. Had this been the case in my state legislature, the legislators would have been more accountable in the funding process.

Legislatures should require a reasonable review period before legislation is brought to a vote. Had this been the case in my state, legislators would have had more time to review it carefully and perhaps detect the concealed special project funds.

States should require full disclosure by legislators of all personal and business income, through annual signed, sworn statements. Such statements were required in my state, but the requirements were vague, and false disclosure was only a minor ethics violation. Making false income disclosure statements a criminal offense might deter reciprocal relationships or pay-to-play schemes. In my investigation, I determined that none of the three representatives disclosed his income from Brooks on annual disclosure statements. Had such nondisclosure been a criminal act, it could have facilitated the prosecution of the case.

About the Author

Gary W. Graff retired from the Federal Bureau of Investigation in 2010 after providing 23 years of service, with assignments in Ohio and Oklahoma. During the course of his career, Gary's investigative work included public corruption, financial crimes, securities fraud, violent crimes, property crimes, drugs, counterterrorism, civil rights and Indian Country violations to include sex crimes and homicides.

Opinions expressed are those of the author and not those of the FBI.

CHAPTER 4

Odd Bedfellows

JON COHEN

As the police diver descended into the cold and murky waters of the Schurizad River, I waited by the shore hoping for a successful search. Approximately one month earlier, Peter Genz had tossed a weighted duffel bag containing eight rifles into the waterway beside a major eastern U.S. city in a desperate attempt to conceal evidence of his crime. Genz had no idea what to do with the rifles and was afraid to store them at home, where his two small children might stumble across them. I waited patiently as the diver began his patterned search of the riverbed, making sure to cover each grid thoroughly while avoiding assorted debris that could ensnare his oxygen hose. After more than two hours of continuously trudging over the rough terrain, he located the duffel and slowly brought it to the surface. I nervously bit my lip while I watched the police officer pull out all eight rifles and the metal barbells that Genz used to keep the bag on the riverbed. As the weapons lay alongside the gravelly shore, we remarked that we now had the "smoking guns" to nail not only Genz but his police officer uncle Fred Wallace.

Peter Genz was the last person anybody would ever suspect of dealing cocaine. The 36-year-old carpet layer was a devoted husband and father and a diligent employee of Branson's Carpet Company, a firm with deep roots and an excellent reputation in the community. Although he occasionally smoked marijuana and was known to hoist a beer after work, Peter was considered a straight arrow with no signs of a darker side to his personality. Genz had started working for old man Branson as soon as he graduated from Eastern High School in a working-class section of Phermont, Pennsylvania, more than 18 years ago. Peter began his employment as a day laborer and general clerk, learning about the carpet business in between sweeping floors and emptying trash cans. The elder Branson immediately took a liking to young Peter, who impressed everyone with his hustle, sharp wit and serious demeanor. Genz politely let everyone know he was interested in advancing himself and was willing to learn from any and all interested parties. This impressed both his coworkers and his bosses, to the point where he was frequently asked to join the installation crews as they plied their trade. Within a few years, Peter had established himself as a quick learner and hard worker, an asset to the Branson firm. This soon led to a promotion as senior installer, not only supervising a crew of four men but handling both customer installation scheduling and employee work shifts as well as adjunct customer consultant. The work was hard but steady, and Peter was earning enough money to finally propose marriage to Bonnie, his longtime girlfriend. Times were good and Peter expected life to get even better in the years to come.

Frederick Wallace — or, as everyone in Telleride, Florida, called him, Fred the Cop — was traveling in a different direction from his nephew, Peter. More than 1,100 miles separated the two men from each other, one an up-and-coming employee at the largest carpet firm in Phermont, the other a bitter, twice-divorced police officer confined to the evidence cage at a medium-size police agency in western Florida. After a tragic on-duty motorcycle accident that left him partially disabled, the highly decorated college graduate was forced to spend his days processing recovered stolen property and assorted seized evidence without any hope for advancement. The 20-year veteran was gradually being eased into retirement, whether he wanted to go or not. Gone were the days when he could aspire to be a detective or a patrol sergeant. No more overtime opportunities or salary increases from promotions. Wallace spent each day as a prisoner in his cage, watching his savings depleted by two alimony checks and five teenage children who never seemed to have enough time to visit him in his tiny efficiency apartment. Every dream Fred ever had was now a distant memory, replaced by the stark reality that he was sinking fast and needed a life preserver just to stay afloat. Fred was spiraling down an abyss that he could not control. Yet all was not lost.

At the largest medical care provider in central Florida, administrator Marvin Yeltson pondered his next move. After a decade of rapid growth, Pine Wood Medical Center had blossomed into a world-class facility specializing in both state-of-the-art cancer treatment and cardiac care. Organ transplant operations now led the way as primary cash cows, enabling an expansion plan to be fully financed without costly bonds or external resources. Pine Wood was the envy of the medical community, ably led by Yeltson and a team of young, super-smart administrators. The biggest problem Yeltson faced was replacing his cadre of talented executives who were constantly being poached by competitors. As soon as he could train them they fled to new opportunities where greater advancement led to higher salaries and ownership options. Despite tighter budgets and reductions in both government and private health care reimbursements, Yeltson had still managed to grow his institution and thrive. But as a man with an insatiable appetite, his goals were never satisfied.

A Pillar of the Community

When this investigation started, I was just beginning an assignment to a federal drug task force that operated in the metropolitan Phermont area. Having been tasked with targeting regional, national and international drug trafficking organizations, I was surprised to be assigned the case of a local independent drug dealer, but I conducted the preliminary inquiries with my usual zeal. As the investigation progressed, I quickly recognized that I would need to call on nearly all the items in my professional toolbox to uncover a unique fraud case.

The investigation began in early spring just as the last remnants of a record-setting winter snow storm were beginning to melt. My partner and I received a call from Sergeant Mason Jarvis of the Phermont Police Department, informing us of the arrest earlier that day of David "Moose" Wickersham, a mid-level cocaine dealer. Wickersham was well known to local law enforcement as a violent man, quick-tempered and feared by many for his boxing prowess as well as a penchant for gunplay. After more than a dozen arrests for numerous violent felonies, Wickersham was unrepentant and said to be emboldened to make an even greater reputation in the Phermont underworld.

I learned that a uniformed patrol officer spotted Wickersham brandishing a loaded AK-47 while standing on a street corner near his home. As if this were not serious enough, Wickersham had the audacity to level the weapon in the direction of the officer. Only at the last moment did Wickersham exercise some common sense and place the weapon on the ground upon a shouted order from the officer. When he got to police headquarters, Wickersham realized the gravity of his situation and uncharacteristically asked to speak to Sergeant Jarvis. Wickersham provided the sergeant with actionable intelligence regarding numerous criminals in the community, hoping to mitigate his own legal problems. Jarvis told me that Wickersham's girlfriend had recently given birth to a sickly baby girl, the third child for the couple, and apparently Wickersham felt a stronger bond with this child than with any of his seven other kids. Consequently, he was desperate to avoid another lengthy imprisonment and was willing to do almost anything to reduce or eliminate the charges he faced.

Unable to pass up such an unusual opportunity to work with a pillar of the Phermont criminal community, I agreed to meet with Sergeant Jarvis and Wickersham later that evening to determine what value Moose could be to me and where we could best apply the information he possessed, as well as how we would "work" him. Over a six-hour period, interrupted only by a fast-food dinner, we sketched out a plan to use Wickersham's drug contacts to target several prominent local dealers, all of whom were rivals of his. Impressing upon him the notion that we would not be used solely to eliminate his competition but would seek instead to eradicate the entire regional drug trade (a noble but highly unlikely goal), we fashioned a plan of attack and agreed to begin implementation the next day.

Prosecution Is Onboard

The following day, I met with a local prosecutor who agreed to supervise the investigation and granted permission for Wickersham to wear a wireless recording device when he met with targets on our behalf. Later that evening, the first of numerous drug deals took place, this one a quarter-pound purchase of cocaine between Wickersham and Melvin Vinson, a highly sought-after target of our agency. Two days later, a second purchase was arranged between the two men that ended in a "buy-bust" arrest of Vinson. In the drug world, word gets out fast when someone is arrested, especially if he is a significant trafficker like Vinson. Law enforcement is forced to act quickly to obtain any relevant evidence before it is destroyed. Knowing this, I immediately prepared a search-and-seizure warrant to locate and confiscate Vinson's contraband and documents evidencing his drug trafficking. Early the next morning we executed the warrant at Vinson's residence and obtained a bounty of evidence, including what are commonly known as tally sheets — handwritten records of customer payments, quantities and costs per drug as well as IOUs. It was the latter category that most interested me, in particular an unusual notation for a Peter Genz. It would be several days before we completely processed all the evidence seized at Vinson's home, but once we did, the investigation took a decidedly peculiar detour.

Although rare, it is not uncommon for allegations of law enforcement officers engaged in illegal conduct to arise, particularly with regard to illicit drug trafficking. When I asked Vinson who Peter Genz was, he told me Genz was a new supplier, capable of procuring kilograms of cocaine from his uncle in Florida. When pressed further, Vinson said that Genz's uncle was a police officer with access to seized drugs and firearms. Vinson also told me that Genz was clueless about how to sell cocaine and was engaging in the activity only at the behest of his uncle, who desperately needed money. Genz admitted to being curious about how much someone could earn selling drugs and sought out Vinson for advice, following an introduction from a mutual acquaintance. The Genz notation on Vinson's tally sheet reflected a $6,000 IOU for a kilogram of cocaine that Vinson had planned to pay Genz for later the same day we executed the search warrant. At the time of Vinson's arrest, a kilogram of cocaine was selling for $32,000 in the Phermont metropolitan area, which is why I found the notation peculiar.

About a week later, Vinson's attorney contacted the prosecutor supervising our case and said his client wanted to cooperate. Vinson agreed to introduce Peter Genz to an undercover law enforcement agent the same evening. Following the introduction, the undercover officer made several small purchases from Genz over the next few days, which led to the execution of a search-and-seizure warrant at his residence at the end of the week. During the search I came across a letter from an "Uncle Fred" to Genz referencing "those things I drove up last weekend." When I asked Genz what the phrase meant, he initially refused to answer. After I reminded him of the gravity of the situation, he quickly changed his tune, informing me that Fred Wallace was his uncle and a police officer in Florida. Fred was experiencing a serious financial burden made worse by a recent gambling trip where he lost almost $5,000. I asked Peter what the reference to "those things" was and he said: "automatic weapons, you know, rifles." Genz said he threw the rifles into the Schurizad River as soon as his uncle left because he didn't know what else to do with them and was worried his kids would get to them.

The next phase of the investigation entailed the repayment of Genz's debt to his uncle for both the cocaine and the rifles. This was accomplished with the assistance of the U.S. Postal Inspection Service, which provided serialized postal money orders for delivery to Wallace. At the same time, the investigation shifted to Florida, where an extended surveillance operation was undertaken. For a week Wallace was continuously surveilled to determine patterns of behavior and observe potential illegal activity. At the end of the week the money orders were delivered, and investigators followed Wallace to a local bank, where he deposited the money into his checking account. Since we had deliberately shorted the value of the money orders sent to Wallace, it wasn't long before he started calling Genz to ask for the rest of the money. These conversations were consensually recorded and monitored and would provide damaging evidence at Wallace's subsequent trial.

The Gambling Bond

For the past decade, Pine Wood Medical Center outperformed its competitors both operationally and financially, a feat that appeared to defy reality. The industry as a whole had experienced significant hurdles, with hospitals closing or reducing staff and operations to stay within shrinking budgets. But not Pine Wood. Where others saw obstacles, Marvin Yeltson envisioned opportunity and plowed ahead, confident he could obtain the necessary financing. When his fellow administrators complained about a lack of available hospital bonds, Yeltson just nodded and remained silent. What his competitors did not know was that for the past five years Yeltson had been perpetrating a massive kickback scheme, demanding increasingly larger payments from many of his vendors. When other hospitals were curtailing purchases and outsourced services, Pine Woods was growing at an unexplainable rate. Vendors were only too happy to remit a small portion of their Pine Woods bounty. It was this unrecorded inflow of illegal revenue that helped offset any financial shortages encountered by a growing medical institution. Over time Yeltson counted on this under-the-table revenue as almost a bona fide balance sheet item, expecting a never-ending revenue stream. Right up to the moment he was arrested, the largesse continued to flow.

In any complex financial conspiracy case, investigators expect to encounter detours and bumps in the road. In this case, the strangest tangent was the road leading to Pine Wood Medical Center through Marvin Yeltson and Fred Wallace. With no apparent connection between the parties, investigators were stunned to learn that Yeltson and Wallace had anything in common, let alone a penchant for gambling away their salaries. It was through this unlikely association that Fred Wallace approached Marvin Yeltson with an offer to "make some scratch," as he put it. In an interview following his arrest more than three months after Wallace's, Yeltson spoke of his bond with Wallace — a gambling riverboat on the Mississippi River. Sitting at a table one night, both men got to talking and soon ordered several rounds of drinks. As each one commiserated over his gambling woes, the talk turned to ways to recoup their losses. Before the night had ended, they agreed to meet again the following week and begin what Yeltson later characterized as "my crazy friendship with Fred the Cop."

When someone's back is to the wall, he will do almost anything to get himself out of a bind. In this case, Fred and Marvin had their backs against the same wall — gambling debts. It's almost unheard of for a police officer to steal evidence, but Wallace was desperate. As with any illegal scheme — financial, criminal or otherwise — hiding it is essential and, to this end, Marvin Yeltson provided invaluable assistance. Wallace's police department had an agreement with Yelston to destroy illegal substances at Pine Wood, including any seized drugs. Over the next several weeks, Wallace and Yeltson hatched a plan to divert kilograms of cocaine that were supposed to be incinerated and instead send them to Wallace's nephew in Phermont, where they could be sold on the street. The scheme relied on sleight of hand to switch real cocaine with a powdery substitute that looked to the average person like the real deal. The cocaine would go to Phermont and the powdery substitute would be incinerated in accordance with standard practice.

As each stage of the investigation unfolded, we followed a routine and thorough method to trace the financial evidence. We tried to corroborate each crucial piece with as many items of circumstantial evidence as possible. For example, every time Genz called his uncle to discuss payment for the drugs, we recorded the conversations and had Genz bring up as many potential evidentiary items as possible to ensnare Wallace. We placed a camera at Wallace's post office, and, each time he retrieved a payment from Genz, we reviewed his bank records for evidence of the deposit. This gave us physical evidence of money laundering, which drove the nails deeper into Wallace's coffin at trial.

We were also collecting evidence against Yeltson, beginning with his deteriorating personal finances. It didn't take long to realize that, like Wallace, he had dug a hole for himself through addictive gambling; only Yeltson's hole was much deeper. After we realized that Wallace and Yeltson were stealing the cocaine that was supposed to be incinerated at Pine Wood, the full picture became clear. Method, motive and opportunity: all three elements were coming together to make Genz, Wallace and Yeltson accomplices. In my mind, a fraud triangle — and the perpetrator triangle — was taking shape.

Pine Wood Audit

The key to a successful financial investigation is to keep digging for more evidence until you've exhausted most every conceivable avenue of inquiry. Knowing we still had some avenues to explore, my partner and I started looking at Yeltson's lifestyle, his assets and the trappings he surrounded himself with. We were used to seeing corporate executives with luxury cars, lavish homes in upscale communities and very high credit card balances, and we found these and much more with Yeltson. However, we also discovered that his income from the hospital could not support his lifestyle. This led us to request a full audit of Pine Wood Medical Center's financial records by the State of Florida, which took nearly six months to complete. The audit results made it clear that massive corruption had been taking place at Pine Wood and that Yeltson was knee deep in the scheme. The auditors found overwhelming proof of contract fraud, kickback schemes, bidding irregularities and double billing by vendors. Despite all of our efforts, we were unable to convince the IRS or state regulators to initiate a tax fraud prosecution against Yeltson, possibly because he had many influential friends.

When we concluded our investigation, the prosecutor charged Peter Genz with several counts of drug trafficking and illegal possession of automatic weapons. Genz cooperated with the prosecution and testified against his uncle and Yeltson. Genz received an 18-month suspended sentence and 36 months of supervised release, plus a fine.

Fred Wallace was not nearly as fortunate; he refused to cooperate with authorities and maintained his innocence throughout his trial. After listening to more than 30 witnesses and reviewing a mountain of evidence, the jury needed little time to return a verdict of guilty on all counts. Wallace was sentenced to 84 months' incarceration followed by 10 years of supervised release. He was also ordered to pay a substantial fine, a requirement he would never be able to satisfy.

Frequently in fraud examinations, the person who was most culpable, the one whose education and station in life should have prevented him from engaging in such misconduct, is not punished in equal measure to that of his co-defendants. But this time, the court levied a sentence on Yeltson that was as surprising for the prosecution team as it was for the defendant. Yeltson was imprisoned for 10 years, to be followed by 12 years of supervised release and fined more than $200,000. He was also ordered to forfeit more than $1.1 million in illegal proceeds he had stolen from Pine Wood Medical Center.

Lessons Learned

This case began as a "normal" drug trafficking investigation but soon evolved into a much larger crime incorporating many elements of a financial fraud. We responded by developing a comprehensive fraud examination inquiry. The results spoke of a plot more insidious than drug dealers plying their trade to helpless junkies and low-level hustlers. This scheme reached into a highly regarded medical center and a police station. Our circle of suspects included three men who suffered financial shortfalls due to poor decision making, character flaws and weaknesses, and who responded in ways most of us cannot fathom.

Recommendations to Prevent Future Occurrences

The auditors at the Pine Wood Medical Center bear some responsibility for failing to apply sufficient due diligence and oversight at the facility. While no audit can encompass all aspects of an enterprise's operation, the individual auditor is the first line of defense against fraud and suspicious financial practices. If the Pine Wood auditor had dug a little deeper during the routine reviews, he or she would have found evidence of Yeltson's kickback scheme, possibly leading to discovery of the cocaine theft as well.

The Telleride Police Department also shoulders significant blame for not recognizing the pressure Fred Wallace was under. If someone had noticed the red flags, he likely would not have been in charge of transporting cocaine for incineration.

Many Certified Fraud Examiners have worked with someone who stopped just short of performing what we consider to be proper due diligence. As investigative professionals, we need to go the extra mile and actively look for any possible signs of fraudulent behavior. To do any less is a disservice to our clients, our profession and our code of ethics.

About the Author

Jon Cohen, CFE, retired in 2007 following a 27-year career in law enforcement, with assignments at several federal, state and local agencies. He is a graduate of Temple University's School of Business Management and earned a master's degree from Fairleigh Dickinson University. Jon earned his CFE in 2008 and is a member of the Philadelphia Area Chapter of the ACFE, where he formerly served as an officer and board member. He also was a contributing author to Dr. Wells' book *Internet Fraud Casebook: The World Wide Web of Deceit* (John Wiley & Sons, 2010).

CHAPTER 5

When Bribery Becomes a Way of Doing Business

AMINE ANTARI

Georges Terrin was a very successful man who loved traveling and meeting new people. Married three times and the father of five, Georges had a big family to provide for. Born in King Falls, a small city in Ireland, he grew up with two brothers and one sister. He was the oldest child and had to work every summer on the farm with his father to make money and help his family. At a very young age, Georges felt responsible for his siblings and wanted them to have a better life.

At the age of 19, it was time for Georges to go to the university and follow his dream of becoming an engineer. The move from a small city like King Falls to a much bigger one, Dublin, was a challenging and educational experience in itself. Throughout college, Georges was an outstanding student and excelled not only in engineering but also in business classes.

His business mind-set and engineering competencies helped him get hired right after finishing his bachelor's degree in civil engineering. Easygoing and charming, Georges was the type of person who seemed to get anything he wanted with just a smile. His savvy and extensive engineering knowledge facilitated his ascension from an entry-level engineer to a vice president position in less than six years. One of the executives of the company, Steve Samson, had noticed Georges at an early stage of his career and had helped him climb the ladder faster than his peers.

Steve Samson was about 60 years old and had been with the company since its creation. Steve was originally from Vermont and was raised in a wealthy Catholic family. He pursued a degree in engineering because his father demanded it. Steve remembers his father telling him when he left for school, "Be a man; it's time for you to make us proud," while his mother cried, already missing her son.

To the delight of his father, Steve earned his degree with honors. Shortly after graduation, he joined an engineering and consulting firm that one of his classmates had just founded. After a year, the new company started growing tremendously, and they needed to hire additional engineers and staff members. A couple of more years down the road, and Steve was appointed the new vice president of the international division in charge of business development activities. His main role was to promote the company across the globe and especially in growing economies. Steve was very intelligent and came across as a nice guy. He traveled a lot internationally to meet potential clients. Most of them were government agencies and ministries. Steve was able to develop strong relationships with government officials and other influential individuals who had a say in awarding engineering contracts.

Steve spotted Georges a few months after he started with the company. Georges was young and ambitious, and Steve needed someone he could trust. Steve took Georges under his wing and brought him on several trips, showing him how to develop client relationships. Dealing with people from other cultures and sometimes in different languages was a challenge, but Georges learned quickly and enjoyed working with his mentor. As the years passed, Steve started traveling less, leaving his protégé in charge of meeting new prospects and maintaining existing relationships. When Steve was appointed president of the international division, it was natural for him to bring Georges on board and promote him to vice president, the position that Steve had held. Georges was not only grateful to his mentor but felt as he owed him for all his help and support throughout the years.

The Merger

CAN Engineering Services was a private company established by Gabriel Solice. The company specialized in providing engineering and consulting services for different sectors, ranging from energy and transportation to forestry and land management. The company started serving clients in Canada and the United States before going abroad and expanding internationally. CAN employed more than 8,000 staff members (mostly engineers) in more than ten countries, mainly in Asia, Africa and Eastern Europe. Headquartered in Mexico, the company used various agents and representatives to perform business development activities. CAN was investigated by an international lending agency for inappropriate practices, but the company was not penalized. Years later, CAN merged with another engineering firm based in the United States called COM, and the result of the merger was a new company called COMCAN Engineering. Senior management at COM was interested in the relationships that CAN engineers had established throughout the years around the world. During the announcement of the merger, Gabriel Solice was named the new CEO of COMCAN.

That company was becoming a leading engineering firm in the world with major projects ranging from construction of oil plants, dams and bridges, to development of cities. Most of these projects were led by local governments in need of modern infrastructures to support growth and attract investors. Organizations such as the African Development Bank were involved in lending money and financing some of these projects to assist local governments. As such, they had their say in the bidding process and the selection of service providers.

Steve and Georges had strong relationships with key individuals in those organizations given their involvement in several projects and the quality of the services rendered throughout the years. They also maintained ties with influential people, such as ministers, heads of state and other government officials and local agents who were hired to assist initially in establishing those relationships.

In the Media

The engineering and construction industry requires companies to adopt specific business practices to win contracts and be successful. But those practices are not always transparent. This case started in March when some competitors started complaining about suspicious business methods used by COMCAN to win contracts in Eastern Europe. These complaints caught the attention of international organizations that were involved in the bidding and selection process of vendors. In addition, allegations of corruption were raised locally against government officials for allowing COMCAN to win a major project related to the construction of a new city. Local newspapers wrote about the case and asked the government to initiate an investigation.

After the merger, COMCAN engineering was headquartered in the United States and had to abide by local and international regulations, such as the Foreign Corrupt Practices Act (FCPA) and the Sarbanes-Oxley Act (SOX). Corporate managers were made aware of the case a couple of days after the local newspaper published the story. Management knew this could cause reputational damage to COMCAN, and it posed a risk to the viability of winning other projects in the future. Therefore, they formed a team with the vice presidents of legal counsel, internal audit and compliance to establish an action plan and propose alternative solutions to the CEO and chairman of the board. Discussions were held and each alternative was evaluated. During one of the meetings held to discuss next steps, the CEO took the vice president of internal audit, Kevin Ford, aside and told him, "I'm not surprised with this.... As you know, in this industry, competition is tough and our competitors are ready to win by any means necessary. You should meet with Georges and Steve; it might a good start for your case. Anyway, I do not expect you to find anything and hopefully this will all go away in three weeks."

The allegations covered a wide range of issues, and an internal investigation had to be initiated to bring the truth to light. The CEO asked Kevin to lead it and to engage other experts to support and assist as needed.

Kickoff Interviews and Analyses

Kevin Ford started the investigation by performing a preliminary interview with Steve and Georges, as suggested by the CEO. Not knowing what to expect, they both answered his questions vaguely. They assured him that COMCAN did not use corrupt business practices and that the city development project in question went through a formal and transparent bidding process. Steve told Kevin, while smiling slightly, "I guess we had the best proposal . . . and our company is well known in the region for the quality of our engineering services."

Kevin had planned to perform a preliminary review of supporting documentation for the project and for a selection of other projects that COMCAN won in the region. However, after few days of review, it was clear that irregularities were present and he needed to take a closer look. He requested the resumes of accountants from three auditing and consulting firms and selected ten professionals to help him; I was one of them. The investigation team included not only accountants and auditors but also lawyers to assist with legal matters. Kevin wanted to keep the investigation discreet and therefore used the pretext with COMCAN employees that we were undertaking a SOX audit of various business processes. To help Kevin determine the scope of the inquiry, I needed to understand how it came about. Could it result in litigation? What was the source of the allegations? The answer to these questions would guide us through our scoping process.

First, we decided to preserve the electronic data to prevent any potential alterations or deletions. We collected e-mails, hard drives from laptops and desktops, phone logs and peripherals from each person who was potentially involved in the case. These individuals were mainly from management and were not aware of the investigation. We established our tasks, which included:

- Obtain a high-level overview of the control environment (e.g., whistle-blower program, code of ethics, investigation protocol).
- Understand accounting processes related to cash advances, expense reports and payments to vendors.
- Review expense reports submitted by management.
- Validate costs allocated to projects in Eastern Europe and their supporting documentation.
- Validate indirect costs, such as marketing and proposal costs allocated to specific accounts.
- Review agreements with agents and subcontractors.

Each member of the investigation team was assigned to a task under the supervision of a more senior team member. I was responsible for reporting directly to Kevin.

A Slow Process

Initially, we held meetings with the controller and some accounting staff to better understand specific accounting processes and to gather information. Other team members began reviewing expense reports submitted by Steve, Georges and other key employees who traveled frequently and were regularly exposed to agents and representatives. These reviews encompassed a variety of steps, from entering data in a standard template to evaluating supporting documentation submitted with each expense. Data analytics were performed to emphasize a few elements: recurrent vendors, high-dollar expenses and duplicate payments. We wanted to use the preliminary findings of this exercise during the interview phase.

While this was occurring, a team of five began reviewing the costs allocated to projects in Eastern Europe. For each payment made to an agent or a vendor, we reviewed the contract to determine if it was in agreement with the scope of the services provided and the terms of payment. Then we compared the total amount of fees paid to a specific vendor or agent with the contract. About ten projects, all of which were partially or fully financed by an international lending institution and including the one in question, incurred extra costs during the past five years (our review period). The team analyzed each expense that exceeded $500 and the supporting documentation. We also looked at indirect costs, such as marketing and proposal expenses allocated to specific accounts. Both projects took us about two months to complete and required tremendous effort from the accounting staff to retrieve all the information we requested. A mandate that was supposed to take three weeks was approaching three months.

After our initial review period, we prepared a set of questions to ask Steve and Georges. We hoped the interviews would help us achieve three things: gather additional information, corroborate our preliminary findings and identify new leads that could narrow down the scope of our investigation. We scheduled five interviews with members of the senior management group — Steve, Georges and three vice presidents involved in business development in Eastern Europe. A representative from internal audit and legal were required at each interview. Most of the questions were asked by the internal auditor, whereas counsel was there to advise the employee if legal questions arose. Some interviews were held in Spanish and others in English, and each one took more than three hours. The interviewees were stressed, but they answered the questions calmly and clearly. When asking the questions, we were very attentive to nonverbal cues, such as tone, inflection and body language. We asked them all if they were aware of COMCAN's whistleblower program to anonymously report acts of fraud and irregularities, and four of the five said they were not.

At that point, Kevin and I felt that we did not have any strong leads and decided to review electronic data that had been preserved at the beginning of the investigation. There were more than one million e-mails to review, many of which had several documents attached to them. Kevin told me, "It will take us two years with an army to look at all these e-mails and attachments!" Instead, we came up with specific keywords based on our preliminary findings and used them to filter out irrelevant e-mails. I gathered a small team of investigators to help me weed through all the remaining messages. I remember a lot of the e-mails I read; some of them were pertinent to the investigation and others were very personal. We were even able to read deleted e-mails and documents.

This exercise provided answers to some of the questions we had, corroborated statements the interviewees made and provided additional evidence for us to investigate. One instance that I recall during the interview of Georges was related to an invoice for medical services submitted through his expense report; COMCAN had paid for dental work for a foreign government official during his visit to Canada. When I asked Georges about the charge, he said, "Mr. Johanescu had an emergency and needed to have a tooth removed to ease his pain. We couldn't let our client suffer. It was a matter of hospitality."

During our document search, we found an e-mail from Johanescu to Georges thanking him for paying his dental expenses. I decided to call the dentist's office to inquire further. Using the invoice attached to the expense report, I was able to get specific information about Johanescu's treatment and learned that he had seven teeth removed. The receptionist also told me when his appointment was made — two weeks before his visit to Canada.

A Different Kind of Interview

We found that expense reports submitted for the questioned contract were not always substantiated with supporting documents, approvals were not formally provided and documented in the standard form and cash advances were not always reconciled. In addition, we found expenses that had no legitimate business purposes. Our review of costs allocated to other projects or other overhead accounts returned similar findings. Some of the invoices Georges or Steve submitted had interesting descriptions, such as gratuity, incentive or reallocation costs. When comparing total fees paid to vendors and agents to budgeted amounts, there were significant discrepancies that could not be explained by the project manager or accounting staff.

We decided a second set of interviews was essential to confront specific employees and get to the bottom of this case. Kevin decided to start with Steve and Georges. We reviewed the statements they made originally and prepared questions based on our findings from the review of electronic data.

This round of interviews would be more confrontational than the first one. We presented Steve and Georges with evidence and demanded explanations. At one point during his interview, Georges started sweating and became very nervous. His explanations were unclear or inconsistent with his previous statements. Conversely, Steve maintained his calm demeanor and answered with very short responses. Both Steve and Georges knew that we had an overall picture and that they could not fool us anymore.

The corruption involved Georges and Steve paying bribes and kickbacks to foreign officials in return for COMCAN winning project bids. They used agents to facilitate bribe payments without being noticed by COMCAN's compliance or finance departments. Fees were paid as commissions to foreign agents and representatives, and then a portion was used to pay bribes and kickbacks to government agents. In addition, fictitious invoices were prepared with a generic description of the services rendered, and payment was made. At the time, project managers did not argue the cost allocated to their projects, given the nature of the expense. These payments were then funneled through the agents to pay bribes to foreign government officials. This approach was well known to senior executives and project managers as well, not just Georges and Steve. In total, the duo paid more than $1 million in bribes to secure contracts.

During these interviews, we brought in external lawyers to determine if there were FCPA implications and to discuss Steve and Georges' options. They were presented with two choices — resign with a settlement package or be fired with no package. They were required to sign a letter stating they would not take civil actions against COMCAN. Steve and Georges both seemed shocked when we gave them their options and told them they had a week to decide.

For COMCAM, the investigation helped identify and remediate control weaknesses, and management realized they needed to change a few business practices. By taking action early and disclosing their troubles to regulators, COMCAN was able to avoid paying fines and being barred from bidding on future projects. Steve and Georges both resigned from COMCAN but were not criminally charged.

Lessons Learned

I learned several lessons from this investigation. First of all, our team included personnel from different firms, which made coordination difficult at times. We held a kickoff meeting to ensure that everyone was on the same page and to align efforts as the investigation evolved, but we still experienced miscommunications. Assembling team members from the same firm might make the process smoother.

(continued)

(continued)

Most of the employees we interviewed were aware of the scheme, but they thought it was a normal business practice that senior management approved. The importance of the tone at the top is a key factor for enforcing a strong company culture and upholding an adequate control environment.

We collected and analyzed a significant amount of data, which extended the case. I learned the importance of defining the scope of the investigation along with the budget to ensure that the team stays on track. To assist with the scoping phase, important red flags should be reported to the investigation team at the outset.

In addition, some accounting personnel involved in gathering the requested information were not always aware of how things worked in the company. It took several iterations to understand the key accounting processes and corroborate preliminary findings. Trained and competent staff members are crucial not only in the course of investigations and audits but also in the daily survival of a company.

Potential compliance concerns, especially in view of the countries CAN operated in, were raised during the merger phase. However, the analysis was never completed, and the due diligence report made note of work yet to be done. All high-risk areas should be addressed before companies merge.

Recommendations to Prevent Future Occurrences

Based on the lessons learned from the investigation, COMCAM established an action plan to respond to various control weaknesses that we identified.

The Whistleblower Program

COMCAM's management decided to improve the whistleblower program to include guidelines pertaining to intake procedures, information retention, evaluation and escalation procedures, case tracking and monitoring, closeout procedures and management reporting. Training was given to employees to ensure continuous monitoring, confidentiality and anonymity. Putting a marketing brochure about the program on the fridge was no longer sufficient to inform employees of their rights and responsibilities. All employees are responsible to report fraud or irregularities to minimize reputational risk to the company. An effective whistleblower program must be well known by employees and used frequently for reporting irregularities.

Due Diligence

Before the merger between two companies, due diligence should be performed to determine if the companies are a good fit. Engineering companies can grow exponentially through mergers and acquisitions, but due diligence is not always performed adequately. To address this, COMCAM leaders established a thorough due diligence process for all new acquisitions and mergers. It included not only standard procedures, such as financial and IT systems review, but also a review of company anti-corruption policies and performing background checks. Management considers several factors in the due diligence process, such as the countries where the company operates, the base (e.g., government entities) and the use of agents to win business. It now takes a risk based approach to reviewing samples of projects and payments made to vendors and agents.

Improvement of Agent Selection Process

At COMCAM, the selection of agents was done by each business unit, and the VP of each unit was authorized to sign agreements with agents; there was no formal process in place. All agreements now have to go through a central review that includes background checks, financial assessments and questionnaires before being approved. COMCAM managers also started using external firms to perform some steps on their behalf. Agreements are now signed for two years and renewed only if the agent is in compliance with the requirements. This approach helps COMCAM standardize agent selection, maintain supporting documentation and minimize doing business with the wrong individuals or companies. Finally, invoices of services rendered by agents or representatives should be more detailed and specific.

Review of Expense Reports

Our review of expense reports took several days to complete due to the sheer number. Numerous weaknesses were identified and addressed by management. Accounting staff now review expense reports on a quarterly basis to identify discrepancies. Supporting documentation is required for each expense, including sufficient details to assess the validity and purpose. Also, travel requests are now centralized to one business unit so employees are no longer allowed to purchase travel tickets themselves.

Corruption is as old as humankind and exists in all human societies. In almost all nations, there are laws against corrupt practices. Regulations are becoming more stringent due to pressure from developed countries and the Organization of Economic Co-operation and Development. Therefore, companies are regulated and obliged to abide by those laws to do business. An essential driver is the tone at the top that could prevent bribery from becoming a way of doing business.

About the Author

Amine Antari is currently a manager in the internal audit department of an engineering and construction company responsible for divisional and forensic audits. His experience is mainly in financial and IT auditing and investigation of fraud and corruption, including anti–money laundering. Prior to that, he was a manager in the consulting and deals practice at PricewaterhouseCoopers LLP. He is a Certified Fraud Examiner and a Certified Information Systems Auditor. He has been a speaker in different conferences with regard to e-discovery and anti-corruption.

CHAPTER

Kickbacks for Comic Books

RAFAEL A. GARCIA

Carlos Diaz was, by all accounts, an ideal son and employee. When his father broke off his marriage and left the family, Carlos helped support his mother and younger sister by taking a job at a local supermarket; he was only 16 at the time. He kept this job all throughout college until graduation, when he began his vocation in the field of banking. Fresh out of school at 22 years old, Carlos took a job as a bank officer for Stone Bank and moved steadily up the ranks. He ultimately settled into a small business banker position, helping local businesses secure funding through loans or commercial lines of credit.

A Close Team

Stone Bank was a fairly large financial institution with more than $50 billion in assets and branches in several states; because of the bank's size, security was divided into two distinct groups: internal and external investigations. I was an internal fraud investigator responsible for cases involving employees suspected of wrongdoing. All other investigations were handled by the external fraud investigations team.

The Corporate Security Miami Field Office for Stone Bank was located in a plain white office building a couple floors up from a Stone Bank branch. Aside from me, there was Joe Valdes, another internal fraud investigator, and Maria Gonzalez, an external fraud investigator. We sat in our own cubicles within earshot of one another.

"¿Quisiera un cafecito?" asked Carlos when I first met him in April. He offered me a shot of Cuban espresso on his way to meet with Maria, the external fraud investigator. She called Carlos over to our office to discuss some commercial lines of credit (CLOC); the tax returns submitted with the initial application had been doctored.

A CLOC is a loan that works very much like a credit card. The lender agrees to lend a borrower a maximum amount of money within an agreed period of time for the purpose of providing working capital to a borrower's business. Generally, a borrower's business assets serve as collateral for the loan. The borrower is not advanced the entire sum of the money up front but instead uses a line of credit to borrow sums in smaller amounts.

Carlos was the loan officer for the CLOCs under investigation but was not yet under any suspicion. Maria's focus at the time was on the borrowers and Cristina Alonso, the Certified Public Account (CPA) who prepared all the tax returns. Maria's investigation started last October. Per the agreement in each CLOC, borrowers must submit their current year's tax returns to continue to prove to the lender that they are still financially healthy. One borrower's returns, however, revealed a huge discrepancy.

I had no intentions of prying, but it was difficult to keep my focus on work with Carlos' bursts of pompous laughter. Rather than meet with him in a private office, Maria had him sit in her cubicle. As he boasted about graduate school and nearing the completion of his master's degree in business administration, I overheard very little relevant information pertaining to Maria's investigation. Nearly 20 minutes after his arrival, Carlos strode his way past my cubicle and left the office.

Maria was still sipping her cafecito when she appeared next to my desk. "What did he do?" I asked her.

"Carlos?" she responded. "Nothing. He was the loan officer on those lines of credit we discussed. He's met with Cristina several times. I was hoping he could offer me some insight on how she referred the loans."

"It doesn't seem like you two got very far."

"No, we didn't. But poor thing! I wasn't about to press him; he's been so busy lately between work and school."

"Did you ever get a final count as to how many loans were falsified?"

"Yes." Her eyes widened as she leaned over my cubicle wall and added, "Sixty-nine loans. That comes out to almost $40 million! It's simply unbelievable!"

She was right. It was unbelievable to think that Carlos, a banker in his mid-20s, just walked into Stone Bank's Corporate Security office with a huge smile, offering coffee to the investigators to distract from the fact that he played a role in lending out $40 million, for which the bank was now suffering a loss. Such a track record was certainly egregious by all accounts, and if it were mine, I would find it difficult to maintain such a jaunty demeanor. It might have been too early for me to speculate, especially since I was not even on the case, but it was certainly a good time to invite myself into the investigation to take a peek around.

Interviewing Made Easy

It was a clear day in May when Maria and I had our first interview with one of the borrowers. Since the investigation began, Maria had been attempting to track down each of the borrowers referred to Carlos by Cristina. Most hired attorneys before they would even utter a word. But then one borrower, Juan, simply dropped in a local branch to discuss renegotiating the terms of his loan because he was no longer able to make payments.

We were sitting in a plain office across town with Juan, an elderly Cuban who spoke very little English. Remnants of his chalk-white hair were thinly laid out across his sunburned scalp; his hands and knuckles were calloused with dirt deeply embedded in the cracks of skin. Though Juan was earning his income through several manual labor jobs, he had initially obtained a loan for his courier business, aptly named Speedy Delivery Inc. The tax returns provided and signed by Cristina, his CPA, claimed his business earned, on average, $100,000 annually. Carlos helped Juan obtain a $150,000 loan to build his company.

Maria slid a copy of tax returns prepared by Cristina across the desk to Juan as she asked him, in Spanish, "How much is your company earning now?"

Juan barely glanced at the tax returns. "I'm no longer running it," he responded. "Business was too slow, so I've had to rely on odd jobs. That's why I can't make any payments on my loan."

"It says here your company earned $100,000 last year," Maria countered. "Has business really dropped off that much?"

"That's a lie," Juan scoffed. "I work alone and operate from a single van. I could never earn that much." While staring down at the tax returns, he asked, "Is that what this says?"

Juan went on to explain how he came to obtain the loan. An old friend approached him about an opportunity to get funding from the bank to help pay for expenses and introduced Juan to Cristina over lunch. To help his chances of obtaining the loan, Cristina advised Juan to list his friend as an officer of the company. The next time he saw Cristina was at her office to sign all the loan documents. He had never signed nor seen tax returns prepared by Cristina.

Once the loan was approved, Juan issued a check for $50,000 to Cristina. Cristina had agreed to also help Juan invest a portion of funds to help him repay the loan. He never questioned the investment as he was being given payments from Cristina every three months as planned. He admitted he thought the whole process was a bit suspicious, but he had a dire need for the money.

I asked Juan about Carlos' role in this process and whether he thought Carlos' actions were anything but sincere. Juan quickly referred to Carlos as a *caballero*, an endearing Spanish term for gentleman or knight. Juan developed this impression even though he first met Carlos only when it was time to sign the paperwork and close on the loan.

Before he left, Maria had Juan complete an affidavit attesting to his story. She also had him sign an Internal Revenue Service Form 4506-T. This form authorized the IRS to release electronic copies of Juan's actual income tax filings directly to Stone Bank. This would confirm what Juan had already acknowledged verbally: the tax returns presented and prepared by Cristina in support of the loan were misrepresentations of his true earnings.

It was June when the investigation was officially turned over to me. I was poring over Carlos' abandoned MySpace web page when Maria broke the news to me in my cubicle. My monitor was displaying a picture of Carlos wearing a sports coat and a proud smile while holding what appeared to be a shot of some amber liquor in one hand and a lit cigar in the other. She was retiring at the end of the month and, because I already had some knowledge of the case, she decided it would be best if I took over.

The Case Becomes Mine

At this point, I wanted to establish my own baseline on the case. With our in-house legal counsel focusing on contacting the borrowers, I decided to concentrate on the internal component (after all, I was the internal investigator). I had Carlos return to our offices for another interview.

As before, Carlos arrived with coffee in hand. This time, I chose a private office with a closed door to conduct the interview. I did not plan on confronting him; I was going to simply gather information from him, even if it was regarding details I already had answers to. I needed to gauge his truthfulness.

"Did you ever accept money or gifts from Cristina, ever?" I asked him after some brief introductions.

He glanced away from my eyes briefly enough for me to notice just before he responded with "No, never. She always offered to give me tickets to a game or to buy me lunch. Is it okay for a client to buy me lunch?"

"If it's within the company limits, yes." I responded.

"Okay, well, yeah, she bought me lunch a couple times, but it was nothing lavish. Sergey and I have actually taken Cristina out to lunch on several occasions to discuss clients."

Sergey was the regional manager for the small business banking division for Stone Bank. He was also Carlos' direct manager. Like most employees in a sales position, Carlos was paid a regular salary, but he also earned an incentive for the number and size of loans he closed. Likewise, Sergey (and Sergey's manager and so on) earned an incentive whenever Carlos successfully closed on a loan. The more money lent to borrowers, the more Carlos and Sergey earned.

"Do you really think I would take money from Cristina?" Carlos directed at me.

"No, but it is protocol that I ask you. I just need to get these sorts of questions out of the way, so that we can focus on investigating those responsible," I offered.

I asked Carlos about Cristina and the borrowers. He explained that for someone in his role, finding a CPA such as Cristina and successfully building a rapport is a coveted goal. A CPA is a gold mine for small business bankers to seek out potential borrowers. He rarely even had to ask her for referrals; she would send him clients regularly. She became his *source*, a term used frequently in small business banking. He claimed he would always meet with the customers at their place of business to visually assess their needs and ability to pay the loan, but he relied on his source to first find the customer.

"Did Cristina ever prepare your personal tax returns?" I asked Carlos.

"Actually, yes. She prepared both my personal and corporate returns for the last three years," he replied.

"Did you pay her?"

He immediately straightened up his posture and replied, "Yes, of course. I paid $100 for the personal returns and $1,000 for the corporate returns." I suspected he knew it was against bank policy to accept free services from clients.

"Tell me more about this corporation. Was this outside employment approved by Sergey?"

"Yes, Sergey knew about it. I own a couple rental properties that I managed through the corporation. I also used to do promotions for clubs."

"What was the name of your corporation?"

"Ladrones Incorporated," he responded. He then offered, "Oh, and Cristina and I had plans to invest in a check cashing store, but that never happened."

"Did either of you ever exchange funds or pool funds together in support of the joint venture," I asked.

"No, it was just something we discussed."

After our interview, I asked Carlos to provide me a written affidavit reiterating the statements he made during our conversation. And, although I had to sit through his boasting about attending grad school, it seemed that I gained some relevant material. It was time to expand my investigation into Carlos.

During the next few weeks, I interviewed several other employees in Stone Bank's small business banking division. In addition to Sergey, I met with other bankers, collections staff, underwriters and even a former classmate of Cristina's who worked as a manager at Stone Bank. The hidden culture of the banking unit was beginning to unfold.

Linda, one of the primary underwriters on several of Cristina's loans, painted a less-than-sanguine picture of her experience at Stone Bank. The taciturn underwriter described how she was often the victim of Sergey's polemics as he demanded she find a way for the bank to close on loans by changing the terms and conditions. CPAs were regularly lionized by the sales staff because they had many potential clients to offer the bankers, potentially padding their salaries. Sales staff viewed underwriters, however, as replete with techniques for denying loans and capping their income potential. Despite Linda's frustrations, nothing she described was either criminal in nature or a deviation from policy.

Between interviews, I had approximately 40 boxes filled to the brim with bank records to review. I had copies of each of the 69 loans and all their supporting documentation supplied by Cristina. I also had about six years' worth of her personal and business bank records as well as those from the borrowers and Carlos, along with copies of canceled checks. It was vital that I had direct knowledge of the flow of money.

As I examined the financial records, clear patterns began to emerge. It was obvious that Cristina played a crucial role in the scheme. Not only had Carlos helped her obtain a $400,000 loan for her own accounting business, she nearly always received a substantial cut from each of the loans. But it was the emergence of a locally based jeweler that truly piqued my interest.

The Diamond Pyramid

Santiago Zaragoza was the apparent owner of at least five separate corporations, each of which received a loan through Carlos for a grand total of $6,750,000. Santiago reportedly operated a jewelry business, but it was unclear whether he manufactured or distributed his products. Of all the individual loan borrowers, Santiago received the most funding. However, as I followed the flow of funds, it seemed that Santiago, like Cristina, also took a cut from each of the other 69 loans. His bank accounts were actually the final destination. And, as Juan had described to me and Maria, a smaller portion of funds was periodically returned to the borrowers. It appeared I was slowly beginning to uncover an investment scam.

It was August in Miami, which meant it was pouring rain every afternoon; a bit of a respite from the blistering heat of summer. It was also the time when responses began pouring in from our borrowers. Stone Bank's legal counsel sent notices to each borrower demanding they repay their loans in full immediately and provide 4506-T forms to verify the accuracy of their original applications. The response confirmed our suspicions: the bulk of the funds were sent to Santiago for an alleged investment in jewelry. Santiago lured victims to invest their money for purported guaranteed fixed returns ranging between 18 and 120 percent annually. He claimed the investments were collateralized by diamonds. However, like a typical Ponzi scheme, Santiago relied on new investors to pay returns to the initial investors. It appeared Santiago was no longer able to find new investors. So, when the investors (our borrowers) demanded to see their diamonds (the collateral), they discovered they were being swindled all along.

Unfortunately for Stone Bank, Santiago teamed up with a CPA to falsify tax returns to help his investors buy into his fraud. And some of the investors claimed a bank employee was in on the whole scam; some even said the unnamed banker received a 10 percent cut. Before I sat down with Carlos again, I needed to find some supporting evidence. Admittedly, I never expected to find the smoking gun.

The Paper Freeway

It's rare for me to have a strong physical and emotional reaction when examining financial records; after all, it's just paper, right? But that's exactly what happened when I came across a single canceled check written from Cristina's bank account.

"Joe!" I was sitting at my cubicle when I called out to the other internal investigator, sitting in a cubicle to my left. "You'll never believe this one."

Joe stood up and responded, "What's up, Ralph?" He was somewhat familiar with my investigation because while I was focusing on this single case, he had to pick up the slack from my other investigations.

"Take a look at this check." I handed him a copy of a check for $7,500. "Cristina issued this check just a couple months after Carlos booked a loan for $75,000."

"Okay, so what's the big deal?" Joe remained stolid. He was careful to never jump to conclusions. He inspected the check, paying close attention to the payee line. "Who's this Ladrones Inc.?"

Joe and I would never have ever thought it possible that Carlos would leave a paper trail for someone to uncover. But here I was, holding a check payable to Carlos' corporation for exactly 10 percent of a loan he had closed for a borrower nearly two months prior. It was more like a freeway than a trail.

Joe remained silent, trying to conceive how Carlos could justify this payment. "Did you compare the endorsement to Carlos' known signature?" he finally asked.

"Sure did. It's a perfect match." Carlos' signed affidavit from our interview served as a fresh comparison. It also served as a stark reminder that Carlos had already been given an opportunity to disclose this payment.

I could have used Carlos as my personal barista during the next few evenings. I spent long hours examining the remaining records. After closely inspecting every canceled check, I found a total of four checks amounting to $29,000 and all payable to Ladrones Inc. All the checks were issued by Cristina, endorsed by Carlos and negotiated at another bank. If Carlos did anything to conceal these payments, it was to deposit them into an account he held somewhere other than Stone Bank.

My next objective was to prepare for my second, and possibly last, interview with Carlos. I assembled a team of investigators. Joe had a proclivity for admission-seeking interviews (during his law enforcement years, he was a certified polygrapher), so he and I would interview Carlos together. The others would search through Carlos' office and computer equipment. Two investigators would collect and catalog all the documents in Carlos' office, while a third investigator and a computer forensics expert would seize and copy all the electronic media.

The search and seizure team arrived at Carlos' office early on a September morning, just prior to Carlos' expected arrival. I called him on his cell phone and asked him to come to my office immediately. He was already in his car, driving to work. Joe and I sipped our coffee, going over our notes and interview plan while we waited.

Carlos arrived at my office shortly after the call. Joe and I sat with him in a closed room. I went first.

The Interview

"Are these your bank statements?" I asked him, handing him copies of the bank statements for Ladrones. Early on, our computer forensic investigator found that Carlos received these bank statements at his work e-mail address.

"Yeah, those are for my company," he responded. He was tense. "How did you get those?"

"They were sent to your bank e-mail address. Are you the sole signer for the account of Ladrones Inc.? Does anyone else have access to your account?" I had to lock him into acknowledging he had sole control over the account, so he could not claim the payments from Cristina were for someone else.

"Wh-what? Yes, of course. I'm the only one on the account."

I asked him, "Did you ever accept any money from Cristina?"

The chair he sat in was immovable. Carlos was desperately trying to find a comfortable position to sit. I recognized this as a buildup of physiological stress due to his attempt to conceal the truth. He finally answered, "No, never."

I purposefully did not show him copies of the checks from Cristina. I wanted to get him to the point where he was comfortable enough to tell us the truth. After that it was up to Joe to seal the deal.

Joe and I took a break from the interview room for a few minutes. When we returned, it was Joe's turn. He began with "A person's character is measured not by the scope or complexity of the mistake he or she has made but rather by his or her actions in the attempt to correct the mistake."

The sermon that only Joe could deliver lasted about 20 minutes. Joe, who was in his 50s, was especially good at building father/son or pastor/parishioner relationships with his interviewees. I have heard Joe's sermon many times before, and it is truly rare for suspects not to break down and confess their sins.

Carlos' physical reaction to Joe's talk was a common precursor to admission and acceptance of guilt. He relaxed into his chair with his shoulders slumped forward as he sighed.

"Okay, okay," he responded. "I was double-dipping."

"Could you explain further?" I interjected.

"Cristina would pay me for just performing my job. I was happy to accept because it was a nice supplement to my regular pay."

"How much did Cristina pay you over the years?" I asked him.

"It was probably about $30,000 to $40,000 a year for about two years."

We continued to interview him, asking him to further clarify how the whole scheme was organized. In the end, he never admitted to any knowledge about the Ponzi scheme or fraudulent tax returns. He maintained that all he did wrong was accept kickbacks from Cristina.

As before, I asked him to again provide a written affidavit, this time with his confession. I informed him he was being placed on suspension pending further action from human resources. He said he had some bank documents, unrelated to the investigation, in his car that he wanted to turn over. Joe and I escorted Carlos to his car, a cream-colored sedan. He popped open his trunk; scattered across the bed of his trunk were about 30 to 40 comic books.

"Sorry for the mess," Carlos apologized. "I'm an avid reader."

He slid the comic books to one side and grabbed a thick folder holding miscellaneous documents that he said he wanted to return before his suspension. He handed me the folder and apologized again. "Ralph, Joe. I'm sorry. I know I got in over my head with this. Thanks for listening."

Presenting a Final Case

After Carlos' departure, I immediately held a conference call with several bank managers, a human resources representative and our legal counsel. I informed them of Carlos' admission. The decision was clear; his employment was to be terminated effective immediately. His manager and human resources would handle the notification.

I prepared all the documents — the 40 boxes of bank records plus Carlos' admission — for my final referral to the U.S. Secret Service. I originally referred the case to them back in June, so by now they had met and interviewed Cristina. She was fully cooperating and also admitted the scam.

It took several more months, but the U.S. Attorney's Office (USAO) obtained federal indictments for Santiago, Cristina and Carlos. The following summer, details about the arrests and the fraud were in the *Miami Herald*. More victims of Santiago's Ponzi scheme began coming forward, including a local politician. It turned out that not all his investors took out loans to buy their way into the scam.

The jeweler, CPA and banker pleaded guilty to their charges. All were charged with multiple counts of bank fraud; Santiago was also charged with securities violations. Ultimately, Santiago was sentenced to 121 months imprisonment, Cristina received 52 months and Carlos was given 30 months.

Both the USAO and our legal counsel attempted to seek recovery from the three defendants and each of the borrowers. The borrowers had nothing to offer; their collateral was business assets, which were too insignificant (and sometimes nonexistent) to collect. Cristina had some property valued at a few million dollars that she turned over. Santiago, who designed the whole scam, was scammed himself. He spent the bulk of his millions supporting a lavish lifestyle and on some allegedly valuable pieces of artwork. The artwork, though, turned out to be fake. None of this was significant enough to make a dent on the bank's loss of $39 million. I wondered whether Carlos' comic book collection was worth anything.

Lessons Learned

This investigation revealed a strong dichotomy between the risk-based and incentive-based cultures. While our underwriters were focused on driving quality loan production by weighing the risks against potential gains of a loan, our bankers were driven by the quantity of loans with the goal of producing sales and being compensated with incentives. There is risk inherent with any loan closed by the bank. The question is: what is the appropriate balance between risk and reward?

This delicate balancing act is further obfuscated when one relies on trust. Carlos was not only motivated by the sales incentive he stood to gain from the bank; he was also receiving kickbacks from Cristina. The bank and its underwriters relied on Carlos to perform his due diligence with his customers, but he abused that trust when he chose to focus on his own personal gain. And, in so doing, he clouded his own judgment, which (intentionally or not) caused him to miss some obvious red flags.

Carlos also extended trust to Cristina and the paperwork she submitted on the customers' behalf. Carlos accepted the documents, including tax returns and bank statements, at face value. If Cristina submitted a document claiming a customer earned $150,000 per year, nobody at the bank questioned it. This was clearly a mistake, as we learned these documents were fabrications.

Recommendations to Prevent Future Occurrences

Building a more risk-based culture can be accomplished on two fronts. First, develop stronger authentication tools to verify a borrower's true net worth and ability to make payments on a loan. Second, change the incentive-based culture by restructuring the compensation packages for bankers — although this suggestion is likely to be met with contention; honest people don't want to make less money.

Authentication/Verification Tools

The bank should have taken the time to verify the authenticity of the supporting documents submitted for the loans. Two cost-effective tools all banks have at their disposal are:

- IRS Form 4506-T: Request for Transcript of Tax Return — used to obtain an electronic transcript of the borrower's federal income tax filings from the IRS
- Fannie Mae Form 1006: Verification of Deposit — used to verify the cash deposits at other financial institutions that the applicant listed on the loan application

Had Stone Bank required borrowers to sign these forms, the information revealed would have put a stop to the loans before they were approved.

Restructure Incentive Compensation Program

It would certainly be difficult to argue against tying bankers' pay to their performance. If you work harder, you should be compensated accordingly. However, the ideal program for incentive compensation is difficult to establish; many banks restructure their compensation programs every few years.

Regardless, there are some key features to building an effective program to help keep bankers focused on quality loan production. The Federal Reserve, the central bank of the United States, addresses three existing methods to make incentive compensation programs more sensitive to risk:

1. *Risk adjustment of awards.* The amount of compensation is adjusted to take into account the risk the employee's activities pose to the organization.
2. *Deferral of payment.* The actual payout of compensation is delayed and adjusted for actual losses or other aspects of performance that become clear only during the deferral period. This may include a "clawback" provision where the employee must return compensation payments after risk outcomes occur.
3. *Longer performance periods.* The time period used to measure an employee's performance can be extended (for example, from quarterly to biannually).

Consideration should also be given to structuring a program that provides incentive compensation based on team results rather than individual efforts. A program encouraging team-based performance as opposed to individual results will likely encourage the bankers to police themselves and their coworkers to seek quality loan production to prevent retributions such as clawbacks from nonperforming or even fraudulent loans.

About the Author

Rafael Garcia, CFE, M.S., has been in banking for 13 years with the last 9 years dedicated to the field of bank fraud investigation. He is a Certified Fraud Examiner. He also holds a bachelor of arts from Florida International University and a master's of science in criminal justice from Michigan State University.

CHAPTER

Interrupted Production

CARL KNUDSON

This case study is presented through the eyes of the Certified Fraud Examiner (CFE) working on behalf of the defense. The author, besides being a CFE, spent many years in the intelligence and federal law enforcement communities, including the Central Intelligence Agency and the IRS Criminal Investigation Division.

Danny and Vicky Lennon huddled together on the front porch of their upscale Beverly Hills residence, trembling in the cold morning fog as the sun peered through the chilling mist. Neighbors began leaving for work and gawked at the Lennons' obvious misfortune. The couple had been ushered out of their own house while the FBI search team completed the execution of the search warrant.

The End of the Beginning

Danny Lennon had produced and directed Academy Award–nominated movies for decades and was intrigued by the prospect of creating a film festival for one of the emerging nations in Latin America. Vicky, his lifelong confidante and office manager of 30 years, knew that Danny was growing weary of the demands of directing and producing movies; in addition, some of his last endeavors, although artistically sound, had not done well at the box office. Danny was the creative part of the duo, and Vicky had a penchant for detail and sometimes an abrasive-pushy demeanor.

Perhaps this could be a new beginning, or at least a good ending. Danny's health wasn't good and he relied on an oxygen bottle that he carried wherever he went; it was a testament to the ravages of smoking for too many years.

Consuela de la Paz, the newly appointed minister of the tourist bureau for the Latin American country of Bella Cora, invited Danny and Vicky and other Hollywood nobility to her estate to celebrate her recent appointment.

Consuela de la Paz was a member of the aristocratic founding family of her country. She grew up in Switzerland and was educated in the finest private schools in Europe. She was fluent in many languages and a gifted concert pianist. She had ambitions to put the Bella Cora Film Festival on the map to rival Cannes. Perhaps her ambitions would ultimately lead to the president's mansion?

Danny knew that putting on a film festival was not too unlike producing a movie — he needed talent and a team of professionals to plan and promote the event. Thus the talks began in earnest over crepes Suzettes and chateaubriand, among the roving mariachis. One thing was for sure, Consuela wanted Danny and Vicky to lead the charge because of their connections to the Hollywood elite who could make or break such an event. So the devil was in the details to be ironed out over the next several months of proposals and negotiations.

Mordida (Bite) por Favor

Of course, as was the custom in some Latin American countries, Consuela de la Paz hinted that perhaps Danny's appreciation for being awarded this wonderful project could be demonstrated with a nice gift, a little "bite," even perhaps 10 percent of the total contract. But "My dear friend, we can work this out once the contracts have been finalized," she demurred.

Of course, Danny had encountered this "accommodation" in many countries where he had filmed movies; even the politicians and union bosses in America's larger cities had to have their palms greased. So you add a couple of ghosts to the payroll, hire a couple of their relatives as "consultants" and charge them off to expenses deeply embedded into the corporate ledgers. The truth was that it was an accepted cost of doing business.

Danny continued his discussions with Consuela's staff over the next few days, and they agreed that there would be four separate projects for the festival: the actual management and production of the event, creation of a website that would have worldwide promotional coverage, brochures and door prizes for attendees and a book that would chronicle the festival's success each year. Each phase would require separate contracts.

Back in Los Angeles, Danny and Vicky excitedly launched their new business venture knowing that their combined creative and business genius would elevate the Bella Cora Film Festival to international prominence.

Let the Fun Begin

Danny knew that once the festival was announced, keeping control of the projects and ultimately the funds would be a huge challenge. And with the beginning of the promotional campaign, the sharks would start circling.

Alain du Pont was a high-strung Belgian who co-produced the Cannes Film Festival over the years but had been let go for reasons not provided by the festival executives. Danny ran in the same European entertainment circles as Alain and so, with some trepidation, he placed a call to Alain with an offer to act as the co-producer of Bella Cora. Danny intentionally did not tell Alain the country where the festival would be held. Alain's expertise in budgeting for a film festival would be invaluable, plus the man had visibility in the industry.

They struck a deal. The only caveat was that Alain would contract with Danny's company, DVL Media Productions, through a company that Alain would incorporate in Switzerland. Alain refused to do business in the United States. Danny called his longtime legal counsel to draw up the contract. It would be no problem to contract through a shell company in Switzerland to accommodate Alain. Many of the big investors from Europe used such companies for asset protection and tax avoidance strategies.

The marketing and media piece of the project was easy: Danny's longtime friend, Jerry Ganz of Ganz Media Consultants, had promoted every one of Danny's films and had an impressive supporting staff to accommodate the demands of a film festival. Ganz Media would create promotional brochures and the book that would be compiled at the end of the first event. Ganz would also provide budget proposals for their work and function as a subcontractor through DVL Media Productions, Danny's company.

What's an FCPA?

The last part of the project was to establish a website for the film festival, which required technology expertise specific to Bella Cora and its question-able telecommunications structure. Danny put out feelers for subcontractors who could establish a reliable and appealing website that also had international browsing capabilities.

Serge "Sugar" Mikhel was introduced to Danny by Alain du Pont as a genius in web design who had worked at Cannes but was also familiar with Latin American computer networks. Serge had been deported from the United States years ago but had an attorney in Los Angeles who could draft up a contract to work for Danny. Danny farmed out the particulars to his longtime legal counsel to iron out the details.

It wasn't until Danny read the contract later that he noticed a provision regarding violations to something known as the Foreign Corrupt Practices Act (FCPA) and foreign officials had been inserted. No matter, Serge would also be a subcontractor working through DVL Media Productions; thus, all of the contracts with Consuela de la Paz would run through Danny's company, and Danny would have control over all of the funds.

Accounting Magic or Not?

Vicky Lennon was the office manager for DVL Media Productions with a small staff of actor wannabes who helped in the office. Vicky kept a tight rein on the office staff when Danny was traveling. Becky Lawson, a family friend and confidante of Danny, kept the accounting records even though she had no experience or training in accounting. Gerry Leib, CPA, had done the business and personal returns for Danny for 20 years and was able to decipher Becky's accounting summaries, such as they were. Like many small business operations, DVL Media Productions was a subchapter S corporation, and all of the ordinary income (or loss) flowed through to the Lennons' 1040s.

The budget proposals for the production, promotion, website and book were completed and refined by Vicky and her staff. The proposed budgets included markups for each of the subcontractors who would bill DVL Media for their actual costs and include a respectable salary. Danny and Vicky then adjusted the numbers upward to include their anticipated profit of 20 percent, at least for the first year; 20 percent of $3.5 million wasn't bad to start with. There were a few expense categories that were intentionally vague, but that wasn't abnormal in the entertainment business. Everyone had to have some wiggle room to maneuver unexpected cost increases.

Make It Happen

Consuela de la Paz's bureaucrats painstakingly reviewed the separate budget proposals. It was a grueling and tedious process because they had no idea what was appropriate for film festival costs, but they challenged each and every line item. Finally, after months of wrangling, the up-front fees were approved and the final contracts were signed in Consuela's offices. The signing was done with much fanfare, and many local dignitaries were in attendance, including the president of Bella Cora. Danny invited a number of Hollywood stars to the event.

Even before the ink was dry on the contracts, Consuela quietly steered Danny to her private study to confirm the payment schedule and routing of her *mordida*. "Let's start with 5 percent of the contract funds paid," she instructed Danny. "I have a niece who is studying in Switzerland and we already have a numbered trust account set up there, so transfers will not be suspicious to the money-laundering fanatics at Interpol." Consuela's niece would be a "creative consultant" for the projects, and Danny received the necessary routing numbers and wire instructions to make it happen. "Fifty percent should go there, but the other half should go to my uncle's company in Bella Cora, which will be a subcontractor for DVL Media Productions," she advised. "Uncle Tomas has an account in Hong Kong." Consuela then provided the routing numbers for the wire transfers.

And with that, the accommodation was complete. The payments would be listed as "commissions" and taken as an expense on the income statements of DVL Media Productions. Danny thought to himself, "I don't think this is Consuela de la Paz's first rodeo."

"Bella Cora Film Festival a smashing success," blared the news release. "Over 6,000 tourists attended the first-ever film festival in Bella Cora. There were many notable Hollywood luminaries in attendance. The Ministry of Finance estimated that more than $20 million flowed into the local business establishments."

Consuela de la Paz was the new superstar of Bella Cora and a member of the film festival elite.

Slings and Arrows

Within days of the invasion of their residence by the FBI search team, Danny and Vicky were contacted by FBI and IRS agents who wanted to interview them at their office regarding violations of the FCPA and also to discuss charges related to money laundering and tax evasion. The FBI and IRS agents worked together and complemented each other's skill sets.

Danny had already contacted a well-respected law firm in Pasadena to get a reading on what was going on. All they knew at that time was what was listed on the application for the search warrant that had been thrown on their kitchen table when the FBI search team departed.

Marilyn Porter, the senior partner at the Pasadena law firm of Porter, Roche and Blackman, had prosecuted many FCPA cases for the U.S. Attorney's Office in Los Angeles and knew what to do. She was as tough as nails but was equally adept at convincing juries that her client was obviously innocent. What really bothered Marilyn was how in the world the FCPA charges began. There was little mention in the FBI case agent's affidavit for the search warrant as to the source, but only a few people in Bella Cora were privy to the arrangement. Gerald Maroney, a top-notch trial attorney from Beverly Hills, was brought in to represent Danny, and Marilyn was to represent Vicky.

Was there an informant in the office? No one from the staff had ever discussed the possibility of some type of illegal activity going on. Becky, their in-house accountant, had asked for the backup to the contracts when the first monies began to flow out to the subcontractors. She was given all of the contracts, even the ones related to Consuela's niece and uncle. Nobody in the office questioned whether the subcontractors performed the work they were supposed to do.

There was no attempt by Danny or Vicky to hide the wire transfer applications or confirmations that had been sent over the past three years to the niece and the uncle. They all sat clearly in a basket on top of Vicky's desk. In fact, the defense provided all of the banking and accounting records to the government without the need for subpoenas since they could obtain the documents anyway.

No one in the office had contact with Consuela de la Paz other than Danny and sometimes Vicky. So were did this allegation begin?

Where's the Mole?

William Prescott (Bill), the FBI legal attaché in Bella Cora, had monthly briefings with Win Scott (Scotty), the Chief of Station, Political Section at the embassy, but most of the time they just swapped war stories of their service in Vietnam. The meetings were always held at the prestigious Tres Vidas Country Club where they rubbed elbows with the local politicians.

On this particular day, Scotty was in a serious conversation with one of the directors of Bella Cora's Ministry of Tourism when Bill approached their table. They had a heated discussion and the tourist director's arms flailed about, his voice unusually loud and profane. Perhaps the director had one too many martinis with lunch. But as Bill sat down, the director bolted from his chair, obviously in a hurry to get somewhere.

Scotty was not amused, and his ruddy complexion was even redder than usual. In a hushed voice, Scotty related what he had just heard from the director — someone high up in the Ministry of Tourism was taking money from a Hollywood producer, the one who produced the Bella Cora Film Festival. Bill was stunned to hear that it had been going on for more than three years right under his nose.

Scotty told Bill he knew who the person was, but the identity could never be revealed. The person was part of the "royal" family that had founded Bella Cora, and it was vital to the U.S. interests in the region to keep the identity under wraps.

If under wraps was really what he wanted, Scotty should have never told Bill. Two days later, Bill sent a message to FBI Headquarters relaying what Scotty had told him because it was a big deal, friendship or not. Bill was summoned back to Washington to meet with the director and the assistant attorney general (AG) at the Hoover Building, and they decided that Bill would report directly to the AG and coordinate the investigation in Bella Cora with local authorities to control the landscape.

Pearls Before Swine

"Call your first witness," instructed Judge Cano to the government attorneys.

The investigating agents from the FBI and the IRS flanked the two government attorneys. The exhibit books, all 360 of them containing over 3,000 documents, were stacked neatly to the right of the jury box. The visual was overwhelming. The government's charts with colorful arrows highlighted the flow of "commissions" paid to the niece and uncle and detailed the millions that had flowed into the bank account of DVL Media Productions from Bella Cora. There was no lack of banking or accounting documentation.

Danny's heart sank as he looked at Vicky; he wanted to clutch her hand, but they were sitting next to their attorneys at the defendants' table. Vicky looked into the audience only to see her beautiful daughters sobbing quietly into their handkerchiefs.

The jury sat stoically averting their eyes from the defense table. Danny did not have a good feeling; this was a jury of his peers? Marilyn had explained to Danny and Vicky that defendants in every case faced this reality. During the opening arguments, Juror 12 was fast asleep. What did that mean?

The first ten witnesses for the government were fact witnesses, government agents, bank employees and employees of DVL Media Productions. The government, as it turned out, had wired Becky, in an attempt to trap Danny or Vicky into incriminating statements, but it didn't work, even after the sixtieth surreptitious recording. Becky told the investigators that she did not know the true purpose of the wire transfers to Switzerland or Hong Kong, not that it would have made a difference in the outcome.

The accounting records of DVL Media Productions listed each and every payment made to the uncle and the niece, which were categorized as commissions. The foreign bank records reconciled to the accounting records and the corporate tax returns. All income and expenses were listed properly by source and disposition.

The evidence showed that Danny and Vicky did not withhold information regarding the transfers to the uncle or the niece from their accountants, but the accountants never asked — a problem that clearly affected the efficacy of taking alleged bribes as "commissions" on the tax returns of DVL Media Productions. This issue had been settled in the 1970s, when the IRS took the position that large military contractors in the United States could not take deductions paid to Saudi Arabian businessmen to gain contracts from the Saudi government.

Marilyn knew that all the government financial witnesses would be devastating. It was telling and probably lost on the jury that all of the money transferred to Switzerland and Hong Kong had never been touched and remained in the accounts up to the trial date. Following the money from the U.S. banks to the foreign bank accounts was not a problem, nor was there a problem in showing who controlled the funds in the accounts. It was also unclear from tax records from the Ministry of Taxation in Bella Cora whether the "commissions" had been properly listed on the tax returns, but that was a matter for the officials of that country.

It was not your ordinary foreign bribery case where the quid pro quo was beyond obvious or where the funds were used to support a lavish lifestyle. There were a lot of unanswered questions.

What was obviously missing from the government's case was a witness from the Bella Cora Ministry of Tourism. Consuela de la Paz refused the U.S. government's request for an interview with her or any member of her staff. Uncle Tomas was suddenly unavailable, and the niece continued her studies in Switzerland.

Finale

"Has the jury reached their verdict?" asked Judge Cano. The jury foreman rose and stated, "Yes, your honor." The foreman then delivered the news that Vicky and Danny had tried to deny: "guilty on count one for violations of the Foreign Corrupt Practices Act, guilty on count two for violations of the money laundering statute and guilty on tax evasion."

Danny had testified and didn't do well under cross-examination. The strain of the trial combined with his failing health was too much. The prosecutor had sensed Danny's weakness and jumped on him like a crocodile on a wounded gazelle; it was ugly. Even Juror 12 woke up for the spectacle.

The Federal Sentencing Guidelines called for a jail term of 60 to 120 months, and the government wanted the maximum. After a number of prolonged sentencing hearings, Judge Cano required more and more documentation regarding case law where the alleged bribe resulted in the foreign government actually reaping a windfall profit from the illegal bribe. There were no cases on the point, and Judge Cano was troubled by this fact. But the government's zeal was over the top. "What do you want me to do?" the judge asked the relentless prosecutors. "Sentence them to death?"

At the sentencing hearing, the courtroom was packed with family and friends and a few diplomats from the Bella Cora embassy who came to view the proceedings. Sadly, it was also the end of the Bella Cora Film Festival. This tiny, emerging country lost tens of millions of dollars in tourist revenue.

Judge Cano finally delivered his sentencing of Danny and Vicky. "After much thought and analysis, I sentence Danny and Vicky Lennon to six months imprisonment with three years' probation." The government prosecutors indicated that they would appeal the lenient sentence but ultimately abandoned it. The restitution is still being litigated.

Lessons Learned

Working for the defense on an FCPA prosecution is a daunting task. The myriad government schedules and tens of thousands of documents can be overwhelming. The attorney you work with will rely on you to interpret all the evidence and then reduce your findings into bite-size pieces for easy consumption in the courtroom.

> The summaries of your analyses will be used as defense exhibits, meaning the work needs to be completely error-free and delivered within the budget and work plan that was agreed on.

Recommendations to Prevent Future Occurrences

Be objective. Continue to hone your skills in accounting, auditing and the investigative processes.

About the Author

Mr. Knudson has more than 40 years' experience in the intelligence-gathering and investigative fields As a former IRS special agent, his storied career included the investigation of bribes to foreign and domestic officials; international drug and money-laundering organizations; organized crime and complex white-collar crime schemes. After retirement from the government, Mr. Knudson worked for two Big Five accounting firms and as an independent consultant. Mr. Knudson has testified as an expert in white-collar crime cases in federal and state court proceedings.

CHAPTER

High-Plains Grifter

CAROLYN CONN, KATIE HOUSTON,
AND BRANDON TANOUS

Skip Martin was an average guy with an average life until he learned how to navigate the grant application process of Oklahoma's State Resource and Environmental Commission (SREC). If you met him on the street, nothing would make him seem out of the ordinary. He spoke with a soft Southern accent. His neatly trimmed mustache matched his salt-and-pepper gray hair. He was six feet four inches tall with a muscular build — except for a little gut his wife blamed on drinking a few too many longnecks every evening. Martin usually wore cowboy boots, jeans and a blue denim shirt. When his wife complained about him wearing work shirts every day, he kidded her, "It's my *best* color. All the women tell me the soft blue matches my eyes."

He and Claudean were married the year after their high school graduation. They had dated since junior high when he ran into her — literally — at a football game. She was a cheerleader and he was a wide receiver. He had gone out to catch a pass and she was on the sidelines with her back to the field. After jumping up to catch the ball, Martin lost his balance as he came down and stumbled into the line of cheerleaders, knocking Claudean off her feet. He picked her up, making sure she was okay. Martin joked with his teammates, "I didn't catch that ball, but I caught the best-looking girl at the game!"

Martin was a truck driver most of his adult life. A week after high school graduation, he started his first full-time job in the shipping and receiving department of a grocery distribution center in Oklahoma City. He helped load and unload the semi-trailer trucks, earning just above minimum wage. But he got by and even saved a little of his take-home pay because he was living with his parents. His mom frequently reminded him he was lucky to have a job with paid vacation, sick leave and health insurance. Martin knew he would not live at home for long. His plan was to save enough so he and

Claudean could get married and for him to get enough work experience so he could move on to "bigger things."

He easily struck up conversations with total strangers and enjoyed talking with the drivers while he was loading or unloading their trucks. Martin asked them what it was like out on the road, driving a big rig. They described the good and the bad. The worst parts were the sleepless nights trying to make it to a destination quicker than they should and being away from their families for long stretches of time. Martin did not like the thought of leaving Claudean, but the good part of a truck driving job was the pay. All he had to do was get a commercial driver's license (CDL) and convince his employer to give him a chance as a driver.

Martin was surprised and excited when he learned that 18 was the minimum age to get a CDL for driving intrastate in Oklahoma. After six months on the shipping and receiving dock, he saved enough to pay for a truck driving course, which he took on weekends. Martin passed the course and the CDL test and persuaded his supervisor to help him get a job as a driver. "You know I'm the best worker on this dock. I'm the only one who gets to work on time, does whatever you tell me to do without any lip . . . and who *doesn't* have a rap sheet a mile long." His supervisor agreed and made a call to recommend Martin for a position. He began making short, local runs for the grocery distribution company, and Martin quickly earned their trust and confidence; within a year he was driving their big rigs across the state.

After a few years of hauling groceries, Martin got a higher-paying job with a refinery driving tanker trucks. He did that for more than 25 years. He surprised himself by staying with one employer so long, but it was important for his family. Martin's dad taught him that family comes first. "You do whatever it takes to put food on the table and keep a roof over their heads." But being on the road, miles from home was tough, especially after his son and daughter were born.

His parting words to Claudean before every trip were "I feel so guilty. You shouldn't have to be both mom and dad to the kids." But it was a good living. They saved enough to buy 50 acres with a wood-frame house in a small farming community about 30 miles from the city. Martin described it as "a place where you can hear the whippoorwills every evening and see a sky full of stars most every night." He enjoyed sitting with Claudean on the front porch steps at night and watching for shooting stars.

They settled into small-town life and quickly became respected members of the community. Claudean taught Sunday school and Martin helped mow the lawn and do small repairs at the church when he was home. His friends described him as trustworthy, honest and hardworking. As Martin neared his fiftieth birthday, he told Claudean, "I think you ought to get your truck driving license so we can start our own company. Both the kids are grown, and we've got enough savings for a down payment on a used rig."

Claudean hesitated. He continued, "We can borrow the rest. We'll make more money going on longer hauls and we can make trips together if you get your license. You know my guardian angel has worked overtime all these years, keeping me safe while driving those tanker trucks. I'd like to stop that." That convinced her. She had worried about him constantly all the years he drove tankers filled with flammable liquids.

Starline Trucking opened for business four months later with an office in the back bedroom of the Martin home; one used rig and two independent truckers ready for hire. Their cargo usually consisted of general freight, building materials, tractors and other farm equipment.

State Grant Program

Oklahoma's SREC was the agency responsible for protecting the state's natural resources with a stated mission of "ensuring the citizenry has clean air, clean water, and that waste is safely managed." It was established as the state's first comprehensive environmental protection agency. In response to pressure from federal regulators to improve air quality in all states, the Oklahoma legislature created and funded a grant program called Clean Air Oklahoma (CAO), which was administered through SREC. CAO was a state-wide initiative to lower nitric-oxide emissions (which create ground-level ozone) by replacing older, high-emitting mobile diesel sources. The primary focus of CAO was trucks used to pull 18-wheel semi-trailers and construction equipment; but program guidelines were written such that other diesel equipment (such as farm tractors and bulldozers) also qualified.

The grant process required completion of an application with a description of the old equipment and a certification as to its current working condition and use, along with a statement by the owner of the number of running hours per year. Applicants were required to specify the brand, model, engine size and cost of new equipment as well as the dealer from which it would be purchased. SREC distributed the funds (up to 80 percent of the equipment cost) directly to the dealer. After a CAO grant was awarded, the applicant went to the specified dealer, paid their 20 percent of the cost and got their new equipment. Though many of the applicants were skilled at truck driving or farming and ranching, few of them understood the grant application process. Thus, many paid a consultant to help complete all the paperwork. Consultants were usually paid a percentage of the grant amount received.

CAO Consultant

Skip Martin first heard about the CAO grants when he stopped for diesel fuel at a truck stop near Enid, just north of Oklahoma City. He went inside to get coffee and overheard several truckers talking about the "free government money." Some of them were applying for a grant so they could get a new semi-truck. Others said, "Not me. I don't want the government meddling in my business. Next thing you know they'll be snooping around, checking on things and telling me what to do."

As soon as he returned home, Martin got on the Internet and found the CAO grant information on the SREC website. Even though he and his wife had been running their used rig less than a year, it sounded like their truck qualified to be replaced under the CAO grant program. He and Claudean spent the weekend filling out all the paperwork and mailed the application and supporting documents first thing Monday morning.

In less than two months, Martin was awarded grant funds totaling $83,928, which went to the truck dealership where he purchased a new Freightliner. "Skip Martin, you're an amazing man," Claudean repeated over and over as they drove home in the new truck. The grant terms required the Martins to use $20,000 of their own cash to go with the CAO monies for purchasing the new truck, which was far less than what they spent when they bought their old, used one. And the CAO money was a *grant* . . . it never had to be repaid.

"I know you're all ga-ga over the engine, foot-pounds of torque and all that guy stuff, but I am *loving* this sleeper!" Claudean sounded giddy as she settled in for a nap while Martin drove cross-country on their first trip in the new truck. If she was happy, Martin was happy. Just a few weeks later, Martin told Claudean, "I can't believe how easy it was to get so much government money for this truck . . . and there's a way to make even more. The state lets people be consultants and charge for helping other folks with the CAO paperwork."

Claudean asked, "How much money do you think you could make as a consultant?" Martin said, "Most of them charge a percentage of the grant received. I think I'd just charge a flat amount, maybe $600 per application. If I did only one application every other week or so, it would be about $15,000 a year." Claudean told her husband it sounded like a great idea and noted he would be helping poor, uneducated farmers, ranchers and truck drivers who might not otherwise be able to afford new equipment. "You'll be doing a good deed," she told him. The next day Martin went to the county courthouse and filed a Doing Business As application for his new venture, OK Grant Consulting (OKGC). As he walked down the courthouse steps, he called Claudean on his cell phone. "You're now married to a *consultant*. This was too easy. I don't even have to get approved by the state!"

Open for Business

Martin's first consulting job was for a neighbor who wanted to replace an old diesel tractor. "Good grief, that thing is almost antique!" Martin exclaimed when he first saw the vehicle. There was no doubt it qualified for the grant funds. Martin knew the rules by heart. The state monies were available to individuals, businesses, nonprofits and government entities for both on- and off-road vehicles that had an engine with a minimum of 25 horsepower. The old equipment had to be scrapped and replaced with a newer, more eco-friendly model. To document the disposal, the owner merely had to include with the application photographic evidence of the destruction.

An additional provision of the grant was a requirement for the owner of the old equipment to report annual usage in prior years and to make a written commitment that the new purchase would operate in the future at least 75 percent of the reported historical usage. The owner also had to certify the use would occur only in eligible Oklahoma counties, which generally were in or near metropolitan areas. Grant applications had to include written bids from three dealers and name the dealer from which the new equipment would be obtained, as well as the make, model and other details related to the purchase. Grants were awarded on a first-come, first-served basis.

It took only a few weeks for Martin's neighbor to be awarded $64,000 in CAO grant monies to replace his old tractor. He told Martin, "Paying you $600 to help with that application was the smartest thing I've done all year!" Word spread quickly through the community that Skip Martin was "certified" by the state to assist in getting government money. Some people in town thought he was an employee of SREC. Martin never corrected anyone who made statements about him "working for SREC." Anything that added to his credibility made it easier to get more consulting business.

A Simple Scam

Martin helped a few of his truck-driving buddies complete applications for CAO grants, but he focused on farm equipment after realizing how easy it was to falsify those applications. Diesel trucks that operated on Oklahoma highways had to be inspected and registered every year. There was no such requirement for tractors, generators and other farm equipment. The paper trail was almost nonexistent, with farmers and ranchers often selling or trading used equipment among themselves. That made it easy for Martin to invent identification numbers and acquisition dates.

The fraud he perpetrated against Oklahoma's CAO grant program was not complicated. A farmer or rancher hired him to assist with a legitimate application for a CAO grant to replace an old diesel tractor previously used for plowing fields or mowing pastures. When he visited their property, Martin inquired about other items that might qualify. He said that equipment that was not in working order qualified for replacement under the grant provisions. This was completely false. The applicants did not mind getting "free government money" for their equipment (running or otherwise), and they did not mind paying Martin a $600 consulting fee for each of their applications. Everyone was happy.

Enter our team of SREC auditors. The CAO grant program was less than two years old, and numerous problems had been identified during post-award audits done by our teams of internal auditors in the first year. We were not alone in our concerns about the lack of controls.[1] We felt that many of the problems were caused by the "shovel" attitude of the CAO program directors. Their primary concern seemed to be to shovel the money out the door (awarding $100 million annually) so they could get good press. The legislature had pressured CAO to award grants quickly so they could report the success of the program (emission reductions) to the federal regulators.

Only one CAO staff member performed pre-award reviews of grant applications, and the volume of work made it impossible for him to identify all the deficiencies in them. The CAO program manager wanted to minimize the negative findings in future post-award audits, so he asked our internal audit staff to help perform pre-award audits. During our planning, the three audit managers spoke with CAO program administrators, who pointed out the seemingly disproportionate number of applications submitted for farm equipment. They were particularly concerned because a significant portion of them had been submitted by one consultant, Skip Martin. Our audit team agreed; applications submitted with Martin as the consultant would be carefully scrutinized.

Three of us worked as project managers on the CAO audit: James Townes, Cindy Wynn and Henry Vance (all with less than five years of experience at SREC). Wynn was nearing completion of her M.B.A. degree and was studying for the CFE exam. We each headed up our own team, assigned to the three geographic regions of Oklahoma that were eligible for the CAO grants. The audit procedures included on-site visits to personally view and photograph the new equipment acquired with the CAO funds as well as the old items that were identified in the grant application as being taken out of use.

"That old equipment is ready to be out of use, all right . . . it hasn't been used in *decades!*" When Townes reported to our audit team what he found during a recent site visit to several farms and ranches, we were in disbelief. "We went to one ranch and found the old tractor out behind a barn with so much grass growing up, you could barely see it." Remarks made by the ranch hand during the visit were informative. "That consultant guy — name's Martin — told us the tractor didn't have to be working to get the state money. I told my brother that didn't make any sense because that tractor hadn't been used in 35 years and we were gonna get caught."

During interviews with grant applicants and surprise on-site inspections, all three of our audit teams had the same findings. Martin had falsified applications to make equipment appear to qualify for the CAO grant program. We examined a total of 120 applications and determined that 75 of them had incorrect or missing identification plates (for the old equipment) and 30 of them did not meet the program's usage requirements. Additionally, 10 of the pieces of old equipment were inoperable and did not qualify for grant monies. One application reported extraordinarily high "current usage" for a tractor on five acres of land — the equivalent of running 12 hours a day, every day of the year. Ownership of all the old equipment was found to be legitimate.

Martin had attempted to defraud the state program by completing applications for real people but for equipment that did *not* qualify. In many instances the owners of the old equipment signed blank application forms that he completed later. For some others Martin forged the owner's signature or had some of the college students working part-time for his firm, OKGC, do the forgeries.[2] Martin made certain that all of his clients, the dealer and CAO staff members felt like they were buddies. He was adept at gaining their confidence.

Another aspect of our audit was to look for evidence of kickbacks and conflicts of interest. On all grant applications submitted by Martin as the consultant, only one tractor dealer was named, J.B. Hamshire Equipment in Stoddard, Oklahoma. It was about a two-hour drive from Martin's hometown. Our audit team checked public records and interviewed grant applicants and Hamshire's owners and employees, looking for a familial or other close relationship between them and Martin. But we were not able to identify any. Martin's explanation for exclusively specifying Hamshire as the tractor dealer was " . . . because they're the only ones who will give me all the details I need about the equipment so I can complete the applications." That explanation was not credible, especially in light of grant applicants who told our team they did not want the brand of equipment sold by Hamshire. Martin misled the grant applicants into believing SREC *required* them to buy from Hamshire.

There definitely was a conflict of interest between Hamshire Equipment and Martin. The company's owner, his sons, managers and employees all applied for the CAO grants. Almost everyone working at or affiliated with the dealer was a grant applicant, and they knew there were few controls on the program. One of them boldly told our auditors, "I've talked to a bunch of people and you don't have any power to do anything anyway." When questioned by us about his relationship with Martin, J.B. Hamshire said, "I don't know how you do things in the state capital; but out here in the country, we take care of our own."

A potential conflict of interest existed with at least one member of the CAO program staff, the one who did the pre-award application reviews. He should have rejected numerous applications that were fraught with red flags. The employee acknowledged to our audit team that he had overlooked problems on applications and justified his actions by saying "It doesn't matter. We're going to fund them anyway." When we learned that his post-retirement plans included working as a consultant at OKGC, the conflict of interest was clear.

Members of our audit team were certain that kickback arrangements existed between Martin and Hamshire Equipment, but we were unable to prove it. As internal auditors for SREC, we did not have subpoena power to obtain bank records and other documentation needed to prove the existence of kickback payments. Upper-level managers at our agency did not want us to spend more time on the audit trying to find evidence of wrongdoing.

Limits of the Investigation

After seeing our audit report, the CAO program administrators took swift action and immediately made a blanket denial of all applications on which Skip Martin was the consultant. The grant monies that SREC could have awarded to Martin's duped applicants totaled nearly $5 million. This figure excluded any consulting fees charged by Martin to his clients.

Our audit findings were forwarded to our agency's environmental crimes unit. They did additional work on the case and submitted it to the county district attorney for prosecution. Martin was arrested, prosecuted and pleaded guilty to charges of organized criminal activity. This included forgery of the numerous grant applications and falsifying several of the accompanying bid quotes from equipment dealers. He was sentenced to five years in state prison.

Because the CAO program did not prohibit consultants from assisting grant applicants and charging a fee for doing so, Martin was not required to repay any of the $600 fees he had charged his clients. SREC did not take any legal action against any of the grant applicants because it was determined that they had relied on Martin's advice regarding equipment qualifications for the grants. The agency chose not to audit any additional grant applications or pursue the possibility of kickbacks between Martin and Hamshire Equipment.

Lessons Learned

"An ounce of prevention is worth a pound of cure." This is an old saying, but it was the most valuable lesson we learned from this case. The state prevented a fraud of approximately $5 million by auditing grant applications on the front end. But the grant monies likely would have not been recovered, even if the fraud had been discovered after the award. This situation also proved that routine internal audits can be effective. As noted in the 2010 *ACFE Report to the Nations*, internal audits are the third most frequent manner (nearly 14 percent) in which occupational fraud is initially detected.

Another lesson we learned was the importance of getting out in the field and looking at the inventory and assets being audited. There have been far too many high-profile cases (such as Crazy Eddie's Electronics and ZZZZ Best) in which auditors did not "put their hands on" assets and other items to confirm their physical existence. The best results come when such inspections are done on a surprise basis.

Earning confidence is essential to the success of any fraud perpetrator. Skip Martin was no exception. He made certain he was well liked and respected. Most people in his hometown regarded him as a "good ol' boy," someone who attended and volunteered at church and did good deeds in the community. But even seemingly upstanding citizens can commit fraud.

The close relationships that Martin cultivated with CAO program staff and the farm equipment dealer made his fraud possible. Yet we were unable to prove his relationships were criminal within the scope of our investigation. It is very difficult to investigate and obtain evidence that proves conflict of interest.

Tone at the top was not what it should have been for this state-funded program. There was so much pressure from managers to award grants (as a sign of having implemented a successful program and to please federal regulators) that lower-level employees had no incentive to question problematic grant applications. Instead, those employees ignored the red flags and approved nonqualifying grant applications.

From the perspective of customers and clients (particularly of governmental agencies), an important lesson is that paid consultants and application fees of any kind are usually not needed; they are certainly not required. Any offer that sounds too good to be true probably is. Be wary of such offers. Perform your own due diligence by asking for and confirming the credentials of anyone making representations that they work for a government agency.

Recommendations to Prevent Future Occurrences

Internal Controls and Staffing

Implement internal controls and provide adequate staffing to help prevent fraud. This includes management reviews as well as training and encouraging employees to look for and report suspected fraud. It is also essential for upper-level management to establish and regularly communicate the entity's anti-fraud policy. They should not put so much pressure on performance that lower-level staff feel like achieving goals must be done at all costs. Management should maintain staffing levels that make it possible to achieve quality work and to identify problems and suspected fraud.

Internal Audits

Both management reviews and internal audits have proven effective in deterring occupational fraud. Internal auditors should be proactive in planning for fraud risk. Brainstorming will help identify the most likely points at which fraud might occur. Going out into the field to look at evidence and conduct interviews is essential.

Inherent Risk and Pressure

Government agencies should be aware of the inherent risk of fraud from subsidies or rebate programs. Some people will have the attitude such programs provide "free money" and may not hesitate to commit fraud because it is government cash. Some

(continued)

(continued)

may even rationalize, "It's my tax money anyway." Also, top-level managers of government agencies should guard against putting too much pressure on their employees to achieve unrealistic goals. Pressures to be successful are typically associated with for-profit entities but can also occur in government agencies. Program directors should not let their desire for good press and results send the wrong message to their employees (i.e., anything goes).

Qualified Consultants

Agency heads and program directors should also give careful thought to allowing consultants to be part of the application process for grants. If this practice is allowed, there should be a vetting process to ensure the consultants are qualified and reputable, and an effective, ongoing monitoring process should be implemented. Governmental agencies should make communications and publicity about their programs easy to understand and widely available via websites, brochures and other media. They would also be well advised to use a hotline so that suspected fraud can be easily reported.

About the Authors

Carolyn Conn, CFE, CPA, is an accounting faculty member with teaching and research interests in the areas of fraud examination and ethics. She has held several administrative positions in the public sector with responsibilities that included investigating occupational fraud. She also works as a consultant and provides litigation support services.

Katie Houston, CFE, CPA, CLEA, is a senior auditor for a state law enforcement agency. She has worked in the private sector as well as for nonprofit and governmental organizations with significant experience in internal auditing. She holds a bachelor's degree in accounting with a minor in economics from Westminster College in Salt Lake City, Utah, and an M.B.A. from St. Edward's University in Austin, Texas.

Brandon Tanous, CGAP, CLEA, is a senior auditor for a state law enforcement agency. During his auditing career with several state agencies, he has focused on internal auditing and occupational fraud. He has a bachelor's degree in public administration with a minor in business and a master's degree in public administration with an emphasis in public finance from Texas State University-San Marcos.

Notes

1. A subsequent audit by the state auditor found that nearly 600 grant recipients who had been awarded more than $50 million of CAO funds did not meet all of the program's requirements.
2. One of the students was forced by Martin to forge one signature and resigned immediately afterward. She did not hesitate to describe the situation to the SREC auditors and later testified against Martin.

CHAPTER 9

Getting a Free Ride

WILLIAM J. KIRBY

Gus Shirani, a 51-year-old father of three, had been driving a cab for 25 years. He was born and raised in Pakistan and arrived in the United States as most immigrants do: full of hopes, dreams and ambitions. However, years of cutting corners, gambling and scamming to make ends meet definitely left their mark on him. Tall and lanky, Gus looked like he bought all of his clothes at secondhand stores and failed to put them through the washing machine when he got home. Always wearing things that did not match, did not fit properly and were a few years out of date, he looked like a newly repatriated refugee as he strolled down the city streets. Most of the time he appeared tired and he always smelled of cheap aftershave, which he obviously chose instead of a shower. Gus lived in a working-class suburb just outside of the city. His driver's license was recently suspended for failing to pay a fine, so he could no longer work as a cabbie. Rather than working on a plan to get his license back so he could earn a living, he spent his time taking the bus to Pakistani cultural centers in town where he would sit around with other natives, drinking coffee, trading war stories about back home and figuring out how to make some money.

Unlike Gus, Sam Hashemi, a 42-year-old from Lahore, Pakistan, did not look like your average cab driver. Sam dressed modernly with a yuppie flair. He wore glasses that made him look studious, and he could have been easily mistaken for a manager at an accounting firm rather than a cab driver. Sam's chauffeur's license had expired several years ago while he entertained other career ambitions — none of which panned out. Having failed to take care of his license in a timely manner, he faced stricter renewal policies. Sam was required to take classes, fill out many more forms and pay some pretty steep fees for classes and renewals. He wanted to return to driving a cab to make some quick cash and was looking for a way to bypass the city's rigid new policies.

85

Steven Williams brought an entirely new meaning to the stereotype of the lazy city worker. Steve had two speeds — slow and stop — and it looked like he had the worst job in the world as he shuffled back and forth behind the counter at the city's Department of Public Transportation and Licensing with a scowl permanently affixed to his face. Steve's official title was Licensing Investigator I, and he had been a city employee for more than 15 years. At age 45, he was in serious financial trouble and had recently filed for Chapter 13 bankruptcy protection after falling months behind on his mortgage. His wife, also a former city employee who worked in the mayor's office of workforce development, had recently died. In his job, Steve had regular, personal contact with city cab drivers seeking to renew their chauffeur's licenses. He was supposed to ensure that they completed the proper paperwork, surrendered their old chauffeur's licenses, that there was a current driver's license abstract on file certifying that the applicant was in good standing and that all of the information was entered into the department computer system. But Steve spent most of his time, as we would later learn, going on extended breaks, smoking outside with cab drivers and disappearing from the office on a regular basis. Those smoking breaks would later have serious repercussions for Steve and the city as well.

The City

Southmoor is a large, diverse metropolitan city with millions of residents. It is a bustling place to live, work and play, and it attracts hundreds of thousands of tourists annually. The city has tens of thousands of employees and an annual budget and local economy that are significantly larger than that of many countries. It contains numerous Fortune 500 companies, top-notch universities, museums, restaurants and sporting teams. As with all cities this size, there is no shortage of crime and corruption. The police department is well versed in conducting investigations of every crime imaginable, and it has a well-storied past. With thousands of police officers and investigators, it has the ability to draw on a wide range of talent, expertise and experience.

Allegations of corruption within the police department are normally investigated by the internal affairs unit. Investigation within the other city agencies, such as the Department of Water, the Department of Planning or the Department of Transportation, is the purview of the inspector general and his staff of investigators. This office is mostly composed of civilian investigators who are trained and experienced in investigating payroll fraud and ghost employee schemes, falsification of time sheets, contract fraud, theft of government funds and property, and other waste and abuse committed by city workers, those doing business with the city and contractors hired by the city. The office is capable of undertaking both administrative and criminal investigations. To conduct criminal investigations, the office has the power of arrest via the handful of city police officers who are detailed to the office. Most cases investigated by the office are handled administratively. Administrative sanctions leveled by the city against an employee, contractor or business could be suspension, termination or removal from a program. Only a small percentage of cases are referred for criminal prosecution, such as bribery, large thefts or official misconduct. This turned out to be one of those cases.

Trouble at the Department of Transportation

It was a beautiful spring day in April when Sam Hashemi arrived at the city's Department of Public Transportation to renew his temporary chauffeur's license. He patiently stood in line as the agents who were attending to cab drivers at the counter examined documents and made inquiries on department computers. "Next," a female employee finally called as she motioned for Sam to approach the counter. As Sam stepped up, his heart raced. "What can I do for you?" she asked. "I want to renew my temporary chauffeur's license," Sam told her, looking at the nameplate in front of her that read Patty. "May I have your documents and temporary license please?" Patty asked. Temporary chauffeur's licenses are issued to new cab drivers and are used until they successfully pass their probationary status, which involves continued testing, evaluation of driver's license records and addressing any citizen complaints made against the driver. New cab drivers normally serve a one-year probationary period and may have that status extended if problems arise during their probation.

Sam slid his application across the counter and informed her, "I lost my temporary license and only have a photocopy of it." "Did you report it to us?" she asked. "I only told my boss," he said. "You must report all losses of your chauffeur's license to us immediately," she admonished, taking the photocopy and entering the license number into the computer system. The number contained on every chauffeur's license, even temporary ones, is driver specific, just as a state driver's license is. Every chauffeur's license also contains a control number used for tracking the actual license, when it was issued and by whom. According to the computer, the license had been expired for three years, and the driver needed to undergo the entire licensing process. Patty looked closely at the photocopy and noticed that her own initials appeared on the temporary license, but they were not in her own handwriting. She looked up at Sam; he had just passed a counterfeit temporary license to the worst person he could have possibly encountered. "Please wait one moment, sir. I have to get a form." She immediately went to her boss' office and informed him of the incident.

The deputy commissioner of public transportation was no city joke. Mark Janis was a bright guy, a straight shooter and a lawyer educated at notable universities on the East Coast. Even though he was only in his third year of city service, he had a thorough and commanding knowledge of the department he was responsible for managing.

Mark and Patty went to the cabinet where temporary licenses were kept and compared the control number on the photocopy presented by Sam to the issue log. It did not appear in the log. Because filing errors frequently occurred, Mark searched for the license among the inventory. It was not there either. This was not what he had been hoping for. About three weeks earlier, he discovered several other licenses missing during an auditing process, which caused him to make some changes in how inventory was stored and handled. Because the licenses were now locked in a new safe, and the license copy that Sam presented had been accounted for before the new procedures were enacted, Mark had to grapple with a manager's worst nightmare: there might be corruption in his ranks.

The Scam Exposed

Sam could see Mark and Patty as they flipped through inventory pages and looked inquisitively at each other just inside an office doorway. He knew something was wrong. His mind and heart raced as he contemplated his next move. Should he play dumb? Plead his case and ask for forgiveness? Run? Sweat started to gather across his eyebrows as he saw Patty point in his direction. Mark looked at him from across the room. Sam was done and he knew it. Mark and Patty approached him.

"Good morning, Mr. Hashemi," Mark said to Sam. "My name is Mark Janis and I am the deputy commissioner of public transportation. Could you come with me, please?"

There was no need for the introduction. Sam knew who Mark was and had heard from other members of the taxi community that he was a stickler for rules and regulations. As he followed Mark to his office, the idea of offering a bribe came to mind. He was desperate and knew that he was thinking irrationally. Would the police be called? Could he go to jail? What penalties might he face? Sam knew the game was over, and his fate now rested in the hands of others. He would have to accept whatever consequences came his way.

Sam took a seat across Mark's large, mahogany desk. Mark wasted no time and got right to the point. "How did you get this temporary chauffeur's license?" Sam made the decision right then and there. He would cooperate with Mark and hope that he would receive some leniency.

"I got it from a guy named Gus Shirani. I know him from the Pakistani community. He can get anything for a price."

"This is only a photocopy," Mark said. "Where is the original?"

"It's in my car," said Sam. "I can get it for you if you'd like."

"How does Gus get them?" Mark pressed.

"He gets them from Big Guy. Big Guy works here."

Mark was flabbergasted. "He works here? Is he here now?"

"Yup. He's the black guy wearing the blue shirt and black pants."

Mark was shocked. Sam just identified Steven Williams.

While Mark surely wouldn't have nominated Steve for employee of the year, he didn't believe that he was the type who would violate the integrity of the office they all worked so hard at managing. Mark recalled that it was Steve who first lent him a hand when he took over the department three years ago. Because Steve was a department veteran, he knew the ins and outs of the office and knew the names of most of the taxi company presidents. He helped Mark learn the office intricacies and made sure he knew of some of the political forces at play. Although he dreaded his next move, Mark knew exactly what he had to do. He reached for the phone and called the Inspector General's (IG's) Office.

A New Case

I had been a city police officer for eight years before accepting the assignment to the IG's Office. My previous assignments had included working as a beat patrol officer and a gang tactical officer. I also did a couple of stints on a burglary mission team and on an aggravated battery mission team, who are plain-clothed officers responding to gang shootings. I had been involved in many search warrants and had already made well over 1,000 arrests. I had been with the IG's Office for a year and a half when I was called into Bruce Fender's office.

Bruce was also a city police officer who had been at the IG's Office for many years. At the office, he was a supervisor of investigations and my boss. A good guy with a great sense of humor, he was instrumental in my learning "the IG way of doing things."

"Hey, kid," Bruce said. "Go see Superman. He has a job that he wants you to look into right away."

"Superman" was Bill Maybrook, a deputy inspector general and a lawyer who was my next line of supervision. Bill was a civilian employee of the IG's Office, but I always felt that he would have been a good police officer had he decided to embark on that career path. Prior to coming over to the IG's Office, he had worked as a state's attorney. Because of this, he had excellent insight into putting a case together from the courtroom standpoint. However, because he wasn't a police officer, many times I had to explain police procedure and reporting to him. Just like Bruce, he was a great boss and a true professional in everything he did.

I walked into Bill's office and caught him as he was still on the telephone. He looked at me and motioned for me to sit down. After hanging up the phone, Bill brought me up to speed on what transpired at the Department of Transportation's licensing office. He told me that he had already interviewed Mark Janis, Sam Hashemi and Patty DeLong. He told me that Sam bought the license from Gus Shirani, his Pakistani contact, for $1,000. The only problem was that Gus was supposed to get Sam a permanent license, not a temporary one. Gus had told Sam that Steven Williams, or "Big Guy," was his contact and that Steve had made the necessary adjustments for him in the Department of Transportation's computer system. Sam was supposed to use the temporary license until it expired and, at that time, Steve would give him a permanent one. Not believing Gus, Sam went to the Department of Transportation office and attempted to get a replacement using the photocopy. He said that he did this because he thought that if city officials discovered that he had a fraudulent temporary license, they would only take the photocopy and he would still have his original to use for driving the cab. Upset that he had been cheated by Gus and facing several felonies, he decided to cooperate. After interviewing all parties involved, Bill conducted an in-house computer inquiry and learned that I was already investigating Gus Shirani for a similar scam that showed up on our radar just three weeks earlier.

"I want you to make this a priority in your case schedule," Bill told me. "Do what you have to do and let me know if you need any help."

I knew much about Gus, including where he lived. Because Gus had obtained the temporary license from Steven Williams and had accepted the $1,000 from Sam, I thought that Gus would be the weak link that I would go after first. If I could find Gus and get him to talk, I would try to flip him and use him as a witness against the corrupt city employee. If he helped me, Gus might walk away from the case without any criminal charges.

Most people have a hard time accepting the fact that a criminal could, or should, get away with a crime without being charged, especially when that person committed several felonies. But as an investigator with the IG's Office, my primary concern was to fight city corruption. To do this, it was fairly common to use low-level criminals as informants and as state witnesses. Some were paid for their services, but most were cooperating because they faced possible incarceration otherwise. Usually they could escape punishment entirely for their cooperation, but sometimes they received reduced charges instead.

Tailing the Suspect

Soon thereafter, I put my plan into action. I headed to Gus' house with Scott Soupy, an investigator I had worked with for many years. Scott was a police officer who used to work the midnight shift with me in a pretty dangerous part of the city. We moved over to the IG's Office around the same time.

Scott and I initiated surveillance on Gus' house in the early morning. He lived in a run-down apartment building in a blue-collar suburb just north of the city. About two hours later, we saw Gus walk out the back door and start walking up the street. Scott followed on foot while I trailed about a block behind in our covert vehicle. About two blocks away, Gus, still followed by Scott, boarded a train and then transferred to a city bus. Scott kept in touch with me via cellular telephone as I raced to keep up with them. In a neighborhood populated with many Middle Eastern immigrants, Gus exited the bus with Scott right behind him. I greeted him at the bus door.

"Good morning, Mr. Shirani. Inspector General's Office," I said as I displayed my credentials. "Can you come with us? We need to talk."

Scott and I placed Gus into the backseat of our vehicle, and we drove a few blocks away before pulling to the curb and parking in a residential area. I joined Gus in the backseat and laid out much of the evidence gathered against him thus far.

"I know that you are selling stolen and counterfeited chauffeur's licenses," I said. "I know who you are getting them from and I am prepared to charge you with bribery, forgery, theft and several other felonies. If you are willing to cooperate, I am willing to take that fact to a state's attorney, and you may have some consideration in your current situation."

Gus looked shocked. After I read him his Miranda rights, he handwrote a 16-page statement implicating himself and Steve Williams. He said that he had purchased temporary chauffeur's licenses from Steve and made color copies of those licenses at a nearby office supply store. He, in turn, sold them to numerous people who were ineligible to work as cab drivers within the city.

I called Bill Maybrook and briefed him on my interview of Gus. He was elated. I told him that I would release Gus and would meet him at the office to discuss our options.

I sat down with Bill and gave him an option that he never once considered. As a matter of fact, it had never been done in the history of the IG's Office.

"I think we should wire Gus," I said.

"A consensual overhear?" he asked.

"Yes. I will write up the affidavit and present it to a judge. Then we will wire Gus and get Steve Williams to admit on tape that he has been accepting bribes. We will also try to buy some more licenses from him through Gus."

Bill pushed back in his chair and pondered the idea. To me, it was normal investigative procedure — a technique we frequently employed against drug dealers and gang bangers. To him, it was uncharted territory for the IG's Office.

"I think it could work," he said. "We have to get permission from Al though."

Al Veranda was the Inspector General for the city. He had been on the job for more than a dozen years and was quite skilled at negotiating the city's political maze. He too was a lawyer and a former state's attorney who knew well how to assemble cases for prosecution and administrative hearings. I talked to Al often and had no problems taking any concerns I had to him.

He was a stand-up guy and absolutely the most legitimate boss I had ever worked for.

Bill Maybrook, Bruce Fender and I met with Al in his office and laid out our proposed plan of action. Al was all for it but he had some concerns. One of them was a big one — we had no ability to do a wire. We did not have covert recording devices and had no experience, as a unit, in wiring an informant. We pondered the many possibilities to get the technical assistance we needed and decided to ask the city, county or state police or the feds for help.

Over the next several days, I prepared the request for a consensual overhear (COH) and took it to the state attorney's public corruption unit. After they reviewed the affidavit, I presented it to the chief judge and it was approved. The state's attorney met with Gus Shirani and agreed to grant him immunity for his cooperation. Because the attorney's office had a relationship with the county sheriff, they got their technical services unit to provide surveillance assistance.

Over the next several months, we sent Gus into the city facility several times and recorded Steven Williams talking about selling temporary chauffeur's licenses to Gus.

The Benefits of Cooperation

Seven months after Sam Hashemi walked into the Department of Transportation's licensing office with a fraudulent license, Steven Williams was arrested in the same building. He refused to give a statement and was ultimately charged with four counts of bribery and one count of official misconduct — all felony offenses.

We were never able to record Steve selling another license to Gus because, as we would later learn, the department instituted new protective measures making it nearly impossible to steal them.

Steve later pleaded guilty and was sentenced to felony probation and community service. He was fired from city employment and was placed on the city's "do not hire" list. His nearly 18-year career with the city ended for what amounted to just a few thousand dollars.

Gus Shirani was not charged, just as the state's attorney promised. But he was banned from receiving a cab license from the city for five years.

Sam Hashemi was never charged. He also received a five-year ban from receiving a city cab license.

Lessons Learned

As is normal in any IG's Office investigation, many of Steven Williams' coworkers were interviewed regarding his performance on the job. While some provided no clues into his alleged misconduct, we were surprised to learn that many of them were afraid of him, thought he was too friendly with applicants and were concerned that he was corrupt. Almost all of his coworkers said that he was lazy and would often disappear from the worksite for no apparent reason. One coworker said that Steve took frequent smoking breaks in front of the office with cab drivers. At least one of his coworkers knew that he was in serious financial trouble and was filing for bankruptcy protection. None were aware that there was an anonymous telephone number they could have called to report corruption, but they all knew that the IG's Office was responsible for such investigations.

Asset control and inventory was lacking in the Department of Transportation. Because temporary chauffeur's licenses were not treated as currency, little consideration was given to properly securing them from theft. Their true value was underestimated and unappreciated by management since they were left in the open and accessible to all agents. The license log was littered with errors and omissions, and it was just assumed that employees were only making mistakes. This was even after several licenses were missing from inventory.

Recommendations to Prevent Future Occurrences

Encourage Creativity

This was the first time the IG's Office used a wire to capture a corrupt employee. While law enforcement has used such tactics for years to show courts and juries the exact actions of suspects, the IG's Office had not tried them. This might have been due to the fact that the office consists mostly of civilian investigators and state law requires the affidavit be filed by a law enforcement officer. Because I felt very comfortable with the civilian management of the IG's Office, I had no reservations about approaching them and proposing this plan of action, which is a compliment to their management style. They were concerned only with getting the job done, not egos. Other managers should encourage such input from employees and solicit creative thinking in investigations.

Play Well with Others

As stated, the IG's Office did not have the ability to do a wire. Having agreements in place with other agencies or companies can reduce the amount of equipment and specialization needed within. There is nothing wrong with asking for help from, or offering assistance to, other law enforcement colleagues. Learn to share resources and have plans in place to do so. The time to hammer out these agreements is not on game day but well before then.

Talk to Your People

Steven Williams' activities could have been curtailed long before he decided to engage in bribery and theft, but the opportunity was missed. He exhibited continual

(continued)

(continued)

workplace rule violations that were never addressed by management because they were not reported. The corruption fight starts from within, and management needs to be approachable. Make sure employees have the ability to report improper conduct anonymously, and post this contact information publicly.

Train, Train, Train

Whether you are in the business of investigating corruption or not, spend time and money on quality training programs rather than losing profits and assets. The ability to think through an investigation and develop enhanced interviewing, report writing and documentation skills is very important in the fight against corruption, and all companies and agencies can benefit from this type of thinking. The more practice you get, the better you become. I was lucky enough to obtain the needed skills on the job due to the sheer number of criminal cases I had investigated. Organizations that aren't exposed to such heavy caseloads should be sure to supplement experience with training.

Fighting corruption is both a science and an art, and it crosses the public/private threshold. Corruption is a disease that plagues both sides of the fence. Ideally, we need to start developing the proper relationships among public and private entities now to ensure a unified effort to address corruption in all forms — and our customers, whoever they are, should demand nothing less.

About the Author

William J. Kirby has been a police officer since 1993 and is currently a criminal investigator with the Arlington Heights (Illinois) Police Department. Bill earned a bachelor's degree in organizational management and leadership from North Park University in Chicago and a master's degree in public policy and administration from Northwestern University. He frequently lectures on gang crimes and conducting municipal investigations.

CHAPTER

Conflicting Interests, Conflicting Cultures

DOUGLAS M. WATSON

onflicts of interest embrace a special category of corruption. They are special because violations speak loudly of an ethical lapse, which cuts to the core of a person's integrity, honesty and professional responsibility. This is a very personal offense, and not infrequently ends with an emotional reaction. That is because conflicts of interest can exist only when there is a breach of trust, a demonstrated lack of good faith. Conflicts carry a double whammy — not only do they impinge on personal reputations, they can also significantly impact business reputations. No one wants to be tagged as untrustworthy, dishonest, unprincipled or amoral, but that can be the result once a conflict of interest is proved. It is a challenge to prove these offenses, but usually no more so than any complex fraud — until you enter the multicultural international business environment, that is, where what may seem obvious and normal to you may not actually be so. That is exactly what happened to Frank Warley and Ali Aziz Al-Obedi and their company, SeizME.

A Forced Partnership

Frank and Ali were an odd team. Pushed together by their company, neither really wanted to work with the other. They were both engineers working in the Engineering Procurement Division of SeizME, a company based in a progressive Arabian Gulf state. Frank was from the United States; tall, tow-headed with a big chin and small pale eyes. To look at him, you immediately came away with the impression, "There's an American." He just looked American — Mom, apple pie, and all that — and would probably disappear in the crowd in any U.S. city. But he stood out in the Middle East and seemed a bit self-conscious about that. His self-consciousness wasn't important, though, at least not to SeizME. To them, what mattered most was what he brought to the table — his Rolodex. Frank was an engineering geologist with a sideline in petroleum geophysics and oil-field experience. He was an expert in developing seismological modeling, which was vital to the oil and gas industry. But the key reason SeizME hired Frank as a corporate consultant was that, after 20 + years of experience in the field, Frank had compiled extensive knowledge of U.S. firms that dealt in oil-industry services, and he possessed an extraordinary ability to assess their potential technical capability to support that business line. Frank's resume of professional contacts was a priceless acquisition for SeizME.

Ali was a different story. An electrical engineer by training, he never adjusted to working in the field. He didn't like the rigs, he didn't like the oil-field culture and he really did not like working with (or for) foreigners. He considered himself to be more the managerial type. He felt out of place in Western clothing, preferring the Arab *thobe*[1] — crisply starched, gold engraved cuff links and all — to the field engineer's T-shirt and jeans. He was most comfortable behind an office desk. Young, short and a bit on the pudgy side, Ali sported a thin mustache with a wispy beard that barely passed for facial hair. His life had always been "privileged." He was, after all, the first son of an influential businessman who was affectionately known as "the Sheik" both by fellow Arab tribesmen and village outsiders. The Sheik had, in the previous year, relinquished control of the family business to Ali. With that inheritance, the Sheik simultaneously bestowed unto Ali the obligation of titular head of the family. These two events caused significant changes in Ali's life, including his sense of loyalty to SeizME.

Together, Ali and Frank looked like a *Mutt and Jeff* cartoon. But when SeizME paired them to work together, their mix was anything but comic.

It was more of a personnel decision than good business. Frank was a solid performer but never seemed to fit in with his coworkers. He kept mostly to himself. After the investigation started and violations began to surface, I asked his supervisors and coworkers why Frank would involve himself in such dealings. They told me they just couldn't answer that question. They were surprised that Frank would do anything wrong. He just did not seem to be the criminal type. He was, however, somewhat of a loner; he never joined in. He didn't have his family with him, and most of his coworkers didn't know if he was married or not. Frank got along with everyone, but he was a private guy and they respected that.

Ali, according to his supervisors, was a marginal employee who simply did not measure up against his peers. Although he was well qualified on paper (two degrees from the United States), he loathed fieldwork and didn't seem to be interested in his job. There was, however, no question among Ali's supervisors and coworkers that he was smart with a keen business savvy. But most thought he was misplaced as a rig engineer. His supervisor told me that he believed Ali was just waiting for a good reason to leave SeizME but that by placing Ali in a more administrative job, he hoped to spark his interest and help develop him.

The idea was to put these two talents together and have them focus on a project that seemed to fit with their personal styles.

Multicultural Ethics

SeizME is no anomaly in this Middle East region. It is an oil company with world-class engineering services drawn from a multinational, multicultural employee background, the majority of whom are of Arab or Middle Eastern descent. The mix of local and expatriate employees is commonplace among companies operating in this region. What set SeizME apart from the rest was the business acumen of its leaders. One of the corporate goals was to enhance oil reservoir management capabilities — a special niche in the petroleum industry. To help achieve this goal, management preached transparency in dealing with national and international vendors. They were ahead of the ethics curve — at least they thought so. This was striking to the rest of the Middle East–based businesses and was a reputational draw for many Western companies, especially those from the United States, eager to increase their Middle Eastern entrepreneurial footprint.

As part of its corporate culture, SeizME formally advocated a Western-style conflict-of-interest policy. Each employee was briefed annually and signed an agreement to disclose potentially conflicting outside business or personal interests and to abide by fair business practices, particularly when dealing with procurement matters. Company doctrine preached loyalty, trust and openness.

Frank and Ali were assigned to work together to identify foreign vendors to supply high-tech equipment. They were afforded direct and continuing access to company operating plans, projects and future expectations to assess the high-tech needs ahead of the industry. Their job was considered sensitive; they were the company's principal source for this critical information — SeizME's linchpin to achieving its goal.

Turns out, Frank and Ali really were the weakest link.

The Sheik

Local trade and importation laws impose a special requirement that any business done with foreign-owned vendors has to be sponsored by in-country "vendor-providers." These are companies that vet foreign vendors seeking to do business in the country. SeizME had arrangements with a number of vendor-providers, among which was a local company called PMPP. According to SeizME records, PMPP was owned by the Sheik. It was a family business that, in the past, had represented a few companies to SeizME.

Earlier in the year, a local influential businessman confidentially approached a personal friend, who happened to be a vice president of SeizME.

The businessman complained that PMPP had almost monopolistic control over certain of SeizME's foreign high-tech vendors. The businessman — very gently — complained that since Ali had taken over control of PMPP, apparently he had refocused that company to represent high-tech equipment suppliers, primarily those from the United States. The businessman asked his vice president friend to look into the matter as a personal favor.

Not long after that, I was called up to my executive director's office. Behind closed doors, he stared at me hesitantly before he began to talk. I didn't really know him well — I had only spoken to him once before, and that was to provide a mission overview of my group, SeizME's fraud investigations unit. We certainly weren't on a first-name basis, at least from my side — I respectfully called him Mr. Naser. He had recently been appointed as director, and my group was one of several divisions under his control. He had come to the security profession from the engineering side of the company, so this was all new to him.

"I think we might have a problem," Naser said as a worried look passed across his brow. "I just received a call from Ahmed, and it looks like we have a situation developing." Ahmed was the vice president for engineering.

He went on to explain about the "personal favor" from Ahmed's friend, adding that Ahmed had done some checking of his own. "It seems as though for the last few months, PMPP has been our exclusive agent for almost anything to do with engineering high-tech. . . . " His voice sort of petered off, and then he added, "And Ali Aziz may actually be in charge of PMPP."

During the ensuing pause, I offered, "If the allegations are true, then this could be problematic." For the next few minutes, we talked about the damage that conflicts of interest can do to firms and some of the steps we could take.

"We want to keep this low key," Naser explained. "The Sheik is a good friend of SeizME. We've known him for years." And then, in a bit more subdued voice, he said, "If there is a problem here, we want to handle it quickly, thoroughly and quietly. Report your findings only to me. We do not want any publicity." Our conversation ended and I left him, staring off into space.

I would meet with Naser several times over the next few weeks. Each meeting went pretty much like the first. He certainly was not pleased with the initial findings, but in the end, he did the right thing.

Reviewing the Records

After getting my charge, I did some basic homework. I checked our indices to see if Ali had a record. He did not, except for a local agency check completed when he was hired that showed he came from a good and respected family. So I contacted a professional and confidential working partner, SeizME's personnel director, Hassan al-Karim, who pulled Ali's official record and also obtained his departmental files.

Over the years, I have learned that when conducting investigations — especially in a foreign country, or involving businesses with locations overseas — the most important thing an investigator can do is develop reliable, honest and trustworthy contacts. Hassan was extraordinary. He was scrupulously honest, and I found I could rely on his counsel. When Hassan was tasked by me, no one knew that but me. Hassan suggested that Ali's records contained more than just paperwork. He was right.

Records reviews are occasionally shunted aside as an obligatory step in the investigative process. Searches, surveillances, interviews and interrogations are certainly more exciting, but in conflict-of-interest cases, the official record frequently contains the evidentiary golden nugget. The elements of proof are fairly clear cut. You must show that: (1) the subject is an employee of the company or comes under the company's conflict of interest policy; (2) the subject has a personal or financial interest that conflicts or appears to conflict with the company's interests; or (3) the subject's conduct, action or interest violates the company's conflict-of-interest and business ethics policy. Ali's records contained his original conflict-of-interest declarations and his entire history with SeizME but revealed no information about PMPP. This, I realized, was what Hassan was implying.

To gain a better understanding of Ali, I discreetly contacted his immediate supervisor. It didn't take long for me to learn that Ali wasn't involved alone. The supervisor told me about Ali and Frank being brought together to form a special consultation team to upgrade SeizME's technology capabilities. I asked about PMPP and drew a blank stare. Seems that no one wanted to acknowledge that Ali had a PMPP connection.

Next Hassan pulled Frank's records, and, when I compared them with SeizME's recent high-tech procurements, a pattern emerged.

Scratching an Itch

To do their jobs, Ali and Frank had unfettered access to SeizME's future needs. Frank, drawing on his past contacts, identified U.S.-based firms with the potential to fulfill those needs. Ali interjected PMPP into the procurement equation.

Using SeizME's automated database, I made a quick check of recent contracts with companies associated with Frank's past. In each case PMPP was the vendor-provider for SeizME. To an outsider, this might appear to be legitimate. To a fraud examiner, it was evidence.

At this point, we believed that PMPP had garnered a lock on certain high-tech contracts with SeizME. We established that SeizME's conflict-of-interest and business ethics policies were clear. But neither Ali nor Frank had declared an interest in any of the companies involved, including PMPP. Frank's

Rolodex was obviously being exploited, but we had no evidence that Frank or Ali was profiteering. Under normal circumstances, we would have seized contract records, conducted commercial registration checks (the Middle Eastern equivalent of doing a Dun & Bradstreet check), examined chamber of commerce records to uncover possible hidden business transactions, reviewed telephone records/Internet/e-mail logs to determine if work time or resources were used to support any conflicting interests and conducted interviews and obtained financial releases to examine bank records for possible profiteering. But doing so would have raised the investigative profile. In this case, we were constrained. *Low key* was the rule.

The Arabs have a gesture that reflects the sometimes-convoluted ways of doing things in the Middle East: use your right hand to reach over your head to scratch the itch in your left ear. We needed to do a lot of abstract scratching.

Instead of going to the source (PMPP records), we went to the U.S. firms — about half a dozen of them. One of my investigators, Tom Wisen, fortuitously, was in the United States on leave. We called him and asked him to contact several of the firms that we believed had been flagged by Frank and Ali. He discovered that the orders weren't big-dollar transactions, but they weren't chump change, either. From an investigator's perspective, it looked like Frank and Ali were operating under the radar of corporate audit review. Coincidentally? I don't usually believe in coincidences.

Tom contacted the U.S. companies that had signed agency agreements with PMPP over the previous 90 days. In each case, we learned two things: (1) They knew Frank Warley and in most cases Frank had recommended PMPP to be their in-country agent, and (2) they knew Ali as the president of PMPP. The firms were not only open and cooperative, but they also backed up their statements by providing Tom with copies of their agreements. As it turns out, Ali had signed most of the agreements.

At this point, I returned to Naser. It was time to interview Frank and Ali. We chatted about the best approach. "I recommend that we interview Frank first," I said. "I think we can relate to him better." Naser sat pensively behind his desk. "As for Ali," I continued, "I'd like to have my best interviewer, Khalid, do his interview."

"Hmmmm," the director murmured.

"Khalid is sharp and completely loyal. He will keep this internal inquiry internal," I assured Naser.

We got the go-ahead.

Opposing Interviews

No one likes being called by the fraud examiner, so Frank's response was telling. "Can I come by now?" he asked almost apologetically. Even though it was late in the afternoon, if I had suggested another time, it would have been like releasing the fish before baiting the hook. "Sure," I said cheerfully but seriously. "Ring the bell when you get here." Our offices were secured from the rest of the company by locked and alarmed doors, with "CONTROLLED AREA" signs prominently displayed in big red lettering everywhere. It was an imposing — and somewhat daunting — entryway.

Frank's interview was shorter than expected. During our pre-interview planning, we had discussed various methods to encourage Frank to talk to us. We knew that he was concerned about keeping his job — something we could use if he became uncooperative. But we also knew that he valued his professional standing in the industry — something we could work with. We planned on a protracted session. Instead, Frank came in, sat down and began to confess.

"Frank, we're investigating some possible irregularities involving the company's relationship with PMPP. You know, the firm that is acting as the in-country representative for several contracts for high-tech equipment and services. Did you know that Ali was actually the president of PMPP?" That's all it took. Frank's body language told the story before his mouth started talking. With his head bowed and shoulders slumped, sadness and resignation drifted across his face. I'd like to chalk this up to my team's exceptional interview skills, but that's just not the case. This was a lesson in remorse. The next hour or so was simply a note-taking exercise.

In a nutshell, Frank said that shortly after they had been paired up, Ali approached him with a "business opportunity" to corner the U.S. market on high-tech equipment. Frank would identify experts with the potential to fulfill SeizME's needs; Ali would have PMPP approach the experts and arrange exclusive agency agreements. Ali and Frank each used their special "insider" information to ensure contracts with SeizME. Frank denied getting any kickbacks; he didn't even know the value of the contracts. He benefited from a good performance rating — that translated into job security. Ali benefited by having his company obtain lucrative contracts. Frank rationalized that SeizME was receiving good service because the U.S. companies were the best and he trusted Ali to make the best arrangements.

Ali's interview was remarkable. Khalid called him up early the next morning. Only with great reluctance did he agree to come to the office. Once confronted, his reaction was striking. He stood up, glared at Khalid and, shaking his finger indignantly, vehemently declared that his involvement with PMPP was done totally and separately from his SeizME duties. He brushed off his failure to report his association with PMPP as simple oversight. He denied any personal profiteering, stating that the PMPP business was a family affair and that he was only a figurehead. He was offended by the accusation that he was using his PMPP business to enhance his SeizME career (or vice versa). Eventually, he walked out of the interview.

Going Their Separate Ways

After the interviews, we were asked to stand down; management would act on the information we had collected to date. The executives weren't interested in determining the magnitude of the fraud, nor were they interested in Ali's or Frank's profiteering. They simply wanted it to "go away."

In the end, Frank received a punitive termination warning notice — one step from being fired. He was removed from consideration for an annual pay increase, received a performance rating downgrade and was reassigned. Eventually, he was released from the company for substandard performance.

Ali received a reprimand for poor judgment and failure to report his private business connections. He was directed to either resign as an officer of PMPP or be reassigned from engineering. He did neither; instead he resigned from SeizME. He remains president of PMPP and continues to do business with SeizME.

That, however, is not the end of the story.

Analysis in Retrospect . . .

Shortly after the interviews were over, the buzz began. All companies enjoy two levels of communication: formal and informal. It is the informal line that feeds the soul of the corporation; it can also be a lifeline of knowledge to the fraud examiner. When bad things happen, or when there is an information void, it becomes the venue for office gossip. In the United States, such person-to-person discussions stereotypically occur around the water cooler or at the coffeepot. In the Arab world, the mosque is where serious face-to-face social networking happens. The hot topic at both locations was what would happen to Frank and Ali, and the discussions were culturally split.

Many Western expatriate employees felt Frank would be a fall guy, whereas Arab and non-Westerners tended to side with Ali. SeizME's corporate culture — what management wanted as the norm for workplace behavior — was crumbling because of a conflict of interest. A corporate culture helps to solidify a business reputation, which is highly valued. SeizME wanted to project a Western ethical model but did little to integrate Middle Eastern mores. Management never considered that deep-seated cultural motivators do not change easily.

Behind the scenes, I learned that immediately after walking out of the interview, Ali had gone to his vice president to complain that we had offended and insulted him and his family. He complained that what he was doing, while perhaps not strictly in accord with the company's ethics policies, most certainly was right and good. He was, after all, simply taking care of his family. Ali explained that his father, the Sheik, had become too old to carry on. As firstborn son, he incurred a moral responsibility to ensure his family was taken care of. Ali implored his VP to understand that he was acting on strong social, cultural and religious grounds, and to imply otherwise was impugning his personal and moral integrity.

I missed that move. I should have predicted Ali's reaction and alerted my boss. Ali was a smart guy and knew which (and whose) strings to pull and how hard. As it played out, Ali's direct approach introduced powerful mitigation into the equation.

The executives who adjudicated the case were Middle Eastern, Western oriented but still culturally bound to Islam. Under sharia, which is the law of Islam and in this part of the world is integrated into every facet of life, the word of a Muslim is considered to be best evidence. Irrespective of his actions, Ali's purposeful and direct denials of any intentional wrongdoing weighed heavily in his favor. Frank's statements did not carry the same weight. In Muslim culture, the statement of a "nonbeliever" is questionable when judged against that of a Muslim. For Frank's statements to carry equal weight, he required corroboration by Muslim witnesses. The investigation did not produce such testimony.

Management acknowledged that our case facts showed how organizational neglect can facilitate fraud by opening the opportunity door. The inquiry revealed that supervisors and coworkers had good reason to suspect Ali was using his SeizME connections to develop his personal business and Frank was overexploiting that priceless Rolodex, but they did nothing. It was only when a PMPP competitor lodged a complaint at a high level that SeizME took action, and then cautiously — the low-key approach.

The SeizME executives were very interested in the *why* of the crime. They wanted to understand motive. Frank's motive came across as self-serving. His implication of Ali was construed as an attempt to deflect blame. Ali's motive might appear to be opportunistic greed, but in his own culture, it is almost unthinkable that he would risk shaming his family by lying.

The "Corporate Answer"

What became apparent to all was that even though Frank was not Ali's supervisor, because of his experience he should have recognized the pitfalls and disallowed the scheme at the outset, pointing out that it would be a violation of business ethics and even fraud. Frank was an experienced consultant, charged with mentoring a young, naive employee who was not familiar with international commerce or to the possibilities of fraud. Frank should have seized the moment to train an inexperienced employee in proper conduct. He failed to do so in the initial stages and participated in the scheme until we discovered it. Consequently, Frank was not only complicit but ultimately owned great responsibility. The company leaders recognized that Ali's acts were wrong, but they were most upset with Frank's failure to take prudent action. They felt betrayed by both Frank and Ali — but more so by Frank because of his experience.

Lessons Learned

The true challenge of this investigation was not proving the conflict of interest; rather, it involved working a case where management was trapped in cultural conflict and did not want to ruffle feathers. It is not uncommon for management to want to maintain a positive image. Corporate culture is very important to the health and welfare of everyday operations; businesses can thrive and die on reputational factors. Executives value their companies' reputations because of marketable economic gain. In this case, management, for local reasons, did not want to impinge on the reputation of the Sheik.

When working fraud in a foreign environment, I learned one must be prepared to address extant cultural and social differences as well as work traditional investigative steps. When I missed Ali's culturally oriented appeal, I hurt the case, because Ali was able to take advantage of cultural markers that impacted on impartiality. Some investigators believe that their job is simply to complete the elements of proof and let the chips fall as they may. But that may not always be true; uncommon circumstances require exceptional responses. SeizME's management team wasn't interested in prosecution, remuneration or jail time. Rather, they wanted to show the Sheik, and the influential businessman who was the original complainant, that they could clean their house without causing undue embarrassment. From an investigator's perspective, it can be hard to pull back on the traditional investigative reins and find subtler ways to get the evidence. Next time, we'll do better. We learned that there are many ways to scratch your ear.

The second big lesson involves recruiting management. Fraud examiners can help management with integrity issues before they occur by explaining the impact of fraud and corruption on business and the bottom line. A close working relationship with the senior leadership is a key element in fraud examination leadership. That relationship must embrace anti-fraud education as a principal tool, and the onus to make it so rests on the team's leadership. The education process is not a simple thing that can be handled by a few meetings, posters or handouts. It's the old "you can talk the talk but do you walk the walk" adage. It has to go beyond training and become integrated into daily business processes. The message from the top must be clear, rational and unambiguously part of both the formal *and* informal corporate communication channels. To do otherwise sends multiple messages to the workforce, which complicates core business functions and undermines effective resource management and sound leadership.

Recommendations to Prevent Future Occurrences

SeizME took steps to show it could "walk the walk." Management reasserted the company's expectation that all employees, regardless of cultural background, must embrace the company's ethical standards, and explained why. To help the process and reinforce that message, the company instituted an enhanced scenario-based training program for mid-level management designed to introduce new managers to the complexities of cross-cultural ethical dilemmas. Finally, it used town-hall meetings to convey concerns about ethics, conflicts of interest and impropriety and to foster two-way discussions. Those certainly were good steps forward. My challenge now is to keep walking the walk.

About the Author

Dr. Douglas M. Watson, CFE, resides in Ankara, Turkey, where he explores cross-cultural behavior dynamics, especially as they relate to ethical dilemmas involving trust and betrayal across cultures. He can be reached at http://dmwatson.homestead.com and on Twitter @550dmw.

Note

1. The traditional *thobe* (also sometimes spelled *thaub*) is a white cotton or linen ankle-length, robelike, long-sleeved garment worn by men in the Arabian Peninsula, Egypt, Jordan, Kuwait, Iraq and most of the Gulf states and in northern Africa.

11

But We Thought He Was *Saving* Us Millions

GARY E. GAUGLER

Michiel (Mick) Segovia had moved to the United States as a child. In his mid-30s, married with two young children, he was an aggressive staff-level buyer. Considered a peak performer in his department, Mick was quietly confident in the workplace but exhibited a consistent neck twitch in interpersonal exchanges. He had been a buyer for more than 15 years and employed at Union & Viceroy (U&V) for almost ten. Taking advantage of one of the company's benefits, he was working toward his college degree at night. Beyond his mild arrogance, he was relatively nondescript. No fancy car; a nice yet modest two-story house; and no reputation for flamboyant clothes, possessions, vacations or lifestyle. He seemed to most observers to simply be a middle-class man living a middle-class life. Soon we would learn that he was a millionaire.

U&V, a successful and growing third-generation manufacturer of metal construction components, had never experienced a significant fraud, nor did we have any reason to believe one had been occurring for almost ten years. It was a tight-knit company where employees were trusted like family members. Although run like a professional and profitable business, the culture could be described as congenial and benevolent. That innocence all changed when our CEO received a Good Samaritan phone call from Greg Angelese, the new owner of HQ Distributors, a former supplier. HQ had gone into bankruptcy and was no longer actively serving us.

Angelese owned other companies in the hardware-component business. He bought the HQ assets from the bankruptcy court and was trying to rebuild the organization under new leadership. Part of his process was studying the business documents that he inherited with his purchase. Angelese suggested that we look into the activities of Mick Segovia, based on "suspicious documents" he had discovered. He also reported that he tried to resume business relations through Segovia but was strongly rebuffed — increasing his suspicions. He then invited us to his facility to review the documents that initiated his call. While our CEO had some doubts about the allegations' veracity, he immediately phoned me, the internal audit director, with instructions to contact the caller and collect additional information. My follow-up call provided enough information to suggest that this was clearly worth investigating, and we arranged for an on-site visit at HQ's location the following week.

A Cautious Start

At the start of the investigation, we formed a small team and agreed to work in the strictest confidence. This was to protect the integrity of the investigation as well as the reputation of the alleged, in case the allegations were unfounded. The initial team was our general counsel, our CFO, our CEO and me. Step one was to verify that if there were indeed kickbacks or improper payments, they would be covered by our insurance program. We contacted Garmin & Company, our insurance broker, to understand the claim-filing process (requirements and timing) as well as to place the investigation under attorney-client privilege in coordination with Garmin's general counsel. No one at U&V had significant fraud examination experience at the time. We wanted to make sure that we performed the process correctly and did not inadvertently corrupt the investigation or defame the accused employee in our process. Garmin engaged on our behalf a seasoned private investigator (PI), Chad Williams, to join our team. After a kickoff meeting with Chad, we were ready to investigate. I was accompanied by Jay and Nick, my two senior auditors, when we visited HQ Distributors' site.

Upon our arrival we were presented with the basis of Angelese's suspicion — numerous canceled checks, computer reports and other documents indicating significant disbursements to a woman named Segovia. A quick cross reference to Mick's personnel file confirmed that the checks were going to his wife, Jenny, and being deposited into the same bank account that his paychecks from us were deposited. Pulses quickened as we started pulling checks deposited into this account and calculated a total. After two days on-site reviewing approximately five years of documents, the verified tally exceeded $600,000. For us, this was a significant fraud. We headed back to the office to update the team and plan our next steps.

Our next objective was to learn more facts. How many suppliers was Mick working with? Were any other employees involved? How much illicit money was being kicked back? Eventually we would need to speak to suppliers, to other employees and of course to Mick, but we needed to focus our approach first. That involved data extraction and analysis. Starting with a list of all of Mick's suppliers, we extracted a multiyear purchase history of each purchase order and item. We were looking for patterns that we could leverage in our future interviews. Knowing Mick's reputation as a vendor-flipping cost reducer, we looked for data patterns where vendors didn't change over time *and* didn't show cost reduction. Of related interest, many of Mick's purchases were commodity items. This suggests they should have had cost volatility consistent with cost movements of the underlying commodity of the parts. About six vendors, including the tipster, met our pattern, and these would be the data points we would eventually put before Segovia when we confronted him. The total purchases in question exceeded $10 million and spanned almost ten years. An interview of Segovia followed by vendor interviews were the next steps required to precisely determine the parties and the total kickbacks involved.

The Interview Strategy

Chad Williams was going to lead the interview because he had extensive prosecutorial experience before starting his own PI firm. He was joined by his associate, Kate Brosious, a Certified Fraud Examiner who complemented Chad's background in criminal law and the judicial process with her wealth of experience in business operations, internal controls and fraud examinations. I was there as the scribe and moderator. We decided on an indirect approach. The premise of Segovia's interview was that I was leading a project aimed at improving U&V's purchasing effectiveness; Chad and Kate were consultants advising on the project, and Segovia was selected to represent his department as the "best practices" performer of vendor selection and negotiation. Mick's head was already inflated by this, and he proudly entered the conference room. Chad and Kate began performing their craft; they spent an hour establishing rapport, building trust and boxing Mick into a corner. Their strategy was to let Mick explain all of his purchasing practices and successes — effectively to confirm that he knew what a buyer was supposed to do and how to do it to best serve his employer.

After Segovia clearly explained how a good buyer should perform, Chad and Kate started asking questions directed at the malfeasance. Chad placed one of our data extracts in front of Mick and asked, "If commodity prices fluctuate as you describe, why have costs been unchanged for this vendor for five years?" After a halfhearted response from Mick, Kate presented a second report and followed, "If you put purchases out for review every two to three years when a supplier's costs haven't decreased, why have you used this same vendor for eight years?"

Mick was now frustrated and finally asked what we were really trying to ask him. When I replied that we had evidence that he had received kickbacks, he said the interview was over and stood up to leave. Kate responded that we could not detain him; he was free to leave if he wanted. But I informed him that our evidence indicated his wife had received and deposited his kickback payments, making her a co-conspirator and legally culpable. Further, we would be providing our evidence against him and Jenny to the authorities, so it might be in his and her best interest if he cooperated. It helped that I had some knowledge of Mick and suspected that he would do the noble thing on behalf of his wife. And he did. He sat back down and proceeded to confess. Mick named four suppliers — HQ, Bucks Bar and Rod, John X. Daniels Supply and Flawless Fabricators, Inc. — and said that he had acted alone, but even while confessing he maintained his innocence. He had rationalized his actions on three bases: the suppliers were fully cooperative; the suppliers lost no money because the fees paid to Jenny were in lieu of commissions that they would have paid to a sales representative; and U&V lost no money because he was still obtaining fair-market prices. He restated his rationalizations throughout the investigative process — to us, the FBI and eventually his counsel.

However, he admitted the apparent impropriety of his actions and said that he assumed he would be terminated (which he was). Kate told him directly that we could make no promises but that his cooperation might look favorable, and we asked for further cooperation — tax returns and bank statements. Then Chad asked him if he still had any of the commission money and said that, if so, we would like to have it returned to U&V. He agreed to the repayment. Kate recompiled my notes into a written statement and Segovia voluntarily signed it. We then arranged for Mick to reimburse us the balance of illicit money in his possession, and the next day a seven-figure wire transfer was deposited to the U&V bank account. A week later he also delivered several years of bank statements and tax returns, as promised.

Uncovering the Corrupt Partners

While the interview explained a lot and a seven-figure recovery was very satisfying, we still had questions about how the fraud was perpetrated, if we had identified all the participants and if we could fully quantify our losses. Our next step was to interview suppliers. This would allow us to corroborate Segovia's statements and better understand how the fraud worked and the role of the suppliers. We interviewed three of the ones Mick named (HQ was of course under new ownership, and the former owner could not be located). We also interviewed the other suppliers that Mick did not mention but who met our pattern and were able to satisfy ourselves that they were not involved.

The discussions with the participating suppliers were almost as interesting as the interview with Mick. They each informed us, independently, of how Segovia executed the process. In each instance, Mick, upon establishing the supplier relationship, created an overstated illusion of his authority at U&V. He maintained this over time by strictly managing the relationship and minimizing their interaction with any other of our company personnel. They confirmed that no other U&V employees were involved. Segovia informed the vendors that he or Jenny would serve as their sales rep. The guarantee of an ongoing relationship at a favorable price (for the supplier) would allow the supplier not to hire a commissioned sales rep; this commission would instead be payable to Segovia. In retrospect, the suppliers expressed discomfort with the relationship and acknowledged that Mick was demanding and overbearing at times — especially when collecting his commissions — but they continued to participate. Often their rationalization was based on Mick's threats to pull the business.

Interestingly, none of the suppliers tried to reach out to anyone at U&V to intercede; perhaps because the profits they received from the relationship mitigated any guilt or angst they might have been feeling. Kate made an interesting observation about the traits the suppliers shared that made them a target for Segovia's scam: each was a family-owned business. Mick would deal directly with someone at the owner or CEO level, and in each case U&V was a substantial part of the vendor's overall volume. In some cases they borrowed money for equipment to meet our supply demands. If they stopped cooperating and Segovia pulled U&V's business, the supplier could suffer layoffs, bankruptcy and family-related embarrassment. How the fraud was perpetrated was now much clearer. But the fact that above-market prices were being paid suggested that our damages might exceed the amount of commissions Mick had extracted. Could we quantify our damages so we might be able to pursue additional recoveries?

After reconciling data from Segovia's bank statements and tax returns, we determined that his total collected kickbacks were slightly below $1.5 million. The total he wired to us from his accounts was about 70 percent of that, so we had a basis to file an employee crimes insurance claim for the balance. We had previously verified coverage, but we had to define, quantify and prove our damages. Were they simply potential savings equal to Segovia's kickbacks, or were our overpayments more than that?

The Final Cost

In conjunction with the U&V Purchasing Department, my team began a project to quantify overpayments. The formula for calculating overpayment was actual amounts paid to the complicit suppliers minus fair-market price of the same items and quantities during the period in question. First we replaced Segovia's corrupt vendors. To determine past overpayments, we could not simply take current prices and remove inflation. As described previously, many of Mick's purchases were commodities, which often do not correlate with overall inflation rates. To quantify these historical market prices, we selected a large sample of products that the corrupt vendors supplied. We then took these to our new suppliers and asked them to provide historical prices for the same or comparable products. We used this sample to develop an index by part and supplier of overpayment percent for each item and calculated the total estimated loss to be $3 million.

It may have been coincidental, but I found it very interesting that our estimation of Segovia's kickbacks approximated 50 percent of our estimated total overpayments — meaning that the ill-gotten loot was split evenly between the buyer and seller. We compiled an insurance claim package consisting of our many spreadsheet analyses of actual purchases, invoices used to build the historical indices and a compelling and defensible narrative prepared by Chad and Kate explaining both the case background and our valuation methodologies. The binder of data supporting our claim was four inches thick, but the insurer, of course, did not simply thank us for the analysis and send us a check. It engaged its own forensic accountant to thoroughly review our presentation. After two weeks of responding to questions, explaining and defending our data and our approach, it agreed with our claim. Net of the deductible and the restitution we previously received from Segovia, we received a check from our carrier for approximately $1.8 million.

Lessons Learned

We learned that fraud doesn't always look like one would expect — Mick did not fit the typical profile of a fraudster. He was not a long-term employee (the fraud started in his first year at U&V) or a high-ranking employee (he was a staff-level buyer). He also did not maintain a flashy lifestyle with significant vices or spending habits, and, fortunately for us, most of his kickbacks were still in his bank account. Mick was also not a college graduate, as most fraudsters are. Also, his relationships with the corrupt vendors were acrimonious; I would have thought a complicit buyer would have pampered his illicit suppliers, but not so in this case. Our most striking lesson was how naive we had been to the risk of fraud. It really *can* happen to us. We had just recovered millions in overpayments from Segovia's purchases, but before the allegations were brought to our attention, we had thought he was *saving* us millions.

Recommendations to Prevent Future Occurrences

U&V's management wanted to do whatever was necessary to prevent the recurrence of such an incident and therefore chose to press criminal charges. Through Chad's contacts as a former prosecutor, we were able to get the attention of the U.S. Attorney's office and presented them with a modified version of our insurance claim. The case was probably 99 percent complete as documented, but the assistance we provided for the criminal case involved pulling data that fit a definable crime. We provided evidence of Segovia's interactions via telephone, computer and mail transmissions to support charges of mail fraud and wire fraud.

In addition, I was deposed by the defense attorney as part of the process. I was so nervous one might have thought I was the defendant. But the process went smoothly, and the case was very clear. I was not privy to the dealings that occurred among the attorneys, but Jenny was not charged with any crimes, and Mick pleaded guilty to mail and wire fraud.

The last legal process before sentencing was a civil claim filed by the insurance company representatives against Segovia. They wanted their money back just as we did. I provided the same data as well as additional assistance to the insurer's attorney. It was the right thing to do to support them, and of course any recoveries they might make would only serve to reduce our loss history (and hopefully our future insurance premiums).

Two years after the Good Samaritan tip, the case wrapped up. We terminated a corrupt employee and four complicit vendors. We stopped a significant fraud that was costing us money and that might have continued indefinitely. We recovered almost $3 million for U&V that, frankly, we hadn't known we were missing. We also recommended that management:

- Segregate duties so the same employee would not control the ordering process, the vendor selection and the price negotiations. This was meaningful because we had excessive stock that Segovia ordered to increase his kickbacks.
- Implement a vendor management system including performance metrics for management review and approval.
- Implement a formal code of conduct with training and written acknowledgment.
- Implement a third-party whistleblower hotline to provide a means for employees, business partners and others to report possible improprieties.
- Require periodic management review of existing vendors and an initial approval of new products and suppliers.
- Implement tools to allow management to monitor cost trends, inventory balances and so on.

And perhaps most important, by being open about the public facts of this incident, we created companywide awareness of what had happened and how it hurt not only U&V but each of our employees. Disclosing the fact that a significant fraud had occurred without our detection was not pleasant, but it was important to address the case and demonstrate our commitment to prevent future occurrences. Some of our innocence was lost, but the company came out better for the experience.

The criminal and civil cases were combined. Chad Williams and I attended Segovia's sentencing, and I read U&V's statement for the court. It acknowledged Mick's cooperation in our investigation, as we had promised during our interview of him. Segovia pleaded guilty and seemed to truly acknowledge his guilt and feel remorse; he even turned to me and apologized for what he had done. The judge sentenced him to three years in prison and two years on probation — less than we expected, but a strong punishment nonetheless. He also ordered Mick to pay restitution to our insurance carrier, although that will likely never be paid in full.

About the Author

Gary E. Gaugler is director of tax and business development for a global manufacturing company, founding its internal audit function. He is a graduate of Lehigh University. As internal audit director, Gary was responsible for the global internal audit program, as well as investigations and compliance. In June 2009, Gary turned over responsibility for the audit function in order to focus his attention on founding an in-house tax function.

The Construction of a Fraud

LORNA LEUNG

Billy Dodd was at his late 40s, married with two children who were about to start high school. He and his wife both worked to support the family, but Billy enjoyed a lavish lifestyle and was always shopping for the next trendy item. Billy had never excelled academically, but he enjoyed hands-on projects and managed to finish his secondary education with average grades. Instead of attending college, he made use of his strengths and enrolled in a building technician program at a trade school and earned a diploma.

Around the house, Billy was a very handy person and seemed able to build anything the family needed: new cabinets, shelves, replaced floor tiles, an extra bathroom and even a completely renovated basement. Despite a limited income, he loved his family and wanted to provide the best for them. He wanted to improve his financial position but was struggling to meet the desires of the average teenagers and maintain his spending habits.

Billy began his career in construction as a carpenter. He worked hard and gained valuable experience. Over the years, he learned how to coordinate with different tradesmen and to resolve many challenges at the construction site. Billy took pride in his skills and enjoyed the completion of beautiful homes with details and craftsmanship. He developed good working relationships with suppliers and his coworkers. Eventually he was promoted to estimator, finishing site supervisor and then site supervisor.

Construction work is physically demanding, and Billy worked long hours; a typical day at site would start at 7:00 a.m. and go until late afternoon. The houses he constructed sold swiftly for hundreds of thousand dollars while he constantly scrambled for more money to support his family and his spending. He dreamed of starting his own business.

Bonfield Homes

Bonfield Homes was established in 1980 by Paul Bonfield. Paul's father was a smart investor and purchased large parcels of land, which Paul inherited and began developing into residential areas. Paul was the CEO, his wife, Mary, was the interior designer and their daughter, Andrea, was responsible for the marketing department. Paul had no formal training in engineering and construction and had to rely on qualified employees in these areas.

A few years ago, Paul had offered Billy a position at Bonfield as the construction manager and site supervisor of a project involving 40 luxury homes. Billy was given authority to handle all ordering, receiving, dispatching of material and management of the construction site in addition to determining estimates for contracts negotiation. It was almost like running a small building business, and Billy was excited to take on the challenge; he gladly accepted the position.

However, his dream of starting his own company did not end with this new opportunity. Because of his limited financial resources, Billy decided the best way to open a company was to enter a partnership. He approached two people he met through his professional network with his idea, and shortly after they began building few small townhouses. One of his partners, Mitchell Durant, worked as a sales agent for the largest lumber distributor in the area and hoped to use his position to the advantage of the new partnership. Billy's other partner was a man named Jake Glade, whom he met at a trade show a few years ago. To maintain his negotiating ties with subcontractors and to ensure a steady stream of income, Billy decided to continue working at Bonfield until the newly formed partnership became profitable. However, expenses incurred at a construction site can be unexpected; Billy soon found that the partnership was short on money to purchase necessary supplies. Luckily, Mitchell turned out to be the lumber sales agent for Bonfield, and Billy was about to be working very closely with him on the contracts for the 40 luxury homes, and, as it turned out, even more.

Launch Reports

At Bonfield, prior to launching a new project, department managers worked together to produce a report that estimated budgets for major categories of the development, such as total hard costs, construction overhead, marketing, finance and administrative costs. Paul thought of the big picture and did not want to be burdened with details. He trusted his department managers and believed that they should operate their department like a business of their own; his philosophy was that "the one who determines the budget should be responsible for monitoring its details."

Prior to monthly disbursements, the accounting department produced a work-in-progress report for each manager to monitor spending against the original budget and reevaluate the cost to complete each building. Every month, Martin Thomas, the senior vice president responsible for land procurement and overseeing the operation, chaired a progress meeting. Each department manager provided an update on contracts, specific issues and significant overruns, and Paul sat in for decision making when it was necessary. Paul and Martin also received the summary cost report, but they only focused on a high-level review of sales revenue and spending. In these meetings, Billy often tried to bring up his concerns about the increasing construction costs, but all that Paul cared about was whether he would make the profit as projected. He insisted that Billy negotiate harder and cut costs where possible. Martin was occupied in land development matters and planning issues with the municipality office, so Billy felt that his concerns were pushed aside.

At the end of each project, the final report included the original budget, contracts committed, revised budget and actual cost incurred for each project. It was used to measure the performance and bonus calculation for each department and employee. With the economy improving and interest rates lowering, the housing market in Toronto was regaining momentum. As sales prices increased, construction costs also rose, but at a more rapid pace. At the same time, the housing industry experienced a shortage of skilled labor, projects were behind schedule and closing dates were delayed. Billy realized that the construction budget for his project was probably going to exceed estimates, and winning a big bonus on the completion of the 40 luxury homes would be almost impossible.

In the meantime, because of limited credit at the bank, Billy and the members of his new partnership needed to come up with additional equity to purchase lumber for the townhouses they were constructing. Billy found himself in a vulnerable position.

The Opportunity

It was early afternoon and a truckload of lumber had just been dropped off at the Bonfield construction site. Because of rain, the framing crew had already left and would resume the next day. Billy stayed behind alone to complete some paperwork. He was stressed and trying to think of ways to fund his side business when he caught a glimpse of the lumber piled in front of the empty lot. He realized he could make use of some of the lumber for the townhouses and get Mitchell to help him with the contract. He picked up the phone and called his partners to bring their trucks over.

The next day, Billy called Mitchell at work and ordered another truckload of lumber; on the delivery ticket, Mitchell wrote "replacement of stolen lumber for Lot 2," and Billy signed it when the lumber was delivered. Two weeks later, he ordered another delivery and Mitchell marked it as "replacement of damaged lumber for Lot 5." The cost for the stolen and damaged lumber in these two orders was approximately $10,000.

Three weeks later, using the Bonfield credit account at a hardware store, Billy picked up $800 worth of building supplies for his side business. On the receipt, he marked the purchase as "miscellaneous supplies and replacement of small broken tools."

Inconsistencies in the Reports

I was the accounting manager at Bonfield Homes and responsible for preparation of financial statements. When a house sales transaction was completed, I reviewed the costs incurred and cost to complete and then determined the cost of sale for each of the houses. As part of internal audit, I conducted routine investigations when the actual cost significantly exceeded the original budget. This review usually involved comparing actual cost against the contracts and budget for each job cost code, such as lumber, drywall and framing. Many times, the overruns were the result of site conditions, building code changes, billing mistakes or simply clerical errors. Occasionally, supplies and material were lost or stolen even though the material was locked in a gated compound. Therefore, our budgets included an allowance for theft and vandalism.

I was reviewing Billy's project records and, by the time I compiled information for the cost of sales and the quarterly financial statement, I discovered the actual costs incurred under "theft and vandalism" far exceeded the estimated budget. Billy's costs in these categories were notably higher than all the other ongoing projects — and this development was in a safe, affluent neighborhood.

I instructed the accounts payable staff members to record transactions in a detailed manner; invoices pertaining to hard costs had to be entered with the lot number and job cost code. Site managers and workers often ordered general supplies for projects as the need arose. When they did, they were supposed to include a job cost code, such as a small equipment purchase, winter cost or theft and vandalism. Bonfield had a policy that these purchases must be confirmed by site supervisor on invoices and delivery tickets.

Again, the actual project cost incurred for this project managed by Billy also far exceeded the original budget. I therefore decided to carefully scrutinize his spending. Something had started to smell fishy.

By this time, about 25 of the 40 luxury homes were already built and sold, ten were in various construction stages and the remaining five houses were sold but construction not started.

I compiled a cost report for the 25 completed houses; each report contained a column for the original budget, contract amount, cost incurred, budgeted cost (actual plus cost to complete) and budgeted cost per square footage for each job cost. Although these houses were not the same model, the structure and specification are similar; therefore, I compiled a similar report for the average house and average cost by square footage.

I scheduled a meeting with Billy to review my reports, and he provided me with an estimate for the final cost of the 40 houses. We determined and agreed on an average construction overhead cost per lot for his project. Since we were undertaking two other projects with similar specifications, I decided to compare their costs to Billy's. I compiled the same average costs and construction overhead to use as a benchmark for comparison.

Suspicious Lumber Invoices

Each of the three projects used the same lumber vendor and had very similar contracts. They all stipulated that additional lumber that exceeded the contract might be needed for grading or various other reasons, but such incurred costs usually accounted for less than 5 percent of the predetermined contract price. However, with Billy's project, the lumber cost for five houses were significantly higher. I began reviewing the lumber invoices and delivery slips and noticed his were the only ones with notations from the lumber salesman, Mitchell. There were many noncontracted lumber shipments for these houses without proper reference; the deliveries were made based on Billy's written remarks on the delivery slips and without specific reasons. After I tallied up these sundry deliveries and deducted the standard 5 percent allowance, the unaccounted for lumber deliveries totaled $26,000.

Since site managers were authorized to purchase small tools from a national hardware company using a credit account issued to Bonfield, Billy had access to it. During our budget review meeting, Billy told me that he was going to exceed his small tools allowance on the project. However, he was unable to provide relevant reasons for the overspending.

I instructed one of my staff members to locate all the purchase tickets that Billy had signed for at the hardware company and list the store locations, dates and times of purchases, amounts and brief descriptions. Many of the purchases were at a store far from Billy's site, in the early morning or in the late afternoon. Those tickets added up to about $8,500. The suspected loss now totaled approximately $44,000.

Interviews

I reported my discovery to Martin Thomas, the senior vice president of Bonfield Homes, and he agreed that for the benefit of doubt, we should conduct confidential interviews with other site workers. We started with Hank, a site foreman who had been a loyal employee of Bonfield for many years.

Hank told us that Billy routinely arrived late or left early from the construction site, but there were also many days that he worked late to finish his paperwork. Hank said that lumber was usually shipped prior to framing but sometimes he couldn't find it when he needed it and had to ask Billy to order more.

Next we interviewed Andrew, a site worker, and learned that Billy was a close friend of Jake Glade, the owner of Tribrooke Homes, a small start-up builder. Andrew also said he suspected Billy and Mitchell were a little too friendly as well. I decided to conduct a business registration search of Tribrooke Homes and discovered that Billy was listed as one of the three directors — along with Jake and Mitchell. Tribrooke Homes was building a few units of townhouses in the area where Billy was picking up many of his hardware supplies.

Good Guys Sometimes Finish Last

Unfortunately, other than the hardware supplies purchased by Billy personally, we were unable to confirm what may have happened to the lost lumber. Martin Thomas and I decided to consult an employment lawyer and a criminal attorney prior to interviewing Billy. We learned that we must obtain evidence that would be beyond reasonable doubt to prosecute him for stolen property.

Billy insisted that the overspending on his projects was the result of grading variances and waste from inexperienced framers. In his opinion, the overspending was reasonable, and he took no responsibility for it.

When he was confronted with the signed purchases from the remote hardware store, the marketing brochure of the townhomes project and the business registration of Tribrooke Homes, he admitted that he may have used the business account for the purchases but claimed that they were unintentional mistakes and agreed to repay $8,500. In the end, he was dismissed from Bonfield Homes, but no charges were filed.

Lessons Learned

This was a small conflict-of-interest case in terms of dollars. But even if it were large, the issues would be exactly the same. Regardless of amounts, the problems normally begin with the tone at the top. Paul Bonfield and Martin Thomas received monthly work-in-progress reports that reflected the costs of each project, but they were concerned only with profits and the verbal reports from construction managers. Fraud schemes can occur when a fraudster thinks that no one is paying attention to the details. Senior management at Bonfield Homes was sending a signal to the staff that the controls were loose and the chances of being caught when committing fraud were low.

Lack of Division of Duties

Billy was the same person making the purchase, signing for receipt the goods and releasing the material for production without restrictions, which created opportunities for skimming and using goods for personal use. It was almost impossible to track how the extra lumber was actually used in the construction. Without eyewitness or surveillance measures, we could not hold Billy accountable for the wasted lumber.

The Fraud Triangle

Donald Cressey describes three factors contributing to business fraud: motive, opportunity and rationalization. All three factors were presents in this case:

1. *Opportunity.* Opportunity to commit fraud and collude with vendors existed because Billy responsible for ordering and receiving materials. There was also no site supervision, and Billy knew no one was checking up on his purchases.
2. *Motive or pressure.* Billy was in a stressful financial situation because he was trying to keep his side business afloat while maintaining his excessive personal spending habits. Billy was relatively new in his position at Bonfield and might have thought his frauds would become unnecessary once the 40 luxury homes were completed. All of these factors could have contributed to Billy's motive.
3. *Rationalization.* Rationalization reduces the fraudster's inhibitions; Billy might have justified his misappropriations out of a sense of being underpaid and unappreciated, or he might have told himself the material he was taking was worth so little compared to the overall contracts that Bonfield would never know.

Recommendations to Prevent Future Occurrences

1. *Establish purchase order procedures.* Since this incident, Bonfield Homes developed policies for contract tendering, negotiating and signing prior to commencement of contract work. Occasionally, construction work completed by a contractor with a long working history may proceed without a signed contract, but the tendering and negotiation must already have been near completion. However, extra material requirements were often left to the sole discretion of the construction manager. This policy worked well to meet hectic construction schedules but was vulnerable to fraud if the construction manager was dishonest. I suggested Bonfield implement a system that required accounting department review and approval from the senior vice president. Also, the

(continued)

(continued)

monthly cost report should be reviewed by the internal audit department or the accounting department for early detection of suspicious activities.

2. *Anti-fraud policies.* Companies should have clear policies about the use of company credit cards and the handling of assets and inventory. The policies should be reviewed, understood and signed by each employee during the hiring process. Senior management should endorse the policies and remind staff of them regularly, along with setting the tone that these matters are taken seriously.

3. *Internal audit review procedure.* Purchasing and receiving should be reviewed by someone in accounting or internal audit to ensure that the proper procedures, including contracts and purchase orders, are followed thoroughly before payment is issued.

4. *Security and surveillance.* Another effective measure is simply to install a camera and surveillance system or hire a third-party security guard to patrol the site after hours. Deterrence and education are better fraud prevention tools than punishment after the fraud occurs. Surveillance and security system implementation will increase the expectation of being caught and will deter these activities.

About the Author

Lorna Leung is a controller at Kerbel Group Inc., a land developer and a home builder. In addition to her CFE, Lorna also obtained a diploma in investigative and forensic accounting from the University of Toronto. For the past 20 years, she has worked extensively in projects analysis, cash flow projections, financial reporting in home building, land development and e-commerce business.

CHAPTER 13

The Summer Bribe

MARK DRON

Summers in London had been progressively worsening over the past few years. Once the pubs and bars closed at 11:00 p.m., desperate drinkers sought solace in unlicensed drinking dens and seedy, overpriced nightclubs. Public transportation was poor and, on a Friday and Saturday, most people were trapped in town until the first train or bus of the next morning.

In this environment, grimy peep shows and all-night sex cinemas did a roaring trade. Avaricious café owners, seeing their chance at easy money, decided to stay open later and later, attracting drunks, junkies and prostitutes with all the problems associated with that lifestyle.

Local legislation required café owners to have a special "night-café" permit to stay open after 11:00 p.m., and the premises had to meet minimum standards of safety, hygiene and security while not exceeding a maximum number of patrons. License conditions were stringent, and the costs could be prohibitive for small businesses. As with any licensed trade, a small group of proprietors decided to chance their luck and operate as unlicensed night cafés.

One of these proprietors was Faisal Hussain. He was a naturalized UK citizen who had been born and raised in Lebanon. Hussain's family had moved to the United Kingdom in the 1960s, when he was a child, and had settled in London in 1973. The family opened a series of cafés and restaurants across the country, catering to the Lebanese expatriates as well as to the burgeoning late-night economy in a number of cities. By the late 1990s, Faisal had become the controller of a network of these cafés, with the crux of operations vested in a number of central London premises.

A Beleaguered City

Premises such as Faisal's — coupled with unlicensed sex shops, peep shows, drinking dens, street vendors and unlicensed cabs — marred the legitimate nighttime economy of the city, dragging certain areas down into vice, persistent violence and antisocial behavior.

It was against this background that the city council, besieged by mounting complaints and rising crime figures, decided to take action. For many years, licensing inspectors had been carrying out round-the-clock spot checks, but these were sporadic and uncoordinated. For the café owners, the threat of fines was minimal compared to the potential rewards of fleecing the city's drunks and party-goers in the early hours. There was only one workable answer: the establishment of a multidisciplinary team (MDT), drawn from all of the disparate enforcement arms of the council, who could work at night and who could provide evidence of persistent illegal conduct for prosecutions and closure orders.

Initial decisions as to the makeup of the team were made by May, and volunteers were in place by early June. These volunteers were drawn from the council's licensing, trading standards, environmental health, noise and nuisance, health and safety, street enforcement and commercial waste enforcement teams. By mid-June the MDT was ready to begin its first weekend of 12-hour night shifts. This was an entirely alien experience for many of the staff, and night work brought with it a completely different clientele than that during the day. By necessity we were working the three most crime-ridden zones in the city center and dealing with all manner of criminality that fell just outside the limit of the overstretched local police. Health and safety considerations called for body armor, mobile communication kits and any number of policies and procedures to keep the volunteers safe. For many of the problem premises, this new brand of enforcement was a shock; council officers clad in body armor and in contact by radio were something few had encountered before. Other enforcement agencies, such as customs and immigration, found our appearance and tactics a little unsettling at first.

Tackling the Problem Premises

We decided to give all our target premises a chance on the first weekend. We would visit all 30 and serve notices of all infringements. Our assignment also allowed for proactive identification of emerging problem premises for MDT action. On that first weekend we issued more than 90 notices for licensing, consumer protection, noise nuisances and health and safety infringements. The proprietors were left under no illusion that failure to rectify the problems within seven days would mean enforcement action.

Life on the MDT was tough; permanent nights and weekends ate into everyone's social lives and eroded our health. However, despite the drawbacks, the team quickly grew into a close-knit group; from a personal perspective, I was really pleased to be working with Mike Saunders again. I had first met Mike, a no-nonsense Scotsman, in the mid-1990s when we worked together on multiagency operations directed at product counterfeiting and social benefit fraud. Those early days of interagency liaison generated considerable success; we were hopeful that working together for the same employer, with a far wider spectrum of powers available, would be an even greater success. It had been starkly apparent, over the months preceding the inception of the MDT, that traditional enforcement methods were incapable of making an impact on the criminality in the problem areas. The occasional visit by a licensing official, followed a few weeks later by trading standards agents and possibly a once-a-year check by the environmental health inspector meant that there was no cohesion to the application of legislation. Nor was there, in general, any real measurable follow-up to notices or warnings. The arrival of multidisciplinary staff was a massive leap forward and it quickly yielded results.

Our evidence was building, as was our arsenal of powers; we were regularly joined by customs and immigration staff as well as officers from other agencies as we needed them. Raids and visits continued throughout late June and early July, and we were so successful that it became necessary to extend our hours to cover other nights of the week and also to recruit other volunteers to assist on an ad hoc basis.

The Bribe

It was against this backdrop of backbreaking work and mounting prosecution files that we first became aware of the Bilal Mansion, a late-night shisha tobacco den that served a wide variety of food. Smack in the center of Zone A, one of the main problem areas, the café was the first of our self-generated targets because it garnered a succession of local complaints. As we patrolled, it became clear that the café was opening later and later on Friday and Saturday nights. The offer of shisha pipes and heavy Arabic coffees was a natural draw to club denizens, who in turn proved a natural draw to local drug dealers and undesirables. Warnings had been issued on various occasions, but we had been unable to identify the owner. The night managers and wait staff proved adept at throwing out a smoke screen to protect their employer. Our usual routes of land-registry searches and checks with the business rates department had led to dead ends and suspected shell companies.

We finally got lucky when we discovered two successive waste contracts signed by the same person, Faisal Hussain. The contracts, combined with the signatory of various infringement notices and the signatory for a Highways Act License application to place obstructions on the highway, led us to the owner. Further checks showed that Hussain and his family were linked to a variety of licensed sites around the city center. It was clear, however, that it was the unlicensed Bilal Mansion that provided them with the greatest customer traffic after hours and, by extension, the largest income. Open-source research revealed that the family had built a chain of cafés and takeout restaurants across the country, with all fingers pointing to Faisal as the boss.

Archive information showed that various individuals had applied for night café licenses on the site of the Bilal Mansion in the previous five years, but based on its proximity to numerous other licensed sites, these applications had been turned down. This lucrative address was therefore a prime site for after-hours sales, and clearly the potential risk of council intervention was outweighed by the benefits of sales income.

Having identified Hussain as the owner, we hand-delivered a letter to the café requiring him to attend the council headquarters for an interview. He did not acknowledge the letter or attend the scheduled appointment. Fair process needed to be followed, so we scheduled a further four appointments; Hussain failed to attend every one. In the end, with the evidence of multiple enforcement visits, numerous notices and surveillance footage of the premises operating in the early hours of the morning, we had sufficient grounds to mount a prosecution.

This situation continued throughout the summer, and as July moved into August, the permanent night shifts and the punishing schedule started to take their toll on the members of the MDT. One night in late August, sickness reduced our team of seven to two members, leaving only Mike and me to cover all the problem premises. Health and safety guidelines frowned on patrolling alone; indeed, for many of the problem premises, the risk assessments prescribed at least three officers for inspection and enforcement purposes. Clearly that wasn't possible this night, so Mike and I agreed that our best course of action would be to split the premises list in two, effectively placing ourselves at opposite ends of the area. We were in touch by mobile phone and we were using the team's motorcycles, so theoretically we were only ever 10 to 20 minutes away if a situation arose.

By 11:00 that night the temperatures were still high, and everywhere I went I could see that the club goers and staff were under pressure. Several of my visits ended in the door staff calling for police assistance, as drunken revelers tried to cause mayhem. The soundtrack to my evening was shattering glass, sirens and the incoherent ramblings of the hopelessly drunk. Not for the first time that summer, I found myself questioning my career choices. By about 4:00 a.m. I had exhausted my supply of enforcement notices and decided to find a sympathetic coffee house to catch up with my paperwork and check in with Mike. Wearily I dialed the number, zoning out as the dial tone clicked monotonously in my ear.

"Hi, mate, how's it going?" I was momentarily startled; Mike actually sounded awake. "It's all been kicking off here. There're fights everywhere, must be the weather."

"Hmmph, you could be right," I grunted through a scalding mouthful of coffee. "It's been the same over my side. I've had the police out to every club on the list. Have you nearly finished for the night?"

"I've got a couple more stops to make, then I'm going to head to the Mansion to see if he's closed for the night." Mike was shouting, his voice almost drowned out by the incessant wail of sirens and the drone of traffic around him.

"Okay, I've nearly finished up; I just have to scope out one more site in the north. If you need any backup at Bilal's, let me know and I'll ride over; otherwise see you later today."

The rest of my night was quiet and uneventful. I dropped off the bike at our headquarters, dumped my paperwork at the office and trudged to the underground station for the first train home. It was about 8:30 in the morning and the sun was already bleaching the grass outside my window when I fell into bed exhausted. Just as my eyes were closing, I was rudely awakened by the insistent tones of my work phone. I fumbled with the phone and croaked, "This better be good."

"It's Mike, hope you're awake. I have a problem!" His voice was steady, but I could tell he was struggling to stop himself from running away with the story.

"Okay, you've got my attention. Is everything okay?"

"I went by Bilal Mansion last night, just after we spoke; he was open and trading as bold as brass. He even had some of the local refuse collectors in there. It was a joke. Anyway I went through the usual crap with the waiters and eventually found Faisal hiding out back. I was cautioning him, when he started begging me to let it slide. Then out of the blue he produces a wad of cash and offers me a thousand to forget this had happened. He wants me to drop the case. He offered me a bribe!" Mike's voice was starting to crack, and I could tell he was seriously stressed.

"Okay, mate, this is serious. We'll need to report this as soon as we can; we won't get any of the bosses on a Sunday morning at this time. Write it all down, everything you can remember, exactly what he said and when. We'll meet back at the office at 3:00 today to try and sort this out. In the meantime, if anyone phones you and you don't recognize the number, ignore the call. Get some sleep if you can and I'll see you at three."

The office was deathly quiet at 3:00 p.m. The only sound was the hissing of the kettle as Mike brewed up one of his industrial-strength coffees. I could smell the heavy reek of tobacco and guessed he had probably been chain-smoking at the back door for at least an hour. So I wasn't the only one who had had no sleep. I keyed in the combination to our secure office and saw Mike watching the street below from the window.

"Afternoon, mate. Any coffee left?"

He gestured to a steaming mug on my desk. "My statement's there too. I suggest you get yours written before you read it."

"Already done. I couldn't sleep so it seemed like a good way to while away the time." I tried not to lisp as the steaming coffee seared my tongue. "Any contact today?"

Mike nodded, sitting down heavily. "Three or four calls, one message from a bloke saying my money was ready when I wanted it; any ideas on our next move?"

I shrugged and dropped his statement on the desk. "We need to get the records of any calls to or from your work phone for the last 24 hours; that shouldn't be an issue. How do they have your number?" I asked this even as I guessed the answer.

"Our bloody numbers are on all our letters and business cards. Anyone and everyone can contact us."

"Okay, we need to call out the duty officer and let him know what's happened and what we have done. I'll get you a new phone. Keep the number to yourself for now. Also, we should let the cops know so that they can start an inquiry." I drained the awful coffee and grabbed the statements.

One complaint and statement to the police later, we decided that it was best to go home and try to get some sleep. Frankly, I was deflated. We knew it was Mike's word against Hussain's, and we had been warned that it was highly unlikely that our complaint would go anywhere.

The Allegation

Monday morning came far too quickly. I met Mike as he was entering headquarters, and his face was like thunder.

"That old phone's been ringing off the hook all night, mostly from unidentified numbers, but two were the same message about my money, and one was from the duty officer calling me in this morning about an allegation."

It was daylight, and a Monday morning; even if our team hadn't been hammered by sickness, the office would have been deserted. I started to brew the coffee when Mike swore and pointed out of the window at the street below. Leaving from the back doors, we saw Hussain with an unknown male in an astonishingly sharp suit. I think we both guessed what he had been up to at once, even as the office phone started to ring.

"MDT office," I answered. There was a brief silence on the line, almost long enough for me to throw the receiver back down.

"This is the duty officer. If Saunders is in, send him to my office immediately," No chance for a response, the connection was cut as the last word was still resounding in my ears. Mike looked at me expectantly.

"They want you upstairs. Do you want me to contact the union?" Mike shook his head and gave a wave as he left the office.

I tried to concentrate on office duties, watching the time crawl slowly onward; finally at 10:00 a.m. the phone rang. No introduction necessary, Mike's Glaswegian brogue was immediately discernible.

"Sol's Café, ten minutes, bring your wallet."

It had been a few months since I had been to Sol's, and I'd forgotten what a struggle it could be to find a seat on a Monday morning. Mike had been lucky; he was tucked into a dingy corner, cradling a massive mug of steaming coffee. I ordered a tea and sat down in the semidarkness. There were several cigarettes stubbed out in the table's ashtray, another was on its way to oblivion, already smoked down to the filter. I waited for Mike to speak; it seemed to take an age. Finally the cigarette crashed into the ashtray and he looked up.

"Hussain has made an allegation that I tried to solicit money from him to drop the case. I explained our side and showed them our statements, but they weren't interested. I've been warned away from Bilal — no more contact, no more inspections. It looks like the case is going to be dropped as well. I've also talked to the police, and they are unlikely to take my complaint if there are cross allegations. We're screwed."

The Investigation

One of the best results to come out of the MDT project was the close-knit team of officers prepared to do what was necessary to ensure we all stayed safe and could yield results. An allegation against one of us might as well have been an allegation against all of us. I called our colleagues and, despite illness, they were prepared to help in any way possible to disprove the allegations. We started with a sympathetic local business owner who had complained on many occasions about the criminality and antisocial behavior at the Bilal Mansion. The empty flat above his business gave us a perfect surveillance point. We had access to a number of cameras and recording devices as well as a competent covert surveillance technical officer, who seemingly could build cameras into just about anything.

We recruited new officers with faces unknown to Hussain and his associates. Their job was to sit for hours inside the Bilal Mansion, drinking coffee and recording the activities on concealed backpack cameras. The footage they obtained was incredibly clear and explosive in content. Temporary enforcement staff, employed to ensure that commercial waste was disposed of properly, were caught using the premises and receiving quantities of cash to ensure that rubbish was disposed of without any legal fuss. This was equally astonishing since the majority of these staff members knew Bilal was on our target list. We even identified senior planning officials from other areas of London frequenting the establishment and engaging in in-depth discussions with Hussain and his managers.

Finally we had a recording device installed on Mike's office landline in a last-ditch effort that we did not believe would yield success. We were proven very wrong. The device captured Hussain calling Mike and offering to withdraw all his allegations in return for all enforcement action against him being dropped, with the icing on the cake being Hussain's comment that he bet that Mike wished he had taken the money in the first place.

The Solution

By the second week of September we had a wealth of surveillance logs, electronic and audio evidence, and witness statements that placed Hussain in a very uncomfortable place. We called a meeting with the internal audit department and detectives from the local police station. We presented our evidence to them and were told to wait for a decision and halt any further enforcement activity. We were given a long-overdue leave of absence.

In our week off, the internal investigation rumbled on, while the police effected the arrest of Hussain and various managers from his café network. In ledgers seized from Hussain's office, he had meticulously recorded payments to refuse staff to overlook breaches of environmental legislation. Police also found evidence that he had retained staff from other government agencies to advise him on handling enforcement activity and how best to approach the legislation he believed did not apply to his business.

While not strictly illegal, these activities did pose serious ethical questions particularly regarding conflicts of interest in enforcement. Perhaps the most damning and worrying were notes seized from his office with detailed personal information about MDT officers. This included home phone numbers, addresses, vehicle details and even certain salary information. The origin of this information is still unknown.

The aftermath of this investigation led to more arrests and the transfer of Hussain's business empire to other more law-abiding family members. The team, with our names cleared and a clear victory, continued to operate for many months; indeed, having evolved through a wide array of guises and operating procedures, the original model survives to this day, albeit under a different name and with a largely fresh crew of officers.

Lessons Learned

This incident, while occurring in one particular authority, in one particular city, was by no means isolated. Indeed, we were aware of myriad similar allegations affecting any number of public authorities. Due to the nature of licensing work, however, and the frequency with which its inspectors put themselves in harm's way, it was obvious that they were vulnerable to such offers and allegations. Within our own authority, a number of steps were introduced to mitigate such risks.

The first step was to ensure that no staff members were ever placed in a situation in which they would have to undertake enforcement action alone. Corroboration evidence was felt to be a primary defense against allegations of corruption. Subsequent to this incident, managers were quick to authorize both covert and overt filming of inspections and enforcement actions. An additional new policy was enacted that removed direct phone numbers from business cards; all future calls had to go through a central switchboard, and were subject to random or automatic recording. Finally, a whistleblowing policy was implemented so staff members who suspected colleagues of corruption or illegality could report them safely and without fear of reprisals.

Since this incident, it should also be noted that there has been a fundamental swing in the United Kingdom in the attitude of the government and governmental subsidiaries toward corruption. New legislation has been implemented to handle official bribery and corruption, as has legislation to tackle similar offenses in the private and financial sectors. These efforts have been boosted by the creation of anti-corruption investigators in audit departments along with anti-corruption police teams charged with investigating both public sector corruption and minimizing its damaging effects upon both public services and society as a whole.

What has been described here was only one of a series of reported cases of bribery and attempted corruption. Although small in and of itself, when viewed with the other cases, it led to a change in the way corruption and those who seek to corrupt are dealt with in the United Kingdom.

About the Author

Mark Dron has served with the UK customs and excise offices, the police and a variety of consumer protection bodies. He has investigated an array of criminality ranging from competition distortion to money laundering and mortgage fraud and has also led a team targeting DVD counterfeiting in the Southeast Asian community. He is currently a police officer involved in the provision of criminal intelligence products within London and across the United Kingdom.

CHAPTER 14

Brazen Bank Manager

ANTONIO IVAN S. AGUIRRE

Helen Van Wyke was assistant vice president and branch manager of Nasdall Bank's East Coast Center Branch. She was an M.B.A. graduate from a top university in her home state and an excellent student during her university days. She prided herself on being a respected community figure, which earned her many customers at Nasdall and the reputation of being a "banker's banker." She was married to Troy Van Wyke, a well-known local businessman engaged in the distribution of consumer goods. Her three daughters were excellent students, all attending Helen's alma mater and set to follow in their mom's high-profile footsteps. Her work ethic was incomparable. Gaining approving nods from her boss at company headquarters, she became the model for what a Nasdall Bank manager should be. She was extremely competitive among the rival local banks and earned the title of "Bank Manager of the Year" for five consecutive years. However, she had a darker side and was manipulative of her peers, subordinates and clients. She also loved the high-finance lifestyle, and it was this love that led her down the road of perdition and corruption.

Helen committed the corrupt practice of abstracting cash from depositors' accounts and bribing other branch employees to remain quiet about it by giving them a percentage of the looted funds. Furthermore, she falsified documents for a friend who could not qualify for loan accommodations otherwise, and he paid her kickbacks to do so. She received a portion of each approved loan — anywhere from 5 to 7 percent. She was able to amass kickbacks worth $1.37 million in five years. They went undetected due to the cover-up and conspiracy she arranged with the other bank employees. It was a classic example of a total breakdown of internal controls due to corruption.

Nasdall Bank

Nasdall Bank had been engaged in commercial banking for more than 50 years and was highly reputed for its efficient service and trustworthy employees. Furthermore, Nasdall emphasized a hands-on style of management and invested sizable sums of money in technological development. The bank had 900 branches and employed 12,000 staff members. Nasdall never expected that one of their highly respected bank managers would turn out to be a criminal.

Helen Van Wyke was a standout at the company, a top performer with no record of wrongdoing. Her region was considered the most profitable and fastest rising. Her branch received top performance awards during her reign, including top deposits and income in the last five years of her tenure.

Suspicious Lifestyle

As the head of special audit at Nasdall Bank, I conducted regular investigations of the bank's fraud cases and red flag issues. In my more-than-a-decade tenure with Nasdall, most of the cases involved petty and white-collar crimes with fairly small losses. However, the nature of this case went well beyond what I was used to, and it adversely affected the bank's standing in the industry.

The case was brought to my attention by a member of my audit team. He received an anonymous tip that somewhere on the East Coast a bank manager was engaged in corrupt practices and might expose the bank to severe financial and reputational damage. No other information was provided. We immediately initiated a lifestyle and reference check on the branch managers in the area. We quickly zeroed in on Helen Van Wyke; various red flags popped up in her lifestyle check, such as large cash deposits maintained at a nearby bank (it was unusual for someone of her stature to maintain cash). However, we knew we were going to have to tread lightly with our audit to avoid raising suspicions in the community. We could not openly speak to bank customers to confirm transactions because we did not want them to become concerned and move their accounts elsewhere.

After a painful review of documentation for the branch's loan and savings accounts, we were able to discreetly contact two bank depositors who cooperated and provided us with information about their dealings with Van Wyke. From the dripping faucet of our anonymous tip we were now facing a massive flow of information about her misdeeds. We began to create a picture of her scheme, which we later used to pin down other bank employees during interviews.

I gathered a team from my special audit staff and we began reviewing the loans and cash position of the East Coast branch. It turned out that there was indeed a group of recently granted loans that became past due almost immediately. This prompted me to send an investigation team to the branch.

The scope of the audit team's work covered all loans granted in the past two years and directly confirming them with clients.

It turned out that 75 percent of the loans were granted without due diligence or appropriate approval and were actually fictitious loans. Helen had corrupted the assistant branch manager and the tellers through bribes and kickbacks, and they turned a blind eye to the fictitious loans. The bank suffered a severe financial loss as a result of the collusion and the failure of its employees to act ethically in response to it.

Documentation Review and Interviews

After gathering the loan documents, we performed a detailed review of them and conducted interviews with clients and third parties. We were able to question some savings account holders who provided us with the fraudulent documents that Helen had convinced them to sign; these documents allowed her to siphon funds from the clients' accounts. They also gave us authentic bank documents, such as promissory notes, deposit certificates, bank passbooks, deposit application forms and specimen signatures, on which the bank officers names had been forged. When we interviewed the branch employees, they all initially claimed to have no idea that Helen was engaged in nefarious activity, but some eventually admitted to manipulating the accounts of various customers in exchange for 6 to 8 percent of the loan proceeds that Helen collected.

Considering the long span of time that Helen's fraud covered, my team and I had difficulties finding source documents. It required a painstaking effort on our part to reconstruct all the evidence due to forgery and fictitious people. We had to dig up deposit and loan records from five years ago and review them one by one. Most of these were already archived, and we had to patiently look at various microfilm and microfiche records to trace the transactions. We spent about six weeks going over the records and establishing the audit trail. At the same time, we were discreet because we did not want to alert the local community that there was an investigation occurring. We also had to maintain a low profile because most large depositors were sensitive to the reputations of their local banks. Furthermore, most of the large customers had relatives who maintained substantial monies at other Nasdall branches and who might threaten to pull out their funds if they heard about the alleged fraud. We coordinated with our public relations officer to ensure damage control.

Identifying Helen's Methods

One of Helen's preferred methods of fraud was to abstract cash by making fictitious loans and depositing the money to accounts that she opened for her personal benefit. The processing tellers allowed Helen to receive the proceeds of the loans rather than issuing the funds to the named borrower.

She forged and misrepresented various bank and commercial documents to secure the loans, and other branch personnel violated bank policies and committed procedural lapses, such as failing to witness the borrower signing the loan documents. In a separate incident, Helen stole money from a trust fund at Nasdall through falsification of documents, misrepresentation and conspiracy with other branch personnel. We also discovered falsified promissory notes and the unauthorized issuance of stolen certificates of deposit. The following are specific activities we discovered:

- Helen prepared a promissory note for a loan worth $120,000 and signed it herself, purportedly for a client named Geraldine Scheer. Then Van Wyke opened a dummy savings account where the loan proceeds were deposited, and withdrew funds whenever she wanted.
- She also stole $150,000 from the savings account of Andrea Carrol and "replaced" the funds with a stolen certificate of deposit supposedly worth the same amount. She used the same modus operandi with other Nasdall customers for a total of $350,000. Eventually when clients tried to convert their CDs to cash, they would learn that they were worthless.
- She misappropriated cash from the trust funds of four Nasdall customers, again by "replacing" the money with invalid CDs, for a total of $250,000. We realized she was able to generate false CDs by stealing and forging the paperwork needed to issue the CDs. She also used her position in the branch to bully unwitting customer service representatives and bank tellers into acting as she instructed, in violation of company policies and regulations.

Staff Kickbacks

Van Wyke was able to manipulate customer accounts because she had recruited a few select staff members to help her — in return for kickbacks. Michael Ball, the assistant branch manager, was paid in return for failing to detect irregularities (such as forgeries) in the transaction documentation that Helen provided for her loans. Tellers Marilyn Taylor, Mary Jane Baker and Lillian Andersen processed transactions that turned out to be fraudulent. They allowed Van Wyke to receive cash withdrawn from customers' accounts and did not verify signatures on the deposit slips. They also processed cash-advance transactions on customer credit cards for Helen without checking the signatures.

Regarding fictitious loans, Michael Ball completed the "Signature Authenticated By" portion of the paperwork for Helen, even without witnessing the client sign the document. The other tellers affixed their signatures in the "Signed in the Presence of" portion of the papers without seeing the client sign.

We interviewed bank tellers to find out how Helen secured their collaboration and found out she paid them kickbacks. Michael Ball, the assistant manager, said, "For the past three years, I got $5,000 from Ms. Scheer's account. I did not touch the money and I will return it." Marilyn Taylor, a teller, confirmed that she too "received money from Ms. Van Wyke, a total of about $2,800." Marilyn did not report Helen because she was afraid of what might happen. Mary Jane Baker confirmed that she received $3,700 from Van Wyke over about 14 months. She stated she was also afraid to come forward; she was worried about getting fired because she was involved. Lillian Andersen, the last teller, received kickbacks worth $3,000. Some of the tellers still had their proceeds, and we were able to collect a combined $10,500 from them.

The Arthur Williams Connection

Next we discovered that Helen forged Geraldine Scheer's signature and those of three other Nasdall depositors on bank forms that granted consent to use their savings accounts as collateral for the loan of Arthur Williams, supposedly just a normal Nasdall customer. Arthur Williams then signed the same forms, making it appear as if he was borrowing money from the bank and had secured collateral from the four customers.

Arthur seemed creditworthy on his loan application, but in reality he was a cash-strapped, unemployed friend of Helen's whom she had intentionally recruited to help her with the loan fraud. Nearly everything on his application had been forged or misrepresented, but Helen knew what she was doing. The loan was approved, the funds were dispersed to Arthur (who gave a substantial kickback to Helen) and the loan immediately went into default.

Helen's collusion with Arthur went even deeper, and existing loan customers at Nasdall soon discovered they weren't safe from Helen's schemes. She convinced eight existing clients with loans to sign incomplete bank documents. She assured them that the papers were required to renew their current loans. However, she actually used their signatures to apply for increased borrowing on their loans and then directed the additional funds to Arthur's account. As a result, these new loans remained unpaid and became past due.

She seemed to gain confidence from her successes and became bolder. She enticed some clients to take out short-term loans against their deposits — for her own use! Helen told the customers various sob stories about a sick nephew or unexpected damage to her home that was not covered by insurance — anything to play on their emotions. She promised that it would be for a short-term loan or for just a 30-day period and that she would pay them back. For such accommodation, she offered them a commission. And she was true to her word and paid them all back in a timely manner. In the process, however, she had them unwittingly sign extra sets of loan documents; when she paid them back for the loans they agreed to, she did the same thing again, but this time without their authorization. As always, the proceeds of the genuine short-term loans or the fraudulent renewals thereof went to her cohort, Arthur Williams.

Admissions

After my team and I had gathered documentary evidence and interviewed staff, I decided we had enough to approach Helen Van Wyke. I wanted to get her to admit to committing serious and well-planned kickback schemes. When she sat down with me in a small conference room, I think she knew what was coming. As I started pulling out the forged documents we had gathered and passed her statements from Arthur Williams' account, she seemed to become angry. After only about 15 minutes of questioning, she threw her hands up in exasperation and said, "Well, obviously I did it! What's the point of this interview? You know everything already; just leave me alone and do what you're going to do." I told her that I needed a signed statement and that if she gave me information about anyone else who helped her with scheme, I would make sure the judge knew she had cooperated with me. She acknowledged in writing that she committed fraud against Nasdall Bank freely and voluntarily and confirmed what I already knew about Arthur Williams, Michael Ball, Marilyn Taylor, Mary Jane Baker and Lillian Andersen. Nasdall Bank terminated Helen Van Wyke immediately.

I prepared a final case report, which included Van Wyke's confession, and submitted it to our chief legal counsel. We then began coordinating with the police and legal authorities. In total, we discovered manipulations of more than a dozen fictitious accounts. Van Wyke amassed a total of $1.37 million in five years, which we were unable to locate. She was arrested and sentenced to five years in jail. Her cohort, Arthur Williams, remains at large at the time of this writing. The other bank employees who helped Van Wyke were also terminated from Nasdall but were not criminally charged. The bank was able to recover around 30 percent of the funds by seizing various assets owned by those involved.

Lessons Learned

My team and I learned the importance of ensuring that internal controls are not only sound but actually being followed at our different branches. Bank employees conduct a huge range of transactions, and each one has a different protocol that needs to be followed. Even slight deviations from accepted practices can leave the door to fraud wide open.

Corruption can be difficult to prove due to a lack of direct evidence. So in this case my team used a method of following the audit trail for loan, trust fund, credit card and deposit transactions, all of which can be used as prima facie evidence in a case of corruption. The judiciary system prefers direct evidence — such as admissions from the person receiving a bribe or kickback from the person who committing bribery — which can be very challenging. We were largely successful in this case because we were able to secure the cooperation and testimony of the bank employees, victims and other friends of Helen Van Wyke to use as evidence.

Recommendations to Prevent Future Occurrences

In general, I recommend strengthening internal controls as the best means to avoid a similar bribery and kickback scheme in the future. Specifically, I recommended that Nasdall institute mandatory reference and lifestyle checks on bank officials, ensure that review procedures are performed for all transactions, strictly enforce the company code of conduct and rotate jobs regularly.

About the Author

Antonio Ivan S. Aguirre, M.B.A., CFE, LPA, CSI, is a chief resident auditor under the Office of Internal Oversight Services, United Nations. He previously worked with the largest bank in the Philippines as the head of special audit and acted on several occasions as an expert witness against numerous white-collar and organized crimes. Fondly known as Tony, he is also a strong chess player and a martial arts instructor.

In Bed with the Tax Man

HANIF HABIB

V an Hoover earned a bachelor of commerce degree in India, majoring in accounting and finance. He worked for a number of private companies in his home country before moving to Tanzania. The high cost of living and unemployment in India prompted a number of human resource agencies to seek recruits among educated Indian workers for overseas clients, and Tanzanian companies were common recruiters. Hoover was married and had a three-year-old son when he moved to Tanzania at the age of 35 to accept the position of financial controller for Amuse Business Machines Limited.

Sam, Deen and Sophia Najuma were the directors and primary shareholders of Amuse Business Machines Limited. They were also siblings who came from one of the most affluent families in Tanzania. The Najumas were known for their wealth — and for not having to work very hard to earn it. They were also known for their "crooked minds" and ability to use their money to get out of various scrapes. The family enjoyed a high-profile social life and squandered money in nearly every possible way.

Amuse Business Machines Limited (Amuse) was a private legal entity based in Dar es Salaam, Tanzania. The company's primary activities were importing office equipment (computers, photocopiers, fax machines, specialized office machinery, etc.) from the United Kingdom, Japan, the United States, Norway and Germany and selling it in Tanzania to large organizations. The Najumas had incorporated similar businesses in Kenya, Uganda, Rwanda and Burundi.

Amuse had elite clientele, including all 26 commercial banks in Tanzania, as well as large hospitals and public companies. A significant part of its business also comprised government agencies. The company was highly leveraged, with much of its capital financed by debt. The company's year-end was December 31, and, according to the Tanzanian tax laws, it was required to have its financial statements audited by a statutory auditor by June 30 following the year-end.

I was employed at an audit firm that had been servicing Amuse for the past three years. We had a policy of rotating clients that often to avoid building inappropriate working relationships, and when I was rotated in as Amuse's audit manager, I had little knowledge of the company or its operations. But the past audit opinions were clean and unqualified, so I wasn't expecting much. Little did I know then that I would be writing an international case study about it.

Early Warning Signs

I began my assignment by contacting Van Hoover, the controller at Amuse, and he sent me the draft financial statements and trial balance — exactly five months after the year-end. We were not off to a good start, and I was concerned about the slow turnaround. A large company with a computerized accounting system and qualified accountants should be able to prepare auditing documents much faster than that. My professional skepticism kicked in, and I began the fieldwork.

Hoover was eager to complete the audit as soon as possible, even suggesting I wrap it up in a matter of weeks. That, however, would be impossible. During the planning meeting he promised to give my firm an exorbitant audit fee if I completed the audit as soon as possible. I was troubled by this offer.

A total of five team members were assigned to the audit with me, and they were all to e-mail planning documents for my approval. After two weeks of fieldwork, I began reviewing the files my team gathered.

Fieldwork

Amuse had ten bank accounts, but Hoover did not provide a single bank reconciliation statement. After I pressured him, he provided the statements for December, but I quickly realized they had been prepared immediately prior to me getting them; the ink used to sign the documents was still wet. The ability to read beyond the characters printed on paper is a very important skill for fraud examiners and is learned over time through practice, concentration and experience.

When I asked for reconciliation statements for other months, Hoover claimed they were not being prepared on a monthly basis to avoid problems with the tax authorities. I wondered what a bank reconciliation statement had to do with tax authorities, but I did not share my thoughts with Hoover or the Najuma siblings.

I asked for access to Amuse's accounting system, but again Hoover denied me; he claimed the server was down. In the meantime, I continued documenting key facts using a mind-map template — a useful tool for illustrating a series of events. It helps identify trends and key connections among separate case facts. It can also help uncover an unknown event or trail.

After my review of other audit areas, I noted that the monthly employment and sales tax returns had all been filed late with the tax authorities throughout the year. (In Tanzania, companies are required to file employment, income and sales tax returns every month with the Tanzania Revenue Authority.) The accounting reports that were supposedly printed from the automated system did not appear to be so. There was no date and time of printing, user name or other identifying information that would normally be included on automated reports. In fact, they looked like printed spreadsheets. I also found that the majority of expenses were not supported by receipts or tax invoices. Some of them were vague in nature — entertainment, sales promotions and miscellaneous expenses.

Hoover wouldn't let other staff members speak with me. When I approached them, they would say, "Kindly let me speak to Hoover and get back to you." Others would simply say, "Please ask Van about that."

Effective investigations and audits cannot be done in a test tube. They require interaction and involvement of people from different departments and units. This exercise often brings to our attention important facts and information that we may otherwise not have obtained. Considering my limited ability to interact with Amuse staff members, I had to take another approach. I spent the night mentally sifting through all the findings so far and made a list of the most suspicious facts:

- Delays in producing financial reports
- Lack of supporting information and documentation
- Missing bank reconciliation statements
- Denied access to the accounting system
- Steered away from key people in the organization
- No date and time on reports produced from the system
- Doubtful integrity and reliability of the financial reports

Based on these observations, I concluded that the financial statements were likely falsified and did not reflect the true and correct state of affairs of Amuse Business Machines Limited. I then asked myself what motivation Hoover had to falsify the documents, and the answer that kept popping in my head was tax evasion.

Amuse was registered as a Large Tax Payer, which meant that the tax authorities would have conducted an annual tax assessment of Amuse in the beginning of the year. In my view, it would have been impossible for the tax assessor to miss the fraudulent financials. Now I started to think there might be collusion as well.

The Audit Becomes an Investigation

At that moment, I made up my mind to confirm my suspicions. As professionals in this field, we sometimes come across an assignment that does not start as a formal fraud examination but turns into one. I think it's important that when we find ourselves in such a position, we pursue the case to its fullest. I had not given any indication of my suspicions to Hoover or the Najumas despite their regular inquiries and e-mails intended to pressure me along to the conclusion of the case.

While I was reviewing copies of the checks used to make all payments from the company accounts, I discovered that the check stubs were blank. I asked Hoover about it, and he said it was not their practice to update the record maintained by Amuse when a check was used. However, he promised to give me all the bank reconciliation statements for verification.

I analyzed the monthly value added tax returns and discovered that they did not tally with the accounting records. The difference was significant—more than $500,000 in one year. I found multiple stamped returns for three separate months, which was unusual because they contained different figures but were nevertheless stamped by the tax authorities. I asked for the documents from the most recent annual tax assessment performed by the authorities, but Hoover claimed they had been misplaced.

Suspicious Behavior

I decided it was time for a meeting with Christopher Sibale, the audit partner, and I was pleased that he shared my concerns after I explained my findings. We forwarded a report to the quality review partner at the firm to get another opinion.

Two days later, Van Hoover visited me in my office. He offered to organize a conference call with the tax officer who was responsible for Amuse's assessments to clear my doubts. This seemed very unusual to me, and I wondered in what capacity the tax officer would speak to me — as a personal advocate for Hoover or Amuse Business Machines Limited or as a representative of the tax authority? I was reluctant so I told Hoover that I had to get permission from Christopher first.

Hoover continued to visit me almost every day to ask about the status of the audit. He could have called me for updates, so his persistent presence in my office told me that something serious was happening.

I moved on to review the prior years' audit files and concluded that they were not done competently. Significant issues were noted in the reports to Amuse's management but were not factored into the audit opinions. I noticed that for the past three years, Amuse's taxable profits decreased — reducing the corporate tax liability. That's when I realized what was going on. Amuse's management team was evading taxes by manipulating the financial statements and, moreover, misappropriating the sales tax they collected.

Essential to the case was Hoover's partner in crime; I suspected he was bribing a senior tax officer.

I called Christopher and explained my recent discoveries. We agreed that we had a professional duty to report the findings to the Tanzanian tax authorities, but I wanted to gather some solid evidence first, in particular to support our suspicions that there might be bribery involved. So far I only had a few unsupported payment vouchers that indicated possible problems. I told Van Hoover to arrange that meeting with the tax officer. He seemed surprised at first but quickly recovered and said he would send me a meeting request.

The Flamboyant Tax Assessor

Samuel Hopkins, Amuse's tax officer, walked in the conference room and introduced himself but did not offer me a business card. His appearance was extravagant, and he had the air of a bossy man. I briefly discussed my findings with him but left out my suspicious of collusion and bribery. His response was to the point, if nothing else: "your observations are baseless. You are wasting your time. Just finish the audit and submit your report to management and we will take care of the rest. You will regret it if you waste time pursuing the matter further. You don't know who I am and what I can do." It was a pretty clear threat, but unfortunately I did not have a witness present.

I responded, "I am not threatened by your words. I can cause much more damage than you can imagine in my current capacity. It would be in your best interests to be honest and confess if you have committed any offense. Better late than never."

Realizing they weren't going to be able to bully me, Hopkins and Hoover took a different approach. They offered me a handsome amount of money to keep quiet and complete the audit with a clean opinion. This indirectly proved my point — we were dealing with bribery and corruption. I told them it was too late and that I had already shared my findings with the audit partner. They stormed out of the office together, pausing just long enough to threaten my life.

I called the audit partner to let him know how the interview went, and he called an urgent meeting with the previous audit team. We asked them why they did not observe similar issues, but they had no answer. Christopher informed the past audit team that he would take stringent disciplinary actions against them. The firm was exposed to high risk based on the clean audit opinions they issued during the last three years. We were at risk of losing the firm's license to practice. I convinced Christopher that, despite the risks to the firm, it was our professional duty to report fraud when we detected it. We had a duty to exercise ethical behavior and responsible judgment in the best interest of our profession and society at large.

Shortly after this meeting, the Najuma siblings sent me a letter offering to double my audit fees if I could issue a clean report as soon as possible, prompting me, in turn, to write a letter to the professional accounting body (PAB) in Tanzania. I asked for advice on how to best handle the Amuse case and received a very positive response. The PAB authorized my firm to refer the matter to the Tanzanian tax authorities. After a lengthy meeting to discuss the case, the board at my audit firm decided to pursue the matter with the tax authorities.

Client Anxiety

At this stage the Najumas, Hoover and Hopkins must have found out we were in contact with the tax authorities because I started receiving threatening calls at work and home. The tax auditors requested access to the files from the last four years (including the current year). After reviewing the case file, the government auditors agreed with my suspicions that the fraud had gone on for a long time and involved collusion with some of their officers. I shared the minutes from the meeting I had with Samuel Hopkins and Van Hoover. According to the commissioner for revenue, there was no employee in the tax department named Samuel Hopkins. This was a new twist in the case.

A few days later the commissioner asked me to go to his office to review the personnel records in hopes of identifying the corrupt tax officer. After hours of continuous review, I finally found him. His photo in the system matched his appearance during our meeting. He was Marlin Junior, Senior Tax Assessor in the Large Tax Payers Department — no wonder he was able to conceal the fraud for so long.

Marlin was called for an interview, and it didn't take long for him to confess. He admitted that he had colluded with Hoover and the Najuma siblings to defraud the tax authorities. They were intentionally minimizing Amuse's tax liability and splitting the unpaid tax revenue. Marlin also said other tax auditors at the government agency had become suspicious in the past, but he always stepped in to offer them a bribe to keep it quiet. After the interview, Marlin was placed on unpaid suspension.

I received a letter from the Najumas asking me to resign as the statutory auditor, which I disregarded. After the letter, I received another series of threatening phone calls, which I also ignored.

The tax agency filed criminal cases against the Najumas, Van Hoover and Marlin Junior. After a month of legal proceedings and court hearings, all the defendants were found guilty, ordered to pay $1,000,000 in damages to the state and sentenced to 20 years of imprisonment each. Amuse was liquidated to pay the damages, and the surplus from the liquidation was remitted to the state.

My employer firm resigned as the statutory auditors of Amuse Business Machines Limited upon the appointment of a liquidator. I also resigned as the audit manager. I needed a break after months of harassment and threats.

Lessons Learned

Dealing with fraud exposes one to sensitive and critical issues that need to be handled with the utmost care. In a corruption allegation, various people are usually involved, and their behavior can be aggressive and unpredictable. These issues need to be clearly managed to ensure that the objective is achieved. This case equipped me with the ability to respond to reactions of different stakeholders.

I also learned how important it can be, when suspicions of fraud are involved, to review files in the field. Due to work pressures and other challenges, audit managers often do these reviews in the office after the fieldwork is complete. I found that constantly reviewing the files as we discovered them kept me up to speed on the case, and I was able to make better decisions under pressure.

I also learned that fraudsters try to be at least two steps ahead of the rest of us. To understand their thinking, fraud examiners need to pay attention to all the details. A seemingly insignificant point might lead to the discovery of fraud.

Professional skepticism is critically important. Fraud examiners should ensure that they are professionally skeptical at every stage of their assignment. Examiners should also observe the personality traits and behavior of the auditee because these can provide important insight.

Recommendations to Prevent Future Occurrences

Keep the lines of communication open and active. Three things are very important in all teamwork: communication, communication and communication. We must communicate upward (to our superiors in the firm), downward (to junior team members) and sideways (to clients and their staff). Communication will keep other team members informed and increase efficiency and effectiveness.

Fraud examiners should assess the following aspects of anomalies:

- Condition: how should things be, in the ideal situation?
- Criteria: what are the essential problems?
- Cause: what are the roots of the problems?
- Effect: what are the consequences of the problems?

(continued)

(continued)

Thinking about a situation from these perspectives will help the fraud examiner assess the case with a 360-degree view to avoid oversight of critical points. While auditing, we must ensure that we have access to the financial statements and their supporting documents.

As professionals in the anti-fraud field, we must read, understand and act on our duties, responsibilities and rights. This will ensure that we perform our work in the most professional manner. We must also communicate our professional expectations across the team to ensure that our associates follow the same standards.

About the Author

Hanif Habib is an audit manager at RSM Ashvir with more than four years of audit, consultancy and financial management experience. Hanif specializes in the delivery of assurance services to the private sector, public sector, civil society and not-for-profit organizations in areas such as internal audits, financial audits, performance audits, investigative audits, pre-disbursement assessments/capacity building, project financial monitoring, internal control reviews, value-for-money reviews, compliance reviews and financial management assistance to projects funded by international donors.

CHAPTER

High-Rise Rollers

RICHARD F. WOODFORD, JR.

Dan Abrams and Mark German were well-established, seasoned facilities management professionals. Working together as the number-one and two procurement officials in a high-profile federal financial regulatory agency, the Trust and Finances Department (TFD), the two were responsible for monitoring a major $400 million construction project for the new TFD headquarters being built within sight of the Capitol Building. The construction contracts had been dutifully put out for competitive bidding, and even though there were some unexpected security cost overruns, the massive building project was moving forward as planned. With three months to go until the grand opening, subcontractors were busy installing fittings and fixtures, and all appeared to be on track. Then an anonymous complaint arrived in the TFD inspector general's mailbox alleging that Abrams and German had steered another contract for an unrelated sole-source construction project for a backup power generator shed at an off-site TFD facility. The complaint alleged that the $350,000 shed contract was wasteful because it cost more than the generator it housed and was actually a disguised payback for various illegal gratuities enjoyed by Abrams and German.

To modify an old saying, where there's smoke, someone usually gets burned. In this case, the careers of these two federal procurement superstars were about to implode into supernovas after it was discovered that they had played fast and loose with the federal government's ethics rules. They accepted illegal gratuities and fostered a culture of "it's okay to accept meals, gifts and favors from contractors because that's how it's always done in the construction business."

At 59 years of age, Dan Abrams had a long and distinguished career in public service. He first served as a young Marine infantry officer in the last year of the Vietnam War and distinguished himself with a medal for valor in the face of enemy fire. After his military service, he became a civil servant and began working his way up as a facilities specialist for the TFD. During the boom years of the market in the mid- to late 1980s, the agency's staff doubled, and Dan gained contracting and procurement experience. He was instrumental in planning the effective use of office space, negotiating telecommunications and utilities contracts, procuring necessary furnishings and office equipment and leasing space to support a rapidly growing organization.

As good as he was at work, Dan was unlucky in love. After his first wife died in an aircraft crash, his second marriage lasted five tumultuous years and ended in a bitter divorce. Soon after the divorce was finalized, he met Ginger, a woman 20 years younger than he, and they quickly married at a Las Vegas casino chapel. Ginger had previously filed for personal bankruptcy due to high credit card debts and several bad investments. Unfortunately, her financial irresponsibility and lavish spending continued in her new life with Dan. Three years into their marriage, Dan and Ginger were heavily in debt, upside down in a mortgaged home, and bankrupt.

Dan didn't disclose to his superiors that he had filed for personal bankruptcy or that his home was in foreclosure. He felt that the government ethics policies were "aspirational" for TFD facilities support staff and that the rules applied only to accountants and attorneys. Dan was known for getting results, but filing disclosure forms and attending ethics training sessions were not priorities for him. Whenever the ethics officer sent over training reminders to Dan's office, they went unanswered.

Mark German, age 39, was a transplant to Washington, DC, from Mississippi. Mark arrived in TFD's headquarters in DC after working for 11 years as a facilities support specialist in one of the regional offices. Mark was a quick study, and, under Dan's mentorship, he thrived in the fast-paced environment.

Mark fared much better than Dan in his personal life: Mark's spouse, Marie, was a CPA partner in one of the larger accounting firms and making a seven-figure salary. Mark and Marie had been happily married for more than 18 years and had three teenage boys at home. They had recently moved into a custom-built, five-bedroom home on a horse farm to accommodate their sons' activities.

Once Mark had tasted the high life and perks that were offered by construction contractors and architectural design firms, he was immediately hooked. It was a floating buffet including expense-account lunches and dinners, golf and tennis outings at resorts, low- or no-fee "site survey" trips, expensive watches, imported cigars and bottles of vintage wine. Mark felt like he had become a member of an exclusive executive club and that there was nothing wrong with accepting favors from his new friends in the construction industry — such as improvements for his recently purchased $1.3 million home.

The Allegation

The TFD was an independent federal agency charged with overseeing the finances and trust accounts of publicly held corporations. It employed financial analysts, accountants and attorneys to monitor and oversee the financial system and ensure an even playing field for investors. TFD received funding by levying fees and fines against violators. The agency was supported by an administrative division consisting of personnel, information systems and contracting and procurement. Dan Abrams was the director of the latter and Mark German was his protégé, close friend and heir apparent.

Unlike most federal agencies, the TFD had been granted independent authority to build, lease and manage its own office facilities and real property. This authority meant that TFD could solicit construction bids and award contracting projects without having to go through the General Services Administration.

I was working as the lead investigator for the inspector general when the anonymous tip about Abrams and German came in. It outlined the following allegations:

1. Dan Abrams and Mark German had steered numerous TFD construction and leasing contracts to several local firms that were run by their buddies and benefactors. The latest award was a sole-source contract for construction of a backup generator shed for $350,000 — grossly more than the cost of the generator it was built to protect.
2. Abrams and German had been wined and dined on a least three separate evenings at expensive restaurants by the successful bidders prior to the awarding of major construction contracts.
3. Dan Abrams had recently purchased a BMW sedan at a deep discount from a local contractor who was one of his lunch buddies.
4. Mark German had gone on several tennis junkets with three construction firm owners.
5. Both men were sporting identical new Epsilon watches worth $5,000 apiece.
6. Mark German had accepted home improvements worth $150,000 from a construction contractor, including a custom-built basement with marble pillars, an entertainment system, a wet bar and a sauna.
7. German was steering contracts to improve his chances of being hired by one of the construction firms at a later time.
8. Dan Abrams was pocketing gifts and gratuities to augment his income because he had recently filed for personal bankruptcy.

The Plan

After my supervisor gave me the anonymous tip to investigate, I met with my colleague Kyle Anderson to develop a plan. Starting with basic steps, we broke down the allegations into the most common denominators and asked ourselves, "In the worst case, if all of these allegations are true, what laws might have been violated and what evidence might be present?" Kyle suggested making a list of each subject and the allegations against him, with some discrete, manageable tasks, such as performing a records review of financial disclosure forms for both employees, reviewing ethics training attendance records and an analysis of contract bids. I also performed a public records check for a bankruptcy or a foreclosure under Abrams' name. When that revealed that he had recently filed for bankruptcy and there were several liens on his property, I knew that at least part of the allegations were valid.

Interviews of TFD staff in the contracting and procurement division also revealed a pervasive, casual attitude toward accepting gifts, gratuities and "goodies" from prohibited sources. Several staff members openly admitted that they believed it was permissible to accept lunches and small gifts from contractors because they had watched both Abrams and German do so — even though most employees could cite the specific ethics rules that restricted or prohibited these activities.

The staff interviews revealed a strong culture of loyalty to Dan Abrams and his aggressive, take-no-prisoners attitude when it came to getting extra concessions and performance from contractors and vendors. Staff members often spoke in a tone of near reverence of "Mr. Abrams' abilities to get the best deal for the government" and how he often would be the first one in the office at 6:00 a.m. and the last one to leave at 6:00 p.m.

It did not take Kyle and me long to ascertain that all eight of the anonymous allegations included indications of possible corruption. For instance, in regard to the alleged "steering of contracts" and the backup generator, there was a full and open competitive bidding process, but what appeared to be the problem was that the three bidders had also won the last three construction bids from TRD. Although there was no obvious evidence of bid collusion or bid rigging, it was unlikely that only three local firms would be interested in a series of large federal construction projects. In one case, a bidder was rejected because he missed a filing deadline by one day. Although his bid was postmarked on time, it was delivered late due to a three-day holiday weekend, and Abrams rejected it. Another bid was rejected for not using a specific type font, even though all the necessary information was provided. We decided that in addition to Abrams, German and TRD staffers, we would interview the owners of the three winning contractors and the two known losers.

The Winners

Our interviews with the winners — Jenkins and Roe Construction, Origin Design Group and Fieldstone Contractors — produced some startling results. Josh Wilson, the president of Jenkins and Roe, freely described three separate social events that his company co-hosted with Fieldstone at upscale restaurants to celebrate major milestones completed during a TRD construction project. Both Abrams and German had been invited, as well as other high-ranking TRD officials. At first blush these events might have appeared to be "widely attended gatherings" or "almost public events," making them permissible by our ethical guidelines. However, as Wilson recalled, most of the TRD staff who attended did not stay long; it was only Abrams and German who spent three full evenings with the contractors while they moved from the reception to dinner, drinks, dessert and later a cigar bar uptown. Wilson plainly stated that he saw nothing untoward in either Abrams' or German's behavior during these social outings and even said he never felt pressured to provide these accommodations.

Jesse Cadena, the owner of Origin Design Group, confirmed that he had sold his 1979 BMW sedan to Dan Abrams for about $1,000. After several convoluted descriptions of the vehicle and the terms of the sale, it turned out that Cadena was secretly ashamed of unloading the car on Abrams because it had more than 300,000 miles and was in poor cosmetic and mechanical shape. Cadena tried to sell it as a collectible classic for $800 without success, so he jumped at the chance when Abrams told him he was looking for a weekend project car. If anything, it appeared that Abrams actually paid more than book value for the vehicle. Cadena also confirmed some of the social events and tennis junkets because he had also participated in them.

Finally, we talked to Chris Fieldstone at Fieldstone Contractors; he had been expecting our call. Fieldstone co-hosted the three extravagant social events with Josh Wilson. Unlike with Wilson and Cadena, Kyle and I immediately realized that Fieldstone was aware of the real and perceived ethical violations in his associations with Abrams and German. In a very open and frank discussion, he told us that he had often warned Abrams that federal employees were prohibited from accepting gratuities and gifts. Fieldstone kept records of the social events for tax purposes, including names of attendees, specific menu items and receipts for accounting. While he confirmed that Abrams and German had both attended three post-project celebration dinners, he was reluctant to provide information that would outright indict either man. He did tell us that at one event, all the attendees came away with a commemorative wristwatch, but he refused to speculate about its value.

When we asked him to confirm our estimates for the dinners and entertainment, Fieldstone hedged. He said he could not remember, but he thought that German or Abrams had offered to reimburse or actually did partially reimburse his firm for their share of the meals and cigars. In either case, the appearance of impropriety was more and more damaging to the credibility and integrity of the TRD procurement process.

Fieldstone then casually said, "In the construction business, it's not uncommon for winning bidders to show some appreciation to their clients by performing personal services like home repairs, remodeling and renovation services at cost." When we brought up the allegation that Mark German had improperly accepted $150,000 of home improvements, Fieldstone quickly asserted that German had paid for all the building materials and also worked alongside the Fieldstone builders to get the job done.

The Losers

At this point, we went to Agile Developers and Heritage Builders, the two losing bidders, to conduct interviews. Surprisingly, both owners admitted that they were also interested in "showing some appreciation" to Abrams and German but were frustrated by their lack of success. Bill Wendall, the owner of Agile, said he had seen the BMW Abrams purchased from Cadena and laughed at what Abrams had paid, stating "That's $800 more than that old clunker was worth for scrap."

Wendell offered us an interesting insight into German's mind-set. He said that German complained of feeling overshadowed by his wife's successful career and larger salary and was eager to leave government service to pursue a more lucrative and entrepreneurial role as a luxury home contractor. Wendell said that he and German had discussed the broad outlines of forming a limited partnership, and German had filed for incorporation, but otherwise, the whole thing was a "pipe dream" that German kept going to satisfy his secret desire to "run with the big dogs."

Michael Lopez, the owner of Heritage, admitted that he had tried to get on Abrams' and German's unofficial "contractor lunch rotation" by bringing by six-foot subs and salad trays to the TRD procurement offices, but he was having little success in gaining access to either Abrams or German. Clearly, Lopez was unaware that Abrams' and German's palates had graduated from the "Subway diet" to more refined tastes.

After our interviews with the winning and losing contractors, Kyle and I sat down and reviewed our notes and the internal records and decided it was time to hear the rest of the story directly from Abrams and German.

The Director

When faced with the eight anonymous allegations, Abrams' initial statements confirmed the worst one: sometime in the last three years he had stopped seeking new bidders and made it known in his department that Jenkins and Roe Construction, Origin Design Group and Fieldstone Contractors were the unofficial prime contractors for all the future major construction and leasing deals. Dan was comfortable with these three firms and saw no need to waste time reviewing bids from others. He was aware of the capabilities of Agile and Heritage, but he did not care for either owner and felt justified in rejecting their bids for being late and using the incorrect font. He had rationalized that if contractors couldn't get bids in early, they wouldn't be able to deliver a construction job on time either. Likewise, if someone didn't use the exact type font and size specified to submit a bid package, how could that person be relied upon to fulfill the myriad criteria in building a custom office space?

Dan was unapologetic and direct in his description of what he called the "minor" social events. He said he attended "one or two" after-work events sponsored by Fieldstone and told his staff that they were welcome too. He also mentioned the frequent deliveries of salads and sandwiches from Heritage and said, because all the staff members were free to partake (or not) in the food, there was nothing wrong with accepting it.

Regarding the BMW, Abrams was genuinely surprised that anyone would question what he considered was a completely arm's-length transaction between two private parties for a fair market price. When we told him the transaction looked like an illegal gratuity or kickback to at least one person (our anonymous complainant), Abrams appeared hurt and confused. He gave me documents showing that he had indeed paid Cadena $1,000 and that the car was currently registered to Abrams with 320,000 miles.

Abrams told us he was aware that his deputy, Mark German, frequently accompanied contractors Wilson or Fieldstone on various trips, including family vacations, weekend getaways and tennis outings. Abrams flatly denied seeing anything wrong with German's close associations and frequent excursions with contractors because he believed that German had always paid his own expenses whenever he traveled.

We asked Abrams if he ever accepted gratuities and gifts from contractors, and he insisted that he had not accepted anything worth more than $20, as required by the ethical guidelines. He specifically mentioned the "knock-off Epsilon" watch he received at one of Fieldstone's holiday parties. Conveniently, Abrams valued the ersatz timepiece at exactly $20.

When we asked Abrams if German ever solicited or accepted home improvements from TRD contractors, his mood suddenly got more serious and quiet. He said he did not know any details but thought German mentioned once that he was paying Fieldstone for materials and labor to finish his basement. Abrams thought German actually did most of the work himself and that Fieldstone had only provided some assistance in hanging drywall and providing permits for plumbing and electrical work. Abrams also alluded to a company named MG Homesteads, which German and Bill Wendell had established.

As for his personal financial problems, Abrams was indignant when we asked why he failed to report his bankruptcy or the outstanding liens on his home. He said he knew it was a violation of TRD policy but insisted that his personal life had no effect on his abilities as a contract and procurement manager. He also stood by his refusal to attend ethics training and said the sessions were primarily for financial and legal staff. At the end of our interview, Abrams agreed to provide a comprehensive written response to each of the eight allegations, but after consulting with private legal counsel, he declined to provide any further information.

The Deputy

Mark German's statements were equally revealing. He explained that he took his cues from Abrams' attendance at the first lavish "post-production celebration" hosted by the contractors and, after that party, he became close personal friends with all three contractors. Whereas Abrams was defensive and unapologetic, German was visibly nervous and eager to clear his name.

German provided us with his credit card statements, which showed that he attended many of the Fieldstone events and paid at least something toward the cost of each outing. He also freely admitted that his family and Fieldstone's saw each other regularly, often dined together in town and had gone on at least two joint vacations. German said that Dan Abrams had given his tacit approval of these activities as well as the incorporation of MG Homesteads. German filed letters of incorporation because he wanted to hold the name for a possible business venture, but he said he was not optimistic the project would go anywhere. He denied soliciting or receiving any gratuities in the form of home improvements and insisted that he paid Fieldstone fair market prices for materials and labor.

Two days after we interviewed German, he resigned from TFD. Our analysis of the contract for the generator shed suggested that our organization could have spent $180,000 with another contractor — roughly a little over half of the $350,000 that had been awarded to Origin and Fieldstone — yet TRD senior managers were reluctant to pursue criminal charges because they did not want to embarrass the agency. Depending on what values were placed on three high-flying dinners, two imitation fashion watches, one broken-down BMW sedan, some building supplies and 40 hours of skilled labor, Abrams might have received between $500 and $1,000, while German might have received between $15,000 to $20,000. Although there were public integrity issues at stake, the paltry plunder that these two federal employees raked in was not going to be sufficient to attract the attention of an assistant U.S. attorney.

At the conclusion of the investigation, Dan Abrams agreed to immediately retire in lieu of formal disciplinary action. Mark German resigned to avoid disciplinary action and is now trying to turn MG Homesteads into a viable business.

Lessons Learned

The appearance of impropriety can be as damaging as any actual violation of law. Managers must lead by example and set the proper ethical tone. When they encourage their subordinates to accept illegal gifts and gratuities, and then "lead" by bragging about what they've personally been given by vendors, it not only sets the wrong tone at the top; it quickly becomes standard and expected behavior.

In this case, Abrams felt that he was too busy to comply with mandatory financial disclosures and annual ethics training — he was more focused on closing business deals quickly with friends and trusted associates. Additionally, over time, Abrams felt comfortable accepting gifts and prohibited gratuities from a few contracting sources that he had dealt with most frequently. His bad example was readily followed by German, which resulted in the unplanned ending of both men's careers.

Recommendations to Prevent Future Occurrences

Federal government employees are held to a different (and higher) set of ethical standards, as they should be. Accepting illegal gratuities opens the door for more grievous ethics violations, including sharing insider information, bid rigging, contract steering and kickbacks. Ethics classroom training is required, but it is not enough; regularly scheduled discussions using real-life examples, spot checks by ethics and compliance personnel and an active anonymous hotline are all key deterrents to prevent or detect future occurrences.

About the Author

Richard Woodford, J.D., CFE, has 29 years of federal service in agencies including the U.S. Department of Labor, the National Science Foundation and the Department of the Navy. Richard is a Regent Emeritus of the ACFE and a frequent presenter of anti-fraud, ethics and leadership training.

Decorum Across the International Date Line

JIM PELCZAR

Harmony, courtesy, manners and respect are hallmarks of Japanese society, as evidenced in the highly civil behavior exhibited by the Japanese
population during the massive earthquake in March 2011. According to
most of the how-to books, Japanese businesspeople are supposedly among
the most ethical in the world and they experience strong social pressure
to do the right thing. Experts advise non-Japanese professionals working in
that country to avoid conflict and embarrassment and help their Japanese
counterparts save face.

But Japanese businesspeople are just like anyone else. The cultural taboo
against dishonesty can produce Japanese wrongdoers who will lie and commit fraud with impunity. But their motive is not always to directly line their
pockets — bribery can take the form of anything of "value," which is not limited to money or goods. Lavish gifts and entertainment, payment of vacation
travel and lodging expenses, payment of credit card bills or loans, promises
of future employment and interests in businesses can all be bribes if they are
given or received with the intent to influence or be influenced. Regardless
of positive cultural assumptions, direct losses to bribery and corruption in
Japan are huge.

Special Materials Build Special Relationships

Noshi Manufacturing was in the specialty materials business, producing
chemicals and compounds that are used in products ranging from aircraft to
sporting goods. Noshi was a joint venture between a large Japanese company
and the U.S. parent company. Although it was a global entity, the Japanese
subsidiary had a 35-year history of operating by its own rules.

George Kim, the global chief information officer of Noshi Manufacturing based in the United States, was about 55 years old and, although he had little charm or charisma, he had an aura of directness and an awareness of his status. Kim regularly communicated with the local IT director in Japan and had close ties with a team of consultants at his preferred vendor, International Business Integrators (IBI). Kim worked with IBI on a variety of projects in the United States, Japan, Southeast Asia and Europe.

Yasushi Mizuhana, Noshi's local IT director in Japan, was a slight, 49-year-old man who smiled and nodded often and spoke broken English. His native Japanese was soft, and his nod was consistent with textbook Japanese business behavior — the nod indicated, to the Japanese, that he was listening but not necessarily agreeing. With George Kim's encouragement, Mizuhana developed close relationships with IBI representatives in Japan. He often received instructions from Kim without the knowledge of local Noshi executives and was positioning himself to follow a career path laid out by Kim.

Takeo Yanagida was the Japanese director of procurement and a close colleague of Mizuhana's. At 44 years old, Yanagida was known around the office for his keen memory and fluent English. He joined Noshi Manufacturing a few years earlier from a major Japanese trading company and had since developed a reputation for being lax about following protocol and for tolerating rule-breaking. He used his English skills like a weapon, especially with his Japanese colleagues who were less fluent. He readily provided quick interpretations and injected his own opinions instead of what was actually said.

The First in a Series

The previous year, Kim, Mizuhana and Yanagida put out a request for proposals for the first stage of a large, three-part project. IBI representatives helped the threesome craft the request, despite also submitting a proposal of their own. IBI won the contract.

Kim, Mizuhana and Yanagida structured the larger, subsequent phases to favor the incumbent contractor. The direct value of the second-phase contract was $32 million. About 32,000 staff hours were expended by more than 200 Noshi employees, which added $12.6 million to the cost and brought the total to $44.6 million. Employee time was spent on planning, interviews, documentation, programming, information system settings and management reviews. IBI sent 25 full-time staff members to Noshi, and Noshi assigned about 30 managers to oversee the initiative.

Learning the Culture

I run an independent management consultancy in Japan, with a primary focus on enterprise financial control and management information systems. In June, a Japanese colleague and I learned that Noshi Manufacturing was undergoing an upgrade to replace its obsolete management information system (MIS). Leveraging my language skills and subject matter expertise, I submitted a proposal to be an independent governance lead on the project. My responsibility would be to make sure the project moved along according to industry standards.

In September, after many negotiations with middle and senior managers at Noshi, I received a call from Bob Fairfax, the CEO of Noshi Manufacturing in Japan. He asked me to come over that afternoon. Traveling east across Tokyo, I thought about how long it took to get Bob Fairfax's attention and how the senior managers resisted and delayed my repeated attempts for a face-to-face meeting with him. Based on my experiences working in Japan for a couple of decades, that's almost always an indicator that the managers are concealing something. The management team also lacked the urgency commensurate with the situation; Noshi executives wanted to overhaul their entire MIS system, which is a huge undertaking.

My meeting with Fairfax started with the traditional courteous exchange of business cards and small talk, and then he quickly turned adversarial. "Look at me; I'm an American," he said, "but I am also running a Japanese company." He raised his voice. "You need to tell me how you think you can handle the subtleties of Japanese culture and address any problems without allowing anyone to lose face. How will you do that?"

Maintaining reasonable eye contact, I said, "This is my 25th year in Japan. I've achieved social standing here, in and outside the workplace; I speak the language and firmly the understand the way business is conducted," I said, "and the key lesson I've learned is that it we must question the status quo, speak our minds and say what has to be said — as long as we say it politely with courtesy, manners and respect."

"Look, here," he countered, "I see you are also a fraud examiner, and I'm not looking for that. I need someone who can effectively manage this project; are you up to it?"

After that tense exchange, Bob smiled, placed his hand on my shoulder and said, "Sorry to be hard on you, but I needed to know you could stand up to pressure and not just tell me what you think I wanted to hear. Welcome aboard."

Getting My Feet Wet

Fairfax put me under the supervision of Yasushi Mizuhana, the local IT Director, who gave me a small desk in an open work area. He arranged several meetings with his project teams, supposedly to build the request for proposals for the second contract, and invited me to sit in on them. These traditional Japanese-style meetings kept 20 people captive for four to eight hours at a time. Only about 5 of the 20 people actually contributed, and the meetings were usually dominated by Mizuhana and Yanagida. In one, I met a loyal company woman named Yuko Hewiagawa. She was among a small core of individuals who had direct access to the CFO, Tadashii Morioka, and upon whom he relied for information regarding middle-management decisions. She recognized Mizuhana's attempt to tightly define my role — against the wishes of Bob Fairfax. A few days after I met Hewiagawa, Morioka called me to his office to see how I was settling in. After a brief conversation, he moved me upstairs to be his direct report. I was out of the little box that Mizuhana prepared for me.

As soon as the second phase of bidding began, Mizuhana and Yanagida and their IBI colleagues took actions to conceal the project status. IBI failed to follow the industry-standard procedures for this type of system implementation. (I discovered this when a South American government helpfully, and in violation of a host of copyright laws, published all the templates for this exact activity on the Internet, and I stumbled across them.)

Kim, Mizuhana and Yanagida refused to apply quality guidelines to the work being done by IBI, and project managers at both IBI and Noshi repeatedly refused to admit that there was any trouble with the project. Such behavior could be mistaken for simple incompetence or mismanagement, but Kim, Mizuhana, Yanagida and their IBI counterparts knew what was expected with this type MIS upgrade and failed to comply — and they didn't think anyone else knew.

If Noshi was part of a strictly regulated industry, regulators would have discovered the anomalous patterns and required corrective action. But Noshi was unregulated, and the trio heading up the project didn't think there was anyone looking over their shoulders.

Reading the Body Language

When it was time to solicit bids for the second phase of the project, Yanagida and Mizuhana again used IBI staff to prepare of the bid request, even though IBI was a bidder. The bid was released and the candidate organizations were all evaluated by Fairfax, his executive colleagues, me and the business unit leaders. George Kim participated by video link. All the major global management consultancies submitted bids. The award was made to IBI, primarily due to their knowledge of the details of the project and because time constraints forced a quick decision. I expressed a dissenting opinion but was strongly overruled by George Kim.

I asked Yuko Hewiagawa why Kim was so aggressive when I questioned the award, citing a possible conflict of interest. She told me that this was the second time that Kim, Mizuhana and Yanagida, without Fairfax's knowledge, worked to structure the bid to favor IBI.

Ryujin Takayama was the Aerospace Business Unit lead and was well known for his fair dealing with everyone at Noshi. His operating unit consisted of 2,000 of Noshi's 4,500 employees. He believed in large meetings only if there were decisions to be made and would summon up to 200 participants on Saturdays so they would not be distracted with daily responsibilities.

The first of his meetings that I attended was about six weeks into my involvement, and I was one of 165 participants representing all the departments. It was a status meeting regarding the second phase of the MIS project. The employees were gathered in the corporate auditorium, seated on small desk chairs 15 levels up. In the center of the room, tables were arranged in U-shape for the four key leaders: Takayama, me and two other executives. I was the only non-Japanese in the room. A podium and screen were set up at the front for the department heads who would speak during the day.

Facing forward, Takayama sat at the bottom of the U, and I sat to the right, diagonally across from him. The two others sat on the left side of the U. Speakers gave the status of procurement, ordering, manufacturing, warehousing, logistics and accounting functions. The accounting manager, Taro Yamamoto, was the first to give his presentation. "Good afternoon to everyone, and thank you for coming on a Saturday." He described how he worked with IBI to clean up cost-code discrepancies, identify existing procedures that would be rolled over to the new system without changes (as-is) and select those that would be improved in the new system (to-be).

"Honestly, we are working very hard to map our as-is processes, even with their slight difficulties, into the to-be processes in the new system." Takayama interrupted. "Wait, just a moment please. In your presentation you mentioned that there were faults with the cost codes, right?" "Yes, sir," replied Yamamoto. Takayama went on, "And you said that you were unable to match procured raw materials to the first-stage manufactured product?" Now clearly nervous, Yamamoto answered, "Yes, sir," and began to slouch. "And you also said, that you were taking the as-is steps and mapping them directly into the new system, correct?" Yamamoto flushed, and tried to reply " . . . but, sir, please . . . " "Stop, just answer my question. I'm not repeating it." Yamamoto quietly answered, "Yes, sir."

Takayama leaned forward with his palms down on the table, far apart. "Okay, let me get this straight. You took flawed procedures, ones that did not allow transactions to be tracked from purchase to at least the first stage of manufacturing, and you mapped those faulty accounting practices into the new system, with the consent of all your peers, information technology and IBI? Is that right? No . . . wait, I'll ask all of you. Do you see anything suspicious about these transactions?" The room fell completely quiet. He didn't look around to see the effect, but it was as if he stabbed everyone in the room. "I am asking the question again. Is there something suspicious here?" More silence.

When he asked the first time, I turned to look at the participants behind Takayama. Many started to glance down. Takayama projected his voice. "One more time, are these transactions suspicious?" Behind Takayama, all heads turned down. Only Yuko Hewiagawa, sitting at the very top of the tier of desk chairs, held her head high and looked straight back at me. It was the most remarkable demonstration of collective body language I ever witnessed. This time I answered. "Yes."

"Jim, what did you say?"

"Yes, Takayama-san, all of those transactions are suspicious."

"Why?"

I continued, "Because, as Yamamoto-san stated, the company cannot match a bill of materials to the first level of finished product. That means ledgers cannot be reconciled from interim transactions to final products. If you can't do that, you don't have financial control over the purchasing and manufacturing. Again, as Yamamoto-san mentioned, the working teams are designing the new system to continue the problems that you have now. That's very suspicious."

Busting the Bid Rig

As the project moved on, Kim, Mizuhana and Yanagida continued to exert influence on team leaders as they prepared to award the third-phase contract to IBI. The first time they channeled business to IBI, it took months to achieve their goal. The second time (where I gave the dissenting opinion), it took only ten business days. This time, they wanted to speed it up even more.

One day while this was going on, one of the older IT staff members, Takahiro Miura, stopped me in the hallway.

"Jim-san, I need to speak with you, please."

"How can I help you, Miura-san?"

"Can we please speak in private, Jim-san?"

"Miura-san, certainly, shall we go up to the executive floor?"

"Yes, please."

We stepped into the empty boardroom and Miura blew the whistle. He confirmed what I had observed — specifically that Mizuhana, Kim and Yanagida were having meetings without the knowledge of Bob Fairfax. He also said that, for a third time, they were going to circumvent proper bidding practices. Miura was anxious as he gave all the details. He informed me that Mizuhana would contact me later in the day to ask me to participate in the bidding meetings as a "referee."

Just after 5:00 p.m., as Miura predicted, Mizuhana called and asked me to go to his office. When I got there, he said, in English, "Jim-san, we are opening the third phase of competitive bidding on the MIS project. We know you are close to Bob Fairfax, and we want you to come to the bidder interviews, please." I replied, "Absolutely, Mizuhana-san, when are these meetings going to take place?" He answered, "Tomorrow afternoon."

Pausing generously before giving an answer, I replied, "Mizuhana-san, who made the decision to do this so quickly, and when?"

"Two days ago, Jim-san, our global CIO, Mr. Kim, ordered this."

"When were the other bidders informed?"

"Yesterday," Mizuhana said.

"Mizuhana-san, who else knew about this decision?"

"Jim-san, we cleared it with Yanagida-san, our procurement director."

"Mizuhana-san, please let me understand. You are opening a bid on a multimillion-dollar contract, and you gave the new bidders only two days to respond?"

"Yes, Jim-san, we've worked this way many times. Besides, Mr. Kim and our local procurement manager said it is okay."

"Mizuhana-san, I can't go to this meeting."

"But why not, Jim-san? We are following our standard procedures."

The muscles under his left eye twitched for a mere fraction of a second; if I had broken eye contact, I wouldn't have noticed.

"Mizuhana-san, I cannot sit in front of large companies with which I might have to do business in the future for what seems to be an attempt to simply give the award to the IBI."

I got up and left. It was pointless to explain to Mizuhana that another perceived unethical action could lead to a huge reputational risk for Noshi Manufacturing in Japan.

Spreading the Word

Returning to my office, I wrote up the incident and e-mailed it to Tadashii Morioka, the CFO. I described how Kim, Yanagida and Mizuhana structured the bid request. I explained all the signs of it being intentionally designed for IBI and expressed my refusal to participate.

I sent the e-mail to Morioka late Tuesday evening and, early Wednesday morning, I printed a copy. At exactly 8:00 a.m., I went to Morioka's office and handed the printed copy to him. I verbally explained why I would not attend any of the bid meetings. He looked at the document gravely and said, "Thank you."

By 10:00 a.m. on Wednesday, Bob Fairfax canceled the bid meetings and took a late-afternoon flight to the United States. It seems that Fairfax had it out with George Kim and forced Kim to issue a formal statement saying he granted permission to his staff to deviate from global purchasing policy and that he personally assumed the associated risks. The contract was awarded directly to IBI. Fairfax was back at his desk in Japan on Friday.

Meeting Marty

Part of my work included an interview with Martin "Marty" Marina of IBI. Marty was sent to Japan from the United States to be IBI's senior liaison with Noshi, at the request of George Kim. Marty and George had known each other since college. I called Marty to talk about the status of IBI's contract with Noshi and to ask why the IBI team refused to admit that there were problems. Martin invited me to lunch. He was polite until I asked him to put his A-team — not his C-team — on the project. I explained to Marty that the results of our investigation showed that IBI leaders fell short of industry standards and, if they continued, Noshi's best interests would not be served. Marty was new to Japan and trusted his subordinates completely, so he was insulted that I questioned his team's performance. From my perspective, the meeting was a failure — Noshi was still stuck with the same IBI project manager, Sanno, whom I knew collaborated with Kim, Mizuhana and Yanagida on the bid-rigging scheme.

Mizuhana, Yanagida and Sanno often worked 11 hours or more in the office together and spent many evenings going out for dinner and drinks. Mizuhana and Yanagida frequently came to work looking worn out. When I asked why, they said socializing with vendors was a common and expected Japanese business practice. These outings were on IBI's expense accounts and often cost more than $1,200 a night per person. Mizuhana and Yanagida didn't earn enough money to maintain that sort of lifestyle on their own.

Bob Fairfax called me into his office a few days after my meeting with Marty. "Jim, what's the matter with you? I told you not to create any ill will among our teams, and now Marty Marina is telling me you are bothering his group and impeding progress!"

The door to his office was open, and a fairly heated exchange ensued.

"Bob, you explicitly put me in charge of making sure that this initiative is a success. I looked at the facts, and the project is heading south. It's a problem and money is falling through all the cracks. Entire categories of transactions, which are now poorly controlled and open to fraud and abuse, are being carried over into the new system without being fixed. How could I perform my obligations to you without approaching Marty and asking for his best and brightest on this project? The team he has now is just not cutting it!"

Bob reflected. "Yeah, Jim, I know. Takayama-san, Morioka-san, Marty and Sanno had a heated discussion about it over dinner the other day."

"Then why are you grilling me on this? You know what's going on!"

He calmed down. "I know, I know, Jim. Don't worry about it. Keep doing what you are doing."

At least we were openly discussing the problem now. Noshi was being saddled with an unjustifiable amount of system customization that Kim approved and that resulted in a profit for IBI (which IBI representatives then funneled back to Kim, Yanagida and Mizuhana in extravagant entertainment). The turning point came when Bob Fairfax forced George Kim to accept the risk of circumventing bidding procedures by signing the policy deviation document. Afterward, Fairfax took a more active role in the endeavor, first by summoning an emergency team to help remediate IBI's failures.

Motivation

The parties colluding to direct Noshi's contracts to IBI had many possible motives. George Kim took material action to direct millions of dollars from

Noshi's foreign subsidiaries to the foreign subsidiaries of IBI. There was no direct evidence of bribery, but our hypothesis was that Kim was planning a career move to IBI. He was on the receiving end of expensive wining and dining in Tokyo, at a much higher level that what Mizuhana and Yanagida enjoyed. IBI often spent $4,000 per person on a single night of entertainment for Kim.

Mizuhana and Yanagida were led to believe that, by following George Kim's directions, they would receive career benefits. They both said they were confident they would be promoted to global leadership positions because of their relationship with Kim. In addition, they enjoyed the lavish entertainment at IBI's expense and, for several months, they lived far beyond their means.

The schemes revealed in this case were consistent with bribery, corruption, collusion, bid rigging, procurement fraud and deliberate obfuscation and alteration of internal controls over financial reporting across an entire enterprise. When they finally came to light, Mizuhana was demoted. It took Bob Fairfax about six months to build a case to fire Yanagida, the procurement director. Japanese labor law strongly protects full-time employees. Noshi suffered residual reputation risk as a result of the shady procurement practices. (Several months after my work at Noshi ended, one of the bid participants and I met by chance. This bidder lost one of the two rigged bids. He told me that it was widely perceived in the community that the Noshi bid was rigged.)

IBI botched the system implementation in Japan and lost the global contract. After accepting the risks associated with breaking the procurement rules, George Kim managed to put several layers of staff between himself and the Japanese locals who engaged in the impropriety, which allowed him to deny any knowledge of the scheme and keep his job.

Estimated direct losses to Noshi exceeded $30 million in license fees, and indirect losses were about $12.6 million in staff hours. Because the first go-around was a failure, executives at Noshi Japan are now under orders to reinitiate the project and align it with global standards.

Lessons Learned

I was able to recognize patterns of suspicious activity in the way Kim, Mizuhana and Yanagida directed the award of so-called competitive-bidding contracts to IBI. In future investigations I will be able to spot similar patterns from a review of contract and procurement records.

Key non-Japanese executives, people who should know better, checked their common sense at the international date line. They tolerated, or failed to question, red flags because cultural experts advised them not to make waves.

(continued)

(continued)

A subculture of systemic corruption, collusion and kickbacks kills the integrity of an organization, discourages honest employees and will eventually cost money through direct and indirect losses. Bribery usually means that money has changed hands. But that isn't always the case; it can occur through inappropriate gratuities and career advancement, as in this situation.

Businesspeople everywhere could benefit from a rudimentary understanding of the principles of investigative interviewing and nonverbal communication. We had a clear example in this case: when Takayama asked employees in a meeting if transactions looked suspicious, almost every head in the room dropped.

Recommendations to Prevent Future Occurrences

Follow policies, standards and procedures and pay attention to deviations from industry norms. We increasingly rely on "instruction manuals" — standard enterprise solutions. Anything that's not in the manual deserves attention.

Look at how other companies handle similar endeavors. What issues did other organizations face in similar circumstances? It is easier than ever to network with peers and learn about their experiences. Ask about similar projects that other professionals have completed.

Set a baseline for performance at the beginning of a project and measure the actual performance against the baseline early and often. Recalibrate the project as needed and keep in mind that it is easier to make corrections early in a project than later.

Keep your common sense, even when you cross the international date line. Suppose you are doing business in a different language. The person you are negotiating with speaks for five minutes, and you get a thirty-second translation. Why? If you think something is out of place, ask. Regardless of where you are, you can say what you think, as long as you say it with courtesy, manners and respect.

About the Author

Jim Pelczar provides operating risk, secure systems, governance, anti-fraud, information security and management strategy solutions to global companies. He develops versatile solutions used by leading financial institutions and organizations in defense/aerospace, heavy industries, pharmaceutical and telecommunications sectors. He has more than 20 years' business experience in Japan and speaks fluent Japanese.

18

The Kickback Mine

J. AARON CHRISTOPHER

It was a typically slow day at the Bellville, West Virginia, Residency Agency of the FBI where I served as a Special Agent. Being the only agent with an accounting background, I was the designated white-collar specialist when new cases arose. I received a call from Crimson Mine's general counsel, George Brent, who told me about the recent discovery that one of their vendors had been overbilling them and he wanted to prosecute. My first thought was that this would be a routine matter of greed by a vendor and I would just need to look at how much was taken and try to get the vendor to confess. However, during the course of my investigation, additional suspects were developed, the scheme took a turn in a new direction, and the "bad guy" turned out to be likable and as much a victim as he was a suspect. It would also be one of the largest frauds to ever occur in Bellville.

The Crimson Mine had been a major employer in the region for more than 40 years. However, recently two of the three mines had closed, which resulted in a loss of jobs in the area. Crimson had been purchased a couple of years prior by a large public company, Diversified Holdings, Inc. It had its own hotline, and the new telephone number was posted in the break room and other places at the mine. Moreover, it subcontracted out mine support construction to local vendors so that Crimson could focus on mining. Over the years, the company had several different vendors, but for the past five years, it exclusively used Richardson Construction because of its prompt response and excellent work.

Keith Richardson moved to Bellville eight years earlier to start a small construction company dedicated to providing specialized metal fabrication to the Crimson Mine and manufacturing companies in the area. When Keith started, he only had one employee, but over the years he had developed the company into a thriving business with 30 workers. Keith was proud of his success but also felt a great sense of responsibility to his employees to earn work to keep them busy and employed. He knew that his success was providing for 30 families, and this responsibility weighed on him more than anyone knew. Because of the limited industries in the area, his work came primarily from half a dozen businesses. The Crimson Mine was his largest account, comprising 30 percent of his total billings.

Because of the substantial amount of work and long-standing relationship Richardson had with Crimson, they established a "blanket purchase order (PO)" agreement. Under the arrangement, when mine supervisors needed work done, they could call Richardson and order it at a prearranged labor rate plus the cost of materials, without the need to obtain competitive bids. The mine supervisor would then approve Richardson's time sheets and materials list and forward the documents to the accounts payable department based on the blanket PO agreement. Crimson reserved the right to review Richardson's time sheets, payroll records and materials invoices at any time without notice.

A few months prior to my call from George, Diversified received a message on its hotline. The tipster stated that Keith Richardson's company had been overbilling Crimson for work done at the mine and that "it had been going on for years." Diversified's response was to seek assistance from the forensic accounting practice of its Big Four external audit firm. The auditors obtained documents from Richardson and performed a review of all of the last two years of billings and compared them to the vendor's actual payroll records.

What they uncovered were overbillings totaling nearly $550,000 over the past two years. This was accomplished through overstating the actual hours reported on the time cards submitted to Crimson for payment. They also found ghost employees listed on time sheets who had either never worked for Richardson or were working on other jobs on the days billed to Crimson. As a result of these findings, Crimson immediately ended its relationship with Richardson, and George Brent called the FBI.

Taking a Gamble

After receiving George's call, my partner and I headed out to the mine to get the whole story. George told us about the message from the tipster and about the work the external audit firm had completed. He had met with Richardson the day before to let him know that they would no longer be using his services but did not detail the audit findings to him. George appeared personally hurt by Keith's betrayal and greed. He had known Keith for a number of years and liked him very much. He knew Crimson had substantially made his company what it was today and also valued the work Keith's company had done at the mine. No safety violations or injury accidents had ever occurred from their work and, as the general counsel, that was very important to him. While he was saddened by the wrongdoings of his friend, George also had a responsibility to the company, and Diversified instructed him to pursue prosecution of the case.

When I arrived at George Brent's office at mine headquarters, he provided me with a two-page summary of findings along with five examples of overbillings. He also told me about his meeting with Keith the day before and that while he didn't accuse him directly, he was confident that Keith knew that the auditors had discovered the fraud. He also told me that all of the audit evidence and working papers were at the auditors' offices back in Texas.

At this point, I had a decision to make. Do I subpoena the detailed audit evidence and spend time wading through several boxes of invoices, time sheets and payroll records, or do I go ahead and interview Keith with the information I have?

I chose to interview Keith. To be honest, this was a bit of a gamble. Keith could tip off other conspirators or destroy evidence. However, I decided not to wait because after George spoke with Keith, he knew the fraud had been discovered. Also, he was no longer in a position to continue the fraud or do further damage. As far as destroying evidence, I knew the auditors already had most of what we needed, and the rest would be found by a subpoena of his bank account. At the time, I was not aware of any co-conspirators, but if they were going to be tipped off by Keith, likely it had already happened.

Special Agent Trace Burrows was the only other agent in the Bellville Resident Agency. Trace had been an FBI Special Agent for 18 years and was enjoying being close to home as his retirement date approached. Prior to joining the FBI, he worked for the Baltimore Police Department and had developed a specialty in violent crimes within the Bureau. While Trace wasn't an expert in white-collar crime, he was an expert at criminal behavior and was a great asset to have on interviews. Typically when we interviewed together, we would strategize and decide who would take notes. For our interviews on this case, Trace took the notes to allow me to focus on developing the questions, introducing the evidence and confronting our interviewee with the fraud allegation. His help and guidance on the case would prove invaluable.

Trace and I asked George to call Keith and arrange a meeting at George's office. Since Keith's office at Richardson Construction was nearby, he arrived about 15 minutes later. He was very surprised to see two FBI agents there but knew why we wanted to speak with him and agreed to sit down and visit with us. I first built a rapport with him and got to know him a little bit. I asked him to tell me about his business and was genuinely interested in learning more about the coal industry and what his company did at the mine. Next I had him tell me about how he got started working with Crimson. By the time I asked him about the fraudulent billings, I presented it as if the allegation of fraud was a fact and just part of the story. I would periodically ask clarifying questions, but for the most part I just let him tell me what happened. I did not want to be confrontational and adversarial with him by leading with an accusation that would be difficult for him to accept and admit to. Instead, by building rapport with him over 30 minutes or so of nonthreatening discussion, when we finally did introduce the fraud allegation, he just incorporated that into his story and proceeded to confess the details of the scheme.

As Keith began to explain the fraud, he started about five years earlier. He was reluctant to involve anyone but himself, but eventually described the first time that the mine manager, Rich Bowden, asked him for some tickets to a big college football game the upcoming weekend. After that, Bowden began asking for money — reminding Keith of all the work Crimson did with Richardson and how much Keith's company would suffer without it. The revelation that someone on the inside at Crimson was involved was news to me, but I didn't let Keith know that I was surprised to learn it. Along the way, I showed Keith some of the billing documents the external auditor had identified as part of their forensic audit. He admitted that they were false and that he had inflated them to provide cash to Rich. At first Rich would ask for money infrequently, but beginning a couple of years ago, he started asking for money on a regular basis and would almost always stop by Keith's office to get an envelope with the cash in it.

As Keith talked, I focused my questions on the "why" of the scheme. As someone who had studied various fraudsters and other white-collar schemes, I had always been interested in that first decision to cross the line and commit fraud. I assumed that he had debts or wanted to buy something and "needed" the extra money. However, as Keith detailed his reasons for the fraud, I actually began to feel sorry for him and his situation. Rich threatened to end his contract with the mine, which would have forced Keith to lay off a number of his workers who depended on him to provide work to support their families. Also, because he was taking large amounts of cash out of his business account and did not have a legitimate business reason or receipts, he had to pay taxes on the withdrawals as if he personally had received the money. Therefore, a significant portion of the overbillings went to the IRS to pay the additional taxes he incurred.

At the end of our interview, Keith promised to cooperate fully with our investigation and answer further questions upon request. Our next step was to go to Bowden's house. We knew it was possible that Keith could have second thoughts about his confession and tip Bowden off to our investigation, so Trace and I wasted no time in trying to interview him.

The Cold Shoulder

As we drove up the driveway to Rich's house, we saw the large industrial building that was rumored to hold his collection of 20 + antique cars. To the left of the house, we noticed a large above-ground pool with a huge deck built around it and a hot tub under a cabana. It quickly became obvious that he was living well beyond his mine supervisor's salary. Bowden was a gruff, mine-hardened man who at 6′8″ could be pretty intimidating. He reluctantly invited us inside to talk at his kitchen table. Unlike Keith, Rich was not in a talking mood. He told us about his 28-year career at the mine and how he was looking forward to retirement. When we turned our attention to his relationship with Keith, he became quiet and seemed to be listening to find out how much we knew. When we directly asked about the bribe payments Keith made to him, he quickly stated, "I don't want to talk about the money." I provided him with my card in case he changed his mind and let him know that we did not need his cooperation with the evidence we had. It was up to him if he chose to cooperate or not. We left shortly thereafter.

Rich's quick, tight-lipped response when accused of taking bribes told me two things:

1. There was money to be talked about.
2. He did not want to cooperate.

This verified Richardson's claim that Bowden was involved, but I still needed evidence to prove it. My next step would be to conduct many more interviews and begin reviewing documents.

Fortunately for me, the external forensic auditors had already done an outstanding job of proving that Keith had been overbilling Crimson. They compared all of the vendor's billings, which included time cards submitted for approval to Richardson's actual payroll. The vast majority of the overbillings had been approved by Bowden, but I began to notice another supervisor's signature on other inflated invoices — Steve Crosby.

As I interviewed other mine workers, they relayed rumors that Bowden had pressured other vendors in the past. They detailed how one vendor had his workers build the deck at Bowden's house and how another had installed the hot tub. They were also suspicious of Bowden's relationship with Keith Richardson and stated that they believed he was also taking money from him.

Since I did not have to do the forensic work on the overbillings, I focused my attention on Richardson's bank statements. The inflated checks from Crimson were deposited into Keith's business checking account, so that was a logical place to look to see where the money was going. What I found surprised me. I saw only small checks payable to Keith personally and on an infrequent basis. Typically, one would expect to find a large amount of money coming out of the account to the primary subject's benefit. I did, however, find regular checks made payable to "cash" approximately every two or three weeks. Richardson's office manager told me in an interview that Bowden would come by Keith's office every two or three weeks and leave with a brown manila folder. She suspected that the envelopes contained cash but never questioned Keith about them. Again, it was more circumstantial evidence of Bowden receiving bribes, but I needed something concrete.

In my search to determine what Keith spent his ill-gotten gains on, I found a few checks made payable to a local credit union. The checks were suspicious and in the amount of $473.54. A subpoena to the credit union revealed that the checks were loan payments on a truck owned by Rich Bowden. Finally I had hard evidence that Bowden had been receiving bribes. He had Keith directly make truck payments for him.

I also found checks made payable to Eugene and Bobby Crosby. The name "Crosby" caught my eye and I remembered the other mine manager, Steve Crosby, who had approved a few of the inflated invoices. It was time to interview Steve.

The Benefits of Cooperation

Unlike Bowden, Steve was very humble and contrite when he came to the FBI office to speak with us. He had been keeping this secret for too long and just wanted to get it off his chest. He told me about how Bowden had promoted him as an individual mine supervisor when he became the area manager. He then detailed how Bowden pressured him to approve false invoices for Richardson and not to ask too many questions. Eventually he too began accepting cash from Richardson. The checks I had discovered were payments made to his two grade-school-age sons. Crosby was completely truthful and fully cooperated. He said he was relieved to have the entire episode behind him and agreed to testify against Bowden if needed.

In reviewing the evidence against Richardson and Crosby, the over-billings and other documents alone would have been enough to convict them at trial. Crosby had no reason to receive checks from Richardson, and the fact that they were made payable to his young sons was even worse. The clear evidence of billing Crimson for workers who were not even Richardson's employees or were working on other jobs on the day billed to Crimson was sufficient evidence against the vendor. However, because they had been truthful and confessed the scheme to Trace and me, they both agreed to plead guilty to a federal information of mail fraud. An information is used in federal court when a subject agrees to plead guilty to a criminal charge instead of being indicted by a grand jury. The federal mail fraud statute was used because the subjects in this case caused the proceeds of their fraud to be mailed by Crimson to Richardson Construction through the U.S. Postal Service. (The mail fraud statute, because it is so broad, is considered the workhorse of federal fraud prosecutions.) As a result of their cooperation, the defendants avoided arrest and were allowed to self-report to court for their hearings. Also, the U.S. Attorney agreed to recommend sentencing on the low end of the Federal Sentencing Guidelines to the judge.

Bowden never took me up on my suggestion that he cooperate with the investigation. As a result of the statements of Crosby, Richardson and Richardson's office manager; Bowden's signature on the false invoices; and, more important, the checks Richardson wrote for Bowden's truck payments, Bowden was indicted by a federal grand jury on multiple charges of mail fraud. I arrested him at his home and took him before a U.S. magistrate for his initial appearance. He was granted release with conditions pending trial.

After reviewing the substantial evidence against him, including his signatures approving the false invoices, Keith's payments on his truck loan and the witness who saw him regularly leaving Keith's office with a thick envelope, Bowden's attorney recommended that he plead guilty to the charges against him. He ultimately did, and all three defendants avoided a trial. The judge sentenced Richardson and Crosby to 12 months in prison, which they served at a minimum security federal prison camp. Although they were given a lenient sentence, the judge explained that they deserved to serve a year in prison because they did not come forward and stop the fraud when they had the opportunity. The judge had harsher words for Bowden, who betrayed his lifelong employer, for failing to take responsibility for his actions. Bowden was sentenced to 36 months in prison, which he served in a maximum security federal penitentiary in another state. All three of the defendants were held jointly liable for restitution for the full $550,000 amount of the fraud.

After sentencing I learned that, out of his feelings of guilt, Richardson arranged to close his business and gave all of its assets, including the real estate, to Crimson in full settlement of the restitution order.

Recommendations to Prevent Future Occurrences

Fraud Hotline

The tip from the anonymous whistleblower led to the initial discovery of the fraud. Had Crimson Mine had a hotline in place prior to the acquisition by Diversified, the scheme could have been discovered much sooner and losses would have been greatly minimized. As discussed in the Association of Fraud Examiner's 2010 *Report to the Nations*, organizations that have fraud hotlines in place suffer significantly smaller losses and discover fraud schemes on average seven months sooner than organizations without such a reporting tool in place.

Early Interview

Often investigators are leery to approach a subject until they have all the facts. This strategy can be useful, but it can also lead to wasted investigative resources and looking for evidence in the wrong places. Because the subject of this investigation was already aware of it and was not in a position to do more harm to evidence or the victim company, interviewing Richardson early paid dividends in investigating the case. Investigators have to evaluate when they have enough evidence to approach a subject with an accurate and knowledgeable accusation.

(continued)

(continued)

Investigative Myopia

Naturally investigators form an initial theory of a case. (In the *Fraud Examiners Manual* [ACFE, 2012], this is known as the fraud theory approach.) However, we must remain open to following the evidence and challenging our initial theory. Rather than being a case of a greedy contractor (Richardson) bilking a customer, this was a case of the greedy supervisor (Bowden) extorting the contractor to pay for his own kickbacks. Richardson profited nothing and ultimately lost everything as a result of the fraud.

Internal Audit

In this case, the internal auditors of the parent company did not provide adequate oversight at this relatively small subsidiary, providing additional opportunity for fraud to occur. Proper internal controls and regular audit procedures might have prevented the fraud or uncovered the losses sooner.

Scope

When a fraud has occurred over a long period of time, it is important to work with prosecutors (presuming criminal prosecution is warranted) early to develop a scope for the investigation. In this situation, even though the fraud was thought to have occurred during the last five years, developing evidence more than the past couple of years would not have added anything to the prosecutor's case. Additionally, complete records older than two years were not available, and only a partial audit trail could have been traced. By limiting the scope of the investigation, I was able to focus on providing clear and logical findings to the grand jury and thereby not overcomplicating the case.

About the Author

J. Aaron Christopher is a Certified Fraud Examiner and Certified Public Accountant. While serving as an FBI Special Agent, he investigated a wide range of crimes from bank robberies and murder fugitives to public corruption and embezzlement. He is currently an assistant professor of business at California Baptist University in Riverside, California. He can be reached at aaron@christophercpa.com.

CHAPTER 19

A Sweet Deal

JASON PETRUSIC

Normally when people think of M&Ms, they picture those innocuous, multicolored chocolate candies and the animated characters used to advertise them. For five managers at Lumbergh Hospitality Group (LHG), however, M&Ms represented a kickback that was a gateway to other illegal activities. Because of weakened economic conditions, many companies were forcing employees to complete more work with less staff and resources. This situation is often a formula for disaster that generally includes a lack of duty segregation and decision-making responsibilities. At LHG, a company that was not immune to this problematic business model, M&Ms represented a selfish act of gratification that ultimately shattered management's trust in its employees.

Brenda Magee was a charismatic, visionary manager capable of inspiring employees to follow her as if she was the Pied Piper. But I always got used-car-salesman vibes from her for some reason. She was nice to me when I would come by for routine reviews and tell me what I wanted to hear, but I felt certain that as soon as I was gone she was bad-mouthing me behind my back.

Brenda was seen as the alpha staff member at Lumbergh, not only because of her tenure but also because of her close relationship with the owner, Eugene. Add the fact that she won more awards than anyone else in the company, and it was as if she could do no wrong. If you wanted to succeed at Lumbergh, Brenda was the one to emulate.

Brenda's direct reports were Tiffany Grubb and Sheila Stoker. Tiffany was a jolly, outgoing assistant manager who was willing to please to fit into the group. Sheila was nearly ten years younger than Tiffany and was easily influenced by others due to her eagerness to learn the hotel business.

Katie Thompson was another longer-tenured manager at Lumbergh, and she was responsible for LHG's sister property across the street from Brenda's. Working for her was John Butterworth, a newer assistant manager who was quickly climbing the managerial ladder that would assuredly have him overseeing his own property one day. John and Tiffany became close friends since they both had the same responsibilities in the two hotels. If one was unable to work or take a deposit to the bank, the other would gladly cover.

All five employees got along well, spending time together not only at work but also at happy hours and weekend activities.

Brenda, though, was not always the easiest person to get along with since she thought she was above answering questions from anyone other than her immediate supervisors. Anytime someone at corporate needed information from her, she *might* have it for them within a week . . . if at all. Besides her disrespect for outside subordinates, there were a few instances when her integrity and business ethics were called into question, particularly regarding some of the awards she won. As a manager, though, she treated her employees like they were her own children, going to any length to protect them, even from corporate questioning.

Inspiring Company History

Lumbergh Hospitality Group (LHG) was founded by Eugene Lumbergh after he received a small inheritance from his deceased parents, but his rise to power did not come easy. For as long as he could remember, Eugene had a job — from cutting lawns to delivering morning newspapers, even dog-sitting the neighbors' pets. His parents instilled a strong work ethic in him at a young age and taught him to appreciate his coworkers, regardless of their responsibilities, in the hope that he would one day become a successful leader.

His hospitality experience started while he was still in high school, working as a busboy at a local conference center. After graduation, he took a night shift position at a hotel so he could go to community college during the day and earn his associate's degree in hospitality management. Thereafter, Eugene began working the front desk during the day and was soon promoted to front desk manager, then general manager, regional manager, and finally vice president. It truly was a feel-good story of an employee working his way to the top after starting in one of the lowest positions in the company.

Upon receiving the inheritance, Eugene left his employer and put all of his money into financing his own hotel. From there, he expanded his business model by building or acquiring the 18 hotels the company currently manages.

LHG became synonymous with excellence. In the company's 30 years of existence, it earned more than 250 prestigious awards for exceptional levels of service and quality. The main reason the company was able to continue its success year after year was its heavy reliance on succession planning, which increased the pool of experienced and capable employees who were prepared to assume roles as they become available.

Because it had a slew of enthusiastic hospitality professionals who began the grooming process the moment they took entry-level jobs, the company was able to save time and money by looking internally to fill available positions. A problem with this business model arose when individuals were inadequately trained and developed an attitude of "that's how it's always been." Such thinking developed negative traits and habits in the staff that were passed from one manager to the next.

LHG's corporate headquarters were based in Lumbergh's hometown of Geistown, Pennsylvania, with the 18 hotels spread throughout the mid-Atlantic region. Each property had five primary managers who were responsible for the day-to-day operations. All other support functions, such as accounting, treasury, accounts payable, and taxes, were completed at the corporate headquarters.

Open Communication and Odd Phone Calls

I was employed with LHG for eight years, primarily functioning as the company's internal auditor, but I frequently was asked to help with other financial and accounting tasks due to turnover. Because of this, I was unable to focus on my primary responsibilities of updating, maintaining and ensuring compliance with the company's policies and procedures. To some degree, I believe the operational managers knew that and began taking advantage of my situation by constantly pushing the envelope on how much they could get away with. Pamela McElroy, however, was not one of these managers.

Pamela and I started working for LHG around the same time, but I was in the corporate office while she was a hotel manager in the operational field. We got to know each other by working on a special remote assignment where I was conducting a weeklong field audit and she was filling in for another manager on disability. After the assignment, it was commonplace for us to call each other when we wanted to know something that we didn't have access to in our positions. We were always respectful about not pushing each other for information but maintained an open line of communication that proved to quite beneficial. In fact, I might not have found out about this unique scheme had Pamela not notified me.

It was a warm morning in late November when I received a call from Pamela informing me of some unusual phone calls/voicemails she recently received from Gibbons, a California-based office-supply vendor. Not only was she confused as to why this vendor was persistently calling her — since LHG had a corporate account through a major supplier — but she was also concerned about *how* they were trying to obtain her business. She was told that if she were to order anything from them, particularly reams of paper, she would receive a three-pound bag of plain or peanut M&Ms. However, if she were to order eight reams, she would receive two more bags of M&Ms for free, as well as a $50 gift card to a retail store of her choice.

She tried to avoid speaking with the vendor directly, but whenever she got stuck on the phone with them, she declined the business proposition. She felt something wasn't right about the situation, and she knew there were at least 27 reams of paper in the back office when she took over as assistant manager (a fact that had puzzled her up until she started receiving the phone calls). After saying no to salespeople multiple times, Gibbons' manager, William Harmon, called Pamela and offered different gift-card incentives to gain her business.

The vendor's persistence worried Pamela because she suspected she had stumbled upon something untoward that her coworkers were involved in. She knew LHG had both a strict ethical policy (each employee had to sign a statement that they are not involved in any type of illegal, unethical business activity of any kind) and a conflict-of-interest policy stating employees were not permitted to use company resources for personal gain. After I received her call that day and took down the facts, I thought to myself, "I hope this is one of those isolated incidents that don't require further investigation." I was wrong.

The first step I took was determining how many times managers had purchased paper from Gibbons. After reviewing the general ledger, I discovered that the vendor was used nearly 200 times in three years by five different hotels.

Because the hotels were spread throughout the mid-Atlantic region, LHG used a document scanning program to catalog invoices. Each hotel was responsible for coding their invoices and sending them to the centralized accounts payable department. After a clerk entered an invoice in the general ledger system, the invoice would be saved into a master data file. Because of this, my next step of retrieving the purchases in question and reviewing them didn't take as much time as I thought it would.

I've spent my entire professional career in corporate offices rather than in the operational field, so I had no idea how much paper the hotels used on a daily, weekly and monthly basis. I needed this information to determine whether the purchases from Gibbons were excessive. I also had to find out if the purchasing methods in question were acceptable by company standards. Due to the volume of daily purchases the hotel personnel had to make, the general managers also served as their properties' purchasing managers. For large purchases, such as air conditioners or washing machines, a corporate headquarters purchasing manager was used to better leverage vendor pricing. Each general manager was also given an approved list of vendors to use to buy smaller items to ensure that the company as a whole received the best prices possible.

I spoke with both the corporate purchasing manager and a few other trusted general managers to get their input. Based on their feedback, I determined that the five hotels in question were ordering approximately double the amount of paper needed. By themselves, the transactions didn't seem altogether out of the ordinary, but when compared to other hotels' usage, it seemed clear that Gibbons and the five managers were not acting in the company's best interests.

I did not want the suspects to get wind of my investigation — they could have contacted Gibbons and warned the staff not to speak to me — so I communicated my findings only to my immediate supervisor and Matt Pinkerton, a trusted vice president who had tipped me off to fraud schemes in the past. Matt was a well-respected confidant within the company and was great at keeping his ears to the ground and his mouth (generally) shut regarding most of what he heard. Sometimes it seemed like employees confided in him if, deep down, they may have wanted to be caught.

The Insider's Deal

One day, Matt and I — disguising ourselves as a new general manager/assistant general manager team working for another LHG hotel — made a pretext call to William Harmon directly. We thought our background story would make Harmon think we already knew of the scheme and encourage him to extend the standard offer to us.

"Hi, Mr. Harmon, this is Matt Farva and Bob Slydell. We're two newer managers working for the Morgantown Sleepytime Inn."

"Hi, Matt, Bob. Please call me Bill. What can I do for you today?"

"Well, Bill, we recently got back from a managers meeting at Lumbergh Hospitality Group's corporate office. At the meeting, we met a few people that you might know — Brenda Magee, Tiffany Grubb, Sheila Stoker, Katie Thompson and John Butterworth — among others.

"Oh, yeah, I know them."

"They were telling us about a great deal you were able to give them on their paper purchases. Could you please tell us more about that?"

"Oh, absolutely! Aren't those guys and gals great?! I'll have to send them each a little something extra for you contacting me. Glad to hear you mention them since we want to make sure only our special clients receive this discount. How much paper are we talking about here?"

"You tell us, we aren't sure how much we need to order to receive discounts or any other perks you might be able to offer."

"Here's what I can do for you guys. If you order a case of paper from me right now at $50, I'll send you a free bag of M&Ms."

"A little bag of M&Ms?"

"No, no, no. A five-pound bag. You know, the kind that should last a month but is generally gone in a week."

"Oh, okay. That's cool. Plain or peanut [kiddingly]?"

"Whatever you guys want, I'm here to help you out and hopefully get us some business as well. Just want to make sure we keep this between us so no one gets in trouble with the corporate personnel, if you know what I mean."

"Absolutely, we'll keep this to ourselves; however, we might want to tell some other managers once we get to know them better so they can take part of this great deal you have going on. What if we order more than one case?"

"Glad you asked, and I'll bet Brenda or Tiffany was the one who mentioned that deal. They take advantage of this all the time. Okay, so if you order three cases of paper at one time, not only will I send you a bag of M&Ms for each case, I'll send you a $50 gift card to a retailer of your choice. It's like buying three cases of paper and getting one for free, even though you're the one receiving the benefits."

"Really?"

"Oh yeah, if you want Wal-Mart, I'll get you Wal-Mart. If you want a store like JCPenney, I'll get you a JCPenney gift card. It's the least I can do for you buying your paper directly from me instead of a big-name store."

"Wow, that's great. This just keeps getting better and better. Okay, one question though: how do we keep this under the radar so a paper purchase of three cases doesn't raise a red flag with management?"

"What I've been doing with Brenda, Tiffany and those other managers is this: if you buy at least three cases within a month, I'll still send you a $50 gift card. So you can buy one case here and there so as to not draw attention to what's really going on."

"Great."

"I know, right? I've been working with Brenda for some time now and told her I'm trying to get more and more of your hotels to buy their paper products from us. We're looking to diversify our business in the future, but we're still trying to build our clientele, and hopefully this is one way we can do that."

"Well, Bill, this all sounds great. Let us look over what we have and we'll get back to you with an order here shortly."

"Great, guys. Looking forward to doing business with you."

We hung up the phone in disbelief but knew we had what we needed.

Small but Significant Outcome

There was no way to prove how many of the approximate 200 transactions warranted a gift card being received by the manager. Looking through the invoices again, I estimated that there would have been nearly 120 instances where a manager would have received a $50 gift card. This $6,000 is probably far less than most of the other cases in this book; however, not only were the managers overpaying for each case by approximately $10 to $15, but a certain level of trust that LHG used to have in its managers was now shattered over free M&Ms and retail gift cards.

I was the one who had to personally break the news to Eugene. I knew this was going to be tough since he and Brenda had such a long relationship. I knew he wasn't going to believe me at first, so I had Matt come with me since he had known Eugene almost as long as Brenda had. The news upset Eugene so much that he had to excuse himself and get some fresh air. Once he composed himself, Eugene immediately called a meeting with the corporate management team to inform them of the situation.

Brenda, Tiffany, John, Sheila and Katie were each called into the corporate office over a three-day period and interviewed. Initially both Brenda and Tiffany denied knowing anything about the M&Ms or the gift cards, but after some harder questioning by Eugene, both admitted to the M&Ms and acted like receiving them was no big deal. When asked if they received anything else, they both said no.

Eugene simply asked them, "What about the gift cards?"

Both literally had the same reaction: "oh . . . those." It must have enraged Eugene to think that two of his most trusted managers tried to get something past him. Brenda claimed she gave them to her employees for going above and beyond expectations. Tiffany said she used them toward purchases, such as lunches, that directly benefited her employees. By that point, though, Eugene didn't believe a word either of them said.

Within a week, after multiple consultations with human resources, Brenda's termination was communicated to LHG. Three days later, Tiffany's was released as well. Both terminations were announced as resignations; however, additional memos were sent out regarding immediate changes to purchasing procedures and policies, as well as a notification for no hotel to use Gibbons for its paper needs. It was clear to everyone at LHG what had happened.

When asked, the other three managers came clean about both the M&Ms and gift cards immediately. When we asked how they found out about the kickback program, it was clear that the trail started with Brenda, went to Tiffany and then forked out to the other three managers. Katie left the company on her own within a month after the first two announcements. A few months after that, John was found swapping bank deposit cash with accounts receivable checks and was terminated immediately. Sheila is still employed with LHG and is still trying to regain the trust management once had in her.

After this case, LHG made some changes to the purchasing function at individual hotels. All purchases have to be made from a list of approved vendors — no exceptions. Two signatures are required on all purchase orders, those of the purchasing agent and their immediate supervisor.

Lessons Learned

Don't place excessive trust in employees. The typical occupational fraud is committed by a middle-age white male in a management position. Even though the majority of the perpetrators in this case were female, they certainly fit the other two criteria and showed that even the most trusted employee can defraud a company if given the right set of circumstances.

Investigate until satisfied. My initial inquiries led nowhere, not only because people weren't willing to give me the answers I was looking for but also because I did not know enough about the subject I was investigating. My persistence opened avenues that led to the discovery of the fraud.

People look out for their own interests. I'm constantly baffled at how fraudulent and criminal minds can justify their immoral actions as if what they're doing is okay. We as humans differ from animals in that we have reasoning to know right from wrong. When someone blurs that distinction, bad things can happen.

Review the no-brainers. Before something like this ever happened, simple checks and balances, such as reviewing vendor validity, should have taken place.

Recommendations to Prevent Future Occurrences

Maintain open lines of communication and confidentiality. Had I not had an open professional relationship with Pamela, she probably wouldn't have called and told me about the odd calls she received from Gibbons. More than likely, an employee who feels disconnected from either management or corporate personnel will say, "That's not my problem. Let someone else deal with it." During my initial conversation with Pamela, I told her that I was going to look into the situation but promised that her name would not come up as the source of information. The peace of mind that comes when employees feel they are free to communicate is priceless.

Install an anonymous hotline to properly handle whistleblower phone calls. A proper channel for employees to report suspicious activity has been proven as one of the first and foremost methods of uncovering fraud. A company can have all the policies and procedures in place, and internal audits and risk assessments can be done regularly, but if criminals want to circumvent the rules, they'll find a way. You need your entire staff helping you uncover frauds.

Centralize the purchasing department. A single accounts payable clerk who reviews each invoice will be able to spot one-off vendors possibly being used for personal gain. This recommendation is based on a high level of trust with said clerk, and, as my case has shown, that level should have limits. Not only could that lone clerk enter invoices for his or her own benefit, but what's to stop a rogue manager from contacting the clerk and striking up a deal to allow certain types of invoices to be processed without question, thus giving the clerk some sort of kickback for his or her services?

A way to prevent this corruption is to have the clerk's supervisor review the approved invoices as well.

Sometimes, depending on the company, centralizing a purchasing department is not feasible. In that case, limit the number of vendors that purchasing agents can order from. This will at least ensure that all vendors should have undergone a thorough vetting.

Finally, review those little odd purchases that simply don't make sense in the back of your mind. I did numerous monthly reviews and had run across Gibbon before. I had an odd feeling about the company but didn't think much of it because multiple LHG branches were using it. I assumed the managers were permitted to make purchases from Gibbon; otherwise, someone higher ranking than I would have said something.

In my mind, the entire incident wasn't so much about the gift cards or the M&Ms; it was about the trust that was destroyed by such a petty kickback. To me, if the corrupt managers were willing to risk their jobs over such trivial items, then what wouldn't they do when it came time to make bigger financial decisions?

About the Author

Jason Petrusic has been working as an accountant and internal auditor for more than 12 years. Along with his ever-growing work experience, his M.B.A. from Penn State University has given him the technical and quantitative skills necessary to successfully handle and deal with fraud. He owes his success to the overwhelming support of his wife and two children. This is Jason's first written publication.

Da' Money

MICHAEL CARR

Dan's downfall was "bling" — specifically, a $14,000 customized Cadillac golf cart. Dan was a purchasing manager for a manufacturing company in the Fortune 500's Top 10 companies. He routinely sourced millions of dollars for goods and services and, ultimately, couldn't resist grabbing an extra slice of the good life himself.

Dan was relatively young for his position, in his early 30s, but he was experienced in purchasing. He was a college graduate, had three young children and a wife, and — I would soon find out — a magnificent new home. He was well spoken, competent, and charming. Dan had risen quickly through the ranks, receiving good reviews along the way. As I came to discover, he was well liked by his managers and peers at work and enjoyed a good party. He also had a reputation for generosity. In fact, he apparently spent so freely that his peers took to calling him "Da' Money."

Dan's company was a vast, international group that sourced contracts that measured costs and revenues in billions. Mammoth, Inc., had a couple hundred thousand employees and had been around for decades. It was big, period.

To its credit, Mammoth had, over the years, adopted a comprehensive set of internal controls. Management had books full of published procedures, some followed more closely than others. Controls were critical as Mammoth shelled out billions each year for goods and services by its huge purchasing group. After all, it was battling against the oft-heard response: "but it's only a million dollars."

In purchasing specifically, Mammoth balanced risks with a series of controls that governed the groups' ability to spend money. Each employee had a specific limit on the dollars that he or she could authorize per transaction, per supplier and in a given period. But with big spending comes rather lofty limits. For instance, Dan, as a first-line manager, had a spending limit of $1 million per transaction. That is, he could spend $1 million at a time without approval from any higher authority. He also had a $5 million per supplier limit on spending without referral to his manager.

A Quick Review

The first sign of trouble for Mammoth, and then Dan, came during a routine internal audit at one of the North American manufacturing plants. While reviewing invoices for goods and services received by the plant, auditors noticed curious supporting documentation affixed to invoices from an electrical parts supplier, Acme. The documents listed services of a type outside Acme's area of expertise. For example, on one invoice Acme had billed Mammoth for painting.

After additional on-site review, internal audit was unable to resolve the apparent inconsistency. Uncomfortable leaving the matter unresolved, the audit manager, Kelly, turned it over to Mammoth's corporate investigations staff, of which I am part.

Given that we had significantly more referrals than could be investigated, my first task was to quickly assess the viability of the information. If it didn't show signs of fraud early, it got tossed in the heap of tips that would not be pursued.

"Quickly" didn't allow for visits to the supplier or the plant or even interviews of employees. It allowed only for a high-level data review. So I began by pulling the purchasing records involving Acme.

Quite simply I organized a spreadsheet with date, supplier/subsupplier, purchase type, amount and Mammoth's purchasing agent. After putting the data in chronological order, a few facts jumped from the spreadsheet. First, the work sourced to Acme had increased dramatically over the past two years — nearly tripling each year. Second, Acme, an electrical supplier, was billing for a wide variety of work outside its area of expertise. And third, the sourcing seemed to be migrating to a single purchasing agent — Dan.

It appeared I was going to take on a new case.

Developing an Investigation

I developed a preliminary fraud hypothesis and investigative plan. Given that it was a "purchasing case" and from the nature of the data I'd seen thus far, the standard hypothesis was that our employee, Dan, was improperly sourcing work to a supplier, Acme, in exchange for something of value. It was already clear, of course, that Dan was sourcing work to Acme, but whether this was being done in exchange for something of value to Dan remained to be seen. Without the "for something of value," I couldn't show the evil intent necessary to support a significant adverse employee action or a possible finding of fraud.

As for the investigative plan, I merely listed the likely productive steps to pursue in a logical order. Typical of a case like this, I intended to first examine any internal sources of information, then turn to vendors and other external sources and finally interview Dan. Admittedly, I'd learned long ago that all this was subject to change as information was developed that supported or debunked the investigative hypothesis or turned it in a totally unanticipated direction.

With a hypothesis and plan, my next step seemed obvious: visit the scene of the crime. Less dramatically stated, a trip to the plant to meet with employees who actually received the goods and services from Acme seemed prudent.

Saying that employees aren't generally thrilled by a visit from corporate investigations is a major understatement. This time, however, they seemed to welcome a chance to voice their sincerely held concerns. The employees weren't happy with Mammoth's new purchasing strategy, which employed far fewer suppliers. Acme, they explained, was one of the suppliers that survived the winnowing process, but they said those actually performing the work hadn't really changed. From the employee perspective, the same suppliers the plant had always used were still doing the work; now they were just routing their invoices through Acme.

With that in mind, I reviewed a sample of Acme invoices. It did appear that Acme was using Mammoth's old vendors as subcontractors. It wasn't obvious that Mammoth was paying more now for the same services, but it could be checked. It also wasn't clear that, even if Mammoth was paying more, it violated any policy.

Leaving the plant's noise and heat behind, I walked to my car with a better understanding of the concerns expressed by the internal auditor and the employees, as well as a fuller picture of the players and processes. But the question of fraud still loomed, so I decided to dig a little deeper into our internal records.

Back at the office, as I looked further into the purchasing details, it did appear that Acme was merely marking up and passing through invoices for others' work. Historically Mammoth frowned upon pass-through invoicing, but suppliers occasionally were used as a conduit to other suppliers for efficiency or expertise gains. In those cases a small markup was allowed. The painting invoice that we've been using as an example had an 18 percent markup. But was I witnessing inefficiency or intentional misconduct? A clue appeared in the data trending. During the past two years, Dan had taken over 80 percent of the sourcing to Acme. More important, Dan had sourced to Acme all of the purchases that seemed outside the vendor's expertise.

From the Plant to the Corner Office

Certainly this trend suggested a lead to pursue, but there could easily be an innocent explanation. It was time to set aside the data and do some talking.

So off I went to meet with the director of purchasing for this commodity, Jamie Lewis.

Nursing a morning coffee in Jamie's eighth-floor corner office, I learned that the company was actively consolidating the number of suppliers and willing to tolerate those working somewhat outside their area of expertise. These suppliers were a "conduit" to subsuppliers and were permitted a small markup, generally 2 to 3 percent. This was offset by anticipated efficiency gains at Mammoth. Related to that, Jamie explained, the purchasing department had experienced significant staff reductions and reorganization.

As I rode down the elevator after the meeting, I realized I might be chasing nothing at all. The new company mandates could explain the trend I had seen relative to Dan taking on a lion's share of the sourcing and expanding the supplier's work into new areas. It was tempting to close the file at this point, but there was still that 18 percent markup.

High-level data and discussion of company policy would only take me so far. It was time to dig into the record details. I needed the electronic files that purchasing maintained for every vendor, in this case Acme. They would contain the details that supported negotiations and sourcing decisions — information that was both confidential and critical to purchasing controls. To avoid raising suspicions within purchasing, I funneled the request through my internal audit contact, Kelly. She had direct access to all purchasing files and could copy entire files for my review without alerting anyone.

Suffice it to say, my fraud antennae sprang back into action when Kelly dropped by my office and explained that there were absolutely no electronic purchasing files for the work Dan sourced to Acme during the past two years.

Kelly and I agreed that this certainly appeared incriminating, but it seemed equally odd that Dan's manager would allow this lack of supporting files. I thought I'd better get some clarification. Back to see Jamie Lewis, the director. Lewis vacillated, explaining that, while it was policy to maintain the electronic files, it wasn't rigidly enforced. A purchasing agent or manager might be "old school" and maintain paper files only.

Leaving the building, I acknowledged that Lewis wasn't turning out to be much help, and I still wanted to see the file detail. My next step seemed obvious: an after-hours visit to Dan's company office to review the old-school files.

I quietly entered Dan's office on a Saturday evening with my laptop and a very large cup of coffee. I was prepared to spend most of the night reviewing files. An hour later, I left with nothing. Dan, it turned out, was old school. He did maintain clearly labeled file cabinets and folders. They were organized alphabetically by supplier and in chronological order by transaction. There were, however, no files for Acme. Nothing.

This finding was a mixed blessing. On one hand, it suggested Dan might be intentionally avoiding documentation. On the other, it meant I had no evidence. This was beginning to get frustrating. The investigation was generating more questions than answers. Of course, I had an apparent policy violation in the lack of records, but this was a fraud examination.

Computer Forensic Review

I decided to change my focus. I would put the data aside and see if I could get some insight into the relationship between Dan and Acme. I knew from experience that understanding such a relationship is often best accomplished by a review of e-mail and the employee's computer. So I put in a request for copies of Dan's computer and e-mail files. Once they were received, I began to sort through the data, slowly piecing together a profile of Dan and pulling out a few very interesting nuggets.

First, the e-mail files helped outline Dan's personality. For instance, there were e-mails thanking Dan for picking up the group's tab at what sounded like a very swanky restaurant. Second, there was an e-mail in which Dan shared a picture of an elaborate landscaping project, complete with cascading waterfall, currently under way at his magnificent new house. I also noted with particular interest that his colleagues, in casual e-mails, referred to him as "Da Money."

I came away with the strong impression that Dan had money and liked to spend it.

The computer forensic review was also productive, turning up a most intriguing image of a customized golf cart. It was customized to look like a bright red Cadillac — very cool! And it appeared the picture was taken in a residential driveway. Pulling Dan's home address from company records and sticking it in Google Earth confirmed that it was most likely Dan's house in the golf cart and waterfall pictures.

Mammoth's computer wizards also recovered a link to a website called Exotic Carts that Dan had visited. Fortunately for me, both the link and the golf cart image were recovered from unallocated space on the hard drive using specialty forensic tools. They had been deleted. I clicked to the Exotic Carts website and saw photos of an amazing assortment of flashy, customized golf carts. The quality, creativity and price tags were amazing. Nothing was less than $10,000.

So I'd gotten a picture of Dan as a free spender, and it fit into my working theory that he funneled extra work to Acme in exchange for something of value, but that fell short of proof of misconduct.

Sometimes It Really Is That Easy

I wondered what Exotic Carts' records might reveal — if they would even speak to me. Only one way to tell. I punched in the company phone number and simply explained that I was trying to confirm the purchase by Dan of a customized red Cadillac golf cart. I provided Dan's name and address, and the helpful sales clerk put me on hold while she checked their computer records. "No purchase by anyone named Dan," she said. Oh well, it had been a long shot. But, she added, the company did deliver a customized cart to the address I had provided. A red Cadillac! The customer was listed as Acme.

Home run! I was gaining traction — I had a link.

At this point, I stopped and assessed what I'd learned. Purchasing records showed that Acme's work with Mammoth was growing significantly and expanding into areas outside its expertise. This was due primarily to Dan, who appeared to be a free spender and had little interest in keeping records about Acme. And I had a direct link between Dan and Acme that appeared unrelated to legitimate business — the red Cadillac golf cart.

Interesting, but still not a slam-dunk case. Where could I find more proof?

I had learned an important lesson over the years. Invariably, when suppliers gave a gift to a Mammoth employee, they billed it back to Mammoth in some form. And, equally as important, they always keep a record because they take it off their expenses. Thus, the Rule: suppliers never eat the cost of a gift, and it's reflected in their records — if you can get to them. I knew it was time to visit Acme.

And Other Times It's Not

I got the name of Dan's contact at Acme, Enrique, and called for an appointment. The next afternoon we met at Acme's local headquarters. Enrique, the general manager, was very cordial and seemed to have intimate knowledge of his company's business with Mammoth. Fending off Enrique's attempts to ascertain the exact issue, I made a request for some fairly sweeping record pulls from Acme's accounts payable and receivable systems. Enrique excused himself and went to get the accounting person to generate the requested records. At this point, I was gauging Acme's response to my visit as much as seeking specific records.

Enrique seemed to be gone a long time, and I wasn't surprised when he returned and informed me that the electronic accounting system was experiencing some technical difficulties. He assured me he had the company's IT guy on it, and he would soon have my records. As we chatted over a cup of coffee, I asked for the hard copy records supporting two specific invoices Acme had recently submitted. Enrique called in a member of his staff and directed her to pull the documents.

I had selected these invoices specifically because they appeared to be perfectly legitimate and I suspected Enrique would be able to find them.

Enrique and I continued to bemoan the recent dismal performance of the local baseball team until his staff member returned shortly with the invoices. When she did, I apologized profusely for my oversight and asked — while the staff person was still in the room — for supporting documents for two more recent Acme invoices. Enrique assured me it was no problem and left with his employee.

These last two invoices were different. I chose them because they were larger dollars and vague in description. I suspected they might have room to hide a gratuity. Enrique returned and explained that Acme had recently closed another office building and shipped all of the records from that building to a storage site. These invoices must be in storage. It would take a few days to retrieve them.

In a nutshell, that's how the rest of my visit went with Acme. Enrique was polite but seemed to have trouble finding the records of most interest to me. I left with nothing but a promise to call when they found the records and fixed their computers.

Driving back to the office, I felt confident that Enrique was concealing something. That was good; it meant Acme had maintained the incriminating records. The fact that they couldn't find them, in a way, was music to my ears. The Rule appeared to be holding true.

While I waited for Acme's call, I decided to firm up the evidence linking Dan and the custom Cadillac golf cart. According to Exotic's records, Dan's house was the delivery point, but what had become of the Cadillac?

As it was a rather sunny day and the office was getting stuffy, a direct approach seemed in order. Google Earth showed that Dan lived in an upscale, new-construction subdivision, just a few blocks off a lake. A short drive to Dan's neighborhood and a conversation with an older lady out walking her cat confirmed the gift. "Sure," she said, "Dan's got that obnoxious golf cart. He's always showing off running back and forth to the lake." A quick peek through the window of Dan's garage confirmed the story.

A few days later, I got a message that Acme had some records ready, and I made an appointment to stop by. Coincidentally, perhaps, Acme's owner, Donna Strong, was also at the office. During my visit, we spoke in general terms about the importance of integrity in business and having confidence in one's business partners. She fully agreed. "Was there anything Acme wanted Mammoth to know about our business relationship?" I asked. "Nothing," Strong assured me.

Taking the records back to the office, I wasn't sure what, if anything, I'd find in them. So I just jumped in. I simply started backtracking each invoice or line item that didn't immediately make sense. After a bit, I found an interesting subsupplier — Best Home Entertainment. Best had invoiced Acme $8,000 for an unspecified item. Acme passed the cost to Mammoth as part of a monthly invoice for assorted parts, which contained only Best's company name, a date and the total amount due.

An Internet check revealed that Best was a retail shop specializing in the installation of high-end residential entertainment equipment. I called Best to follow up and got completely shut down; the manager refused to provide any records or information.

It can't always be easy.

Undaunted, a few days later I drove out to visit Best's showroom. When I walked through the doors, the first person I encountered was a young salesperson. In response to her offer of help, I simply presented a copy of the Best invoice and pointed out the company had failed to detail the nature of the purchase. She quickly pulled the file and informed me it was a complete home entertainment package and installation. I pointed out that Acme wasn't a home and it didn't have, to my knowledge, any room with an entertainment package. I misunderstood, she explained. The installation occurred at a residence; Acme had simply paid the bill. Although I was reading it upside down, the delivery address on her work order looked familiar — Dan's house.

It was becoming pretty apparent that Da Money's relationship with Acme needed some explaining. So I called and made an appointment to meet again with Donna Strong, Acme's owner.

When I arrived, I was ushered into Strong's cluttered office and introduced to Acme's attorney, Phil Woods. I explained to them that I had some documentation that suggested Acme provided "something of value" to Mammoth's employee, Dan. They stammered a bit and then demanded to see my proof.

I declined, explaining I knew what had happened and was now interested in why. I offered a choice. Had Acme corrupted Mammoth's employee or vice versa? I stressed the importance of trust in the partnership between our companies while letting slip just enough facts to suggest that I had a good picture of the impropriety between Acme and Dan.

They asked for some time alone.

Complete Candor

Following a brief private discussion, Strong invited me back into her office. Standing tall, she announced Acme was through capitulating to Dan's demands and wanted to come clean. She produced records showing payments to a subsupplier for "consulting services." Maintaining my game face but smiling on the inside, I realized I had struck a new vein of gold. This subsupplier, 21st Tech, was a one-man firm owned by Dan. Acme's records showed it had made five payments to 21st Tech, totaling about $110,000.

Strong further explained that these periodic payments to Dan's company were to ensure the continued growth of Acme's work with Mammoth. In reality, Dan had done no consulting work for Acme. Strong assured me it was exclusively Dan's idea. Acme, she explained, felt trapped and capitulated only out of fear that Dan would stop using it as a vendor for Mammoth.

I expressed disappointment on behalf of Mammoth that our employee engaged in such conduct and asked if there was anything else we needed to discuss. Any other problems? "Nothing — that's all there is," she assured me. So much for complete candor, I thought as I walked to my car, picturing the custom red Cadillac golf cart in my mind. But I was definitely making progress.

Returning to the office, I reflected on another potential problem. The "consulting" paperwork didn't have any identifiers linking the firm to Dan. However, a quick check of the state's business incorporation records showed that Dan had incorporated 21st Tech about two years prior. Interestingly, the state also showed a second company incorporated by Dan — Engineering Excellence. I'd seen that name before on another Acme invoice.

Curious, I compared the dates of Acme's "consulting payments" to Dan against Mammoth's sourcing of work to Acme. It was readily apparent that Acme rewarded Dan shortly after Dan sourced a significant new project to Acme, a classic quid pro quo relationship in purchasing.

Admittedly, I felt pretty comfortable that the evidence was coming together solidly in support of the original investigative theory that Acme was providing Dan with something of value in exchange for contracts. But I still had unfinished business with both Acme and Dan. We didn't have it all on the table yet.

I wanted to take one more shot at Strong and her attorney. After all, they still hadn't owned up to the Cadillac golf cart, the home theater or Dan's second company. The tone of the second meeting was strikingly different from the first one. Only Acme's attorney, Phil Woods, participated in this meeting. All his documents were well organized and, I suspected, carefully screened, but he gave me records showing payments to both consulting companies, as well as the cart and home theater system. It had taken awhile, but we'd finally gotten complete candor — I think.

The Obstacle to a Confession

It was time to talk with Dan. I set up the interview and brought a partner. It turned out to be a marathon. Dan's tactic: deny, deny, deny. I dipped deep into my toolbox of techniques taught at interview schools and still nothing. Dan had his heels so deeply dug in he was plowing furrows in the title floor.

Even in the face of compelling documentation and Acme statements, Dan continued to deny. I paused; there was something keeping Dan from confessing. But what was it? I put aside the facts and began to probe for the obstacle. Soon Dan grew quiet; he was thinking. And then he offered, "I'm not worried about my job; it's done. But there are some things I don't want the IRS to know."

I explained that we weren't working for the IRS but simply resolving an employee/vendor issue. There were several more minutes of silence, and we simply waited. With his head down, Dan was clearly looking inward. And then he began talking. He eventually acknowledged everything we suspected.

To wrap it up, we asked Dan to write a statement explaining, in his words, what had happened. Dan initially declined but eventually agreed to sign one produced by my partner, who had fortunately taken extensive notes.

We had it all: documentary proof, Acme's statements and a signed statement from Dan.

The case was solved but the work far from over. Now it was time for reports and meetings to present our findings to human resource and purchasing management. In the end, Dan's employment was terminated for violating Mammoth's code of conduct regarding gifts.

Dan's direct manager had some explaining to do while sheepishly acknowledging he was aware that Dan was "always going to lunch with suppliers" and that his peers called him "Da Money," an apparent reference to his flashy spending and lifestyle. But he held on to his position. As for Acme, we realized it was a replaceable vendor and Mammoth no longer required its services.

Lessons Learned

Looking back, it was easy to see there were two significant gaps in the control environment that allowed this inappropriate behavior to flourish. First, management oversight was seriously lacking. Jamie's failure to monitor and note that Dan maintained none of the required purchasing files was truly egregious. Management should have periodically reviewed the files, although an automated alert system tied to purchases made without a corresponding electronic file would serve better.

Additionally, management should have picked up on Dan's flashy behavior and excessive lunches. Arguably, the lunches were a minor policy violation. However, in an environment like purchasing, they are often the first indicator of a general disregard for policy, which can lead to more serious violations — such as bribery and extortion.

The second gap was Mammoth's failure to account for the impact that downsizing personnel and consolidating work would have on the control environment. This change resulted in higher spending thresholds, fewer file reviews and more autonomy for buyers. Mammoth failed to provide clear guidance and controls in the new operating environment.

Fortunately, while Mammoth's preventive and detective controls failed in this instance, the second-line fraud defenses held. Mammoth's routine internal auditing of the always-risky purchasing cycle unearthed the suspicious activity, and the auditor followed our escalation process to pursue matters that could not be resolved.

I used those tried and true tools in the fraud examiner's toolbox to crack this case. Analyzing internal purchasing data with readily available software, searching public records online, performing site visits to review original paperwork and employing the interview techniques taught by experienced professionals all proved — once again — to be reliable pathways to the truth.

And, I'm pleased to say, the Rule held up. Acme didn't pay for Dan's bribes and kickbacks; they were on the invoices submitted to Mammoth. In the end, no one won. Dan got greedy, his manager got sloppy and the supplier either conspired with or acquiesced to clearly inappropriate conduct.

Recommendations to Prevent Future Occurrences

There are steps any company can take to minimize the risk of corruption, such as:

- Promote an ethical culture.
- Enforce the code of conduct.
- Ensure active management oversight within operations.
- Utilize automated alerts.
- Have an escalation process for investigating unusual activity.
- Clearly communicate conduct expectations to suppliers.
- Have a mechanism for suppliers to anonymously report ethics concerns.

Collectively, these controls help safeguard company assets and might help prevent the next employee and supplier from slipping into fraudulent behavior and losing his or her livelihood. I suspect it was just too easy for Da' Money and Acme to conspire to defraud Mammoth.

About the Author

Michael Carr is an investigations manager, licensed attorney and adjunct college and police academy instructor in Michigan. Mike retired after 25 years in law enforcement and has been a manager in white-collar fraud investigations for the past ten years. As a proud Certified Fraud Examiner, Mike knows one can't substitute controls for integrity.

The Seemingly Upstanding Citizen

AUSTINE S. M. ADACHE

Jawu Bayamilada was a successful 55-year-old businessman who attended college in Zaria, Nigeria, and later enrolled in the London School of Economics to train as an administrator and economist. After fulfilling his duty to the Nigerian National Youth Service, he went into corporate private practice. A few years into his career, he accepted a position with Blue Sky Marketing, where he rose to marketing manager and later resigned to join the government.

His public career began with his employment as a senior administrative officer in the Management Commission. He later moved to the National Development Authority (NDA), where he served in different capacities and was later appointed director-general. Jawu was married to Munara, and their marriage was blessed with four children, Jana, Phalama, Junana, and Esasina.

Many of his colleagues heard Jawu philosophize over the years about his post-retirement goal "to retire but never to tire of public service." When he did retire, he wanted to go after his dream.

Jawu decided to run for an open senate spot in the Nigerian congress. He believed Nigerian politics were highly monetized, so he was prepared for intense electioneering during his campaign. As a prelude to his bid for office, he joined the Patriotic People's Party, the dominant party at the time. He started earning a favorable reputation with the local chapter by donating his time, money and expertise as a career administrator. News of Jawu Bayamilada's dedication to the party and skills spread up to the state offices, encouraging Jawu in his political aspirations.

Jawu's wife, Munara, began complaining about his increasing absences from the family and was completely against the idea of him venturing into politics. Every time the subject was discussed, they would end up in a heated argument. Still, Jawu hoped that, in time, Munara would support him.

Munara had always been a supportive wife and an excellent mother. She also worked as an accountant for a private business until she decided to apply her knowledge to her own endeavors. With the help of a dedicated staff, she opened and ran a successful boutique and salon. She received regular shipments of beauty products from foreign suppliers, which necessitated acquiring a large warehouse. Her local success had her contemplating expanding operations into other Nigerian states, particularly in the major cities.

As a senate hopeful, Jawu had envisioned a better and more respectable life for his family. The night before our encounter with him, he attended a late-night meeting of the party caucus to fine-tune his campaign strategy. The event ended in the wee hours of the morning. He had returned home and quickly fell asleep. He was still sleeping, deeply snoring, when there was a banging at his door.

This was the morning that my team and I had come to execute a warrant for search and arrest of the Bayamiladas. It was the culmination of intense, long weeks of discreet investigation.

Weeks Earlier

It was a beautiful Monday morning. It had rained heavily the night before and the weather, though clement, was misty and cloudy as if it might rain again.

I was an investigative detective with the Nigerian Economic and Financial Crimes Commission working under Alada Ayoja, head of the investigations unit. I was running late to the mandatory weekly briefing, wishing that traffic hadn't been heavier than normal. When I finally made it to the office, I rushed to the conference room while returning greetings to fellow staffers. I was sitting down just as Ayoja entered. The meeting was convened to review the department's previous assignments and to chart new courses of action for the week. It was also a forum to discuss challenging ongoing cases. At the end of the meeting, just as he was stepping out, Ayoja beckoned me. "Adache, see me immediately, please."

"Yes, sir," I replied. Over the years of working with him, I have come to understand that that means a high-priority summons.

When we got to his office, he asked me to sit down. He said that we had received a complaint against the recently retired director-general of the National Development Authority that suggested corruption. "I would like you to handle the investigation. I want a thorough and discreet job. Get started and keep me apprised of every step and development. Draw up your plan of action and let's review it together, please."

Getting the Ball Rolling

Once I got to my office, I looked through the petition file. It contained information, conjectures and allegations. The petitioner preferred anonymity. The gist of the complaint centered on corrupt enrichment, embezzlement and bribery involving Jawu Bayamilada. From the tone and the nature of some of the documents, it appeared that the anonymous whistleblower was an insider who was privy to confidential information.

The summary of the complaint was that Bayamilada:

- Corruptly enriched himself through contracts he awarded for the construction of the ultra-modern office complex of the new headquarters of the National Development Authority in Abuja
- Owned properties in the federal capital territory that ordinarily he could not have afforded as a public servant
- Operated proxy accounts in which stolen public funds were lodged
- Operated shell companies that were used to siphon public funds

After a careful study of the petition, I formed a mental picture of possible leads and approaches. As a matter of practice, especially for this kind of case, our suspects are our last stop after we have learned enough about the allegations against them. The goal was to use as much discretion as possible to obtain all the pertinent facts before confronting anyone.

I summoned my team members and briefed them on the contents of the anonymous petition. I instructed them to execute the investigation discreetly. We discussed all the leads, specifics and their verifiability. After careful evaluation, I came up with a plan of action. We ran through the plan and made a draft.

Once the case file was ready, I headed straight to Ayoja's office. We discussed the approach, and, after thoroughly scrutinizing each of the steps, he approved it for action.

Following the Money Trail

Preliminary checks were done on the addresses of the two properties mentioned in the petition. The first home turned out to be a newly renovated, semidetached duplex. There were no occupants except for a gatekeeper who seemed to know next to nothing about the owner of the property.

Without raising suspicion, we learned that the gatekeeper was hired a few months ago by the caretaker of the property and that the duplex was already being advertised for rent. This was confirmed by the advertising sign we saw hanging on the gate containing the name and contact information of the agent: Jabila Estate Agency. Before leaving, we photographically documented the building.

The second property was a beautifully landscaped compound with a terraced row of five three-bedroom houses. All the houses appeared to be occupied except for one. Posing as potential tenants, we found out that the building was owned by a company called Jamiyada Odula & Sons Limited and that it was originally meant for the staff of that company. But for some reason, the flats were rented to individuals. The caretaker's phone number was given to us.

After taking photographs of the building, we called the number and discovered that the caretaker was also from Jabila Estate Agency. The discovery was quite striking—the two properties were managed by the same company!

We wrote to the Corporate Affairs Commission to request information on Jabila Estate Agency and Jamiyada Odula & Sons Limited, both of which were registered companies. The first had been in existence for the past 15 years and seemed to be a reputable agency. When we were satisfied with that information, we turned our attention to Jamiyada Odula & Sons Limited. The company had been incorporated about a year and half ago with registered business activities of "general merchandizing." The directors had the same surname — Bayamilada — and Munara Bayamilada was the executive director. The other directors listed were Jana, Phalama, Junana and Esasina. After checking the address, we realized that it was a store or some sort of warehouse.

Meanwhile, we received information from the Abuja Geographical Information System Unit of the Federal Capital Development Authority about the properties in question. According to the databases, Mikartarbu Teki, managing director of MT Oil & Gas Ltd., and Polamali Jingir, a commercial farmer, were the owners of the two properties, respectively. We eventually traced and contacted both of them, and each confirmed to have sold his property to Jamiyada Odula & Sons Limited. Both of the transactions were facilitated by Jabila Estate Agency.

From the documents supplied by the Corporate Affairs Commission, we learned that Jamiyada Odula & Sons Limited held an account with Bond Bank. We requested the account details and statements. From studying them, we saw that the company maintained another account with a different bank to which money was often transferred. It had three withdrawals for the amounts of $500,000, $400,000, and $130,000 during the period we reviewed. One was to Mikartarbu Teki, the second to Polamali Jingir and the third to Labi Wajala. The last recipient turned out to be the head of the procurement unit of the National Development Authority. His account showed the money was still in it.

Munara Bayamilada was the sole signatory on the two accounts we traced to Jamiyada Odula & Sons Limited. There were disbursements that we traced to a foreign construction company, Sahenli Lisiona Limited (building and civil engineering contractors). Payments ranged from $130,000 to $160,000 within a year, totaling $1.6 million. Money to the Sahenli Company was traced to the capital expenditure account of the NDA at the Nigerian Central Bank.

At this stage, I paid a visit to the NDA to ask some questions. I met with the acting director-general, Pelmona Gidoin, a very perceptive man by my summation. He fully cooperated and was forthcoming with details, facts and documents when I requested background information regarding the relationship between the NDA and Sahenli Construction Company. He told me that, by the authority's records, Sahenli built the NDA's new office complex and conducted renovation work of the official residence of Bayamilada. Gidoin said that the total contract sum was $3.7 million. Incidentally, at the time of my visit, Wajala was on annual leave.

In one of our routine surveillances of the Bayamiladas' home, a new vehicle caught our attention. Their two cars that we knew about were a 1998 Camry and a rickety Mercedes. This one, a Toyota sport utility vehicle, looked brand new. We noted the plate number and ran it through the licensing unit of the Federal Road Safety Commission. The registration showed that the SUV was bought with a fleet of five others from Sana Danga Motors, a major Toyota dealer in Kaduna. The purchasing papers showed that it was bought in the name of Sahenli Construction Company but registered to Jawu Bayamilada.

Having traced the properties and accounts to Bayamilada, we requested the last asset declaration form he filed with the Code of Conduct Bureau at the NDA before he retired. Government officials were required by law to submit personal financial information every four years. Bayamilada's properties, company, accounts and SUV were conspicuously not included on the final declaration he had filed three months earlier.

Bringing the Investigation to the Suspects' Doorsteps

The eventual arrest of the Bayamiladas was preceded by the separate arrests of Labi Wajala and of Heinz Schmidt, the managing director of Sahenli Construction Company who represented the company during the negotiations of the whole conspiracy.

During the arrest of Schmidt, I read him his rights and allowed him to call his country's embassy. The embassy's legal attaché came and was briefed. We later officially wrote to the embassy to explain the circumstances of Schmidt's arrest. His travel documents and international passport were taken into custody.

After we showed them our findings during separate and intense interrogations, the three suspects admitted to using government funds for renovation work on Bayamilada's home and explained how they conspired to divert money to build a four-bedroom country home for Wajala — a fact we already knew.

Because of the evidence that we gathered and presented, their confessions came pretty easily. Bayamilada tried to defend his actions and deny wrongdoing, but to no avail. We had rock-solid evidence given the fact that we had the two properties' original documents, sale documents of the SUV, the SUV itself, the bank statements and the checkbook from which Wajala was issued the check for $130,000.

At my office, Jawu Bayamilada wept like a baby. "I am finished!" he cried. "I am finished! Oh! Oh my God, what have I gotten myself into?"

With these words, Bayamilada's confession was recorded. He pleaded that his wife should not be included as she was not privy to his wrongdoing and had no knowledge of it. He claimed that it was all his doing.

Following up the next day, armed with a warrant and accompanied by Wajala, we drove five hours from the capital to his country home to see the house that this scheme provided him. It was a four-bedroom home within the Wajala family compound and was complete except for the perimeter fencing. It was not furnished yet, but Wajala's younger brother was staying there as a caretaker.

As we were taking photographs of the home, we noticed that the garage was heavily padlocked, indicating something was in it. We demanded it be opened. Wajala claimed he did not have the key, so we forced it open and discovered a car covered with a tarp. Upon uncovering the vehicle, we saw that it was a brand-new SUV —just like the Bayamiladas' new car — with the factory polythene cover still on it. So Wajala was also a beneficiary of the SUV bribe.

At first he maintained it was a gift from a rich friend, but the engine number matched one from the fleet that Schmidt purchased with Sahenli funds. All our findings were appropriately documented, and the SUV was taken into custody to use as an exhibit.

Figuring Out the Jigsaw Puzzle

After weeks of painstaking investigation, culminating in the arrests of Bayamilada, Wajala and Schmidt, and their confessions, we had pieced together the jigsaw puzzle of the corruption case. The facts that emerged had brought to light the key components of this fraud:

- The federal board of National Development Authority approved the construction of its new office complex.
- The contract was awarded to Sahenli Construction Company for the sum of $3.6 million.
- Added to the contract was the renovation of the official residence of then director-general Bayamilada for the sum of $100,000, making the contract worth $3.7 million.
- Sahenli Construction Company "won" the contract through a bidding process facilitated by the procurement unit of the NDA, headed by Wajala.
- Before the contract was finalized, there were negotiations between Bayamilada and Wajala and the Saheli Company to inflate the contract

sum from $1.85 million (a possible bid price if they had done their due diligence) to $3.7 million — an increase of 100 percent —and to include the SUVs for Bayamilada and Wajala.

- The surplus funds from the contract were funneled to Bayamilada through his front company, Jamiyada Odula & Sons Limited, and used by the wife, Munara, to pay for her luxuriously furnished boutique and salon.
- The construction work commenced, and, as Sahenli Construction Company was paid in installments, remittances were accordingly made to Jamiyada Odula & Sons Limited. With these payments, the properties were bought and Wajala was paid his kickback of $130,000.

Awaiting Justice

I knew we had an airtight case against Bayamilada, Schmidt and Wajala. It was corruption that included conspiracy, bribery, diversion of public funds and money laundering. Once the case file was compiled, I sent it to our legal and prosecution unit. It was vetted and sent to court, where the three men are currently standing trial.

Through our legal unit, we successfully executed an ex parte application order to force the suspects to forfeit all the traced assets and properties to the federal government. In addition, we requested that the government blacklist Sahenli Construction Company. Our suggestion is currently under consideration, and government agents are reviewing the previous contracts it had with Sahenli.

As the investigation and arrests became public knowledge, we formally contacted the NDA and briefed it. The acting director-general pledged full cooperation and insisted that there be an internal investigation to ascertain the level of management involvement and inherent inadequacies within the system. He formally requested that we shine our searchlight on the NDA in this regard. To this end, I conducted a diagnostic review of the processes leading to the award of the contract. For a proper and clear approach, I restricted my checks to the operations of the procurement unit and the contracting process.

I examined the functioning of the unit in relation to the existing legislative framework and procedures laid out in the Public Procurement Act of 2007. I immediately noticed that the Procurement Planning Committee was chaired by Bayamilada and that Wajala was the secretary. Additionally, the committee was not fully staffed, and it did not meet the requirements of the law.

After a review of the processes leading to the award of the Sahenli contract, we saw that NDA did not have appropriate controls, fraud prevention strategies or proper bidding processes in place, making the system susceptible to corruption. It became easy for a cozy relationship to develop among bidders and between the contractor and government officials.

Consequently, we found evidence that the selection of Sahenli Construction Company was not done through competitive bidding. This evidence included the facts that:

- Adequate notice, as required by law, was not given between the time of the advertisement for prequalification tender and the submission of bids.
- The selection process was not properly and fully documented.
- The other four companies that bid with Sahenli Construction Company had, in the past, all bid in four other different identified contracts, and each had won one. This was a sign of a possible bid rotation or a complementary bidding scheme.
- One of the companies had close ties to Sahenli Construction Company, indicative of bid rigging.

Lessons Learned

Every new assignment presents fraud examiners with an opportunity to improve their planning and investigative skills. This one was no different. My organizational skills improved by tracing funds and the acquisition, study and evaluation of documents with regard of their evidentiary value.

This case brought into perspective the money laundering processes of placement, layering and integration, all in an attempt to hide the source — corruption. The investigation also showed the effectiveness of gathering documentary evidence, conducting interviews of secondary witnesses and working your way toward the main suspect(s) to confront and impeach them with the facts to evoke confession with ease. The confessions of the suspects in this case were easily obtained by laying all the facts and evidence before each of them.

Discretion was also important to my approach — where it was possible. Most of the inquiries were to government and corporate establishments, which helped maintain the desired secrecy so that the suspects did not know they were under investigation until their arrests. This approach gave them little time to cover their tracks and destroy evidence.

Recommendations to Prevent Future Occurrences

Based on my findings in this case, I presented the following recommendations for consideration:

- A comprehensive overhaul of the NDA's procurement unit and the appointment of qualified and well-trained expert personnel

- The reorganization of the procurement planning committee to follow the provisions of the Public Procurement Act of 2007
- A review of the operations of the unit
- The implementation of procedures aimed at promoting close monitoring of the activities of the procurement unit
- A comprehensive review by management of all contracts awarded during the tenure of Bayamilada and Wajala
- The enactment of adequate internal control measures and structures

This case showed the different forms that corruption can take. We all have to contribute to the difficult task of fighting bribery and corruption — because the fight is one for change that starts with and comes from each individual.

In conclusion, staff of both public and private institutions and members of the general public with useful information and tips should be encouraged and incentivized, if possible, to come forward and help the fight against fraud. Without the anonymous whistleblower in this case, uncovering this corruption would have been impossible. We must all work together if having a corruption-free, fraud-free world is our goal.

About the Author

Austine S. M. Adache, MCMP, CFE, is a senior detective superintendent and a lead investigator with the Economic and Financial Crimes Commission (EFCC), Nigeria. He has been involved in fraud investigations since 2005 and has varied experiences in law enforcement and investigation, especially in advance-fee fraud, bank fraud, Internet fraud, public corruption and money laundering, and has acquired numerous local and international certificates in related courses and training.

The views and opinions expressed, and the pattern of presentation in this case study, do not necessarily represent those of the Economic and Financial Crimes Commission, Nigeria, or the federal government of Nigeria, but are the author's. Therefore, they are not to be considered an official endorsement of factual accuracy, opinion, conclusion or recommendations of the EFCC or the government.

CHAPTER 22

Big Dangers from a Small Vendor

KIMIHARU CHATANI

James Dugan, executive vice president of Naritomo Automotive U.S., sat in his corner office watching the endless stream of cars passing by. He never appreciated the sight before and now stared blankly at it, lost in thought. As he faced his imminent retirement, he reflected on one unfinished task — a relationship mired in deceit, duplicity and corruption. He had played the role of executive vice president, second in charge of operations, for the past two decades while an unsuspecting line of CEOs and directors of the board came and went, but those who knew him well were aware that he played a prominent role in a web of supervisory fraud and manipulation. He needed to cover his tracks one more time because his new marketing director, a numbers guy, had begun questioning the anomalous business relationship and billing practices between Naritomo Automotive and its longtime vendor Topline Performance.

Topline Performance, a small company in comparison to Naritomo Automotive, was the exclusive vendor of engine parts for Naritomo and represented its products in various shows and events; Topline was treated like family by Naritomo executives and derived all of its revenue from the auto maker through 100 percent reimbursement of its operating expenses and from the sale of its highly successful racing-engine parts. It did not take a lawyer to recognize the potential vulnerability of the "legal corporate veil" being penetrated; Topline was nearly a de facto subsidiary of Naritomo. How and why this unusual relationship was formed points to a major fraud scheme that began serendipitously and subsequently grew deeper and stronger, thanks to a number of self-interested, venal mercenaries in the executive ranks. James (Jim to most people) had worked all of his adult life at Naritomo and was one of the biggest fish in the relatively small pond; nonetheless, he wielded power that froze new sales associates in their tracks. He had built an empire that extended beyond the four walls of the company into the complicated and sometimes seedy world of high-performance engines. Jim's close-knit network included partners from a large law firm that Naritomo had under retention as well as current and former employees and family members. He seemed to have all the bases covered as he contemplated his approaching retirement.

Naritomo

From its humble beginning in the early 1900s as a joint venture between Shikoku Electric Company in Japan and Monmouth Engine Company in the United States, Naritomo Automotive moved on to exponential growth during World War II as one of the major suppliers of engine parts to Japan's Air Force. In the early 1960s, Naritomo began expanding its global reach by establishing representative sales offices in the United States and elsewhere. Cheap engine parts with precision quality quickly became the hallmark of the company. During the growth decade of the 1970s, Naritomo acquired a small engine manufacturer in Tennessee and was finally able to establish a firm presence in the United States. Naritomo geared up to tackle the massive U.S. market that had been dominated by domestic manufacturers.

Just off Naritomo U.S.'s lobby was a small museum that showcased the company's history and products. Visitors with ample time to spare before an appointment occasionally browsed through the dimly lit museum, and only the most observant would notice a picture on the wall from the first sales class of 1975, which included a young and ambitious James Dugan. Jim had even forgotten about the picture by now. He had been the only member of the starting class to last so long at Naritomo.

As Naritomo entered its second decade of the new millennium, all efforts were focused on reaching the new sales plateau of $2 billion, a goal that Jim spearheaded. With everyone's efforts dedicated to reaching this objective, irregularities in the $2 million plus budgetary relationship with Topline were within the margin of accepted error and escaped the scrutiny of external and internal auditors. Many employees at Naritomo, including the Japanese CEO and Jim Dugan, treated the business relationship with Topline and its foray into the racing-engine market as an expensive hobby or an ineffective marketing campaign, something that was inherited from the prior regime — except that this hobby was not inherited; it was cultivated by Jim to bring riches to his inner circle of friends.

The New Kid

It was an unusually warm December day, even for Southern California, as Jim sat at his office window looking at the flowing traffic below. The wall clock indicated that it was 10 a.m., time for a meeting with the latest marketing director in charge of the Topline relationship. As Jim swiveled his chair to face the door, he heard a soft knocking; it was Mike Jenkins. At the urging of Topline's owners, he had dismissed the previous marketing director for being inept and unmanageable but only Topline and Jim knew the real reason for his dismissal.

Mike Jenkins had been the marketing director for only four or five months when he noticed a number of peculiarities. The existing practice was for Topline to submit an annual operating budget of $2 million that would be prorated monthly and paid in full throughout the year. Any overage or savings to the annual budget would be adjusted at year-end. However, to Mike's astonishment, in the past ten years, there had been no variance on even a single line item — unusual to say the least. Mike's analysis of past financial transactions and Naritomo's relationship with Topline made him uneasy and prompted his request for a meeting with James Dugan.

He walked into Jim's office with his financial analysis and a rudimentary sketch he created of the "social-network relationships" he discovered among Naritomo and Topline personnel. He was concerned there could be conflicts of interest and family ties among Topline's ownership and long-term Naritomo employees. As Mike made his case and recommended an audit of Topline, Jim stared at him in silence. After what seem like an eternity, Jim looked directly at Mike, dismissed his request and told him the meeting was over. Stunned but unable to respond, Mike quietly left Jim's office. Little did he realize that this was the beginning of a two-year journey that would shock Naritomo's staff and management to the core and launch an unprecedented internal investigation. He would soon learn the magnitude of a fraud that was 20 years in the making and reached the highest levels of Naritomo's management.

After leaving Jim's office, Mike quietly walked to the desk of Daniel Gains, Naritomo's internal auditor. It did not take long for Daniel to grasp the potential enormity of the situation and recognize that Topline also serviced the company's competitors openly at racing-engine events, which was prohibited by the contract — or so he thought.

Armed with suspicions of irregularities, misappropriation and kickbacks, Mike and Daniel went to see the CEO, Ken Okada. Okada had come to Naritomo with great hopes for change, discipline and growth. He was expected to lead the company's unprecedented growth for the next several years and return to the headquarters in Japan as a key member of senior management. Mike and Daniel were hopeful that Ken would live up to his reputation and initiate an investigation. They didn't realize the extent to which lax governance, an overall culture of self-interested leadership and weak ethics and compliance enforcement had created a breeding ground for deceit and conflicts of interest.

Vendor Audit

Ken Okada immediately ordered Daniel to form a team of experts to investigate Mike's discoveries. Ken told them that the investigation should be conducted in secrecy and the only internal parties privy to the case should be himself, Mike and Daniel. I had worked with Daniel on an unrelated Naritomo project a few years ago and we had a good rapport, so he recommended my services as a Certified Fraud Examiner to Ken. After a brief meeting with me and my partner, Dawn Underwood, Ken agreed to bring us into the investigation. Dawn had significant experience working with global investment banks in the quasi-compliance/operational group and was very familiar with money laundering, illegal payments and fraud. I felt that she would be an asset to the case.

We began by conducting a vendor audit based on a clause in our agreement that allowed us to do so without warning or cause. We hoped to understand the extent of potential illegal activities, identify the members of the inner circle and recreate the intricate and often complex web of muddied relationships among the players. It soon became clear that kickbacks, deceptive business practices and tampering of internal personnel issues by Topline executives were occurring. Jim and the owners of Topline had a long-standing personal history that went back several decades, but no one knew or understood the full extent of that relationship. Topline CFO, Jenny DeWitt, had previously worked for Naritomo, where she formed close ties with key members of the organization. Among her inner circle was her brother, an up-and-coming young salesman at Naritomo. Ted Ballard, the CEO and co-owner of Topline was a master puppeteer; he not only skillfully manipulated the DeWitts' family relationship, but he was also able to convince Jim to hire his daughter-in-law to be the lead manager of Naritomo's newest and most promising product. She was in a position to advise her managers on cost, and she used their trust in her to suggest pricing strategies that worked to the advantage of Topline — and to the disadvantage of Naritomo.

It did not take long for us to realize that Naritomo's marketing tactics and strategies had been leaked to Topline. The sales impact from the compromised cost information could have resulted in lost revenues of $3 to $4 million annually over the four years that the main product, an engine, was on the market. The initial year's audit identified more than $500,000 of questionable expenses charged to Naritomo by Topline personnel; the company and the cumulative financial impact of these padding and kickback schemes during Naritomo's over a 20- year relationship with Topline could have reached $10 million. Our team pored over thousands of expense records, payroll information, bank accounts that identified questionable accounting, nonsupported invoices and nonbusiness expense charges. The "black-bag" investigation of the company's systems helped identify the extent and level of the web of deceit that not only compromised the company's financial performances over the past 20 years but also compromised the company's ethics and integrity standards. As the vendor audit clearly confirmed Mike's and Daniel's suspicions of fraud, it became imperative that our team add independent outside legal counsel.

Double-Cross

The vendor agreement prohibited Topline from supporting Naritomo's competition or providing them services for obvious reasons, and everyone associated with the agreement knew it. But during one of the vendor agreement renegotiations, Ted Ballard flooded changes to the draft agreement at the eleventh hour and managed to successfully eliminate the noncompete clause. Unaware that his longtime friend would double-cross him, Jim blindly signed and executed the agreement, allowing Topline to establish another company, under the same ownership, to service Naritomo's competitors. Topline continued to provide service to Naritomo while using the same employees and subcontractors to work for Naritomo's competition. While this was occurring, Ballard's daughter-in-law continued to funnel Naritomo's sales and marketing strategies to Topline, which Ballard used to the benefit of his other customers.

Under Dawn's direction, we hired the law firm of Kemper and Hogan to assist with the investigation, and we continued under the watchful eyes of our attorneys. We started classifying our findings under the attorney-client privilege.

Topline's other owner had a long and complicated relationship with executives of Naritomo. Takara Okayama came to the United States as a college student 30 years ago and started a small import and export firm with the backing of his father, who had ties with executives at Naritomo. Takara leveraged his father's position well and earned the support of important people at the company. Over the years, he had provided enough favors to Naritomo executives that his questionable business practices at Topline were allowed to pass unquestioned. Our investigation team was unaware of the connections between Takara and various Naritomo executives. Takara used his influence throughout the investigation and ran interference in the background while Ted Ballard did the same at Naritomo. No one at Naritomo was above suspicion as evidence of the kickback scheme between Jim and Ted Ballard surfaced. When questioned, Jim vehemently denied the allegation.

Complete Turnaround

Our preliminary report of the investigation included recommendations to overhaul sections of Naritomo's organizational structure and decertify Topline as a vendor. The report broke out the amounts of suspected kickbacks and listed conflicts of interest. Initially the CEO, Ken Okada, approved our recommendations and threw his support behind us, but pressure from the Naritomo office in Japan and threats to his own professional advancement caused him to abruptly terminate the investigation and reaffirm Topline as Naritomo's exclusive service vendor. One day Ken walked into the office I had been using since the case started and told me he was going to meet with Takara to "look into his eyes and soul" to see what type of man he was. My recommendation — and that of the lead counsel — not to meet with Takara fell on deaf ears; Ken was determined. I waited with the other team members for Ken's return, and I could tell I was not alone in sensing the changing tides in our case. Ken called a meeting with the team when he returned and in a stern voice told us that Takara's eyes "told a different story." Ken was now convinced that our "mountain of evidence" did not matter. After months of investigation, Ken ended it and resumed normal business relationship with Topline. No changes in personnel took place either; our work was for naught. In fact, after the case was closed, Ken appointed a Topline insider to succeed Jim after he retired. The new boss fired Mike Jenkins and replaced him with the brother of Topline's CFO. Now the fox was indeed guarding the henhouse.

Ken Okada had just finished his third year at Naritomo, but his tour of duty was cut short after our examination and he returned to Japan. I later learned that he was put in charge of an obscure division with limited opportunity for advancement.

Lessons Learned

Containment is absolutely necessary in any internal examination. Containment of losses, kickbacks, fraudulent charges, spheres of influence in conflicts of interest, collusion and individuals' self-interest need to be factors in every case. In our investigation of Naritomo, we identified many of these elements, but in the end we were not privy to or aware of the intricate relationships that existed between Naritomo and Topline and the survival instinct of Ken Okada.

Company executives not only decided to turn a blind eye to the overwhelming evidence of employee and vendor misconduct but willingly participated in the fraudulent scheme by silencing employees who dared to question the unscrupulous vendor relationship. This case demonstrated the astonishing ability of one small yet corrupt vendor to penetrate multiple levels of mid-, senior and executive management of a well-known corporation, to the point where even C-level officers were willing to disregard their fiduciary duties in order to maintain the illicit relationship.

Recommendations to Prevent Future Occurrences

Fraud often begins and ends with self-motivation of the perpetrators and decision makers. Instead of weighing the ethical and financial results of fraud, they base their decisions on self-interest and a desire for wealth. Human emotions and ethics are at the core of these problems. Only long-term training programs and ethics practices might convince individuals to weigh the consequences and come to an ethical decision when confronted with an opportunity to make gains illegally. We should refocus our culture of "succeed at all cost" to embrace the spirit that participation, not winning, is the ultimate goal. However, on a practical level, there are also business practices that could make it more difficult for such a fraud to occur.

- Strengthen company standards of ethical behavior and conduct regular employee training.
- Regularly review vendor contracts, regardless of the length of the relationship.
- Rotate executives and employees who manage vendor relationships.
- Conduct surprise audits to look for conflicts of interest.
- Perform regular and surprise vendor audits.
- Establish an internal legal department to review and approve contracts and monitor questionable business practices.

Society should instill the worth of ethics in individuals' professional and personal lives. Until we are able to distinguish right from wrong, the roles of CFEs, CPAs and regulatory agencies will be necessary to help act as our conscience.

About the Author

Kimiharu Chatani, CFE, CPA, CFSA, CIA, FCPA, has more than 25 years of experience as a former audit and consulting partner at notable organizations such as Arthur Andersen, LLP, AT Kearney, Inc., and BearingPoint, Inc. (formerly KPMG Consulting). He is bilingual in Japanese and advises global executives on enterprise initiatives involving strategy and operations, compliance and technology. He is a recognized authority in fraud examinations, audit, IT strategy, systems integrations, business process improvements, business continuity management and IFRS.

CHAPTER 23

A Drop in the Ocean

LUDMILA GRECHANIK

I t can be difficult to pinpoint one primary culprit when a fraud occurs in a culture of corruption. That is the case with this story. Blue Ocean was a gigantic, international manufacturing firm that produced diverse equipment for other businesses. It had branches in Europe, the United States and Asia-Pacific. In Eastern Europe, the company had subsidiaries in Moscow, Saint Petersburg and Kiev, all of which were subordinated to the head office in England. Managers at the Blue Ocean branch in Moscow had established a system of fraud a decade ago and developed it over time. Despite having different leaders throughout the years, the framework remained in place and active, and new managers were encouraged to continue the tradition.

I was employed as an external investigator at Blue Ocean in the corporate headquarters when I first heard of Marina Karpova, the CEO at Blue Ocean Moscow. Karpova was in her mid-30s, married and had two children. She began working in the finance department of Blue Ocean Moscow when she graduated from college and had worked her way up the ranks to become CEO. She was smart, well respected and lively. She was a nice person and well educated, and she gave me the impression that she understood my questions before I even finished asking them. However, she also appeared to have gotten herself and the company in quite a bit of trouble.

Puzzling Payments

The first time I met Karpova she was at a coffee shop in Moscow, where she had agreed to meet me and tell me what happened at Blue Ocean. She was smoking nervously and kept saying "I only wanted what was best for the company. I worked hard to resolve all the issues and clean up the mess that previous management left, and look what happened — I'm out of a job!"

The previous November, Karpova had contacted Nigel Anderson, the regional director at the UK headquarters, to tell him that she intended to

217

make a payment of approximately $200,000 to a children's charity. She did not explain why she wanted to make the payment; she simply stated her intentions. Puzzled at her odd behavior, Anderson refused Karpova's request and informed her that she was not authorized to make such payments. When Karpova told him she wanted to proceed with the donation anyway, Anderson warned her that she would be dismissed for such an action. Karpova ignored his warning, issued the charity payment and subsequently resigned from Blue Ocean. After the funds had been transferred to the charity organization, Karpova sent an e-mail to Anderson and other Blue Ocean executives explaining her motivation. She said the payment in question was necessary to secure the ongoing cooperation of the tax authorities, given the Russian subsidiary's potential tax exposure in previous years. She also wrote that future payments would be needed to keep the tax auditors quiet. This e-mail triggered our investigation.

Records Review

As a senior investigator at Blue Ocean's corporate headquarters, I was given Karpova's case to look into. I started by gathering publicly available information about the charity to which Karpova donated company funds because I had never heard of it before. I started digging, but I could not find any records. I knew charity structures in Russia were complex and that state officials often demanded bribes from businesses to be funneled through such "charitable" organizations. This might corroborate Karpova's claims that the payments were in fact directed to Russian tax authorities, not the charity itself.

Then I discovered internal records that indicated the Blue Ocean Moscow office had made use of bribes — passed through charity organizations — in the past to avoid taxes. Previous investigations had resulted in personnel dismissals but not prosecutions, and it appeared that the company's executives preferred to address the problem quietly. From what I gathered, past Moscow managers had committed tax violations that greatly exceeded the one Karpova was trying to cover up.

I gathered a team of experts, including a computer forensics specialist. Our first step was to image Marina's computer. While reviewing the files we recovered, we identified a spreadsheet labeled "Moscow Unofficial Cash." It was as if the document had been prepared specifically for us and our investigation! It contained information on how bribe money was generated and applied in the past, covering nearly a decade. We discovered that in previous years, someone from a UK subsidiary of Blue Ocean would routinely withdraw cash from the corporate bank account and physically hand it to a senior executive of the Moscow branch. The Moscow executive would then carry to money into Russia, where the cash would be used to pay various bribes. The Russian management team annotated the spreadsheet with notes on how the funds had been applied and then e-mailed copies to various managers in the United Kingdom.

The bribery spreadsheet also contained a separate list of transactions not recorded on the official books. I established from the file that illicit payments had been made to the tax authorities several years before, in forms that went beyond the regular cash payments. The list included payments to customers, business trip expenses, presents for the tax inspector and rent for warehouses in Moscow.

When I interviewed Karpova and showed her the spreadsheet we discovered, she was close to tears. She said, "I have two children and I don't want to go to jail. I had to make this payment to halt the tax investigation!" She explained that the previous year's tax auditor had uncovered a parallel-import scheme occurring at Blue Ocean Moscow, along with illegitimate purchases from intermediaries to avoid customs taxes. While parallel imports are not illegal in Russia, they do raise serious tax liability issues. A *parallel import* is a non-counterfeit good that is imported through a number of intermediaries for the purpose of underdeclaring its cost to reduce the customs payment. By using a number of intermediaries, it becomes more difficult to determine if the customs duties were paid appropriately.

Karpova quickly realized the extent of the potential fines and the possibility of her own liability. She reached out to her personal connections and was put in touch with an individual with considerable clout at the Russian tax office who agreed to help her. He instructed her to make monthly payments to a children's charity, and, in return, he would instruct the tax auditor looking into Blue Ocean's history to close the investigation. Karpova had made payments to the charity for more than a year, in the end totaling $1.5 million. These did not appear on the bribery spreadsheet that Marina maintained, but we assumed management was aware of the arrangement because no one questioned the payments. What we could not figure out was why Karpova decided to seek permission for the corporate headquarters for her last payment. But it turned out the bribes were just the tip of the iceberg.

Black-Cash Operations

While the charity payments were questionable, they were not the only significant and dubious expenses that we discovered on Karpova's spreadsheet. Cash outflows included business trips, medical expenses, presents for customers, staff parties, warehouse rent and phone charges. Some of the entries were marked "SP," which I discovered meant "special payment" and represented a customer facilitation payment (i.e., a kickback to the customer company's procurement manager).

We reviewed not only how cash was applied but also how it was generated. Initially, senior executives carried the money into Russia themselves.

However, over time the system matured, and a number of third-party companies were brought into the scheme. Their purpose was to generate cash in Moscow by submitting invoices to the UK subsidiary. It appeared the consulting invoices were the primary billing mechanism employed by these third-party vendors. During our review we identified a number of questionable consulting contracts. For example, my team and I found numerous consulting agreements with unregistered companies that we had not heard of before, and public records searches returned no information on them. We figured they were shell companies established for the sole purpose of moving money from the United Kingdom to Moscow. The largest of these payments was $100,000, paid to a company called Dolphin for consulting services. However, the invoice for this payment had a handwritten note from Marina showing her cash conversion calculations. Cash conversion is illegal in Russia as it helps companies reduce Russian taxes and might be used to fund inappropriate activities.

The following example illustrates how cash conversion works. Blue Ocean entered into a fictitious agreement with Dolphin to buy consulting services for $100. Blue Ocean transferred the funds to Dolphin but did not receive the service. Instead, Dolphin provided Blue Ocean with an invoice for $100, which Blue Ocean submitted to tax authorities to reduce its value-added tax (VAT) and corporate tax. Dolphin then returned, in cash, approximately $92 to $95 to Blue Ocean and retained the remainder as commission. Blue Ocean managers could then use this cash to pay bribes without fear of attracting the attention of the Russian authorities.

Logistics, Customs and Parallel-Import Schemes

We examined Blue Ocean Moscow's suppliers and were surprised that the corporate headquarters in England was not on the list. Instead, the Moscow branch purchased equipment from a number of curious Russian companies, and these companies changed from time to time.

For a number of years, Blue Ocean Moscow imported equipment via intermediary companies. Imports were carried out as follows: goods were shipped from a European plant, invoices were issued by the Blue Ocean UK subsidiary and the goods were then imported to Russia through a chain of intermediaries that provided customs and transportation services (customs brokers). As this system was opaque and operations were insufficiently documented, we immediately suspected it to be a tax-evasion scheme.

As can be seen from the diagram, Blue Ocean UK would issue an invoice to an intermediary company, which would then engage a second intermediary company before the product finally made it to Blue Ocean Moscow, along with an invoice from the second intermediary company. It was not clear why this structure was used, what took place between the two intermediary companies or whether other intermediary companies were used in between.

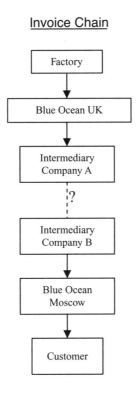

Invoice Chain

Karpova explained that outsourcing customs clearance and transportation services to a broker cut the related costs in half; however, she did not provide us with any calculations to support the assertion. She explained that customs brokers were able to negotiate import charges in ways that private companies could not, apparently through bribes, and that it was beneficial for Russian businesses to use brokers. Both Blue Ocean's Moscow and St. Petersburg offices employed customs brokers when they were importing goods.

In her interview, Karpova said that the accounting staff at Blue Ocean Moscow did not retain any documents confirming these import transactions with Blue Ocean UK and the intermediaries. Karpova herself did not know if contracts among the parties even existed, as she had never seen them. In any case, she explained that her staff members would not keep payment documents or bank statements related to such transactions because there would be a tax risk associated with them, in the event that they were subject to a tax audit.

We did discover that the UK invoices to intermediaries were actually issued from the Moscow sales department, using an invoice template with the UK letterhead. We found that in most cases Blue Ocean UK received money from unknown companies on behalf of the intermediaries. Karpova explained that Moscow managers did not follow up regarding which company made a payment. Normally, someone from the UK office e-mailed or called a sales administrator in Moscow to confirm that an invoice had been paid. If payment was delayed, the UK employee asked the Moscow administrator to verify the reason for the delay and the date when payment would be received. The sales administrator would then phone a contact person in the customs broker group of companies and ask them to transfer money. We wanted to speak with the customs broker, but the sales administrator refused to give us a name and suggested we talk to Karpova. When I asked Karpova for the information, she said it was confidential.

We identified that in some cases Blue Ocean Moscow made special payments to intermediaries from its petty cash. Karpova could not explain the reason for the payments, though it was clear that they were related to the customs process and tax-evasion scheme.

In many cases the intermediaries charged the full amount of customs duties from Blue Ocean Moscow although they paid the "negotiated amount" to customs. Karpova said she presumed the use of third parties was a mechanism to extract cash from Blue Ocean and mentioned that a number of the contracts contained a commission payment of up to 30 percent for the third-party company. When we asked who established this system, Karpova said that she thought it had been created by the former deputy general manager. Regardless, it had been in practice for years and a series of executives had participated in it in the past.

Kickbacks to Customers

As mentioned earlier, certain customers were marked as "SP" on the spreadsheet, which I assumed represented a customer facilitation payment. We compiled a list of all the SPs and noticed some well-known multinational companies and several state-owned companies, which could mean potential Foreign Corrupt Practices Act violations. We also found spreadsheets recording cash receipts by sales managers (with handwritten notes stating "cash received amounting to X"). The receipts corresponded with special payments to customers and were usually a percentage of the facilitation payment. The total amount of kickbacks to sales managers was $230,000, and individual amounts varied from $200 to $26,000.

We discussed these printouts with some of the sales managers and a sales administrator, but none of them said they recognized the files. We were unable to talk to either of the IT system administrators, who might have been aware of this program, since they had both resigned by the time our review began.

While we were looking through the documents in Karpova's office, we actually came across a kickback policy. The file stipulated kickback rates to be granted depending on a contract's value and the necessary approvals that had to be obtained before the kickback could be paid. The presence of this policy confirmed senior management's knowledge and endorsement of corruption throughout the company.

Culture of Corruption

The principal irregularities we identified in this case included:

- Improper use of intermediary companies to transfer funds between Blue Ocean Moscow and Blue Ocean UK
- Payment of bribes to customs officers
- Payment of bribes to a Russian tax official to abandon a tax audit
- Payment of kickbacks to various customers
- Acceptance of kickbacks by various Blue Ocean sales personnel

We submitted our case report to Blue Ocean's corporate office in England, and Karpova's resignation was accepted. However, the rest of the management in Moscow (the majority of whom resigned when we began our investigation) was reinstated, much to my team's dismay. The reason offered by the corporate executives was that Karpova was the driving force behind the corruption in Moscow and, with her gone, things could return to normal. They seemed to think the other corrupt managers would begin conducting operations ethically, but they failed to acknowledge that the bribery scheme had been in place long before Karpova assumed the role of CEO. No criminal charges were filed, and the Moscow office was not audited by tax authorities.

Blue Ocean leaders decided to investigate other branches in light of the fraud uncovered in Moscow, and they began with the St. Petersburg office. The company president released an official statement to all branch managers, instructing them to halt any potentially illegal or unethical practices immediately. The UK office that facilitated the bribes in Moscow was closed permanently.

Lessons Learned

The main lesson I learned from this case was that management often looks to past practices for guidance on handling current issues. In this case, the managers seemed to be saying "This is how things are done in Russia. We have to go along with protocol." They even had a bribery policy in place for years before the fraud came to light. From this we concluded that once the managers perceived a need to keep corrupt funds on hand, it became nearly impossible to prevent their use and equally impossible to prevent the company from becoming involved in fraudulent activities.

Recommendations to Prevent Future Occurrences

This was a classic case of a failed tone at the top. Blue Ocean Moscow had been subjected to bribery and kickback schemes at the hands of its managers for years, as enshrined in a corruption "policy" and documented on the bribery spreadsheet. Each new executive in Moscow was introduced to the standard practice and encouraged to continue it. To avoid similar circumstances, corporate executives should actively encourage ethical behavior in managers and other branch officers. Companies should have an ethics policy in place, and managers should regularly communicate it to staff to ensure the employees are aware of it. It is also helpful for companies to have an anonymous hotline in place for whistleblowers to report suspected fraud. If Blue Ocean had had a hotline, perhaps the scheme would have come to light much earlier.

As for Blue Ocean's processes, they should be more transparent to prevent future frauds. For example, it is acceptable to use customs brokers in Russia, but managers are expected to conduct proper due diligence before hiring a broker. If a broker has a dubious reputation or there is no information about the company in the public domain, it would be a good idea not to contract with such a broker. Management should periodically request a random sample of customs documents from the broker to verify that duties are being paid correctly. If there are signs of wrongdoing, it is best to conduct an internal investigation and to stop working with the supplier.

The internal audit and accounting functions need to challenge the procurement team about suppliers. If there is no proof of performance (e.g., in case of fictitious consulting contracts) or if major suppliers substantially change from year to year, controlling or accounting personnel should start asking questions. If a branch office does not have a local internal audit department, potential wrongdoings can be investigated at the company's headquarters.

About the Author

Ludmila Grechanik is a partner in the forensic department at KPMG Russia. She graduated from the Financial Academy under the Government of Russia with a degree in accounting, audit and financial analysis. Having obtained accounting and audit experience in a number of companies, she joined KPMG Forensic in 2003. Since then Ludmila has engaged in a number of fraud and anti-bribery investigations in Russia. Ludmila also has extensive experience advising clients regarding fraud risk management and internal controls.

24

The Professor and the Deputy

PAUL KEYTON

Erik Gutenbourg was a middle-aged engineering academic who was known as the professor by his colleagues. After spending 20 years in the ivory tower, he decided to swap university life for what he hoped would be fame and fortune in private industry. He was a precise, energetic and small-framed man who had a beard and restored and drove vintage English sports cars as a hobby. And regardless of the situation, he always thought he was right.

I never had the privilege of lengthy conversations with him because he had been unceremoniously dumped from his position as CEO of Fabrica prior to my engagement. His offense was to have presided over the company's first major — and very large loss-making — contract in specialized engineering applications, an action that did not endear him to executives at ADK Gruppen, the European conglomerate that counted Fabrica among its many subsidiaries.

Gruppen also decided to dispense with Max Klein's services when it fired the professor. Max the deputy, as I always thought of him, was in his mid-30s, tall, jowly, balding and defensive. He had been with Fabrica for several years; before that, he had had a respectable if not exciting career in manufacturing. Becoming the assistant to the professor meant making it into the big leagues to Max. Unfortunately, this was to be the pinnacle of his career as, tainted with failure, he was fired alongside his supervisor.

While I favor firm and decisive action in response to employee wrongdoing, Gruppen management's firing of these two men before it had all the facts seriously impeded my investigation. I only ever spoke to them face-to-face in the company of their lawyers, which led to stilted, formal conversations. But one message was clear from the beginning. They claimed they had acted with the full knowledge of Gruppen's senior management and were not about to be made fall guys.

Stefan Laudrup was a middle-aged, urbane, widely traveled senior employee at Specialista, a multinational corporation that frequently used manufacturing vendors for million-dollar contracts. Laudrup was a key procurement officer at Specialista, and he awarded Fabrica the loss-making contract that ultimately cost the professor and his deputy their jobs. Laudrup was also closely involved in implementing cost-cutting programs designed by his friend, mentor and leading Specialista board member, Mike Gurman. Laudrup shared his boss's appetite for slashing suppliers' margins and imposing draconian delivery and financial terms. He had a reputation as a ruthless negotiator, wielding the knife on hapless suppliers, calmly and matter-of-factly. He was also regarded as unassailable. He and several other senior Specialista colleagues had previously worked under Gurman at Nortia Machine, where they were credited with turning around the company's fortunes. Nortia was a major competitor of Specialista's.

Nortia had been hemorrhaging money through wasteful, inefficient purchasing and antiquated production techniques, but Gurman and his team recast relations with suppliers and overhauled the production processes, resulting in savings beyond everyone's expectations. Their methods were regarded as revolutionary but also caused some unease. Specialista's powerful chairman wanted that firepower for his company, and in a remarkable, though unethical, coup he induced Gurman, Laudrup and colleagues to quit Nortia without notice and relocate to Switzerland, where Specialista was headquartered. As far as the chairman was concerned, Gurman could do no wrong and, by extension, neither could Laudrup.

Setting the Scene

Fabrica was a minor subsidiary of the European conglomerate ADK Gruppen and specialized in providing robotic solutions to third-party organizations. It was a relatively insignificant player in the market, a state of affairs that senior Gruppen management wanted to change. In a pep talk to Fabrica's management (including CEO Gutenbourg and his assistant Klein), Gruppen leaders had emphasized the need to win some of the million-dollar contracts up for grabs in the market.

The first contract that the professor and his deputy bid for after this pep talk was one offered by Specialista. People at Fabrica were initially thrilled when their company won the bid, but once negotiations began, it became clear that Gurman's group was implementing cost-cutting strategies at Specialista and cowing suppliers into submission. Specialista leaders were enjoying significant savings, company share prices were up and the board regarded Gurman and Laudrup as saviors.

ADK Gruppen was a massive, worldwide conglomerate and a leading player in heavy manufacturing. Its leadership was extremely well connected, and its board members frequently accompanied government ministers on overseas trade missions. With the company predicated on continued growth, Gruppen management aggressively pursued every opportunity to expand market share and, as Professor Gutenbourg and Max found out, did not tolerate failure.

Breakthrough Turned Disaster

I was engaged by ADK Gruppen's internal audit department to help investigate the circumstances surrounding massive losses in the fixed-price contract with Specialista. When Specialista, through Laudrup, awarded Fabrica the prestigious project, it seemed to be the breakthrough the company needed — but it had turned into a disaster. Delivery was behind schedule and losses were mounting. Most of the team was concerned with analyzing bid documentation and engineering specifications to determine if a design or engineering failure had contributed to the losses; I was trying to determine if there were any financial irregularities.

Project records showed millions of dollars in payments to various subcontractors, engineering specialists and consulting companies, but one series immediately stood out to me. Fabrica had made substantial payments to an IT consultancy that appeared to be located in a residential area and whose invoices, when I examined them, were vaguely worded. The payments seemed to have the hallmarks of a scam.

A surreptitious visit to the company's address confirmed it was a house in a quiet village not far from Fabrica's factory. I pulled public records on the company and conducted a background check on the registered owner and found no indication of IT expertise.

If the professor and his deputy had been complicit in making false payments to the consultancy, there was no time to lose. I did not know the precise relationship between them, and they might have already tipped off the IT subcontractor to alter or destroy records. However, the next day when a senior internal auditor and I, armed with copies of the company's invoices, knocked on the door to ask for explanations, we received a big surprise.

Instead of aggression and noncooperation (which we expected) or weak excuses, Martin Huber, the resident director, cheerfully admitted the invoices were false. He explained that he provided a service to many companies wanting to make large, untraceable cash payments. For a commission of 5 percent of the invoice total, he would supply companies with false invoices. Once a payment cleared, he would withdraw the funds in cash from his bank (less his commission) and contact the requesting company to arrange collection.

His records were precise; he charged and accounted for the correct local sales taxes and reported his profits to the tax authorities. He confirmed that the professor and Max had both collected cash from him. According to his records, their collections amounted to more than $3 million during the last nine months.

Preliminary Interview

Armed with this information, I decided to interview the professor and Max. I could not see them simultaneously, so I started with Gutenbourg, whom I thought would have little loyalty to his former subordinate and might give him up to save himself. Strangely, in collusive fraud (which this case immediately appeared to be), subordinates can be very reluctant to implicate their bosses, but the favor is generally not returned. I thought if I played Max a recording of his former boss denouncing him, any loyalty he might harbor would evaporate and I would be more likely to get to the truth.

I interviewed Gutenbourg in the presence of his lawyer and confronted him with the evidence showing that he had embezzled. He admitted to picking up the cash from Martin Huber but vehemently denied embezzling the money. He said he paid the funds to "the network" in return for Fabrica winning its contract. According to the professor, the network consisted of senior Specialista procurement officers based around Europe who awarded contracts to suppliers in return for kickbacks. Failure to play ball in one country meant a supplier was barred from winning business elsewhere. According to Gutenbourg, Laudrup ran the network, set prices, distributed bribes and maintained an orderly process. The professor named a very senior Gruppen director and alleged that he knew of and approved the arrangement but had not wanted to know the details.

I thought his story sounded far-fetched and tried to probe further to find out why the contract, if it was corruptly awarded, was losing money and how he interacted with and delivered cash to the network. However, Gutenbourg's lawyer advised him not to answer any more questions.

The Intermediary

The next day I received a letter at my office in Basel, Switzerland, from a man named Dietrich who stated that Fabrica owed $400,000 to unnamed but powerful individuals and, unless management paid quickly and in cash, these individuals would not award Fabrica the generous contract amendments it needed to turn the Specialista contract around and make a profit. The letter instructed me to use the special paper enclosed to reply to a local address. Curiously, it was signed. I researched the name and found it belonged to a local headhunter with no overt connection to Laudrup or Specialista. Apart from his membership in a Swiss Napoleonic Wars reenactment society, there was nothing notable about him.

I was skeptical and thought the letter was simply an elaborate diversion, but I nevertheless had it examined by an expert. It was written on expensive paper with a complicated watermark and could not be photocopied. Unfortunately, it was not exclusive; three Swiss companies produced it, and it was impossible to trace their customers.

This was either a ruse or a possible indication of corruption within Specialista. If it were the latter and I could prove Laudrup was orchestrating extortion on a grand scale, as the professor claimed, it would be invaluable to Gruppen's senior management. I wrote to the address and included my phone number. I said Fabrica would pay the $400,000 but that I wanted proof it was not just a scam first.

Of course, I had no intention of paying $400,000 to anybody (nor could I have done so, in any case), but I wanted to excite the greed of the letter's author and see where it led. So with the help of a colleague, I prepared an attaché case — just like in films. We bundled plain, stiff paper cut precisely into the shape of $100 bills and topped them with real money. I intended to flash the case at the right moment to "prove" I had the money and demand Laudrup contact me before I handed it over.

Paradeplatz, Zurich

A few days later a man identifying himself as Suter, Dietrich's associate, called me and told me to meet him that day at 1:30 in the center of Paradeplatz in Zurich. He timed the call to allow me enough time to catch the train to Zurich and make the rendezvous but left no time to spare. I guessed he intended to thwart any plans I might have had for surveillance by limiting my time and choosing the location. Paradeplatz (which means "parade ground") is very open, surrounded by banks and expensive shops and has numerous streets leading off it. It would be difficult to cover all the exits and easy to spot a tail walking across the wide-open space.

I had a surveillance team on standby but events outside my control prevented the members from fully deploying. Operatives had been called away or were stranded elsewhere, and I ended up with just one man, Felix, who made his way independently to Zurich.

The Bearded Man

I was on time and stood in the dead center of Paradeplatz. A stocky, middle-age man in a leather jacket and cap approached me and introduced himself. He was medium height, calm and low key and, although his English was not great, he nodded when I opened the case, showed him the money and said I could hand it over only after Laudrup had contacted me to prove the deal was bona fide.

We went our separate ways and I phoned Felix, who was waiting in the vicinity, to give him Suter's description and route. I was pretty sure I was not being watched and I could see Suter walking away calmly. He did not seem on guard and Felix acknowledged his description and exit route. I headed back to Basel and waited for him to report.

A few hours later, Felix came by my office and told me he had followed Suter to a residential address. This was good news — I could check him out and see where it took us. However, he also criticized me for not giving him a better description. Apparently I had failed to mention Suter had a beard. As calmly as I could, I explained that I had not thought to mention his beard because Suter did not have one. Felix had followed the wrong man all afternoon.

The disappointments continued. The next day Dietrich the headhunter called and berated me for doubting his connections. All bets were off; there was no chance of Laudrup contacting me, and Fabrica would continue to suffer losses on the contract. Dietrich said Fabrica would never have another chance with Specialista and it was my fault.

The Lucky Break

My subsequent interviews with Max and the professor produced nothing new. They were adamant that they paid the network with Gruppen's full knowledge and their lawyers advised them to say nothing more. With senior Gruppen management firmly denying they authorized bribes, I was at a standstill, so I passed my evidence to the company's lawyers and moved on.

However, two days later, the secretary of Paolo DiMetti, one of Gruppen's vice presidents, called to say a Gruppen manager in Barcelona had just called DiMetti for advice about a sensitive issue. A local lawyer he knew called him and said he represented Laudrup and wanted to meet to discuss the ways Gruppen could receive "assistance" to obtain Specialista contracts throughout Europe. What was he to do?

This appeared to be a golden opportunity to establish my credentials with the network and possibly tie Laudrup into the extortion racket. DiMetti was also eager to take advantage of the situation, so I called the manager in Barcelona and told him I was a special consultant and that DiMetti wanted me to attend the meeting alone. He read between the lines: DiMetti was head of European operations and one of Gruppen's most senior and powerful executives. If his private secretary routed sensitive calls to me, it meant I was highly trusted and DiMetti authorized the meeting. However, no Gruppen employee would be present to implicate the company and as a consultant I was deniable, which was perfect.

Off to Barcelona

A few days later I was in Barcelona waiting in my hotel room for a phone call. I was unsure if Laudrup would be coming or if he would leave the initial meeting to his lawyer. I had rigged the room with tape recorders and arranged for some unobtrusive backup, if I needed it — a tough, streetwise, French ex-cop who was, at that moment, driving in from the airport.

Time was getting tight when my backup called. He had been flagged down by two men on a motorcycle who pointed out he had a flat tire. When he got out to check, one of them snatched his overnight bag and jacket from the passenger seat and they rode off. He had no cash, credit cards, clothes or passport. Angry at being so easily fooled, his temper had kicked in and he was in no fit state to help me or anyone else.

It got worse. Laudrup and his lawyer called from the lobby and insisted on meeting in the hotel coffee shop, so my carefully rigged room was useless. I hurried down with a recorder in my jacket hoping the background noise would not drown out our conversation and Laudrup would not spot the red recording light glowing in my pocket.

It turned out I did not need to worry. I had been vouched for: the $400,000 in the attaché case had been reported so Laudrup seemed to consider me semi–bona fide, but the clincher was the DiMetti connection.

Laudrup was relaxed, and in just over an hour I learned as much as I could have reasonably expected. To have tried to talk numbers in public during the first meeting would have been too pushy and suspicious, but Laudrup volunteered the rest. Contracts were available across Europe, not only with Specialista but also with rival manufacturers. The network appeared to be real. Laudrup boasted of his extensive contacts and how some contracts were managed industry-wide to ensure that manufacturers' costs in certain areas were comparable and avoid suspicion. We agreed to communicate further through his lawyer and arranged to meet again after I had Gruppen's response. It was clear that the professor and Max were complicit in Fabrica's corrupt contract but were only the couriers, not the architects. Laudrup also intimated that it might be too difficult for him to ensure Fabrica recovered all its losses now, but he was confident any shortfall would be more than compensated for later.

Attempted Extortion

I reported the meeting to DiMetti and handed over the recording and transcript. I recommended arranging further meetings to record Laudrup offering proprietary bid or negotiation information for a specific project in exchange for money. I reasoned that this might help identify other alleged network members and irregularities in Specialista's procurement department and give Gruppen the most leverage in negotiations between the two companies. However, it was not my call. I asked DiMetti to consider my recommendation and let me know how he wished to proceed.

Within a few days I found out. DiMetti told me nothing but went ahead and aggressively confronted Specialista's board, demanding compensation for the Fabrica contract and the dismissal of every Specialista employee associated with it.

However, DiMetti did not anticipate Specialista's reaction. Instead of embarrassment and compliance, Specialista's board members resisted his demands. The chairman made it clear he had no sympathy for a company that admitted to bribing its employees and then demanded compensation for its losses. He flatly refused to pay anything, saying he would otherwise be rewarding bribery.

DiMetti then clumsily threatened to leak the investigation findings to the media but again misread the chairman's mood. The chairman was very auto-cratic and reacted emotionally under pressure. Unknown to DiMetti, he was having troubles with his board. Specialista's reputation was suffering as sup-pliers publicly and often bitterly complained of their treatment. And Nortia Machine, unhappy about Gurman and Laudrup jumping ship, was threat-ening legal action for breach of contract and industrial espionage, alleging the men stole proprietary cost and production information before leaving.

The chairman was not the type to admit he made mistakes, and he interpreted his board's criticism as a personal attack. He also interpreted Gruppen's publicity threats as a plot by some board members and DiMetti to replace him. So he dug his heels in.

Laudrup Flees

After this meeting, Laudrup left Switzerland and reportedly fled to Brazil, well away from media scrutiny and further investigation. However, DiMetti acted precipitously and did not have the evidence to prove corruption at Specialista. Laudrup did not disclose proprietary information or explicitly ask for a bribe during our meeting. Nor did he name other conspirators or identify specific projects he could influence, and when he left, there were no obvious lines of inquiry to pursue.

Gruppen did receive other reports from its subsidiaries alleging Special-ista employees extorted bribes from them, but it was too late. Everyone knew of the investigation by now, and no one was going to do anything risky. The trail went cold.

With Laudrup gone and production costs massively reduced, Special-ista's chairman was able weather the storm. He explained the Laudrup affair as an aberration by one trusted employee but hinted it could have been a misunderstanding or even an attempted entrapment. He also categori-cally denied the possibility of organized corruption within Specialista on the grounds there was no evidence of inflated costs.

However, despite his semipublic and vociferous defense of his employ-ees, the chairman was a realist and, when it came to protecting his legacy, utterly ruthless. Gurman, widely believed to be the mastermind behind Lau-drup's action, was let go on purported health grounds with a very generous severance package; four of his senior colleagues were also let go. By this time, Specialista had a cadre of procurement and production specialists well versed in Gurman's methods and most likely able to maintain the momentum to keep Specialista highly competitive.

Firing the Gurman group helped, but Specialista management eventu-ally had to buy off Nortia with a sweetheart deal. It also eased up a little on suppliers, helping some to implement their own cost-savings and softening contract terms with others. Specialista's board gave a sigh of relief and decided to back its chairman. Gruppen dropped its loss claim and received some favorable deals in return.

Fingers in the Cookie Jar

This left the professor and Max jobless and out on a limb. The professor was threatening to sue for compensation and to expose Gruppen senior management's complicity in the original bribe. But Max was less aggressive and, because he had a young family, decided to confess to Gruppen's in-house counsel. He admitted Fabrica's contract was corruptly awarded but said the idea came from another Gruppen executive with Specialista contacts.

The deal was simple. Fabrica would bid low, win the contract and pay the requisite bribes. Specialista would then change the engineering specifications and pay inflated prices for the amendments, guaranteeing Fabrica a healthy profit. According to Max, the professor jumped at the offer and saw an opportunity. He boasted that he could underpay the network by saying internal controls prevented them from generating enough false invoices to pay the whole bribe. He appeared to assume the network would settle for less and award the amendments anyway. Max thought this typical of the professor's arrogance, and he believed at first that the professor wanted to save project funds, increase profits and make himself look good. However, later he became suspicious.

Although both men collected cash from the fake IT consultancy, the professor insisted on delivering it alone, traveling by train to swap bags with a courier at an airport terminal or other public place — or so he said. Max was concerned about security with only one person carrying the cash, but the professor brushed aside his worries. Max's unease continued until one day he searched the professor's office and found correspondence and a statement from a private Swiss bank showing he recently rented a safety deposit box. The pieces fell into place. Max copied the documents and saved them as insurance, marveling at the professor's insouciance.

It was all Gruppen needed. They prosecuted the professor, while Max was allowed to leave quietly and get another job. I don't know the details as I am no longer living in Switzerland, but I heard that, true to form, the professor tried to blame Max, but inconsistencies in his story betrayed him.

Lessons Learned

The obvious lesson is neither businesses nor individuals truly prosper by unethical conduct, and short-term fixes almost always lead to long-term regrets.

(continued)

(continued)

Another lesson is less obvious but extremely important. In pep talks to the professor and Max, Gruppen's leadership continually urged them to aggressively chase business. The message they heard was "Do whatever you have to do to win business." In one meeting, the professor suggested using "unorthodox means." It was obvious he was alluding to bribery, and the director responded with "You should not talk like that in front of me."

I interviewed the director in front of legal counsel and head of audit. He told me he meant there was no place in business for that kind of behavior. Unfortunately, that was not how it was interpreted. To Max and the professor it meant "I don't want to know the details" and was regarded as tacit approval to bribe.

The director was a decent, highly intelligent man, but his lack of leadership and failure to delineate what was acceptable and unacceptable led to an extremely damaging episode. It also cost him his job.

Recommendations to Prevent Future Occurrences

This case illustrates how vital tone at the top is. Gruppen had ethics, conflicts of interest and other relevant policies, but they were not properly disseminated within or outside the organization; nor were they properly enforced.

Senior management must endorse and emphasize proper business conduct and give firm leadership, setting out clearly and concisely what is and is not acceptable. Breaches of codes should be rigorously investigated, and, regardless of rank, offenders should be sanctioned. This did not happen at Gruppen.

There can never be guarantees against malpractice, but inculcating a culture of honesty, high ethical standards supported by tight internal controls and effective oversight will discourage malpractice and help unmask corruption when it occurs.

About the Author

Paul Keyton is a British Chartered Accountant who has specialized in fraud prevention, detection and investigation for over 25 years. He has worked on complex cases worldwide and in multiple sectors, and his clients include major financial institutions, multinationals and government departments. He is based in London.

CHAPTER 25

Calling for Kickbacks

ANIL KUMAR

I spent my first few days at DS Ventures, my new employer in New Delhi, meeting people and settling into the environment. Rajat Malik, a tall, handsome young manager, would catch anyone's attention the moment he walked through a door. Even I noticed him as a promising young employee. Rajat was a hardworking guy, generally the first one in the office and the last one to leave. He seemed like a self-starter who could be an example for his peers and the fresh management trainees inducted into DS Ventures. Rajat had a natural flair for stocks and commodity trading and often consulted with his peers and supervisors about market movements in the early morning.

Rajat was married and had a young son. He had worked as an engineer at a well-regarded organization before starting at DS Ventures and had earned a degree in business management from one of the finest institutions in the country. Rajat had rich experience in business planning and project finance. This, coupled with exceptional business knowledge and flair for hard work, helped him position himself as a confidant of the top management team.

Strong industrial growth in India, booming stock markets and emerging business opportunities resulted in significant foreign investment into the country. Most of the entrepreneurs in India were dreaming big and aspiring to scale up their companies, given the positive industrial sentiment and availability of abundant capital.

DS Ventures was part of a reputed industrial conglomeration in India with diversified business interests. However, DS Ventures had not experienced much growth in the past few years when compared with similar companies in the industry. With the next generation of entrepreneurs now taking keen interest in business, DS Venture's new directors were quick to realize the importance of retaining their industry market share and embarking on major growth plans. At this time, the organization had already initiated new projects in one business segment that involved a capital expenditure of more than $100 million.

After having spent a number of years in my struggle against corporate fraud, corruption and white-collar crime, I accepted an assignment with DS Ventures as a member of its top management team to oversee corporate strategy, as well as to head the assurance and audit function. Given the ambitious business plans and enormity of the capital investment projects that DS Ventures' management were juggling when I was hired, I knew I would have enough on my plate to keep busy. After having spent only a few months in the organization, I was summoned by one of the directors on the board, Gaurav Jain, to discuss a rather sensitive issue.

Gaurav knew of my prior experience with fraud investigations and shared his suspicions about the commercial negotiations process for ongoing development projects. He had received complaints from unsuccessful vendors that the contracts were being awarded unfairly and some vendors were being favored. Gaurav, a man with a positive outlook and a strong belief in his team and their integrity, wanted to confirm that the complaints weren't true. He told me, "I also hired a professional detective agency about two months ago, but they haven't been able to figure out anything yet. Prem Mishra, the department director who is in charge of these new projects, has been with the company for 29 years and his integrity is beyond doubt." Gaurav wanted me to investigate the complaints and confirm for the board of directors that there was nothing wrong with the procurement process.

Too Close for Comfort

The integrity of the team members working on the DS Ventures development project was of utmost importance because the possibility of contract manipulations was high. In addition, plenty of vendors were willing to go that extra mile to oblige procurement officers to help them secure valuable contracts.

My time-tested rules of investigations — "don't believe anyone" and "keep your eyes and ears open to any possible leads" — came in handy in this case. My first thought was "How could Prem Mishra, a department director who had been managing routine operations all these years, be put in charge of a procurement project of such large value without prior experience?"

Operations and project management are two different tasks and require different skill sets. Therefore I suspected Prem must have felt the need to hire a few people with the experience to help him. My intuition was correct. A review of the latest organization chart and personnel files reflected a few new members in Prem's department. I looked into their hiring documents and saw that they had proven experience in project execution.

Rajat Malik was one of the specialists Prem had hired to oversee the development projects as part of the core team. Incidentally Prem had a great interest in the stock markets, and he and Rajat chatted often about market movements, which made them close. But many times Rajat used Prem's official laptop to send e-mails on his personal investments.

Prem was a short man, partially bald with a medium build; he had a good sense of humor, which ensured him the frequent company of his colleagues. He also had a large number of external visitors, including vendors waiting to meet him in the lounge of his swanky office on the 21st floor overlooking the beautiful greens of New Delhi. He was often in one of the meeting rooms adjacent to the reception area with visitors or his "cabinet of ministers" that formed the central procurement and development group. Occasionally, I also happened to enjoy his hospitality during the regular project status meetings he held.

Prem strongly believed in empowering his team members to make decisions and in sharing information liberally with his commercial partners and staff to ensure they were up-to-date and worked together effectively.

Initially I wondered whether I should involve anyone else in my investigation but decided to go it alone, at least at first. Confidentiality was essential, and the internal audit team was not in place yet — we were busy interviewing people for this function.

The Direct Approach

Thus began my fact-finding mission. I began by interviewing people within the purchasing function and compiling a list of project orders to understand which ones were finalized and which were pending. I organized a meeting with Subrat, one of the purchasing managers. In our discussion, Subrat mentioned that during the bid-solicitation phase of the current manufacturing facility expansion project, a potential vendor called him and reported being contacted by someone named Sanjay Kalra. Sanjay claimed to work for DS Ventures and said he could help the vendor secure the contract. We didn't have any details, and it had happened so long ago that the vendor was no longer in operation. Nevertheless, I pulled the contract file, which involved cable vendors, and found the contact information for the bidding company's sales manager, Girish Sachdeva. I called Girish and, after some hesitation, he confirmed that he had received such a phone call, but said he had not recorded the caller's phone number. Girish said that the caller claimed to be a representative of DS Ventures and said that a kickback was necessary if he wanted the contract.

When Girish asked the caller to prove he actually represented DS Ventures, the caller gave him complete details of his confidential bid, including the first and the revised rates he quoted. The caller gave him the names of the people who accompanied Girish to the DS Ventures office, the exact time they had come for the meeting and the room where they met. All this information was sufficient for Girish and his supervisors to believe the caller was a genuine DS Ventures representative and this was the way the company conducted business. Since his organization refused to adopt such unethical practices, it lost out on the contract (and eventually business dealings with DS Ventures).

Scrutiny of the other cable bids revealed that the contract had been issued to a vendor at a price that was only marginally lower than the second lowest bidder's, and not just for one item but for all items in the bid document. This gave me sufficient indication that the vendor who was finally awarded the contract had a good idea about the other quotes DSV received.

Further inquiry revealed that another purchasing officer, Debashish, had once received a similar complaint from another vendor. When I spoke to Debashish, he explained that a bidder, Vineet Singh, claimed to have received a phone call from someone demanding kickbacks in return for helping him secure the contract. Vineet said the person's name was Sanjay Kalra, the same name mentioned by Girish. Sanjay had told Vineet that he was working on behalf of DS Ventures.

Vineet and Sanjay exchanged a few more phone calls, and Sanjay asked for a 4 percent kickback in return for confidential bid information. Vineet tried to accommodate the request, but his company's bid was already as competitive as it could make it; there was no room for the kickback. The contract was eventually awarded to another bidder. Vineet gave me the cell phone and landline numbers from which Sanjay had called him, and I compared them to DS Ventures personnel files, but they did not match any employees' phone numbers.

When I looked into the other bids that Vineet was competing with, it was clear that the winner had been privy to insider information. The winning price for each item in the contract was revised to be marginally lower than the second best bidder. I arranged a meeting with the vendor who won the contract to ask if he had been contacted by Sanjay Kalra. He immediately denied any involvement, but his facial expressions were enough to raise suspicion.

Launching a Full Investigation

It was evident that all was not well in DS Venture's contract negotiations and awarding process, and it was time for a detailed investigation. I contacted Subrat again to understand in detail how contracts were awarded. I wanted the full process — coming up with a list of requirements, floating the request for proposal, identifying potential vendors, receiving quotes and proposals, preparing comparative charts, conducting technical and commercial evaluations, putting bids before the decision-making authorities, negotiating and finally awarding the contract. I also wanted to know who had custody of bid documents and other people on the team who had access to such information.

While most of DS Ventures' procedures seemed to be in line with generally accepted principles, I noted three areas of concern. First, bidders were not identified from an existing database or through an appointed consultant. Most potential contractors were suggested by new appointees on the project team. Second, bids received were compiled into a technical and commercial comparison sheet in Subrat's computer, which was neither password protected nor physically restricted. Third, there was no centralized record of the bids received.

Subrat seemed honest and had cooperated with my investigation promptly, but he was at the helm of all the contracts and I could not rule out the possibility that he was Sanjay. Subrat told me he was normally in the office around 10:00 in the morning and left by 6:30 in the evening. Since his e-mail account had no password protection, anyone could access his messages. I went to Subrat's floor to see who sat near him and who could possibly overhear his conversations with contractors and colleagues.

Rajat Malik occupied the workstation right next to Subrat's. Rajat was also working on the project team, and Subrat had a high regard for him. Subrat said Rajat often suggested potential new contract bidders based on his experience working with contractors in the past. Moreover, he had superb qualifications and was a highly paid executive, which led Subrat to believe that he could be trusted to keep information confidential. Rajat was not part of the procurement team, so he was not directly involved in the contracts and the negotiations. Nevertheless, Rajat frequently asked Subrat about the various bids received from vendors.

While Subrat was telling me this, his face clouded over for a second and he said he just remembered something that had made him uneasy. He told me about an incident when multiple e-mails were forwarded from Subrat's e-mail server to Rajat's personal address on a Friday evening after Subrat had left the office. When he came in Monday morning, Subrat received delivery receipts for each of the forwarded messages, sent automatically from Rajat's personal e-mail address. Surprised by the receipts, he looked to see if the messages were in his Sent folder, but they were not. Apparently someone had accessed his computer in his absence, forwarded the messages and deleted them from the Sent folder without realizing that Subrat's e-mail account automatically requested receipts for sent messages. All the messages contained contract bids received electronically from potential vendors.

When Subrat asked Rajat about it, Rajat initially claimed he did not know anything. However, Subrat brought it to the attention of Prem Mishra, who independently asked Rajat about it. Rajat admitted that he accessed Subrat's computer but said it was out of normal curiosity and to get estimates for cash-flow planning. Rajat apologized and assured Prem that in future he would ask the appropriate person for any information he needed. No disciplinary action was taken.

This was enough to set off my alarm bells. If Rajat genuinely needed the information for cash-flow projections, he would not have forwarded the messages to his personal e-mail address. Even if he had done it in an emergency, he would have informed Subrat and not denied it when first asked. Further, deleting the message from Subrat's Sent folder was very suspicious. The second concern for me was how lightly Prem had handled the issue.

It's All in the Phone Calls

I contacted the telephone company and obtained the past six months' worth of records for Subrat, Rajat, Prem and Sanjay Kalra. I spent hours poring over the files and discovered that Rajat Malik made frequent phone calls to Sanjay Kalra's cell phone, not only during office hours but late at night as well. Similarly, Sanjay Kalra often called Rajat and vendors who had bid for DS Ventures contracts.

Clearly there was some sort of connection between Rajat and Sanjay, and it appeared that they could be involved in a kickback scheme together. Rajat might have provided insider information and Sanjay used it to extort kickbacks from vendors.

Subrat also mentioned that, during the course of contract negotiations, there was a fair amount of precision in revising the bids by certain vendors to make them marginally below the second best offer. Having submitted the revised bids, these vendors were very clear that they could not further revise their quotes even if it meant losing the contracts. This was certainly surprising for the procurement team and seemed out of the ordinary.

Now that I understood what appeared to be the scheme, I needed to find conclusive evidence; the phone records would not be sufficient. I went to Rajat's supervisors and presented my findings so far. They were shocked, and Prem was unwilling to believe that one of his brightest team members was engaging in such practices. However, the evidence could not be ignored.

I was given Rajat's personnel file to review his past employment, salary and so forth. We consulted with the legal department to create a plan of action to confront Rajat. We decided to interview him the next day, after we had a chance to plan a rough list of questions. During the interview we intended to have teams search his desk and computer for more evidence. Finally, we agreed to ask a police officer to be present in case there were any physical confrontations.

The next morning I met up with the company's director of the board, Gaurav Jain, to update him about our findings and the planned course of action. I also requested a copy of Rajat's bank statements (which we had obtained through a private detective) to understand his spending and investment patterns. I learned that he was investing hefty sums of money into stocks and commodities every month.

Around 3:00 p.m., I asked Prem to call Rajat into the conference room; it was time for the interview. While we were gathering, Prem borrowed Rajat's cell phone on the pretext of needing to make a call and having forgotten his own phone. He left the conference room and took the phone to my assistant, who copied the text messages and call logs. While Prem had the phone, Sanjay actually tried to call Rajat, but Prem disconnected the call. As this was happening, another team was deployed to take possession of the personal and official documents in Rajat's desk drawers. The IT department picked up his laptop, backed up all his data and began to create a proper audit trail.

Showdown in the Conference Room

In the meantime, I began the interview in the conference room with a police officer sitting outside. Rajat initially reacted to the questions with surprise and feigned innocence, but quickly became aggressive and began challenging my authority and the basis of my allegations. Piece by piece, I presented the evidence to him for explanation. After three hours of rigorous interrogation (by which time Prem had joined us and returned Rajat's phone), he realized that we had done our homework well before questioning him. He finally admitted that he knew Sanjay Kalra but denied any involvement in contacting potential vendors.

During the interview, the IT director, Sujit, informed us that he had found confidential, personal documents belonging to Prem and Subrat on Rajat's laptop. He also reported that Rajat had remote access to Prem's laptop, which enabled him to access Prem's e-mails and confidential data. Rajat pleaded innocence and said he had no idea how that information came to be on his laptop.

Rajat finally realized how much evidence we had against him and decided to quit lying. He broke down and admitted that he was indeed party to the kickbacks and operated through Sanjay Kalra. He admitted to leaking confidential data for quick financial gains. He said that he had been carried away by his desire for the luxurious lifestyles of the wealthy. He always thought he deserved to be a rich man, knowing that he had the brains to do it.

He asked to call his wife, and we let him call privately from an empty office. He returned ten minutes later and said he understood that he could not continue working at DS Ventures but requested he be allowed to resign rather than be fired. He also asked that we not file criminal charges.

The Grand Total

The contracts that Rajat and Sanjay manipulated with various vendors amounted to $900,000, which netted the duo shared kickbacks of nearly $40,000. Documents found on Rajat's laptop revealed that he made significant expenditures in the past few months in the names of his wife and other relatives. We also found details of other bank accounts in which he parked his kickback money before channeling it into other investments. Large unusual sums of cash had been deposited into his bank accounts at frequent intervals and then invested in stocks and commodities.

We allowed him to leave the office without going back to his workstation and told him that anything personal found at his workstation would be returned to him. We also told him that management would decide whether to file a criminal complaint. He did not look surprised by what was happening; it was like he anticipated being caught eventually. Security escorted him out of the office.

We moved his belongings to a separate room to be reviewed, and I kept the keys to the room with me. I suspected Rajat had an accomplice in DS Ventures helping him, so I asked security to monitor all the incoming calls. The next day Rajat contacted one of the office assistants and asked him to retrieve some personal documents left behind. When I questioned the office assistant, he admitted that Rajat used to tip him for photocopies of sensitive documents, but he had no knowledge of the importance of the files. He was given a warning and returned to work.

Lessons Learned

Out of curiosity, I conducted a reference check with Rajat's previous employer and discovered that they had a fair idea about his suspicious interactions with vendors, but no one from DS Ventures called them before Rajat was hired. In the end, management decided not to file criminal charges because they did not want to attract the media attention, particularly not at a time when they were trying to expand operations. They were unable to collect any restitution from Sanjay or Rajat but accepted the loss as a necessary cost of learning. This case taught DS Ventures executives a few important lessons:

1. Proper documentation procedures must be followed and audit trails established for transactions.
2. Interviewing suspects is valuable, particularly in this case because we were able to hear Rajat's excuses firsthand and immediately counter them with evidence.
3. Use of law enforcement agencies can be helpful when interviewing fraud suspects.
4. Planning during the investigation and interviewing phases is critical to success.
5. Flexibility during investigations is necessary when faced with roadblocks and the need to create alternate plans.
6. Establishing the fraud and obtaining a confession from the perpetrator requires a well-planned strategy.

Recommendations to Prevent Future Occurrences

DS Ventures' board of directors enacted a new anti-fraud policy after this case, and it included the following points:

1. Confidentiality and security of documents during contract negotiations is essential.
2. Vendor selection should be an independent process, and recommendations must be thoroughly evaluated.
3. Proper reference checks should be conducted before hiring new employees to establish their integrity.
4. Information about commercial matters should be kept confidential by the people involved in negotiations.
5. Channels of communication should be kept open, especially for unsuccessful vendors who bid for contracts.
6. Lifestyle checks on employees can reveal possible red flags.
7. Do not assume that high qualifications translate to high integrity in employees.

Corruption is widespread throughout the world. In some places it has even become a way of life and an accepted norm. There are innumerable cases in which people have adopted unfair means to acquire wealth to lead a lavish lifestyle. Many young professionals are lured into such methods to make a quick buck, expecting a fortune but ending up in a mess.

Development projects attract significant capital investments, but they also entice specialized fraudsters who are on the lookout for organizations making large investments for obvious reasons — the larger the value of projects, the greater their take. The more experience members of the anti-fraud community gain through investigations, the better equipped we will be to prevent future schemes.

About the Author

Anil Kumar is a Certified Fraud Examiner with more than 24 years of experience in consulting and fraud investigation. He worked as executive director and head of audit and investigations for large multinational corporations in various sectors, such as media, telecommunications, pharmaceuticals, manufacturing, automobiles and consulting. He currently heads the strategy and consulting practice at the consulting firm Potential Search and is also the CEO at MySource Innoventures Pvt Ltd.

CHAPTER

Going Green in Mexico

RONALD L. DURKIN

Viento Manufacturing Company sold electricity-making windmills throughout the United States and in more than 25 countries. Viento's customer base included individuals, companies of all sizes and governmental entities. The heightened focus on going green had increased windmill sales, and the company's marketing efforts focusing on carbon-footprint reduction and environmental responsibility had proved worthwhile.

All was on the up-and-up for Viento. The company had been founded as a labor of love by Peter Viento about 20 years earlier when he left a stable and well-paying job as an engineer to devote his efforts to developing products that would make energy cheaper and cleaner for the masses. Over the years, the company enjoyed slow but steady growth based on the values of innovation and quality. Peter had a lot to be proud of, including the VMC2 windmill, a design he personally engineered a decade earlier that remains atop the list of most popular windmills sold in the United States.

Viento's history of selling windmills in Mexico went back more than 20 years. Although the windmill market had become more saturated every year, Viento maintained market share by consistently beating the competitors' quality and delivering excellent customer service. Viento's sales record in Mexico for windmills and replacement parts in the past 20 years was in excess of $35 million.

From the beginning, Peter managed all facets of the company from design and manufacturing to the back-office operations and accounting. He maintained a very small group whom he trusted deeply. They largely consisted of family members and friends. Five years prior, Peter brought in his first highly skilled employee to the accounting department to fill the role of chief financial officer. John Scrivener was a CPA and a former auditor with a major accounting firm. Soon after the hire, Peter relinquished the accounting responsibilities to Scrivener and all was going well. . . . or so he thought.

245

The Salesman

Francisco Javier was very successful in Mexico, and his agency, Quality Sales, had been in business for more than ten years. Francisco had friends in high places in the Mexican government, and these relationships provided his business with a steady flow of contracts and impressive sales figures. Francisco operated in a particularly lucrative niche of energy-sector clients. Word spread of Francisco's ability to deliver contracts from state-owned enterprises in Mexico, and a successful track record brought him a long list of happy customers.

As Francisco's success in the marketing and sales of goods and services grew, he faced a growing challenge of serving two different types of clients with competing values. On one side were the companies that provided goods and services based on the model of creating electricity by burning fossil fuels. On the other side were those that provided "green" technologies, such as wind and solar power.

To handle this challenge and better appeal to both kinds of clients, Francisco decided to set up a separate company called Superior Sales. Superior was to handle the "green" clients, and Quality would focus on the more traditional customers. It was Francisco's intention to keep Quality's and Superior's business relationships separate.

Francisco's wife, Juanita, was an integral part of both companies, which had become family businesses. Francisco focused on fulfilling sales, and Juanita maintained the books and records, paid the bills and signed sales contracts.

When not in the office, the Javiers lived in a quiet community outside of Puerto Vallarta, and all was well, or so Francisco thought.

Unknown Exposure

Viento used a third-party sales agent in Mexico for many years, but Peter was unhappy with him because he did most, if not all of his work, by phone. He rarely went outside his office to sell products or services to his clients. Since Mexico is a very large, geographically and economically diverse country, physically reaching out and setting in-person meetings in areas needing windmills and replacement parts was critical for Viento's success.

After learning about Francisco and Superior Sales from a friend in Mexico, Peter decided to interview Francisco and determine whether he would be suited to Viento's needs. Francisco convinced Peter that he was on the road most of the time and would be the man to market and sell Viento's products. Francisco dropped a few names and mentioned that he had strong professional relationships with officials in the Mexican government. When he explained that his company, Superior Sales, focused on green energy providers and knew how to market that initiative, Peter was convinced that Francisco was the right agent for Viento.

Francisco asked that his contract be structured with a commission plus reimbursement of travel costs. After discussing the actual components of the contract, the sales expectations and other details, the deal was finalized. Francisco was to receive a 20 percent commission with a reimbursement of travel costs not to exceed 10 percent of the sales contract. Depending on the extent of travel costs incurred, Francisco could receive a 30 percent fee in some cases.

During the six years that Francisco sold windmills and replacement parts for Viento, he earned more than $3 million in commissions and reimbursements. He did quite well as a sales agent for Viento, and they were pleased with his work.

Francisco was one of the best sales agents in Mexico. He knew everyone in positions of power and treated his friends very well. Lavish meals, fishing trips, tickets to sporting events and other gratuities made Francisco a powerful force. No other sales agent in Mexico had his connections nor did they have his marketing prowess; he was an agent's agent.

But agents who pay gratuities to government officials or shower them with gifts and promises of more lavish treatment can get themselves and others in big trouble. Since Francisco was a Mexican citizen and not knowledgeable about the Foreign Corrupt Practices Act (FCPA), he created a huge exposure for himself and his clients.

The Secret Hiding in the Books

Alps was a global, heavy-construction company located in Florida. Alps built power-generation plants and installed generators in commercial projects such as high-rise buildings and shopping centers. Alps used sales agents in various parts of the world to identify opportunities to sell their construction services. Alps also used Francisco in Mexico as their lead sales agent.

In doing their routine internal control review over compliance with the FCPA, Alps' internal auditors identified certain weaknesses and therefore expanded their testing to determine whether there were any potential violations of the FCPA. To their shock they identified payments made to certain Mexican government officials through Francisco. In their opinion the evidence was conclusive; they saw expense reimbursements for lavish vacations and luxury items such as jewelry and fine art and knew it was a big problem.

After conducting an internal investigation and determining the extent of the corruption scheme, executives at Alps went to the Department of Justice (DOJ) and admitted their wrongdoing. Doing so would help Alps and its management limit exposure. The DOJ wanted to know the entire story and who was involved. After demonstrating that Francisco was intimately connected to making the alleged bribe payments, the DOJ focused on Francisco's other sales agency, Superior Sales.

For context, the FCPA is a federal law that prohibits U.S. companies from offering or providing, either directly or indirectly through a third party, anything of value to a foreign government official for the purpose of obtaining or retaining business. The FCPA has two provisions. The first deals with anti-bribery. The second provision addresses accounting and internal control issues. The anti-bribery provisions of the FCPA apply to all individuals, employees and agents of U.S.-based entities. The accounting provisions relate only to U.S. registrants (publicly traded companies).

Assumed Kickbacks

The DOJ and federal agents subpoenaed bank account and other records so that they could see who else was doing business with Quality. The agents found out that Francisco owned Quality Sales and Superior Sales. Each had separate bank accounts and separate customers. Quality handled Alps-related sales and Superior handled Viento-related business.

The federal agents determined that Francisco used Quality's bank account to pay bribes to foreign officials. The bribes included a Rolex watch, diamond bracelets and a series of rare and valuable artwork for a government official who worked at a large utility company in Mexico. They also determined that Francisco *might* have used his other company, Superior, to bribe foreign officials in Mexico.

As a result of their findings from the investigation of Quality, the DOJ and the United States Attorney's Office indicted Francisco and Juanita. Additionally, because Viento conducted business with Superior, they also indicted Viento (the business) as well as Peter and John, the CFO. One of the key issues that surfaced was fact that Francisco was receiving roughly 30 percent of the sales contracts from Viento. Instead of viewing Francisco's fee as a combination of commission and cost reimbursement, the federal agents deemed the entire amount as a 30 percent commission. As such, they suggested this was the kickback that Francisco was receiving from Viento for securing the sales.

Although Francisco and Juanita lived in Mexico, Juanita was arrested in the United States while she was attending a meeting with her investment advisor. She was ordered to stand trial along with Peter and John, who were not incarcerated. Since Juanita was a Mexican citizen and considered a flight risk, she was denied bail and had to spend her time in federal prison prior the legal proceedings. Her husband, who had been indicted but not arrested, was secure in his native country of Mexico and therefore was never in a position to stand trial.

Conflicting Evidence

I was approached by Viento's defense counsel to act as a defense witness. Previously, I was an FBI agent specializing in white-collar crime cases before joining the private sector. Knowing that the government was on the other side and was nearly impossible to defeat in court, I still accepted the engagement but as a consultant, not an expert witness. The reason I decided to accept was to help the defense determine whether any of the payments made to Viento's sales agent went to bribe foreign officials. Defense counsel was of the belief that no payments were made to purchase luxury goods, nor were any payments made to Quality, the other entity controlled by Francisco.

To accomplish this goal, I had to determine the flow of funds both into and out of Viento through a process called *tracing*. Briefly stated, tracing of cash is an analysis of the flow of funds from bank account to bank account for the purpose of identifying specific transactions, purchases, sales or other attributes.

Using a data analysis tool, I uploaded receipts and disbursements for the period under review and began the process of determining the sources and uses of funds. The first step involved examining payments made to Viento under contracts with clients in Mexico. Because of the existing relationships and long history of sales in Mexico that existed prior to Francisco's tenure as sales agent, those sales were also considered in this analysis.

The second step was to examine all payments made from Viento by check or wire transfer for the period under review. After using the data analysis tool to list payments to vendors and others, I scheduled them from largest to smallest (dollar amount). I also used a search function to run the names of Francisco's sales agencies, Quality and Superior, to determine the number of payments, dates of each payment and description of the dates of service and contract information.

To demonstrate completion of my work, I made sure that the database and its totals tied out to the bank statements, which they did without exception. I was now ready to compare these results with the government's charts and diagrams. Although the government claimed that Viento made large payments to Quality, I determined that was totally untrue.

I also reviewed various affidavits prepared by federal agents as well as grand jury testimony of agents and others to determine what evidence there was to prove that payments were made by Viento and its agents to foreign officials.

When I was unable to trace any payment from Viento to a foreign official for any luxury good or service, I presented my results to the defense team. But after a five-week trial, the jury convicted all of the defendants, including Viento and Peter, of violations stemming from the FCPA.

The government agents alleged that the funds from the Mexican sales contracts were the result of bribes paid by Francisco to government officials in Mexico. According to the government, and contrary to evidence proven in our tracing procedures, Viento allegedly supplied the funds to purchase the luxury goods for the government officials. Additionally, the government argued that Francisco was receiving an exorbitant fee from Viento for his services. By looking at Francisco's commission and travel reimbursement as one total fee, the government contended that this was all an inflated commission payment and kickback for securing the sales in Mexico.

The case was appealed by the defense based on procedural as well as factual issues. After a thorough review of the facts and the evidence, including the pretrial, trial and post-trial conduct on the part of the government, the District Court judge dismissed the case against the defendants. The judge found that the government misrepresented key facts in the case as well as allowed agents to testify untruthfully during the trial and to the grand jury to obtain the indictment.

Lessons Learned

Any U.S.–based company conducting business in a foreign country is responsible for adherence to the FCPA's provisions for all of its officers, directors and employees. The company is also responsible for the adherence to the FCPA's provisions of any and all third-party agents and business partners with whom it is affiliated. Unfortunately, many businesses do not know this.

In addition to the FCPA, all organizations are required to meet the provisions of the U.S. Federal Sentencing Guidelines (FSG) by having an effective compliance and ethics program in place. The program should be designed to prevent and detect criminal conduct and promote an organizational culture that encourages ethical conduct and a commitment to compliance with the law.

Companies need to have knowledgeable people within the organization who understand the risks of fraud and misconduct to ensure compliance with the laws. This oversight function should be assigned to a high-level person in management. Even smaller organizations like Viento need to have compliance and ethics programs in place.

The fact that Viento was a small company cannot excuse the lack of this important oversight function. If Peter created an effective compliance and ethics program, the risk of a possible FCPA violation might have been identified prior to the execution of the contract with Francisco. Knowledge of corruption risks associated with doing business in foreign countries is critical to avoid entering into questionable contracts with sales agents or government officials.

Recommendations to Prevent Future Occurrences

Management of companies operating in a foreign country should*:

- Develop and promulgate a clearly articulated and visible policy against violations of the FCPA, including anti-bribery, books and records and internal controls provisions. Include similar foreign laws; the policy should be memorialized in a written compliance code.

- Ensure that senior management provides strong, explicit and visible support and commitment to its corporate policy against violations of the anti-corruption laws and its compliance code.
- Write and promulgate compliance standards and procedures to reduce violations of the anti-corruption laws. Encourage the observance of ethics and compliance standards against foreign bribery by personnel at all levels of the company (and any affiliates). Notify all employees that compliance with the standards and procedures is their duty. Standards and procedures include policies governing:
  - Gifts
  - Hospitality, entertainment and expenses
  - Customer travel
  - Political contributions
  - Charitable donations and sponsorships
  - Facilitation payments
  - Solicitation and extortion
- Define these compliance standards and procedures, including internal controls, ethics and compliance programs, on the basis of risk assessment addressing the individual circumstances of the company.
- Review anti-corruption standards and procedures annually and update them appropriately.
- Assign responsibility for implementation and oversight of the anti-corruption policies to one or more senior executives. Such officials should have direct reporting obligations to independent monitoring bodies such as internal audit or the board of directors.
- Design a system of financial and accounting controls to ensure the maintenance of fair and accurate books, records and accounts to prevent their use in paying or concealing the payment of bribes.
- Communicate effectively the anti-corruption polices, standards and procedure to all directors, officers, employees and agents and partners. Include periodic training and annual certifications.
- Establish and maintain an effective system to:
  - Provide guidance to directors, officers, employees, agents and business partners on complying with anti-corruption policies, standards and procedures, including when they need advice or in any foreign jurisdiction in which the company operates.
  - Offer internal and, where possible, confidential reporting and protection to all potential whistleblowers.
  - Respond appropriately to reports of suspicious behavior.
- Institute disciplinary procedures to address violations of the anti-corruption laws and code, policies and procedures of the company.
- Establish due diligence and compliance requirements pertaining to the retention and oversight of all external agents and business partners, such as:
  - Applying properly documented, risk-based due diligence pertaining to the hiring and regular oversight of agents and business partners.

(continued)

(continued)

- Informing agents and business partners of the company's commitment anti-corruption laws and of the company's ethics and compliance policies.
- Seeking a reciprocal commitment from agents and business partners.
- Where necessary, include standard provisions in agreements, contracts and renewals thereof with all agents and business partners to allow the company to:
  - Require anti-corruption representations.
  - Conduct audits of the books and records of the agent or business partner.
  - Terminate an agent or business partner as a result of any breach of anti-corruption laws.
- Management should conduct periodic reviews and tests of its anti-corruption compliance code, standards and procedures to evaluate and improve their effectiveness in preventing and detecting violations of anti-corruption laws.

United States of America vs. Panalpina Transport (Holding) LTD Deferred Prosecution Agreement, www.justice.gov/opa/documents/panalpina-world-transport-dpa.pdf

About the Author

Ron Durkin, CFE, CPA/CFF, CIRA, is a partner at CliftonLarsonAllen LLP. Ron has more than 30 years of combined experience in public accounting and as a special agent with the Federal Bureau of Investigation. He has testified in accounting, financial and bankruptcy matters in U.S. District Court, U.S. Bankruptcy Court, U.S. Tax Court and various state courts. He earned a bachelor's degree in accounting and a master's degree in business administration from California State University, Sacramento. He is a frequent presenter of anti-fraud education.

A Wolf in Sheep's Clothing

DANIEL NITA

Adrian Marinescu was a young man who seemed outwardly like any other growing up in Brasov, Romania. He finished high school in town, attended college and was looking for a job. His family called on their collective professional contacts to try to get Adrian a job out of school and help him off to a good start as an adult. Both of his parents had strong careers and networks of associates; his father was a retired military officer and his mother was still active in the army. Opportunity came Adrian's way when a distant relative, Mary Anne, offered him a job that would allow him to settle into a quiet and safely engaged life.

In the beautiful mountain town of Brasov, people enjoyed simple, peaceful lives. As in many other small towns, the local economy received important support from credit institutions. One such establishment in Brasov was the well-rated Astar Bank. Founded in 2000, Astar achieved a strong market position in a few short years and was one of the top ten banks in the nation for several years in a row. Astar was a well-organized company with a professional management team and very strong employees occupying key positions.

Two factors helped Astar Bank hold its position: a skilled sales team and a strong control group, consisting of internal control, anti-fraud and compliance teams. Mary Anne led the internal controls department at Astar and had earned top management's trust in her professional and leadership abilities. She had just one weakness — she loved her family and had unconditional trust in them. All of them.

Thus, young Adrian received a job offer as a client advisor from Astar, thanks to Mary Anne. No one seemed to mind that he had no experience in banking (really, no work experience at all) and was woefully unqualified for this position.

Credit Spikes

In Astar Bank, one of the permanent activities of the anti-fraud department I lead is to constantly monitor sales activity by reviewing periodic reports. One day I noticed a significant increase in credit cards sales in one of the bank units. Generally, this can be a sign that something suspicious happened in a branch or region, so I decided to pull the records of 40 customers who obtained credit cards in this unit during the time frame.

My conclusions after this first check were:

- The same four companies issued certificates of income (e.g., verifications) for all 40 individuals.
- All the customers shared the same phone number.
- The customers' reported wages were too high and not consistent with the realities of Romanian incomes and the job listed (generally taxi drivers, maids and bricklayers).
- The advisor for all 40 clients was Adrian. He contacted only one customer and wrote in the file, "He didn't want his phone number entered in the computer system." That was Adrian's reason for using the same number for all the rest.
- When I called the phone number listed on the records, the person did not know any of the customers, Adrian or Astar Bank.

Following these initial discoveries, I decided to conduct an on-site review. My objective was to get as much insight from unit employees into how they issued new credit cards and to identify other cases that followed the same pattern. To cover more activities in the same time, I asked Oana and Marius — two of my colleagues in the anti-fraud department — to accompany me on my first visit.

During the visit to Adrian's branch in Brasov, we identified several sets of incomplete records that nevertheless were used to issue credit cards with various credit limits. I stressed to Oana and Marius that one of the most important tasks on our plate was to preserve the chain of custody for all the evidence we uncovered, should any of it turn out to be essential to proving the case.

I asked Radu, the staff member responsible for monitoring card activity, to identify all cards issued by the Brasov branch that had similar circumstances as my 40 suspicious accounts. At this time, Radu proactively called the security officer who monitored the branch's video surveillance and asked him to check all the footage from the suspicious time frame. Radu's search identified more cards issued by Adrian with the same associated phone number. We checked the history for the cards and found that many of them were used at the same ATM on the same day, and the first transaction on each was a $150 withdrawal. "That's very interesting!" I said, reading Radu's report. Armed with a suspicion, Radu and I watched the video footage of the ATM and — surprise! — it showed Adrian Marinescu withdrawing money at the ATM with the customers' cards.

We could not believe what we were seeing on the monitor. Nobody wanted to think that this nice young man from a good family, recommended by the internal controls department coordinator, could steal money from customers. I quickly realized that we needed two things. First, discretion: I told everyone involved in the investigation, "Until this case is closed, we are all forbidden from discussing it with anyone else." Second, respecting the professional ethics of investigators, we had to perform more checks to confirm our suspicions. I wanted to rule out any doubts that this could be a misunderstanding or a coincidence. Perhaps the card holders asked Adrian to make the withdrawals as a way to activate the cards. Admittedly, that was a slim possibility. Or perhaps we really had another problem — an insider in our organization colluding with someone outside the bank to commit fraud.

And, of course, I had to inform Marku, Astar's president. Every investigator knows that this is a sensitive moment, when you have to present bad news about an internal employee. But it is part of the job, so there I was, in the president's office, summarizing the evidence.

"Incredible! Are you sure? Adrian? I just received a proposal from his superior to increase his salary and offer him a promotion. There's no doubt that Adrian was at the ATM?" I explained the investigation and our evidence so far, and he asked me what effect the case would have on Mary Anne.

I told him my team and I had plans to maintain confidentiality while further establishing Adrian's full involvement and that, if necessary, we would extend our investigation to other possible conspirators. I summarized the plan and requested permission to use an external investigator to assist, which Marku approved. We parted, and I promised to keep him updated about each step we took.

Expanding the Team

After obtaining the president's permission to bring in third-party assistance, I contacted my old friend Emil, who used to work at Astar and was now a private detective. I described the case in detail, and he agreed to join the investigation team. Together we developed an action plan with clearly defined steps and tasks for each person involved. We went to work — me with my team and he with his — always keeping in touch. Each day ended with a short debriefing between Emil and me to analyze our results and fine tune our plan.

After analyzing documents, talking with branch managers and client advisors and tracking the video surveillance images, we found the following:

- Most of the 40 credit cards had been requested, issued and delivered in violation of the bank's internal controls procedures. Customers had not submitted written requests, and Adrian bypassed the mandatory checks required by Astar's policies. The accounts were not approved by the branch manager.
- In none of the 40 cases was a contract completed and signed; there were no account opening agreements either.
- Adrian Marinescu received a copy of the identity card and a certificate of income from a person who — according to Adrian — was the customer's employer (although the clients were employed at different companies). It sounded like a joke to us, but Adrian told us very seriously that the person assured him he was committed to repaying lines of credit if the borrowers defaulted.
- The clients never went to the bank. Adrian activated the cards and distributed them outside the bank, to the leader of a criminal group, as it turned out. We later identified him as the "employer" of all the account holders.

At this point, I asked for support from my colleagues in the sales department to verify all the records associated with the 40 credit cards. The objective was to determine precisely what documents that were missing from each file in the hope of obtaining a complete picture of all the violations. The result was spectacular: fraudulent credit limits totaling $225,000. The issuing conditions were, in all cases, those mentioned above.

As this research was occurring, my daily meetings with Emil continued to bring new data. At the end of the investigation, our combined evidence established and proved:

- How this attack was planned
- Who the people were and how deeply they were involved
- How the culprits divided the money obtained

Delivering the Bad News

It was time to give Marku the whole picture. He postponed a scheduled meeting to give me half an hour of his time. Knowing how much he valued Mary Anne, I had a feeling that he would be anxious to know if she had been involved in any way. My answer — "Yes, she was involved, and has been involved from the beginning" — hardened the president. He called his secretary and asked her to reschedule all his meetings that day. "Do not disturb us for anything!" were his last words to his secretary as she left us.

Broadly, the report said the following.

Two crooks devised an ingenious plan to earn money dishonestly. They ran employment ads for various jobs in a construction company, and the "owner" of the company copied the applicants' personal documents, such as ID cards, driver's licenses and educational diplomas. These documents were then presented to a bank to request lines of credit on behalf of those people — without the applicants ever knowing. The perpetrators would split the money and leave town.

There was just one hitch for our con men, named Stefan and Mircea. They knew the bank would not accept photocopies of documents, especially without the applicant appearing in person. However, Stefan caught a lucky break when he discovered than an old friend of his, Mary Anne, worked at the local Astar Bank. He called and set up a meeting.

Mary Anne agreed to help Stefan and Mircea in return for a very large kickback from each credit account Stefan and Mircea opened. She brokered the meeting between the two fraudsters and Adrian Marinescu — the perfect fall guy to help with the scam. Adrian assumed that if Mary Anne was involved, the plan had to be legitimate. She was in charge of internal controls, after all. Moreover, Adrian was enticed by the "bonuses" Mary Anne promised him for helping with the credit cards.

Shortly after he was hired, Adrian and branch manager Amalia Anghel began a close relationship. Amalia turned out to be a co-conspirator; Adrian told Mary Anne about it and said they would have no problem getting approval on the credit applications now.

Marku was still not convinced of Mary Anne's involvement. "From what you've presented so far, all I can tell is that Mary Anne introduced two potential clients to a bank employee. There is nothing wrong with that." I understood that he was having a hard time accepting the news about a favored employee. However, I could not hide the results of the investigation, and I presented the last evidence:

- Mary Anne's bank statements from accounts she held at two other financial institutions showing large deposits immediately following the activation of each fraudulent credit card
- The two cards attached to these two accounts, issued on behalf of Mary Anne, along with some video images taken from different ATMs showing her using the cards to withdrawal large sums of money

The evidence was enough for everyone, including Marku. He immediately called the members of the board of directors and set up a meeting for me to present my findings. The very next day I found myself in a conference room facing Marku and all the board members. Marku introduced me and said, "Daniel has some information that we need to share with you."

I described the investigation and our findings as briefly as possible by saying:

- We had a case of corrupt employees colluding with external fraudsters to perpetrate a crime.
- The external participants were two con men (Stefan and Mircea) who convinced the internal controls supervisor to help with their crime by offering her kickbacks.
- The internal players were a client advisor (Adrian), the internal controls supervisor (Mary Anne) and a manager (Amalia). They signed up customers for credit cards without their knowledge and based on false or forged documents. They also accepted a kickback from Stefan and Mircea for every credit account they opened.

The truth was hard to accept. The person who was supposed to identify, combat and prevent violations of the bank's internal regulations, the internal controls supervisor, was the one who cooperated with the external group to commit fraud. "No way!" "Not Mary Anne!" and "You are kidding me!" were some of the reactions of board members after I presented the findings.

I continued to explain how the fraud was committed. Mary Anne introduced Adrian and Stefan, and they agreed on the terms of their scheme (each player would receive one-quarter of the proceeds collected from the false credit cards). Stefan and Mircea began sending Adrian the "employment" documents they gathered from their false job advertisements, and Adrian used them to complete credit applications. Stefan and Mircea also provided Adrian with documentation to attest that the individuals were employed. Adrian would then ask Amalia, with whom he had a personal relationship, to sign off on the applications as the branch manager. The applications would then be processed and approved, and Adrian would intercept the delivery of the cards. He would activate them using the ATM at his bank branch and pass the cards on the Stefan or Mircea.

A routine control would not have prevented the fraud because of extensive collusion. Moreover, if anyone noticed something amiss with an application, it would look like an honest mistake or, at worst, employee negligence.

Adrian violated regulations regarding customer communications and other bank internal rules. In the end, the total losses suffered by Astar Bank were only $30,000. But the potential damage was more than $150,000, taking the approved credit limits into account. We were able to limit the losses by blocking all the suspicious accounts as soon as we discovered them, before the fraudsters were able to access the full line of credit.

The board of directors voted for a disciplinary hearing against Amalia, Mary Anne and Adrian, which resulted in all three being terminated. The executives at Astar also filed a criminal complaint against all the offenders.

Lessons Learned

I think the most important lesson this case taught me was that, regardless of an employee's reputation at a company, nobody should be above suspicion. I also learned the importance of conducting background checks and solid interviewing of potential new employees. Astar's management relied on Mary Anne's recommendation of Adrian, even though he was clearly unqualified for the position. Perhaps he was hired primarily to assist her in the scheme.

Recommendations to Prevent Future Occurrences

Crime obviously can't be completely eliminated from our day-by-day life. But it is important to find different ways to prevent it. This is our job as anti-fraud professionals — to make recommendations to top management to ensure a proper framework is in place to prevent, discover and investigate such offenses. After this case, I sent the board the following proposals:

- Change internal controls to include a monitoring system that reviews branch activities at the central office, specifically including a random sample of approved credit applications
- Move the power of credit card and loan approvals to the central office, meaning individual branches would no longer have that authority
- Modify hiring procedures and improve the background checks for people recruited for top management positions

The board enacted all of my recommendations, which shows that Mary Anne's story shook their trust in human behavior, just as it shook mine.

About the Author

Daniel Nita is from Pitesti, Romania. He earned a law degree from the police academy in Bucharest in 1997 and worked as a police inspector for five years. He also gained experience managing private companies before accepting his current post as the director of bank security at a large Romanian bank. His specialties include fraud prevention and identification. He has collaborated with the Romanian Banking Institute to conduct seminars on bank fraud. He believes that fraud is everywhere and we should be prepared for it at all times.

CHAPTER

Dances with Fraud

HANK J. BRIGHTMAN

The desert has a way of playing tricks on the mind. From a distance, there appeared to be rolling, lush green hills — thicker and denser than the most perfectly manicured fairway at Pebble Beach. Yet, as I drove mile after mile on the pockmarked and rutted roads of the reservation in my "lowest government rate" rental car that was clearly ill suited for the endeavor, it became apparent that I wasn't seeing forests, but rather the periodic piñon and scrub that jutted out from the stark white and gray rock faces against an endless expanse of cloudless pink and orange sky.

It seemed nearly impossible to fathom that just a week earlier I was sitting in my office in Jersey City, New Jersey, grading my students' final examinations in my undergraduate white-collar crime course. Moreover, less than 48 hours later, I was receiving briefings from a spate of mid-level government officials at the U.S. Department of the Interior's Bureau of Indian Affairs (BIA) Headquarters in Washington, D.C., each seeking to impress upon me the challenges of managing environmental remediation and infrastructure enhancement projects from more than 2,000 miles away.

Isolation and rural settings were nothing new to me. Having spent nearly eight years with the National Park Service working in resource protection and environmental contractor fraud enforcement, I had grown accustomed to such venues — from the endlessness of Alaska's Denali National Park to the impenetrableness of the Florida Everglades. However, this experience was profoundly different. There was a sacred mystique traveling this lightly mapped terrain where GPS feared to tread. The stark beauty of the landscape made me question what expectations, if any, I should have about those I was going to meet with. Would Anzarki chief Stephen St. Cloud greet me warmly, seeing my visit as an opportunity to clearly document his tribe's accomplishments in the remediation of asbestos from the three tribal schools so that he could move forward with Phase II of this BIA-funded project?

261

How would the Anzarki superintendent of schools, Dr. Shirley Manyfeathers, and her political champion, Daniel Yazzite, a seasoned tribal council member and school board president, perceive this official office call? Perhaps they would simply consider me a necessary nuisance forced upon them by the requirements of the $2 million grant awarded in accordance with the Tribe Education Amendments Act of 1978 to mitigate asbestos hazards in tribal schools. I pondered whether each of them would be as hard and weathered as the landscape that surrounded me, especially since they had all been born and spent the better part of their lives working on "the rez" (reservation) — an accomplishment unto itself, given the Anzarki Nation's high unemployment and decaying physical infrastructure.

Unlike many of their sister nations, the Anzarki did not have casino interests or large commercial holdings; rather, many of its members were employed in the agricultural and livestock sectors at both the labor and — to a lesser extent — managerial levels. The tribe also received considerable grants and subsidies from the federal government through the BIA. Because there was not much incentive to remain on tribal land, many of the younger members of Anzarki Nation sought employment far from the reservation, especially those who had graduated from all three of the reservation's schools.

Unfortunately, a substantial number of Anzarki's Flat Top High School graduates found themselves ill prepared for either college or successful careers in corporate America. Indeed, it was this challenge that prompted three-term superintendent of schools Manyfeathers to promise widespread reforms in terms of both academic content and the environment in which this learning occurred. Manyfeathers had found an ardent supporter in her quest for both physical infrastructure enhancement and curriculum reform in Daniel Yazzite, a senior member of the tribal council and president of the school board. Through their combined advocacy and sheer tenacity, Yazzite and Manyfeathers were able to convince Anzarki Nation Chief Stephen St. Cloud to petition the BIA for a multiphase grant to improve the physical infrastructure of the three tribal schools.

The equally persistent and politically astute St. Cloud was able to garner a multimillion-dollar, phased, facilities-improvement grant from the BIA. Phase I provided the Anzarki Nation with nearly $2 million to mitigate asbestos hazards, including friable insulation, ducting and floor tiling, in Running Bear Elementary School, Wandering Brook Middle School and Flat Top High School. Following a very brief bid announcement in the Anzarki newspaper, the tribal council and school board had selected Whylaway Asbestos Control, Inc., owned and operated by Patrick Whylaway, to perform the asbestos mitigation and remediation project in accordance with the 1986 Asbestos Hazard Emergency Response Act (AHERA). Randall Uryechee, occupational health and safety officer for the Anzarki Nation, supervised the project.

Friend of the Tribe

Whylaway was well known to the leadership of the Anzarki Nation, having been afforded the title of "Friend of the Tribe" nearly five years earlier in recognition of his faithful service to the community. In addition to hiring a large number of the tribe's senior high school students and recent graduates for both skilled and unskilled positions in his business, Whylaway personally oversaw the refurbishment of several of the Anzarki Nation's tribal leaders' homes, including Chief St. Cloud's and Daniel Yazzite's. Indeed, the high quality of Whylaway's work, which included a vast granite solarium complete with an ornate marble sundial on the St. Cloud property and a rich mahogany-paneled recreation room at Yazzite's home — all for prices that seemed impossibly low — were enough to convince Randall Uryechee to contract with Whylaway for a new in-ground swimming pool that was constructed last fall.

Interestingly, much of Whylaway's work beyond the reservation consisted solely of small-scale residential painting, drywall and roof repairs — certainly nothing of the scope or magnitude required for the mitigation of serious asbestos hazards at the three school buildings and four storage facilities that comprised the Anzarki education district. Despite this lack of experience, records signed by Uryechee and filed with the BIA earlier that year attested Phase I of the project had been properly completed not only in a timely manner but also that Whylaway's crew had actually finished ahead of schedule — qualifying the contractor for an early completion incentive bonus.

Meet the Tribe

"For the record, Professor, we don't appreciate you sticking your nose in our private affairs." Even as Chief St. Cloud chided me for my intrusion into what he perceived to be tribe business, I could not help but sense his aura of affability — he had an almost apologetic air since, on some level, he was aware that I was authorized to conduct this verification audit on behalf of the BIA. However, the chief's tacit understanding was countered by the icy, dagger-laden stares of Dr. Manyfeathers and Daniel Yazzite. Manyfeathers said, "It is beyond the realm of comprehension why you people from Washington have to come here so close to the start of our new school year to disrupt our preparations." She neither blinked nor varied her stern tone — a stalwart pitch she had perfected by years of teaching and school administrative service.

Yazzite added, "As Dr. Manyfeathers has so eloquently stated, your unanticipated, unannounced visit can only be seen as a sign of the mistrust and lack of confidence that you bureaucrats have in our tribal leadership. I can assure you, Professor, that the feeling is mutual."

For a split second, I contemplated offering a firm but gentle response. After all, I could have reminded them that unannounced audits are a matter of BIA protocol, a grant provision that each of them was more than happy to sign and have notarized in triplicate. Yet my attention was drawn to the unassuming figure in the corner of St. Cloud's spacious office. Although he never looked directly at me, I could sense Randall Uryechee's seemingly downtrodden demeanor. Politely excusing myself from the three tribal leaders, I made my way over to Uryechee. He was a tall, thin man with a wisp of white hair and soft hazel eyes that contrasted with his sun-soaked skin. My guess was that he might have been in his mid-40s although he looked about ten years older. One of the few Anzarkis to have earned both a bachelor's and master's degrees (in civil engineering and industrial hygiene), Uryechee had spent nearly ten years with the Department of Occupational Safety and Health before returning home to serve as the nation's health and safety officer. Hoping to inspire the next generation of Anzarkis to achieve academic and professional excellence, Uryechee was a frequent visitor to the reservation's classrooms — where he showed the children personal protective equipment and environmental monitoring gear, often allowing students to don the Darth Vader–like respirators and "moon suits" that had become part of his traveling collection. However, for a man who had sought to inspire so many future scholars, he seemed decidedly sad, almost beaten. As Uryechee handed me the thick manila file folder containing invoices, contract modifications and floor plans for the asbestos project, he whispered, "I would appreciate it if you would please review these tonight, Professor. It will make the process go far more quickly. I will meet you at my office tomorrow morning at six o'clock. Please be sure to bring your environmental sampling equipment and a camera."

School Visit

Dawn broke exceedingly early at the small motel adjacent to the Anzarki Nation's visitor center. Two black and tan dogs that appeared to be part German shepherd and part Labrador retriever — with possibly a little coyote mixed in for good measure — scratched at my door, lured by the smell of the apple and cinnamon breakfast bars on the nightstand of my cramped, 1950s-style room. Prior to the age of superhighways and GPS shortcuts, such quaint lodgings served as welcome respites for weary truckers and tourists alike. The inn was now sparsely inhabited and falling into neglect.

I left the room and offered my last two breakfast bars to my canine alarm clocks. Fifteen minutes later, I had arrived at the double-wide trailer that served as Randall Uryechee's occupational health and safety office. Although nearly halfway through his thermos of coffee when I arrived, Uryechee appeared even more haggard than the day before.

"Did you look over the materials I provided to you yesterday?" Uryechee asked flatly, referring to the heavy folder replete with official-looking certification stamps and signatures.

"Yes, although admittedly everything seems to be in order." The pre- and post-contamination sampling certainly suggested the work was done correctly by Patrick Whylaway's crew. Indeed, I had spent the better part of two hours the previous evening in my musty room combing through the pile of documents that Uryechee gave me — although, admittedly, there wasn't much else to do since the television didn't work.

"You brought your industrial hygiene gear and a camera." This was more of a statement of fact than a question.

"Of course," I responded.

"Good. Then go get them and we will take a tour of the schools."

Twenty minutes later, we had left his office in the official Anzarki pickup truck assigned to him (which offered a considerably smoother ride than the rental vehicle I had been using) and had pulled up at the entrance to Running Bear Elementary School. Although nearly three weeks remained until the start of the new school year, and there was not a teacher or administrator in sight, Uryechee was emphatic that I begin my sampling immediately. Upon entering the boiler room, it was evident that sampling was not even necessary: thin, prism-like brownish wisps clung to the metal pipe and boiler surface — a few even danced merrily in the breeze offered by the large air-handling unit in the maintenance area. I immediately left the room, donned a powered air-purifying respirator, white coveralls, gloves, and hard hat, and returned to begin collecting air and wipe samples from the pipes and porous and nonporous surfaces within the room.

Post-sampling analysis confirmed violations of the Asbestos Hazard Emergency Response Act (AHERA), the National Emissions Standards for Hazardous Air Pollutants and the Occupational Safety and Health Administration procedures and permissible exposure limits. As I snapped a few pictures of the pipes and boiler, I asked less than politely, "Where is the removed material?"

Uryechee walked me to the exterior of the recently renovated vehicle maintenance bay, past the school buses that sat in various states of repair in the yard and out to a rusted, 30-cubic-yard dumpster. Inside I saw the savagely torn chunks of amosite asbestos insulation— some wrapped in green trash bags, others exposed to the end-of-summer heat. Perhaps more interesting than the insulation was the mountain of ceiling and floor tiles— some shattered into small fragments revealing their soft, curly, poisonous fragments — that took up at least half of the container.

"I didn't see any evidence of asbestos tiles in this building. Where are they from?" Of course, I could hazard a guess what his response would be.

"Mostly from the middle school and high school," Uryechee replied nonchalantly. He had apparently passed the point of trying to keep the tribe's dirty little secret. "Although some of them are also from the police station and jail that Whylaway worked on a few months ago. I can take you there if you want."

I decided not to continue my tour with Randall Uryechee and instead asked him to drop me off at my rental car so I could continue the investigation on my own. I also chose not to visit the police station and its holding cell at that time. However, I did visit the Wandering Brook Middle School and Flat Top High School and collected air contaminant and surface samples. These tests confirmed that asbestos-containing materials (ACM) still existed in both facilities in concentrations well above the regulatory limits.

Unsubstantiated Violations

If there was one bright spot in my inspection, it was the plethora of new flammable-materials safety cabinets and the satellite hazardous-waste storage area constructed near the school district's administration building. By my estimate, these containers, along with miscellaneous personal-protective items, such as respirators, gloves, goggles and spill-containment response kits, accounted for less than $350,000 of the $2 million that had been allocated by the BIA for this project — and their procurement was not authorized in the grant. However, there had at least been some effort on the part of the tribal leaders to manage their chemicals, paints and solvents in a responsible manner and ensure the well-being of the workers who handled the materials.

Still, I remained deeply troubled that an entire district of schoolchildren, from kindergarten through high school, had potentially spent the better part of a semester exposed to significantly elevated levels of ACM. According to the records that Uryechee had provided, much of Whylaway's asbestos mitigation and removal activities had occurred during the winter recess. Judging from the condition of the insulation and tiles in the dumpster, this time frame appeared to be right. ACM removal or mitigation requires notification of students, parents and employees under AHERA, but I did not think such a notice had been sent out by Manyfeathers. Accordingly, I figured if I were able to demonstrate an awareness of this asbestos hazard on the part of the tribal leadership and obtain a notice of violation from AHERA regulators against the Anzarki tribal council and school district, perhaps, just perhaps, I could convince the U.S. Attorney's Office to enforce criminal penalties on each of the council members. In my estimation, Randall Uryechee, Daniel Yazzite, Shirley Manyfeathers and St. Cloud were all possible defendants. The maximum fine they could each receive was $25,000. In some very rare cases, imprisonment could also result from AHERA violations. To do so required joining the applicable regulatory notification provisions of the Comprehensive Environmental Response, Compensation, and Liability Act of 1980 (CERCLA) with AHERA provisions. Specifically, Section 103 of CERCLA allows for prison sentences of up to three years for the first offense and up to five years for subsequent convictions. However, as an experienced environmental fraud investigator, I understood that these criminal penalties were almost never sought by the U.S. Attorney's Office (or even considered as part of the initial plea bargaining process). Moreover, the tribe itself was considered a Local Education Agency (LEA) under AHERA, and there are no known cases where an LEA has been charged in aggregate with imprisonment.

In fact, even after discounting imprisonment and criminal penalties as options, I assumed that efforts to invoke the civil provisions of AHERA against the tribe leaders would also be pointless. Given the defendants' lack of assets, employing the AHERA provision that afforded penalties of up to $5,000 per day for each school building in violation, any efforts at settlement would simply end up with one federal agency (U.S. Department of Justice) seeking recovery from another (BIA).

As for Patrick Whylaway and his employees, I would need to find hazardous-materials manifests, job orders, invoices or other documents bearing his signature. Although several of the documents that Uryechee had given me bore Whylaway's stamped signature, none was signed in original ink. Moreover, Uryechee himself had completed the majority of documentation attesting to the removal of materials from the site, not Whylaway. Uryechee had provided a wealth of materials that implicated no one other than himself. My greatest hope rested in obtaining a notice of violation and then using that to entice statements from tribal leaders St. Cloud, Manyfeathers and Yazzite.

Accepting Defeat

"Welcome, Professor. Please sit down and make yourself comfortable." Manyfeathers' tone was no longer as cold, flat and unemotional as it had been at our first meeting; instead, it dripped with sarcasm. She was joined in her office by Daniel Yazzite. Stephen St. Cloud was attending a reelection function for the state's governor.

I had been on the reservation for nearly three weeks and had turned up nothing else. I was exceedingly lonely. I missed my wife and stepdaughter on the East Coast, and other than the two dogs who appeared far more interested in my daily breakfast bars than they were in me, I was utterly alone. I had only a few days of summer vacation remaining. At least I would soon be back at work teaching — a welcome respite from my unfulfilling experience serving as a practitioner for the past month.

None of Patrick Whylaway's employees would speak to me, on or off the record, because jobs were hard to come by in this little part of the world. Whylaway had gently but pointedly referred me to his personal attorney if I had any questions regarding his business practices. Although the U.S. Attorney's Office had initially expressed interest in my case, he changed his mind quickly after receiving a call from the U.S. senator who served the reservation, asking him to reconsider. Even my last hope — that a notice of violation for failure to alert residents of the asbestos hazard, in accordance with the reporting provisions of AHERA — had been thwarted. Nearly a week earlier, Manyfeathers provided me with a copy of her signed letter to parents, students and faculty, dated from the previous January, advising them of "ongoing asbestos remediation activities in the Anzarki Tribal District," and referring them to her, Board President Yazzite or Chief St. Cloud if they had any questions or concerns. Although I suspected that Manyfeathers' letter had been predated shortly before I arrived on the reservation, I was unable to interview any parents or school officials to confirm my suspicions. I had also been unsuccessful in finding invoices or receipts to support my belief that funds had been siphoned off for improvements on several individuals' personal residences.

As I noted in my final investigative report, the only signed purchase orders and delivery receipts were for the flammable-materials storage lockers, the hazardous-waste facilities and related supplies totaling about $350,000. Although these items were not authorized by the federal grant, BIA officials in Washington were comforted by the fact that at least some of the money went to resolving health and safety issues on the reservation.

I had completed my assignment as a contracted government investigator tasked with providing the BIA with a comprehensive report detailing my findings. Through photographic evidence and environmental sampling, I provided overwhelming evidence that almost none of the $2 million allocated for the mitigation of asbestos hazards in the three tribal schools had been expended for this purpose. However, I was unable to definitely prove where the money went. The BIA chose not to further investigate this matter criminally or civilly, instead opting to allocate additional grant funding to supplement ACM mitigation in Phase II of the projects. To this day, I do not know if this reallocation included more stringent oversight or if the later phases of the multiphase grant were ever completed. For obvious reasons, I opted not to serve again as an independent contractor with BIA subsequent to completing my report.

Lessons Learned

Although the outcome of this investigation was personally frustrating because further action was not taken against the suspected perpetrators, this case demonstrated that practices such as stringent records review and evidence collection serve as the workhorses for corruption and fraud investigations. Sadly, the victims in this case included the students attending the three schools and the U.S. taxpayers who spent nearly $2 million on services that were evidently not rendered.

Perhaps simply alerting others to the incident of suspected corruption that occurred within the Anzarki Nation will raise awareness that such incidents do occur and afford a broader understanding of the challenges that tribe members face in their daily lives. As a result, future generations of students attending tribal schools may not have to face the hazards of improper asbestos remediation, which will provide a better life.

Recommendations to Prevent Future Occurrences
In essence, this case taught me that fraud examiners may follow all of the right procedures and still come up short. However, it is important not only to learn these lessons but also to persevere in the face of adversity and to continue to engage in sound fraud detection practices.

About the Author

Hank J. Brightman serves as professor and director of Applied Research & Analysis in the War Gaming Department of the U.S. Naval War College. He was previously an associate professor and chair of the Criminal Justice Department at Saint Peter's College from 2000 to 2008. Hank has more than 20 years of varied experience in law enforcement, investigations and intelligence analysis with the U.S. Department of the Interior, U.S. Secret Service and U.S. Navy. He is highly regarded for his nontraditional approach to teaching complex subjects such as economic crime theory, corruption control and applied social science research methods. Hank currently serves as an adjunct faculty member at several undergraduate-, graduate- and doctoral-level institutions.

The views and opinions expressed in this case study are the author's, and do not necessarily represent those of the Naval War College, Department of the Navy or the U.S. government.

CHAPTER 29

The Corrupt Public Servant

SANDEEP MEHRA

Jay Verma was a high-ranking officer in the Government of India, working in a remote location. When he was offered a job managing a state employees' retirement fund in Mumbai, he jumped at the chance to move his children to the city, where they would receive a better education. His wife, Sheila, was a stay-at-home mom to their two teenage daughters, 15-year-old Neeti and 13-year-old Preeti. The new job required collecting retirement contributions from various government employees, matching the same with the government's contribution and investing the entire amount in government securities to get the highest rate of return and for easy liquidity. Jay had scant knowledge about investments, so he knew he would have to rely heavily on someone.

The new job was nothing like his previous one, where he had been in charge of safekeeping and transportation of food grains. Jay ensured they were distributed correctly and that suppliers were paid on time. In other words, his old job was drab and offered him no financial gains or excitement. Above all, it required that he and his family live in a rural part of Maharashtra, India, where his wife often complained about the upbringing of their daughters and the lack of opportunities for their growth. Hence his eagerness for this new job opportunity, even if he did not have the expected experience.

His wife had been a Chartered Accountant and worked in Mumbai for some time before marrying Jay. She maintained ties with friends in the Mumbai financial world who, on learning about her husband's new position, offered to help.

One such friend was Sunil Kapoor, who headed an investment company in Mumbai by the name of Infra Investments, dealing in the brokerage of government securities. Sunil visited Jay's office shortly after Jay began work and boldly offered him a kickback for every investment he made with Infra Investments; he didn't even ease into the topic. Jay was reluctant, but he felt like he couldn't refuse his wife's longtime friend. And greed for quick money got the better of him. They agreed that Jay would earn a personal commission of 0.5 percent in cash on whatever investments he made through Sunil. The state retirement fund totaled $22 million, and Jay quickly learned that the best way to earn extra commissions was to invest and reinvest the funds with Infra every few months. What Jay failed to realize and question was that every reinvestment he made resulted in a loss to Infra Investments. Why would Sunil be encouraging a strategy that caused his own company losses?

I, being a government investigator, received a tip from an anonymous source that there was a problem with the retirement fund. I started inquiring discreetly, but Jay soon learned about my questioning. To save his skin, he filed a complaint with the government that Infra Investments had not delivered any government securities to the fund against the invested amount. By then, I had already discovered that Jay had not received investment certificates from Infra since they began trading together. Since we were dealing with $22 million, we opened a full investigation.

The initial complaint was filed by Jay against Infra Investments, but I soon realized how close Sunil and Jay were and that Jay had acquired a few expensive properties since he moved to Mumbai. When I visited the government office, I learned that securities certificates for the retirement fund had not been delivered once since Jay took over as the fund manager four years ago. In lieu of the certificates, contract notes from Infra Investments that simply said "we bought/sold for you [security]" were delivered. Jay was aware of the circumstances but he chose to keep the board in the dark, stating that it takes time to transfer securities to the fund, hence the delays. I also learned that the day before a security certificate was supposed to be delivered, it would be sold for another one. Jay would receive another contract note showing the sale of one security against purchase of another of the same value.

Initial Searches

I set out to prove that the securities were never delivered and that Jay was an accomplice in the offense, even though I knew it would be a difficult task. The office records were maintained in such a way that it was impossible to prove whether the securities had been received. The book of meeting minutes was my only clue; during every meeting Jay mentioned which securities were on their way, and the minutes reflected this information. Also, although there were two audits each year, the auditors had not verified the securities certificates. I started interviewing the officials connected with the investments and consistently received verbal confirmation that the securities were never delivered. However, I knew testimony would not be enough to carry a case, so I started looking for documentary evidence. As the amount in question was huge (the full $22 million), I knew the defense attorneys would have a field day cross-examining witnesses I provided for the prosecution.

Believing my intuition, the next day I obtained search warrants for Jay's home and Infra Investments' office. Initially, my search at Jay's home was not fruitful, until I noticed that one of his personal bank statements listed a different home address. When I looked up the address, I discovered the home was registered to Sheila Verma, Jay's wife. This was surprising because I knew Sheila had no income of her own. The house was locked when I went to search it, and Jay and Sheila denied having the keys. I had no option but to break open the lock, which is permissible by law for such investigations. After entering the house, I recovered title documents for four more properties and investment documents for various accounts, bonds and so forth in the names of Sheila, Neeti and Preeti. The investments and properties were worth an estimated at $1.5 million and I could not imagine a legal means to explain such a large amount, considering that Sheila was unemployed, the daughters were minors and not earning income and Jay had no inheritance.

The searches at the office of Infra Investments were also fruitful. My team found Infra's books, which revealed deposits in the amount of $22 million from the government retirement fund. The company received funds from other entities as well, and segregating them was a difficult task. The search also revealed a file containing details of securities purchased by Infra Investments and delivered to various clients. But the file showed none to the retirement fund Jay managed. However, substantial amounts were invested in shares of other companies. There was hardly any income reflected in the accounts. Instead, funds were used for advertising campaigns, research trips abroad and so forth. I was starting to understand where the money from the retirement fund was going.

After analyzing the evidence from searches for next two days, I started collecting "negative evidence." I had to prove that the securities Jay and Sunil claimed as part of the government portfolio had never been purchased at all or, if so, had been delivered to a third party. First I researched the historic rate of each security on the date Sunil purportedly purchased it for Jay. To my dismay, the securities appeared to have been purchased at market rates. Had there been a difference in the rates, it would have been easier to prove that the securities were fictitiously purchased.

I decided to get more information from the Reserve Bank of India (RBI), the regulator of the government securities. An agent looked up a list of securities I provided but said he could not find a trading record for most of them. My spirits lifted until the agent said they could be off-market transactions, which would not be recorded at RBI (off-market transactions are done privately between two parties rather than routed through the regulator). High-fund, off-market transactions are irregular — especially for a government retirement fund — but not illegal. Based on what I'd gathered so far, I would not have been able to prove my case.

Second Round of Searches

I needed stronger evidence, so I turned my attention back to Infra Investments' books. There were plenty of copies showing sales of securities to Jay but no record of Infra having purchased those securities to sell. If Sunil had not procured the securities for Jay, how could he sell or deliver them to the retirement fund?

The files were enormous. There were at least 17 government securities that were supposedly bought and sold ten times or more. The records showed Infra's investments, advertising campaign costs and research trips along with documents for investment properties in Jay's wife and daughters' names. I collected these to present to the court in case of a trial. Next I pulled records from the retirement fund office, including minutes from the board meetings in which Jay had assured board members that the fund was earning profits with Infra and stating that the securities certificates were in the office. As per Indian law, each document presented in court must be offered by a witness who has generated that document or was conversant with it in his job. Therefore, my next task was to identify any connected witnesses and secure their testimony for court.

I also started analyzing the retirement fund's records. To my dismay, I found that on the last two occasions, the entire set of securities was sold and bought through a different investment company called Alice Securities, which had no connection with Sunil. Now technically, the defaulter company was Alice and not Infra. Jay's complaint was against Infra Investments, and I was not ready for this twist in story. I had never heard of Alice Securities before, and it did not exist in RBI's records as a registered investment company. The contract notes issued by Alice were computer printouts with a fictitious address. Jay's staff informed me that the contract notes were sent directly to Jay through the mail and that he passed them on to an assistant to file.

I had pursued my investigative avenues and was left with no choice but to take Jay and Sunil into custody to interview them. In India, investigators are required to seek permission from the court if they need to keep a suspect in custody for more than 24 hours. Armed with my evidence against both Jay and Sunil, I arrested and produced them before the court and requested a hearing.

Custodial Interviews

By this time the case was garnering significant media attention, and word of my custody order spread almost as soon as the judges agreed to it. When I walked out of the court, I realized how bad being in the public eye can be. The reporters had no respect for my "no comment" shouts and kept following me, Jay, Sunil and the escorting staff through the courthouse. Based on years of experience, I knew the best confessions were obtained on the first day of custody, so I began my interviews that night, despite being very tired.

I spent the first hours in the interview room listening to the suspects, who had been separated, repeat "I don't know" over and over again. I started with Sunil and flatly told him that because he was the beneficiary of fraud, we were making Jay an offer if he would testify against Sunil. I also told Jay that Sunil promised to repay the entire amount and that therefore we were going to make a deal with him. Considering Jay's position as a public servant, I could only assume he would lose his job and be tried for criminal misappropriation of public funds. Also, I pointed out that Jay invested the defrauded amount in his family members' names, which meant they could face jail time too. On top of it, I told both Jay and Sunil horror stories about jails in India and about the juvenile detention centers where Jay's daughters would be kept if convicted. I also played upon Jay's sense of guilt by reminding him that the funds he stole were the hard-earned retirement savings of government servants. After the first hour of interviewing, I asked staff members to serve them sandwiches and coffee in their respective rooms. While they had their dinner, I rested in my office and ate as well. I took an hour break but asked my assistants to engage the accused in conversation and continue telling them stories of jail.

I got my break at 11:30 p.m. One of the staff members told me that Jay wanted to see me. When I got to his room, I could tell he was really upset. When I walked in, he started weeping and said that the guilt was killing him. He said that whatever happened, he was to blame. However, he only benefited from a small amount of the funds. Sunil took most of the money. I got a glass of water for Jay, and when he calmed down, I told him I was ready to listen to any information he had but warned that I would need evidence to support any of his claims. He agreed and began recounting the events at midnight; he kept talking until 5:30 a.m.

The Full Story

Regarding Jay's association with Sunil, he told me nothing new. He explained his wife's connection to Sunil and how he felt obligated to accept his initial offer of kickbacks. I asked him how he converted his cash kickbacks into checks, knowing that the properties he purchased could be bought only with checks. He explained that he received kickbacks in cash from Sunil amounting to 0.5 percent of the total transaction each time an investment was made or changed with Infra. Sunil gave Jay the cash through an intermediary — a chartered accountant named Neel. This accountant had many clients who wanted to show less income on their books to avoid income taxes. Neel would take Jay's cash, give it to his other customers, and they would write a check for the same amount to Jay's wife or daughters, fictitious vendors on the companies' books. For this service, Neel charged a 1 percent commission from Jay and the other clients. Jay gave me the information I would need to follow up with Neel and the clients. To validate his claim, I needed the account statements of the clients and recordings of their interviews, as they could be used as witnesses to prove the case against Jay.

Jay also told me that he and Sunil were showing profits in their books for each switch, so the board members did not start asking questions. To avoid having to pay profits to the retirement fund, Jay showed them being reinvested in government securities, which again were never delivered. This is how the original investment of $17.23 million grew to $22 million while Jay was managing it. But this crime was, in essence, a Ponzi scheme. The board members only required that Jay provide financial statements showing profits. He was able to falsify documents well enough that he never raised any doubts in the minds of the board members.

As for the auditors, Jay told me he knew in advance when they were planning on coming by, and a day or two before the audit he would record the sale of an old security and the purchase of a new one. When the auditors questioned the transaction, Jay would tell them that the new security had not been delivered, and therefore he could not provide proof of the trans-action. Jay would show them the contract notes he made in the financials, which satisfied them. The accounts were audited twice a year, but, as a general practice, the auditors were rotated each time to avoid developing close relationships with clients. Jay took advantage of this to pull the same trick during each audit.

Jay told me that Alice Investments was a fictitious company fabricated by Sunil. As the retirement fund grew, Jay and Sunil planned to shift the invest-ments to Alice, which would take the fall if they were discovered. Jay told his staff that to earn the maximum return on the investments, they should look for other companies. His staff collected proposals from different companies, and Jay slipped in Sunil's proposal for the fictitious Alice, which of course offered the best returns. However, Jay knew his staff would question this company no one had heard of before, so he asked Sunil to hold an informational session to convince them. Sunil arranged a meeting at a five-star hotel and presented numerous bogus recommendations for Alice Invest-ments, supposedly from different government agencies. He also arranged for a friend to introduce himself as the director of Alice Investments and give costly gifts to the concerned staff members. At the end of the meeting, the staff unanimously agreed to Alice, and Jay had what he needed to begin moving the investment over. This sneaky move supposedly protected Jay in the event that Alice failed to deliver the securities — he thought he could not be held responsible because his staff chose to work with the company; it wasn't his decision.

This was Jay's full story. But to prove the case we needed evidence, and the statement of the accused in police custody is not sufficient in India. However, Jay had given me what I needed to collect proof. I had the details of accounts and I obtained the bank records, which clearly showed the transfer of money from the retirement fund to Infra and further on.

The Finishing Touches

Next I met with Jay's chartered accountant Neel, who provided me with the account statements and addresses of his clients, who were responsible for the conversion of cash to checks. There were 17 in all, and I recorded the testimony from each one and Neel, in which they admitted to the transactions. They gave me access to their account statements and transfer vouchers. I was able to match them to cash deposits in Jay's account, and they corresponded with transfers from the retirement fund to Infra. Jay purchased his properties and other investments from these funds.

I collected the account statements for the retirement fund, Infra and Alice from their respective banks, along with transaction vouchers and checks. These documents provided evidence of the transfers of funds. I obtained a business address for Alice from the company bank statements and discovered it was a guest house registered to Infra Investments. This was sufficient to prove the connection between Infra and Alice. Bank statements and checks also proved that the funds received from Infra were reinvested with Alice. Additionally, Infra's account statements demonstrated how Sunil used his proceeds of the scam — on advertising campaigns and "business" trips, among other things.

Favorable Judgments

After getting the documents lined up and statements of witnesses recorded, I presented the charge sheet to the government prosecutor. He confirmed that it was a strong case for prosecution. We maintained a clear chain of evidence to link each transaction and the flow of funds. I also identified the properties that Jay purchased with the proceeds of his kickback scheme and linked them with the dates of investments. The court passed a judgment in favor of the government. We were able to recover a considerable amount of funds by freezing the bank accounts of Sunil's family members. The government was also granted ownership of Sunil's and Jay's properties. Jay was prosecuted for criminal conspiracy, cheating, misappropriation of government funds and abuse of official position as public servant. Sunil and Sheila were prosecuted for criminal conspiracy and cheating. They can all face up to ten years in prison, and their sentencing hearings are ongoing.

Lessons Learned

This case taught me about the complex trading of government securities, how extensive the records are for government transactions and, perhaps most important, that fraud examiners should reserve skepticism even for the complainant, in case he might be the culprit.

Recommendations to Prevent Future Occurrences

I made the following recommendations to the government office in charge of the retirement fund:

1. Investment certificates should be physically checked by the auditors and contract notes should not be accepted as proof that they have been received.
2. Investment of government funds can be a very lucrative job. There should be a group of people making the decisions, not one person with sole responsibility.

About the Author

Sandeep Mehra, an ex-national swimmer from India, joined the Indian Police at the age of 22. He excelled in police training and was judged the best cadet. He served with uniformed police for six years and thereafter was picked up by the premier investigating agency of India, Central Bureau of Investigation (CBI), as an investigator. With CBI, he continued to excel and investigated major financial crimes between 1994 and 2009. He was judged best investigator of India in 2007 for his investigation of the stock market scam. He currently works with the Royal Bank of Scotland as Vice President, Investigation.

CHAPTER

30

Romance, Jewels and Kickbacks: All in a Day's Work

DENNIS THOMAS

I had the opportunity to meet Margaret Alexander years ago while I was attending a company networking function. She was an accomplished professional and highly regarded in the jewelry industry in general and at our company, Gem World, in particular. She was in her mid-50s but could easily pass for early 40s. She was exquisitely dressed and manicured from head to toe. At first she appeared to be a Harvard-educated attorney.

She was well liked and people were drawn to her when she began a conversation. She seemed to be a devoted mother to her two children and a caring wife. She readily admitted lacking a college degree but instead became a learned professional through the experience she gained working as a manager for a large department store corporation, which she wore as a badge of honor. Margaret believed her street smarts enabled her to exceed in areas where academics didn't compare, and she preached the importance of hard work and perseverance to her subordinates and anyone she met who would listen.

Margaret was recruited to Gem World by a long-term manager who believed in her ability to sell and close deals. Margaret began as a jewelry consultant at Gem World and rose through the ranks to district manager. Her reputation at the company was flawless, and she was the last person I thought would become the subject of an investigation.

Gem World was a family-owned operation established in the early 1900s by Dave and Cecile Levitt. They started the business as a young couple with small children as a way to manage their own schedules and commit to time with family. The couple opened the business on a tree-lined street of Williamsville, New York, a suburb of Buffalo.

The Levitts loved the area and the ability to raise their children while being self-employed. As the years passed, the company saw rapid sales increases and huge growth, and it eventually became a regional corporation that operated several different business segments. The Levitts moved the operation from Buffalo to Dallas, Texas, to be close to their son, who attended the University of Dallas to obtain a degree in journalism. Gem World expanded rapidly thanks to the increased population the Dallas metropolis offered. The company was purchased by an investment firm and went public shortly thereafter.

Out in the Field

I was one of 18 regional field investigators employed by Gem World in North America, and I was assigned to internal and external investigations in the northeastern United States. My cases included robberies, burglaries, frauds, internal theft and dishonesty by employees and vendors. I spent a large amount of time conducting training seminars for executives and employees on not becoming victims and identifying potential areas to decrease loss exposures. I also had the pleasure of instructing law enforcement agencies on the investigation of crimes specific to the jewelry industry.

The training aspect of my job gave me an opportunity to interact with the managers in a nonadversarial atmosphere and build personal relationships. Over the years the trust I developed with the staff in these meetings and trainings became beneficial; they would provide me with additional leads and information during investigations because they believed they could trust me.

It was a hot July day and it was only 8:00 a.m. when I sat down at my desk to open e-mails. The warm breeze and sunshine distracted me from the routine. My thoughts drifted to the beach as I sifted through the several dozen e-mails. It was then I saw that one of them was a hotline call received by corporate and assigned to me for investigation. As I read the report further, I was shocked. I couldn't believe Margaret Alexander was the subject of the hotline call.

The hotline caller claimed that Alexander was romantically involved with a vendor and that they appeared to be orchestrating an elaborate fraud scheme dealing with the falsification of repair orders and transactions. The whistleblower observed the delivery of cash payments to various other employees involved in the scheme but failed to provide further details. The caller refused to identify himself but said a thorough investigation would confirm his accusations.

Interviews and Invoices

Initially, I believed the call would be easily explained, and I was certain the caller was misinformed. However, as the preliminary investigation progressed, I began to uncover information that did not exonerate Margaret or her suspected paramour, William Mack. I began by interviewing several of Alexander's subordinates and learning the full scope of the relationship that had developed between Alexander and Mack, a jewelry-repair vendor.

William was married but going through a divorce and was the father of three boys. He worked out regularly and did not appear to be near his age of 56. Most people who met him, including me, believed he was in his mid-40s. He had been a bench jeweler in the area for years and was well respected in and around the community. He was a Boy Scout troop leader and volunteered regularly at the local soup kitchen and pantry. William was also known to provide quality service with a smile. The few times I had met him he was cordial, respectful and engaging. Whatever the topic, William would offer a concise and well-thought-out perspective.

Gem World largely used independent contractors in an effort to limit costs associated with having an in-house jeweler on the payroll. William maintained a solid reputation in the area and seemed like the right external addition to the business.

Using a third-party provider to conduct jewelry repair has its ups and downs. One of the negatives is that the company cannot fully manage the flow of goods as it can with in-house jewelers. Also, negligence on the part of the jeweler can amount to serious customer-service issues for the store if the pieces are lost or stolen, and the company has limited controls to review the quality of the work being performed. One of the positives is that many of the vendors are local and can provide direct, personal service to the stores. The jewelers are able to build strong working relationships with the stores and in many cases will interact with customers while they are in a store picking up repaired items. William gained this sort of trust with the employees and customers in Margaret's region.

As I continued interviewing staff members at Gem World, I learned that Margaret and William often had lunch together and that Margaret regularly received calls from William that she would take in her office for extended periods of time. The investigation took a major turn when one of Margaret's employees told me that Margaret was using William's personal credit cards to purchase thousands of dollars of jewelry and for daily living expenses, clothing and vacations.

I pulled copies of all the invoices William had submitted to Gem World in the past six months and began reviewing them for suspicious items. I immediately noticed some repair work that looked unnecessary, either based on the other work listed on the invoice or the type of jewelry. I kept a stack of all the suspicious invoices and discovered another similarity: most of the invoices were processed by Margaret, although there were a few other staff members who appeared to be involved as well. As the fraudulent invoices began piling up, I learned that Margaret and William were earning thousands of dollars each from their lucrative scheme.

After reviewing William's invoices for the past six months, I went farther back. The mixing of fraudulent invoices into legitimate customer repair work had gone undetected for years! The payment of the repair invoices did not appear suspicious simply because of the sheer number of repairs that were completed in the region, and the internal controls failed to identify the additional line items that William added to the repair work. The profit margins were consistent throughout the region, and it actually looked like Margaret's region was driving additional sales through the repair business. The scheme added a small expense to the total repair cost, which on its face didn't appear to be fraudulent. Although this expense was not material to the company as a whole, it was significantly increasing William's overall annual income.

During my interviews with staff members, I learned that William was covertly bribing other Gem World employees to order unnecessary repair work that was ultimately paid for by the corporation. These were the same employees I identified earlier as processing William's inflated invoices.

I determined the employee kickbacks were an effort to silence staff members who discovered the couple's scheme. The employees would authorize the service invoices, and Margaret was in a position to pay them directly at the store without sending them to the corporate office for review by an auditor or accountant. They believed they had devised the perfect plan but didn't take into account the strong morality of some of Gem World's employees. In the end that would prove to be the undoing of William and Margaret.

Unable to Stop

After I accumulated the necessary statements and corresponding invoices, I conducted interviews with Margaret and William. Margaret admitted her marriage was crumbling and she was flattered when William began paying attention to her. She said a relationship had blossomed. At first they shared long talks but then progressed to secret dates and ultimately to a romantic relationship. She also admitted to using William's personal credit cards because her ex-husband had removed her from his credit accounts during their divorce proceedings. At first Margaret tried not to use William's cards too much, but she admitted that eventually her spending became a daily habit.

As their relationship progressed, William confided to Margaret that his business was floundering and he was experiencing a downturn in revenue after losing several major accounts. The lease on his repair shop was also going up, and he faced mounting legal expenses because he was trying to win custody and visitation rights to see his sons. He was also having a hard time supporting Margaret's use of his credit cards.

They both believed their personal financial situations were spiraling out of control. Pillow talk quickly turned into an active conspiracy to target Gem World. They came up with many ideas but decided that padding invoices with unneeded work was least likely to be identified by auditors. Margaret and William considered the crime to be victimless and thought the scheme would help them get back on their feet.

At first they conducted several small transactions to test the waters. When these invoices went undetected, they increased the frequency. They agreed to end the scheme after six months, but when six months came, they couldn't bring themselves to stop. They both said they had become dependent on their increased (and nontaxed) income.

Margaret stated William was much more receptive to allowing her to use his credit cards after they began colluding because she was, in effect, helping to drive up his profit margins. When an employee began to suspect the collusion, William offered him a kickback if he started to inflate repair invoices as well. From there, it was only a matter of time before other Gem World employees joined the fray.

Margaret additionally admitted to violating the company's code of ethics. She justified her actions through a series of rationalizations ranging from financial need to years of service without appropriate compensation. In the end, she admitted to knowing the scheme was not only defrauding Gem World but also the customers she prided herself in serving.

William admitted his involvement but insisted the idea was entirely Margaret's. William said he only agreed to the scheme to continue his romance with Margaret. He admitted to feeling excited and having his "blood pump" when he was handing over a kickback to a Gem World employee.

At the end of my interview, William agreed to return all current repair work in progress for Gem World. I obtained written confessions from both Margaret and William. All shipments to William's repair shop were canceled throughout the organization, and he was placed on the banned-vendor list.

During interviews with Margaret's subordinates, I learned that some employees were brought into the fraud subtly. They were told it was a program designed to increase repair profit margins, and the kickbacks they received were "incentive payments." Some of them became suspicious when they received their payments in cash and the totals were not reflected on pay stubs. Nevertheless, it took several months for the first employee to come forward and call the hotline.

I presented my findings to senior executives and human resources at Gem World, and they immediately began a nationwide investigation for similar activity in other regions. Thankfully they did not find other corruption cases. We implemented a prevention and detection program to identify various patterns that were prevalent in this case. Margaret was fired, and all future repair work with William's company was terminated nationwide. Due to the complexity of determining exactly which repair work was fraudulent, no criminal charges were pursued. The investigation revealed the scheme was operating for at least a year (although I suspect it began three years earlier) and cost Gem World thousands of dollars in unnecessary repair work.

That money went directly to Margaret, William and a handful of employees who also participated in the fraud.

Lessons Learned

This case taught me a lot about the investigation of a kickback scheme, which I had little experience with previously. I learned that identifying personal relationships of suspects is a crucial component. In addition, I now review transactions conducted by known vendors and look for particular patterns in invoices. In particular, I look for patterns over a set time frame rather than in specific transactions. I determine if generic coding was used that might allow an invoice to be padded with unnecessary work, and I check for the same work being performed on a large collection of invoices for different pieces of jewelry. I also review the invoices being paid to determine if additional line items are being added after the repair work is performed. This case taught me that critical internal controls need to be enforced at all levels of the organization to prevent future incidents from occurring. This means a review of invoices at several points through the payables process.

I now regularly review social networking websites for information about suspects. Margaret and William were connected on such sites and even communicated plans for their corruption online. Specifically, they set up delivery dates of the payments via these websites. Some of Margaret's employees openly discussed online how uncomfortable they felt with the transactions.

Recommendations to Prevent Future Occurrences

Although it is difficult to identify kickback schemes like this one, it is not impossible to investigate them. I would make the following seven recommendations to identify similar frauds.

1. Maintain and advertise an employee hotline and provide a financial incentive for reporting dishonesty and ethics violations. In this case, the financial incentive Gem World offered whistleblowers exceeded the repeated small payments William was offering participants in his fraud, which provided incentive for someone to come forward. Unfortunately, most of the employees did not know about the hotline because Margaret was in charge of informing her staff of it.
2. Have multiple procedures for reviewing and paying vendor invoices to identify patterns of charges and determine the authenticity of the work performed. In this investigation, I observed that many invoices were paid locally by the stores in the region. This kept the scheme off the company-wide radar.
3. Unannounced visits to vendors can ensure that work is being performed in accordance with company standards. If Gem World randomly inspected its contract jewelers, we might have detected Margaret and William's fraud much earlier.

4. Have a policy in place that clearly defines and restricts relationships between vendors and employees, along with a strong code of ethics that delineates acceptable business practices and provides reporting mechanisms when violations occur. Define appropriate gifts from vendors by dollar figure and list unacceptable items (such as cash payments, vacations and tickets to sporting event over a certain value).

5. Regularly review social media websites for inappropriate vendor and employee relationships. You can create an account to view the subjects' personal pages and befriend them online to access private communications.

6. Identify pressures in employees' lives. In this case, both Margaret and William were going through expensive divorces and were under much stress as a result. Knowing the financial strain they were experiencing might have prompted a greater review of Margaret's exception reporting.

7. Identify revenue and expense lines that exceed department, region or corporate averages, along with third-party credit card transactions used for employee sales through the exception reporting practice. These fraudulent practices also have a direct effect on the income statements, balance sheet and cash flow statements of the organization.

About the Author

Dennis R. Thomas is currently a regional loss prevention manager and certified field trainer with a major specialty jewelry firm overseeing investigations in the Northeast, mid-Atlantic and Puerto Rico. He has more than 20 years of experience in the loss prevention field. Mr. Thomas is a licensed New York State Private Investigator. Mr. Thomas holds a bachelor's degree in business management and economics from the State University of New York and currently is an M.B.A. candidate at Utica College specializing in advanced economic crime investigations.

Power Corrupts and Absolute Power Corrupts Absolutely

JIM CALI

Steven Griffin spent most of his life earning slightly more than minimum wage while being employed at a variety of fast-food restaurants, convenience stores and gas stations. He was a hard worker who routinely put in 60 to 70 hours per week, often working nights, weekends and holidays. Steven was very dissatisfied with his current situation but, with only a high school diploma, his career opportunities were limited.

Steven had been working at a convenience store near the county jail for approximately two years and was acquainted with many of the jail's employees. One day, while working a double shift, he began complaining about his job to one of his regular customers from the jail. The jail guard listened to Steven's temper tantrum while he carefully selected his morning doughnuts and prepared his extra-large coffee with four servings of hazelnut creamer. As the guard paid for his breakfast, he told Steven, "Hey, man, why don't you come work at the jail? I know they're looking to fill a supervisor position in the inmate commissary." Steven laughed so hard he began snorting like a pig. He was able to choke out, "Who, me? Work in the jail? I am not a cop." The guard explained the supervisor was a civilian position and that running the commissary would be like running a convenience store.

After working his third double shift in seven days, Steven called in sick. He polished his shoes, put on his best shirt and tie and drove over to the county jail to apply for the job of supervisor of the inmate commissary.

In the Slammer

It appeared that shortly after Steven Griffin was hired as supervisor of the inmate commissary, he acquired a dose of entrepreneurial enthusiasm as he began to negotiate with vendors to provide the wide array of commissary items. In other words, if you wanted to sell your products to the commissary, you had to give Griffin expensive gifts, tickets to sporting events and eventually cash. You would think that an employee of a law enforcement agency who takes a solemn oath to protect and serve the community would be honest, trustworthy and maintain the presence of mind to do the right thing. Well, think again.

Inmates have a "bill of rights" that governs their residential accommodations, meals and access to medical treatment. In accordance with various provisions within the inmates' bill of rights, all jails must provide each inmate with the ability to purchase various personal hygiene items; writing paper; envelopes; postage stamps; and a huge array of snacks such as candy bars, potato chips, cheese puffs, chewing gum and the ever-favorite fried pork rinds.

To regulate the sale and distribution of these items, jails operate an inmate commissary that for all practical purposes resembles a modern convenience store but without gas pumps and cigarettes.

Our case takes place in the luxurious county jail located on the scenic banks of a river, surrounded by majestic royal palm trees in sunny Florida. The facility was no ordinary county jail, for the daily population averaged 6,500 inmates. To satisfy the snack-food cravings of such a large captive audience, the county jail's commissary unit was a complex operation that required eight to ten staff members. The commissary employees were responsible for maintaining the inventory of products, filling inmate orders and delivering the items to the inmates. Even with the limited selection of items, the commissary generated more than $1 million in sales per year.

The supervision of all the employees, the selection of all commissary products and the selection of the vendors to supply these products was all vested in one person: Steve, the commissary unit supervisor.

Any entry-level auditor could have easily spotted the weaknesses in the internal control environment of the commissary unit; however, none of the CPA firms engaged to perform the annual audit of this law enforcement agency ever looked at the operations of the commissary. By the auditors' own admission, the dollar value of the commissary's annual sales was "immaterial." In fact, the commissary was considered so insignificant that its income from operations was reflected as "miscellaneous" revenue on the books. The old sayings "Out of sight, out of mind" and "Who is watching the store?" certainly applied in this case. In reality, no one was watching the store, which created the perfect opportunity for Steven to "do his own thing." In addition, most of the county jail's senior managers were career law enforcement officers who had skillfully worked their way up the paramilitary ranks; therefore, they lacked the necessary business experience to govern the inmate commissary, a commercial enterprise.

Steven was allowed to select the vendors he wanted without using a competitive-bid process. The commissary supervisor also had the authority to place orders, receive merchandise, maintain inventory records, bill inmates, process vendor payments, write off obsolete and/or damaged inventory and approve payroll time cards and overtime hours. In short, Griffin had complete control of the operation without any managerial oversight.

A Diamond in the Rough

In the analysis of this case, we will use the concept of the Fraud Diamond to illustrate the culture of corruption the inmate commissary supervisor was able to create.

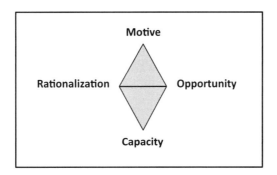

The Fraud Triangle — Motive, Rationalization and Opportunity — is the classic explanation for occupational fraud. But the Fraud Diamond goes further to include Capacity. The elements of capacity occur when the individual:

- Is in a position or function within the organization that gives him the ability to create or exploit a unique opportunity that is not readily available to others
- Understands the internal control weaknesses, and his position or function allows him to take advantage of these weaknesses without being questioned
- Has great confidence that his scheme will not be detected and believes that, if questioned, he can easily talk himself out of any trouble
- Can use his authority to convince or coerce others to commit, conceal or simply ignore the fraudulent activity.
- Lies effectively and consistently to avoid detection
- Possesses an ability to keep track of the lies to maintain a consistent and believable story
- Is able to successfully deal well with stress (committing, managing and concealing a fraudulent activity over a long period of time can be extremely stressful)

In applying the elements of the Fraud Diamond to this case, opportunity and capacity appear at once.

> *Opportunity.* The lack of adequate internal controls and managerial oversight created a magnificent opportunity for Steven to execute his kickback scheme.
>
> *Capacity.* As the commissary unit supervisor, Steven was given the sole authority to manage the entire operation. In this capacity, he developed the weekly work schedule; designated all employee work assignments; and approved all vacation requests, sick time usage and overtime hours. Steven also had the power to select the vendors, award purchase orders, sign vendor purchase agreements, amend the offering of commissary products, sign for the receipt of inventory, process and approve inventory adjustments, such as writing off damaged goods and snack products that had reached their expiration date. Steven also had the authority to approve all vendor requests for payment.

Steven's kickback scheme was simply brilliant. In all the years he spent in the convenience store, he developed close relationships with a handful of dry-good and snack-food sales representatives and vendors. Now, as commissary supervisor, when a purchase order with the incumbent vendors was about to expire, he would notify his cadre of corrupt snack-food sales representatives to submit a bid. Using his authority, he would award the purchase order to one of them, even if it meant amending the offer to conform to the information in the corrupt vendor's bid.

With no segregation of duties and no independent managerial review of the bids that were submitted, Steven had carte blanche to pick the vendor he pleased. Because the system granting all the power to the commissary unit supervisor had been in place for many years, Steven truly believed that he could run his scheme handing out lucrative purchase orders for commissary products in return for personal gratuities without ever being detected.

It appears that Steven began his kickback scheme small by taking tickets for himself and his wife to sporting events and concerts. Over time, as he gained more confidence, he modified the commissary unit's purchasing policy from purchasing small quantities of goods from many vendors to issuing large-dollar contracts to fewer and fewer vendors. This change in purchasing policy led to some protests from vendors who had held a contract to supply the commissary, but the protests were dismissed as sour grapes.

All Clear

As the chief audit executive for the Sheriff's Office, I was contacted by detectives from Internal Affairs, who requested that I perform a forensic analysis of the overtime expense for the inmate commissary. Our investigation revealed that a deputy sergeant was recently given the task of looking into complaints from a vendor who lost his contract to provide snack food products. The deputy sergeant's report stated that Steven was questioned about the modifications to the procurement policy and was able to justify his actions by explaining that the issuance of larger purchase orders to fewer vendors was more efficient and saved the organization money. The deputy sergeant dismissed the complaint as unfounded, noting that it stemmed from the vendor's unhappiness about legitimately losing the commissary's business. The deputy sergeant's investigation into Steven's new procurement practices failed to uncover any wrongdoing because he lacked knowledge of internal controls pertaining to the submission and evaluation of merchandise obtained through sealed bids. If he had examined the bid documents, he would have discovered that the majority of the winning bids were dated a day or two after the losing bids. And many of the products on the winning bids with the lower prices were in fact for merchandise packed in smaller quantities; for example, a winning bid listed six-ounce packages whereas the losing bid quoted prices for the same item in eight-ounce packages.

Once the investigation into Steven's new procurement policy was dismissed, his confidence that his scheme would never be detected must have grown by leaps and bounds. Based on our analysis, shortly after the deputy sergeant's investigation was closed, Steven developed a healthy appetite for cold hard cash instead of the usual gratuities from his corrupt vendors.

Steven was living the dream. That period of working 60 to 70 hours a week in the convenience store was over. He finally had a good job with excellent benefits along with the perfect scheme to demand and receive kickbacks on a regular basis.

But Griffin's dream quickly turned into a nightmare when Deputy Webster, one of his loyal employees, learned about the bid-rigging scheme from one of the corrupt vendors and demanded that Steven give him a "piece of the action" to keep his mouth shut.

You Have the Right to Remain Silent

Steven had a huge dilemma on his hands. His new, high-flying lifestyle consumed every bit of his ill-gotten cash, leaving nothing left to buy Deputy Webster's silence with. Steven knew that he could not hit up any of the vendors for additional kickbacks; therefore, he had to devise with another source of hush money or he would risk losing everything.

One evening after work, Steven secretly met with Deputy Webster at a neighborhood bar and offered to add extra hours every week on Webster's time sheet. Steven explained that he would not have to actually work any extra hours; all Webster had to do was submit his time sheet with the extra hours and Steven would approve it. Steven explained to Webster what a great deal this was because he was going to be paid all of this overtime at the premium rate.

Webster was not keen on the idea of submitting falsified time sheets. He told Steven, "No way. Someone downtown would question the overtime, and then what? I want some of that cold hard cash you're getting."

Steven told Webster that bogus overtime was actually better than cash because it would give him plenty of extra income each payday and it would increase his annual earnings, which in turn would boost the basis for his pension benefit. So Webster, by agreeing to the bogus overtime scheme, would be much better off.

After some thought, Webster agreed to the overtime scheme on one condition. He said, "If the overtime hours get questioned and are cut by the folks downtown, then you will have to come up with some cash, or else I blow the whistle."

For approximately two years, no one questioned why Deputy Webster had been working so much overtime. Yes, Steven's bogus overtime scheme to buy Webster's silence worked like a charm. Steven and Webster believed they would never get caught, and both set out to live the good life.

Anything You Say or Do Can Be Used Against You

Working in the commissary unit was considered one of the most desirable assignments in the jail. The commissary unit employees worked Monday through Friday 7:00 a.m. until 4:00 p.m. with weekends and holidays off. In a police agency, having such a regular schedule is a very rare occurrence; therefore, turnover in the commissary unit was practically nonexistent. In reality, once someone had enough seniority to capture one of these coveted positions, they stayed until they retired. The prestige of working in the commissary unit helped to foster an esprit de corps among the close-knit group.

The commissary employees routinely ate lunch together, talked sports and, every Friday, frequented their favorite bar after work for happy hour. Because they had worked together for so long, they all knew each other pretty well; therefore, the other employees picked up on the sudden changes in Webster's lifestyle quickly, and they were ruthless during their happy hour interrogations of him.

No one knows for sure if Webster had one too many Jack Daniel's or if the skillful interrogation technique of Deputy MacDaniel got the better of him, but on one fateful evening, Webster bared his soul. He told his colleagues all about Steven's kickback schemes with the vendors and how he concocted the hush money payments through the submission of bogus overtime hours on his weekly time sheet.

Shortly after Webster's happy hour revelation, his colleagues cornered Steven. They informed Steven they knew about his bid-rigging deals and the vendor kickbacks. They too wanted in on the bogus overtime scheme or else they would blow the whistle. Knowing that no one was paying attention to the overtime expenses, Steven agreed and began falsifying the payroll records for all three employees.

You Have the Right to Speak to an Attorney

The fourth commissary employee was Deputy Carmichael. She was the only female employee in the unit and had worked there longer than any of her male coworkers. She rarely socialized with the other employees. She ate lunch alone and never attended any of the happy hours.

Being a single parent, Carmichael paid close attention to her wages, and when she heard her male coworkers talk about all the overtime hours they were getting, she approached Steven and requested the opportunity to work overtime. She kept detailed records for every request she made, and just about every one of her requests was denied without an explanation.

In response to continually being denied the right to work overtime, she filed a gender-discrimination complaint with the Department of Internal Affairs. She stated that only the male employees of the commissary unit were given the right to work overtime. She claimed she was a victim of gender discrimination and that the only reason why she was being denied the right to work overtime was because of her gender. It was the investigation of this complaint that brought the corruption in the commissary unit to light.

In reviewing the last two fiscal years' worth of financial statements, it quickly became evident that the actual overtime charges were substantially greater than the budget for overtime. When I asked management for an explanation for the excess overtime, I was told it was immaterial because every month the inmate commissary realized a healthy profit.

A further analysis of payroll records confirmed Carmichael's allegation. Male employees of the commissary unit were being paid for 16 to 24 hours of overtime in each and every payroll period, but Carmichael received only a few hours of overtime during the two years I examined.

I began the investigation by looking at a small sample of the overtime slips submitted to payroll. Almost every slip in the sample lacked the proper managerial approval and required justification. I took a second, much larger sample, and it mirrored the findings of the first. With such a large number of exceptions in two samples, I examined 100 percent of the overtime slips submitted to payroll.

The analysis confirmed the disturbing pattern we discovered in the samples. Almost every overtime slip lacked the proper approvals and required justification to explain the reason for why the employee worked overtime.

If You Cannot Afford an Attorney, One Will Be Appointed for You

The beauty about working an investigation within a secure facility like a jail means you have access to plenty of control logs that capture the date, time and name of every visitor and employee who enters and exits the facility.

In performing a simple date match, it was obvious that the commissary employees did not work the hours of overtime claimed. For example, Webster's normal hours were 7:00 a.m. to 4:00 p.m., Monday through Friday. Therefore, on a certain day when he claimed to have worked four hours of overtime, the control log would have shown him entering the facility before 7 a.m. or leaving after 4 p.m. The video surveillance footage consistently failed to provide such corroboration.

Equipped with this evidence, I began to question the commissary employees about their overtime hours. One by one, they quickly confessed that they had indeed submitted false time sheets claiming the bogus overtime hours. Each one was willing to work out a deal to save himself from criminal prosecution by testifying against Steven to expose both the bogus overtime scheme and his shady vendor kickback deals.

Follow the Money

To build a case against Steven Griffin, I needed evidence to support the claims from the commissary employees that he was receiving the cash payments from vendors in return for giving them sweetheart contracts.

One of the best means law enforcement agencies have to identify and track cash transactions is to request information from the Financial Crimes Enforcement Network (FinCEN). It is a division of the U.S. Department of Treasury that was created in 1990 to help federal, state, local and international law enforcement agencies fight money laundering and other financial crimes. FinCEN researches and analyzes information obtained from financial institutions under the provision of the Bank Secrecy Act to establish a financial trail for investigators to follow as they track criminals, their banking activities and their assets.

Using information from FinCEN, I was able to locate the bank accounts for Steven Griffin and the vendors implicated by the commissary employees in the kickback deals.

My second request to FinCEN produced the most incriminating evidence imaginable. FinCEN records over a two-year period revealed a number of currency transaction reports where large sums of cash, greater than $10,000, were withdrawn from the vendors' bank accounts. Within a day or two of the vendors' cash withdrawal, a similar amount of cash was deposited in Steven Griffin's personal bank account.

With the signed confessions from the commissary employees stating that the bogus overtime scheme was really hush money to cover up Griffin's vendor kickback deals, coupled with the detailed financial information from FinCEN showing a series of suspicious cash deposits, I was certain that I had a strong case against Griffin and the corrupt vendors. The only thing left to do with this investigation was to present it to the district attorney and file the appropriate criminal charges, or so I thought.

Justice Is Blind

The detectives assigned to this case did their best but were unable to obtain a single confession from any of the vendors. Each of the vendors was able to concoct a reasonable business purpose to explain the large cash withdrawals in question.

Without a signed confession from at least one vendor, the district attorney refused to move forward with any criminal charges against Steven Griffin pertaining to the bid rigging or vendor kickbacks.

The rationale for the district attorney's decision was twofold. First, due to the Safe Harbor provision of the Bank Secrecy Act, I would be unable to present the bank account information and cash transaction reports obtained from FinCEN at trial.

In accordance with federal law (31 U.S.C. 5318(g)(3)), the Safe Harbor provision provides complete protection from civil liability for all reports of suspicious transactions made to appropriate authorities, including supporting documentation.

Specifically, the Safe Harbor law provides that financial institutions, and their directors, officers, employees and agents, that make a disclosure of any possible violation of law or regulation, including in connection with the preparation of suspicious activity reports, "shall not be liable to any person under any law or regulation of the United States."

Furthermore, the Safe Harbor law forbids a financial institution, and its directors, officers, employees, and agents who report suspicious transactions, to notify any person or business associated with the suspicious transaction and that it has been reported.

Second, without the ability to present information about these cash transactions that was obtained from the bank employees, it would be too difficult to prove the cash withdrawals identified from the vendors' bank accounts were in fact the same cash that Griffin deposited into his personal account.

On the strength of the signed confessions from the commissary employees pertaining to the submission of fraudulent overtime slips resulting in the payment for overtime hours that they had not worked, the district attorney did charge Steven Griffin with one count of official misconduct, a third-degree felony.

As for the commissary employees, in return for their cooperation with the investigation and for agreeing to testify against Griffin, the district attorney did not file criminal charges against them. However, they were terminated and required to make full restitution to the Sheriff's Office for the amount of the bogus overtime they received, plus the cost of the investigation.

Lessons Learned

This case taught me the importance of consulting with the district attorney throughout each stage of the investigation rather than waiting until the end. Even if you have conducted your investigation in a most professional manner, if the district attorney has any doubts, the suspect will get the benefit of the doubt.

Granting individuals who do not possess the required knowledge, skill or ability for a job the authority and responsibility to oversee general business functions based solely on their seniority and/or tenure with the organization is a recipe for disaster.

There is no magic number for "materiality." Making decisions based on artificial dollar levels without understanding the nature, scope and magnitude of the business enterprise is a dangerous course of action. Griffin's fraud flew under the radar for so long because his department's costs were not considered material by the prison system.

It is important to investigate even minor exceptions from established policies and procedures. Failing to adequately investigate them may prevent you from identifying a problem that the system of internal controls has detected.

Recommendation to Prevent Future Occurrences

Historically, the top management positions in jail have been assigned to police officers. These individuals understand crime prevention and law enforcement techniques, but they do not necessarily have the business experience necessary to oversee a multimillion-dollar operations budget. As a result of this case, I recommended that a position of business manager be created to manage and oversee all of the jail's fiscal affairs.

The Payroll Department's only concern was making sure the paychecks were ready on time. It did not have the resources to investigate exceptions. As long as the payroll appeared to be reasonable and had a manger's approval, it was processed without question. I stressed the importance of, in the future, stopping the process and questioning all errors and exceptions.

I also recommended performing regular risk assessments on business units that involve cash or cash-based transactions. It is also important not to allow vendors to conduct business with only one individual. Last, we now require the utilization of a form of competitive bidding for the procurement of all goods and services.

About the Author

Jim Cali, CPA, CFF, is a well established internal auditor and forensic accountant who has worked in law enforcement since 1983. His forensic accounting experience includes investigations for money laundering, embezzlement, insurance fraud, mortgage fraud, terrorist financing and arson for profit. In 2007, he received an Outstanding Law Enforcement Officer of the Year Award from the United States Department of Justice. He currently teaches forensic accounting at the University of Missouri.

CHAPTER

For Love or Money?

JOHN R. HOLLEY

Sandy Benedict, maiden name Lee, grew up in central Washington outside of Yakima and graduated from a local high school. Sandy had shoulder-length brown hair that she always kept neatly pinned up at the back of her head. She wore very little, if any, makeup most days because of her strict upbringing by her deeply religious parents. She had an uneventful childhood and was not a cause of concern for her parents through her teenage years.

Sandy's first job was in a fast-food restaurant where she worked as a cashier. Although she enjoyed working with the public, she hated the long hours and the little pay that she received. Sandy was described by her family, friends and employers as being trustworthy and dependable. After high school she attended and graduated from a Seattle-area college, where she majored in business administration. She had several clerk jobs during her college days to help pay for her education.

Sandy met her husband, Ted Benedict, in college, where he was also studying as a business major. After their graduation from college, Ted became a pilot in the Air Force. Ted and Sandy got married after he graduated from flight school and was stationed at a base in Anchorage. In Alaska, Sandy took an entry-level position at one of the local title insurance agencies as an escrow assistant.

Sandy liked the work because it allowed her to interact with customers daily. She became very good at her job and developed an extensive list of repeat customers, mainly contractors and real estate developers.

One of the happiest days for Sandy was when she passed her written insurance examination and obtained her title insurance license. This allowed her to have an increased role in real estate transactions.

Sandy was approached by Lisa Shields, who had recently acquired the Caribou Title Insurance Agency in Anchorage, to join her team as the escrow manager. Sandy accepted the position; she liked her new responsibilities and the trust that Lisa and upper management placed in her.

299

Sandy was responsible for implementing a new computer software program at Caribou Title and was given complete access to all sections, titles, escrows and financials of the program. Because she was trusted completely, her access was never changed or withdrawn. That turned out to be a mistake.

While flying a private airplane, Ted was injured in a crash. The crash left him a paraplegic and largely dependent on Sandy and others for his daily care. Sandy was distraught over Ted's injury but reacted by distancing herself from him physically and emotionally. In an effort to deal with her faltering relationship, Sandy threw herself into her work. The local real estate market was booming so there was more than enough work to be done. It was not unusual for her to be the first person at the office in the morning and the last one to leave at night.

Sandy would be in the office on Saturdays and Sundays and never took a vacation or a day off. She had the only key to her office, and it was not unusual for an employee to go to the file room for a particular document only to find it was not there because Sandy had it in her office.

Sandy was well acquainted with John Adolf, a local contractor and real estate developer, because he was one of her frequent customers. A friendship developed between the two, and they often went to lunch together. John would also bring Sandy gifts as a token of his appreciation for her good work.

Sandy declared to the other office staff that John was her customer exclusively and no one else was allowed to handle his business. Sandy kept all his files in her office, and no one was allowed to review them. Her behavior provided much fodder for the office rumor mill, and it was widely speculated that Sandy and John were having an affair.

At a meeting in her office late one night, John told Sandy that he needed $750,000 to develop some property. Exactly why they were meeting late in the evening was also the subject of speculation. But whatever the reason, John said to Sandy that he could not obtain the necessary funds through the normal commercial means because he had defaulted on previous loans. Sandy gave a smile reserved only for John and knew that she would help him.

Sandy's Special Customer

John Adolf had an uneventful early childhood that led to rebellious teen years. When he turned 16, John dropped out of high school and started working in construction. He discovered that he liked the work and developed quite a knack for it. John learned the tricks of the trade from his boss, Ray Seton, who became John's mentor. Ray had quite an operation, which John envied. John dreamed of the day when he would own his own company.

After inheriting a small fortune when his parents died, John used the money to finance his own construction company. This was the time when the real estate market was at its lowest and distressed properties were ripe for the picking. John was able to buy some of them cheaply and flip them for large profits.

With the significant amount of money that was coming in, John purchased several large homes and cars for himself. He also developed an expensive addiction to drugs and alcohol. He quickly squandered all the money and other assets in his company on his drug habit and was unable to borrow from banks or other financial institutions because he had defaulted on several loans. Although he knew that borrowing money from private lenders was costly, his situation forced him to do so to support his business and personal expenses.

John used his charm and rugged good looks to persuade others to give him what he needed, including money. That included Sandy.

Caribou Title

Caribou Title Insurance Agency, Inc., had been founded ten years earlier by Andy Fredericks and Steve Anchor. Because of the surging local economy and real estate market, its share of real estate transactions grew from 3 to more than 30 percent. Andy and Steve sold the business to Lisa Shields, a local Realtor who owned several real estate offices, and Steve remained with the company as vice president.

Because of its steady increase in its share of the real estate market, Caribou Title soon outgrew its office. This forced the company to move into a new, larger space, sharing a building with its sister real estate agencies and a mortgage company that Lisa had acquired.

In an effort to cut down the amount of time required to conduct the title history examination (a necessity when issuing a title insurance policy), Lisa decided that the history would be reviewed only back to the time of the last policy issued. This allowed Caribou employees to process title examinations in half the time it took their competitors. That turned out to be a big mistake, but at the time, business grew exponentially.

Common States Title Insurance Company was the chief underwriter of the title insurance policies that Caribou Title issued. Because of the large volume of business Caribou Title was generating, Common States required it to pay a smaller-than-normal percentage of the premium; the rest was kept by Caribou Title as its commission.

To Lisa and the upper management at Caribou Title, the future looked rosy indeed. All they needed was more capital to grow.

Private Lenders

In October, Nelson Marlow, a local physician, decided to try his hand as a private lender in an effort to increase his retirement fund. Nelson knew a fellow physician, Roger Gallagher, who had done quite well as a private lender and asked Roger to help him break into the trade.

Because the list of individuals willing to serve as lenders was so short, it was not long before Sandy heard about Nelson's interest and contacted him. Since Sandy wanted to help John get his required $750,000 and because she had complete access to the computer system at Caribou Title, she devised a plan. She told Nelson that she had a real estate developer who needed a loan and could put up more than the $750,000 in real estate collateral. She then called John to get his thoughts on the plan. She would use John's existing legitimate transaction with Leroy Thomas (another private lender) and the property in question but change the title report to reflect a clean history on the collateral. Sandy also manufactured a bogus deed of trust and settlement form. John was hesitant, but he needed the funds and figured Sandy knew what she was doing.

Nelson agreed to lend John the money after Sandy assured him of the collateral properties' value. She provided him a title insurance policy that listed John Adolf as the sole owner of property (Lots 1 through 10 of Valley Springs Subdivision) with no existing loans or liens against it.

In late December, the loan was closed in Sandy's office at Caribou Title. Nelson gave the funds to John, and Sandy gave Nelson copies of the closing documents. According to the documents, all of the costs associated with the transaction were paid for by John. John was to begin monthly repayments to Nelson the following January. Sandy did not receive funds from the transaction, but she was confident that she had gotten John's attention and that their relationship would grow.

Shared Collateral

When John failed to make his first payment in January, Nelson contacted him directly to see what was going on. John said he had experienced building permit delays but promised that the money was coming. However, he failed to make his payments in February and March and gave Nelson the same excuse and promises of repayment.

In early April, Nelson was at a dinner party at Roger's house when he overheard a mutual acquaintance, Leroy Thomas, make a comment about John Adolf. The mention of the name piqued his interest when he overheard Leroy say that he was going to have to foreclose on some property because John had defaulted on a loan that Leroy had made to him. Nelson spent a sleepless night thinking about Leroy's comments. He wondered if the property he had as collateral for his loan to John Adolf was the same property as Leroy Thomas's.

The next business day, Nelson contacted Sandy about Leroy Thomas, but Sandy assured him that there was nothing to worry about. She said John's loan from Leroy had nothing to do with the transaction between Nelson and John.

In late April, because John had failed to make the required payments and was no longer returning his messages, Nelson called Sandy to discuss his options. Nelson told Sandy of John's inability to repay the loan, and she assured Nelson that she would talk to John.

In mid-May, Nelson still had not received any money from John, so he called Sandy again. This time Sandy was out sick, recovering from surgery, so he was transferred to Deb Jackson, the title manager.

To research the transaction, Deb asked Nelson to bring her copies of his closing documents because she couldn't find them. Knowing that Sandy kept John's files in her locked office, Deb called her at home to obtain more information. Sandy became angry and started cursing at Deb for even speaking to Nelson about the transaction; she accused Deb of trying to steal her customers.

Deb was dumbfounded at the reaction she got from Sandy, so she called the underwriter, Common States Title Insurance Company, to research the transaction from that angle. Deb was told by Common States that no such title insurance policy had ever existed involving Nelson Marlow and John Adolf.

Deb next went to speak with Lou Romero, the president of Caribou Title, and informed him of her investigation and what she had learned regarding Nelson's transaction.

Lou had Deb pull a title report concerning the collateral property. That report indicated that John was indeed the owner of the property, but there were multiple liens against it and Nelson Marlow was not listed as one of them. There was no record of the loan to John Adolf by Nelson Marlow.

Lou contacted John about the transaction, who told him that he was indeed behind in his payments to Nelson and that Sandy had handled the paperwork in the transaction. John denied knowing anything about the fictitious title insurance policy.

Lou informed Steve Anchor, the vice president of Caribou Title, about the transaction, and they agreed to talk to Sandy about the matter. The meeting was held with Sandy on a Sunday at the Caribou Title offices. After being advised of their findings, Sandy gave them a prepared letter of resignation that was effective immediately and refused to answer any questions.

Lou and Steve were both dumbfounded by Sandy's resignation. They mistakenly allowed her to clean out her office and even left her alone to do so.

The next day, Lou went through Sandy's old office, looking for the missing files, but did not find any trace of the transaction. He ordered an examination of Sandy's computer by Caribou Title's internal information technology department, but it did not reveal any record of the transaction either. After discussing the matter with Lisa, other upper management and the corporate attorney, Lou reported the incident involving Nelson, John and Sandy to the State Division of Insurance.

State of Fraud

When I was working as a fraud investigator for the State of Alaska, I was contacted by Brenda Thompson, director of the State of Alaska Division of Insurance, who told me that Lou Romero and Lisa Shields of Caribou Title were coming to her office to file a complaint. I knew Brenda as having been a former school teacher and insurance agent who had a conservative approach to issues but always placed consumers' interests first. She wanted me to sit in on the meeting with Lou and Lisa.

Lou had prepared a written outline of what he determined had occurred among Sandy Benedict, John Adolf and Nelson Marlowe. After the meeting, Brenda called again and informed me that she wanted me to investigate the complaint.

I interviewed Nelson regarding the transaction with John Adolf, and he supplied me with copies of the documents Sandy had given him. The documents reflected a title insurance premium of $3,100, an escrow fee of $750 and a total of $150 in recording fees associated with the transaction. Nelson stated that John paid all those costs. Nelson also added that he had filed a claim with Common States for the $750,000, but it was denied because the policy did not exist.

In my review of the transaction documents supplied by Nelson, I noted that the title insurance policy appeared to be on stationery bearing the logo of Common States and that the policy number was 3344. I also noticed that on the settlement statement, the internal Caribou Title file number for the transaction between Nelson and John was SSS-12345SB.

Conspirator or Victim?

I interviewed John Adolf and explained what I had learned about the transaction between him and Nelson and the false documents that Sandy had prepared. John denied any wrongdoing and stated that Sandy had handled everything. He said he trusted her professionalism and assumed the transaction was legitimate. John said that he had paid all the fees associated with the closing to Caribou Title through Sandy. Regarding his relationship with Sandy, John admitted to being close with her but adamantly denied a romantic connection. During my interview, John promised to fully cooperate with my investigation. But I tried to contact him on several later occasions, and he failed to respond to my requests.

I tried to interview Sandy about the transaction, but she refused to talk to me and walked out of the interview. She failed to respond to any of my later requests, and, during the course of my investigation, she allowed her title insurance license to expire.

At first Caribou Title was very cooperative with my requests for information. I interviewed Deb Jackson, Lou Romero, Steve Anchor and other staff members. That is when I discovered evidence that Caribou Title was not conducting thorough title history examinations. I also learned that there was very little supervision of employees by upper management. Caribou Title ceased cooperation after I started asking questions about these issues.

I obtained a search warrant for all records, both physical and electronic, from Caribou Title concerning the transaction between Nelson Benedict and John Adolf. The warrant also demanded all of Sandy's files, including her personnel files. With the help of other members of the investigative staff at the Division of Insurance, I served the order and physically carried out the records.

Our review of the information uncovered e-mail messages among members of the upper management discussing whether they "should cooperate with the investigation and cease our activities, or make all the money we can." In an e-mail message between Lou Romero and Dave Holden of Common States, Dave referred to the title insurance policy that Nelson had submitted a claim against as being a "fake" and that a real policy should be issued to him.

Save It for a Rainy Day

Our review also detected the presence of a so-called slush fund to which unaccounted-for, or surplus, funds were directed and then withdrawn when needed to balance a transaction. From the review, it was evident that the slush fund was controlled by Sandy — all the deposits and withdrawals involved transactions with John Adolf. There was no evidence of any payments to Sandy from the account. It appears that her actions were for love, not money.

We also discovered that the title insurance policy #3344 was issued to a transaction between Leroy Thomas and John Adolf that took place in September. Leroy loaned John $500,000, and in exchange John put up the title to Lots 1 through 10 of Valley Springs Subdivision as collateral. Sandy Benedict was the escrow officer in charge of the closing, and the internal Caribou Title file number for the transaction was SSS-12345SB — the same insurance policy number and file number as Nelson's loan. The state recorder's records reflected the transaction between Leroy and John, but there was no record of the transaction between Nelson and John.

Caribou Title's bank records failed to show any evidence that the money belonging to Nelson Marlow was processed in the same manner as funds from other transactions. I was also unable to find evidence of transaction fees paid to Caribou Title from Nelson's loan.

Sandy's personnel records indicated that before December her performance evaluations had always described her as dependable, trustworthy and delightful. These records also revealed several notations, since December, regarding complaints from customers and employees about her unprofessional, uncaring attitude and lack of dependability. The records also contained a signed note dated mid-May that read "I, Sandy Benedict, do hereby resign my job as of this date."

The Hope of Civil Recovery

After reviewing the evidence, I wrote my report and forwarded it to the prosecuting attorney for consideration. Because of a lack of sufficient evidence, no criminal action was taken against Sandy or John.

Steve Anchor, vice president of Caribou Title, was forced to resign his position because he had failed to adequately supervise Sandy. Because of this, administrative action, consisting of sanctions and fines, was taken against Caribou Title.

Common States put Caribou Title on probationary status and reserved the right to randomly examine Caribou Title's records. Common States' management also required Caribou Title to pay an increased premium for the policies it issued.

Sandy Benedict was forced to surrender her insurance license and is permanently barred from renewing it. Caribou Title underwent a drastic downsizing, both in the number of personnel employed as well as its market share.

Nelson Marlow was forced to pursue legal action civilly against John Adolf to recover the $750,000. His case is still working its way through the court system. Not promisingly for Nelson, John Adolf filed bankruptcy in federal court under Chapter 11.

Lessons Learned

In the process of my investigation, I learned a great deal about the proper way to conduct real estate transactions and the pitfalls encountered if these business deals are not correctly handled.

I also learned how important it is to maintain proper documentation, both in electronic and hard copy form, and how to successfully build a case of negligence against a corporation. I learned the vital importance of a computer program to reflect and track any access or changes to documents created and stored in the program. Finally, I learned that no file would contain details of the kind of personal relationship that existed between John and Sandy. That can be uncovered only by asking the tough questions.

Recommendations to Prevent Future Occurrences

I made the following recommendations to Common States and Caribou Title management:

- Hire an internal auditor to review all transactions for thoroughness and correctness.
- Review random files with the same goal to ensure proper handling of all transactions.
- Change the employee manual to require that all staff and employees take all their vacation time yearly.
- Acquire new computer software to monitor and track all changes to records in the system.

About the Author

John R. Holley has over 20 years of law enforcement experience both in Georgia and Alaska. He has conducted hundreds of financial and other fraud investigations during that period. He is a member of the Alaska Peace Officer Association (APOA) and Association of Certified Fraud Examiners (ACFE).

CHAPTER

Ethical Governance: A Mandate for Outsourcing

JYOTI KHETARPAL

arketing, operations, human resources and accounting are recognized as essential functions for a business to run smoothly, but there are other divisions that support these departments and are necessary to operations. Radel Crowe headed one such division, procurement, in the organization in which he was employed. Radel joined Rhodo Industries in its second year of operations. He was hired to be the procurement manager based on his substantial industry experience. As a staff member who had not been with Rhodo since the very beginning, he felt the need to prove himself and to consistently exceed expectations in his daily work. He wanted the recognition and approval of the leadership team.

Radel was from a small town and had not attended college or obtained professional credentials, but his loyalty and honesty made him popular with senior officials. He also demonstrated an ability to achieve great results in his department without needing too much guidance. As a result, he was given more responsibilities to shoulder and began reporting directly to the president.

Although management respected Radel's work, his peers and subordinates considered him to be rude because he set the rules for his department and strictly enforced them; violations often resulted in job loss. Others resented Radel's rapid ascension up the career ladder and suspected there was favoritism at play.

Opportunities in Outsourcing

Rhodo Industries was founded in a developing country with the purpose of securing outsourcing services for third-party companies so they could benefit from the local cost savings. Rhodo hired experienced local personnel to lead different departments under the umbrella supervision of an expatriate named Michael.

Department heads were selectively recruited from the industry. They were all experts with hands-on experience in their area. Rhodo management was planning to outsource many more processes over the years based on the success of its pilot project, which went well and created more efficiency than was expected. Rhodo had spent a good amount to support its outsourcing infrastructure. The leadership was extremely happy after learning of the reduced overhead in the first year for their clients. It raised salaries and levels of many managers and base employees to boost morale.

The company's plans were on track, and management was ready for future process migrations. It had to increase the team size rapidly and of course the infrastructure. After learning the success of the pilot project, prospective employees were more than happy to join Rhodo, and the company quickly became known as one of the best places to work in the industry. That was when Radel Crowe joined the organization.

The Things You Can Learn over Coffee

Michael was invited to speak at a seminar organized by an industry regulator for the purpose of discussing the benefits of outsourcing. Executives from other organizations were also present.

After the seminar sessions, there were informal discussions over cocktails and dinner. While talking to a group of other business leaders, Michael realized that although Rhodo was saving money with its processes, the company could cut costs even more. Michael discovered that while Rhodo was paying the best salaries in the market, the high-ranking officials were not saving as much for Rhodo as their counterparts at other companies. Meanwhile, every year Rhodo's budgets increased across the board, especially for procurement. The reason his staff gave him was rising inflation.

One evening Michael invited Victor, an executive from another organization, to join him for coffee after dinner, and they started talking about their experiences at their offshore centers. Victor said, "There are plenty of opportunities in this country. The abundance of educated personnel, top-notch facilities and low costs are making our plans more successful."

Michael said, "We've also reaped great results. The only drawback I've discovered so far is the inflation rate. It seems very high and results in huge procurement and administration costs for us each year."

Victor agreed and said, "Yes, the inflation rate is high, but I've experienced different trends at my organization. I've seen a steep drop in cost per full-time employee in terms of facilities and administration since we've increased our staff after our pilot program. Maybe it is because we are working in a different domain than Rhodo."

Michael asked if Victor could give him specific areas where he had seen cost savings, and Victor responded, "Sure. For example, cafeteria costs per head have been reduced due to discounts offered by the vendor because his sales increase with the more staff we have. And the most interesting is transportation costs; they have reduced drastically. You must be aware of the way transport is handled there. Though this industry doesn't operate by the best ethical standards, the competition among vendors has made our costs very low."

This made Michael question the way things were handled at Rhodo. During the course of his discussion with Victor, he also realized that he had not been made aware of certain practices in the local market, which caused him to think about the integrity of his staff and the associated processes they had implemented. However, he decided he needed to research and understand the local market better before discussing his concerns internally with his department heads. He did not want to alarm anyone with his doubts if they turned out to be unfounded.

Process Evaluation

My supervisor, David, had known Michael since he started his career at Rhodo. After gathering information through his internal control department on various functions, Michael contacted David for help.

I was appointed case manager for an internal inquiry with the objective of finding potential malfeasance in the processes that various managers at Rhodo followed. It was a tedious job of screening each procedure and measuring it against standards or benchmarks. I chose the best team members considering the level of trust Michael had for David.

My team and I selected only transactions that involved disbursements. We left the technical processes completely alone and focused on HR, legal, administration, procurement and accounting. We started by looking at how the budgets were created, approved and followed for each expense. We also mapped the role of each employee in the departments we were analyzing. An overview of available information revealed a few gaps.

We noticed that in the procurement department, the person responsible for requesting vendor bids was in charge of approving them as well. There was no separate team for screening the bid documents. The legal department was, at times, signing agreements without reading them. Agreements were renewed beyond their original time periods. Fresh bids were not invited regularly. Market surveys were not conducted to find out current market rates for products and services. Negotiations were not carried out to benefit from the economies of scale. Vendors were hired without background checks, and there were no minimum qualifications for them.

HR personnel were also hiring new staff without conducting background checks, leading to many family members of vendors being hired at Rhodo.

We also noticed that family members of employees were hired as vendors for certain services. Further investigation revealed that, due to overburdened legal and finance departments, proper procurement procedures were pretty much ignored. These conditions were ripe for kickbacks. We discovered that our own people openly asked for "commissions" for awarding contracts for transportation, building maintenance, event management, training, cafeteria service and even from HR consultants. When we conducted discreet checks, we found that employees would often share a percentage of commissions received from vendors with others in the company.

Happy Outcome

When we told Michael, to our surprise, he laughed loudly. He explained he was laughing because he was relieved — the problem was only with lower-level staff, which could easily be fixed. He said he had been worried his trusted, senior team members might be involved.

Michael asked us to suggest improved standard operating practices for different processes, and we created standard checklists for all the critical procedures, supported by detailed manuals. We also defined industry-specific clauses to be incorporated in the request-for-proposal documents and final agreements.

Michael was exceptionally satisfied with our work, particularly with the fact that Radel's name came up repeatedly as an honest manager of the procurement team. Michael had a separate confidential meeting with Radel in the presence of my boss, David. Michael and David agreed that Radel should be promoted to the most senior position in the department and report directly to Michael. Radel was put in charge of the procurement and administration budgets and cost-cutting initiatives.

Radel readily accepted the additional responsibility. He reviewed the manuals we created and implemented the new processes immediately. With the help of the internal controls team and the finance department, he identified the procurement employees who were involved in financial malfeasance. Radel personally interviewed them in the presence of HR and internal control representatives and, after giving them an opportunity to defend themselves (which they were unable to do), he fired them.

Radel hired replacement personnel after conducting background checks on them. The vendors were advised that they would have to participate in the bids based on qualifying criteria. Radel sent my team details for shortlisted vendors and we conducted "know your vendor" checks. Even after that, the approved vendors underwent significant due diligence by Radel.

Radel made sure that there were no loopholes in the system and kept the internal controls team informed. The result of this overhaul was significant savings for the company. Michael was impressed with Radel's work and rewarded him with a pay raise. Radel soon became a close confidant of Michael's.

However, this entire exercise was in vain as it was a precursor to a much larger corruption.

Returning to Rhodo

During this first investigation, we identified many loopholes in the coordination of the HR, legal, administration, procurement and accounting departments. The roles of the departments were vague, so we redefined the expectations of each department and hired new staff where necessary. A few employees involved in the corrupt practices were asked to leave the organization.

With Radel's promotion, we thought our assignment was finished. However, two years later things turned ugly once more, and this time the corruption was much bigger than we could have imagined. There were rumors of employees being involved in kickbacks again. The allegations were a surprise for Michael and for us, especially because many of them indicated Radel's involvement.

Initially Michael disregarded the accusations; he attributed them to employee dissatisfaction with Radel's strict nature and possibly some disgruntled ex-workers who were trying to harm his reputation. But when the allegations began coming in from different employees across departments, he couldn't ignore them anymore. He asked David and me to form our team again, and we embarked on an investigation that was much more complicated than we planned for and ended up lasting six months.

Investigating When the Suspect Knows

Radel knew of the allegations against him because he had a close-knit team that made him aware of the latest chatter in the grapevine. Immediately after hearing the rumors, he contacted Michael to clarify the situation. Michael explained to him, "See, Radel, since the complaints have reached HR and are coming from so many different people, I have to investigate them, even if I believe you are innocent. If you haven't done anything, you shouldn't be worried about it."

Since David, my boss, was traveling at the time, Michael called me to relate Radel's curious phone call. He wanted to know how I would prefer to go about it now that Radel knew we were investigating him. My suggestion was to carry out an internal investigation using staff from the internal controls department. I wanted my role to remain unknown to Radel because I did not want him to know about the external investigation yet. We wanted to check his earnings and lifestyle independently.

Michael liked the idea and asked the head of the internal audit department, Cindy, to initiate the investigation. He also advised Cindy to stay in contact with me in case she had questions about local or industry operations. Cindy had never started an investigation in which the alleged perpetrator was aware of it, so she and I talked on the phone to come up with a plan.

On my suggestion, she asked the accounting department to generate a list of the top 50 vendors used by Rhodo, in terms of expenditures. Her team prepared an analysis chart and identified that, after Radel's appointment, there had been a drastic decline in payments made to these vendors. Radel said he had renegotiated rates with vendors and cut out the "customary" bribes that they used to charge to secure contracts. If this was true, Radel's position looked even stronger.

My Team's Turn

My team started our discreet investigation after two weeks. We wanted to understand the staff complaints and the reasons behind them. Our on-the-ground examiners, after various rounds of discussions with security guards, transport vendors, employees and ex-employees, reported that "fingers are still pointing toward Radel. Various stakeholders in the supply chain think he is not as clean as management likes to believe."

When we compared the results of Cindy's internal analysis and our examination, nothing matched. According to Cindy's report, Radel had saved a lot for the organization, processes had been properly implemented, the roles of each department were defined and procurement had become transparent. Our investigation suggested that Radel and a few of his close associates could be involved in financial malfeasance. However, the extent and type was not clear.

Cindy and I decided to look into the accounts more deeply. When we asked for a complete record of vendors from the accounting department, it gave us a list of more than 1,000 companies. It was difficult for us to analyze payments made to all of them, so we decided to start with vendors that had been begun working for Rhodo after Radel's promotion. We discovered that there were many small vendors providing "maintenance services" that were introduced into the system recently. When Cindy asked the staff what kind of services these vendors were providing, no one knew. Before confronting Radel and informing Michael, we decided to search further.

Rounds of interviews with employees, ex-employees and vendors revealed that Radel had become overambitious after receiving his promotion, but he took an unusual path to fulfill his dreams. He saved money for the organization where he was expected to and found other unexpected avenues to generate money for his personal benefit.

As he was involved in defining the rules and procedures, Radel conveniently ignored or twisted them in his favor where he felt necessary. He represented a unique case of corruption while presenting himself as the most loyal and dedicated employee of the organization. He also once expressed to Michael his wish of becoming CEO of the entity and asked for his advice.

My team conducted a background check on all the suspicious vendors and on Radel as well. This time, not to our surprise, we found out that the small vendors were owned by Radel's and his close associates' family members. The background check on Radel revealed that he had financial difficulty some time ago and had created a few of the companies with his wife. He had first used the same vendors at his previous employer. When questions arose, he quit his job and joined Rhodo. In the meantime, he transferred the ownership of his businesses to relatives to avoid future scrutiny.

Breaking the Bad News

After gathering this evidence, we decided not to confront Radel and instead went to Michael. Michael confirmed that he had approved the new vendors Radel suggested because Radel assured him the services they provided were necessary. Michael trusted Radel and, although he did not like that the companies were owned by Radel's relatives, he was of the opinion that if services were unsatisfactory, they could simply change vendors. When we informed him that the services had never been rendered, he was stunned. We told him that, in total, Radel's corruption had cost Rhodo $75,000. All he could say was "But why? What was the need? He saved a lot for the organization and was growing within the organization. Why?"

My reply was "This might not be just for money but to prove his power. Corruption is normally considered a form of financial malfeasance; however, abuse of authority is also corruption. He might have been trying to help his relatives, but he abused the system that he himself designed and implemented."

Michael scheduled a breakfast with Radel outside the office in a private meeting room. Radel had a fair idea about the outcome of the investigation through his rumor-mill informants. On the table, Michael placed names of the vendors owned by Radel's relatives and asked him why he did it.

Radel tried to defend himself: "Michael, these vendors have been hired to monitor the services of other vendors. To put the system in place I wanted people I knew and trusted to give me honest information. Their role was kept quiet because they were inspecting others' services."

Michael countered: "You know you hired your relatives as vendors while company's policy manual clearly states that no relative, distant or close, can be employed with the organization either as an employee or third-party vendor. And even worse, they did not render any services."

Radel said, "I know. I messed up, but my intentions were honest. Otherwise, how could I have saved so much money for the company? I did this for Rhodo. I do not care what others think about me. You have seen my work and I want to know what you think about me."

Michael looked away in disgust and said, "I don't think highly of you anymore."

The next day Radel resigned from Rhodo. One week later, two of his close associates from the procurement department also resigned. We knew the repercussions and had already decided on replacements. Michael hired new employees and defined their roles clearly. No single person was given authority over the full procurement process after Radel left. However, management decided it was not worth the costs and reputational risks to pursue criminal or civil charges against Radel or the vendors. It cut its losses and vowed never to let such corruption occur again.

Lessons Learned

Before investing in an outsourcing venture, conduct due diligence. In some closely knit societies, people are obligated to ensure benefits for their relatives, even if it is to the detriment of their employers. Familial concerns might not appear to be important to a business executive when deciding to outsource operations, but, as this case demonstrated, neglecting to conduct due diligence can have serious financial repercussions.

We learned that before considering new locations, investors need to research the social environment in addition to financial, legal and demographic advantages. Processes should be introduced based on the local culture while meeting international standards. Potential employees' acceptance and adaptability to the organizational goals and ethics are important factors in the hiring decision.

We also learned that it is important to repeatedly reinforce organizational values to staff through HR policies. Employees should be motivated to make integrity a part of their job, and those who are adhering to such values should be rewarded.

Recommendations to Prevent Future Occurrences

After the investigation, we made the following recommendations to Michael:

- A strict internal controls system is mandatory in any organization based on its values.
- Background checks should be conducted before hiring employees and vendors.
- Industry trends in the local markets should be studied in depth before formulating internal policies and procedures.
- Clear and strict procurement policies can help many companies avoid corruption.
- Organizational values should be reinforced repeatedly, particularly integrity. After Radel's departure, we created a checklist of integrity rules and Michael disseminated it to the staff.

- Positions that entail significant responsibility and power might be better allocated to more than one person. Michael divided the procurement process into subprocesses and appointed managers for each task under a committee, which directly reports to him.
- Job rotation can prevent and detect frauds. After Radel, Michael began rotating employees regularly to unearth potential skeletons in the closet.
- Managers and directors should also be supervised. No single person should have enough authority to manipulate a system in his or her favor.
- Process governance or ethical governance checklists should be introduced and regularly disseminated to employees.

About the Author

Jyoti Khetarpal is an India-qualified Chartered Accountant with more than 13 years of corporate experience with Dun & Bradstreet and American Express. She has been instrumental in outlining risk management methodology, analytics and assessment. Currently she is working with Alea Consulting providing reputational due diligence, corporate (fraud) investigations, intellectual property protection, KYC and related advisory services.

CHAPTER 34

Friends and Lovers in High Places

RICK HOYE

Cindy Pomeroy was like many executives at small, government-funded organizations whose missions were to provide public assistance to those in need. She applied for and obligated the group's finances. She reported to a board of directors made up mostly of local government officials. She was directly accountable to a state agency charged with disbursing federal funds. However, unlike her contemporaries in this small, midwestern state, Cindy managed to provide herself with a financial compensation package, albeit illegal, that exceeded the combined salaries of the governor, lieutenant governor, secretary of state and the state treasurer.

Pomeroy grew up in a town of 350 people, most of whom worked in jobs associated with the endless surrounding fields of corn and soybeans. Some families did better than others financially, but no one in town was considered rich. She dropped out of high school at the age of 15 to get married but later received her GED certificate. Like many young people of her generation, she had dreams that could never be satisfied in a small town. She moved to the state capital to find the opportunities that might lead to personal and financial success.

Over the years she married and divorced three times, had two children and used her management and social skills to achieve a comfortable and rewarding lifestyle. She started working for a group that helped the unemployed get practical training and productive employment. She gradually worked her way up the ladder from a clerical position to become the director of the agency. Cindy Pomeroy was good at her job, but it was her ability to develop and charm a support network of well-placed colleagues that shielded her schemes to pay herself salary and bonuses far beyond any reasonable standard.

Roger Thurston was the son of a small grocery store owner and grew up in a large family in the state capital. Even before he graduated from high school, he was training to take his place in one of the city's major political clubs. This was nothing like the powerful, legendary political organizations of New York, Chicago or Baton Rouge. Rather, it was a cohesive group of party officials and officeholders who generally thought alike and were committed to watching each other's backs. They sometimes used their positions and political skills to help folks in the neighborhood with a little inside information here, a job reference there or some other favor to ensure that voters remembered them at election time.

Thurston was married with six children, and he demonstrated the kind of skills needed to take a leading role in the organization. He became the youngest-ever councilman and spent more than 30 years as part of the six-member city council. This afforded him opportunities to sit on numerous other boards, committees and task forces that had great influence on how the city was run. He received numerous awards and tributes, including having a community center built and named in his honor. Like many big-city politicians, he was satisfied with the job he had and never attempted a campaign for a higher office.

Training for Corruption

The Regional Employment Training Alliance (RETA) was a quasi-governmental entity with a board of directors made up of representatives appointed by city and county governments. It was organized under state law and considered a governmental agency; however, it functioned as a private nonprofit organization.

Over the years the number of employees varied from about 40 to 70, depending on funding. The annual budget usually ranged from $5 to $7 million, most of which came from the federal government. State, county and city governments provided funding as well, and the agency received some private donations. Cindy Pomeroy was RETA's executive director. Roger Thurston was the chairman of its board of directors.

RETA's mission was to provide job counseling, training and placement services to the unemployed and to other disadvantaged groups. The primary government organization overseeing their receipt and use of money was the state Labor and Workforce Management Administration (LAWMA). Most of the state and federal funds were channeled through LAWMA, which also monitored similar organizations around the state. RETA was conveniently housed in the same state office building as LAWMA, allowing easy access to the officials with the money.

A few other key players in this story were Oscar Hirschorn, RETA's chief operating officer, and Geri Tate, the group's chief accountant. Pomeroy knew she needed these individuals to go along with her compensation scheme, and they were rewarded handsomely for their participation. Pomeroy also brought RETA board member Jeff Frazier into her circle.

Carolyn Montague was the assistant director of LAWMA. Its director reportedly liked to travel and leave the daily grind of running the agency to

Montague, who gladly seized the opportunity and aggravated many employees with her authoritarian management style. She might not have been very popular with her staff, but she had the categorical approval of Pomeroy and Hirschorn.

Trying to Keep It Quiet

Carolyn Montague was a strong manager but lacked the ability to maintain strict control over the hundreds of LAWMA employees the way Pomeroy could at her small agency. During a routine audit, LAWMA analyst Tracy Frank uncovered some startling data about salaries and bonuses at RETA. This was not as easy as it might seem because LAWMA auditors studied individual programs rather than RETA's activities as a whole. Frank discovered that, by channeling money from dozens of different grants and programs, Cindy Pomeroy and Oscar Hirschorn had concealed the amount of funds flowing into their personal accounts. It also helped that Hirschorn's wife had been contracted a few years earlier to "modernize" RETA's accounting software, while reportedly making it much more difficult to retrieve relevant data.

When Frank started asking questions at RETA about compensation, Pomeroy immediately called Carolyn Montague. Pomeroy put Frank on the line, and Montague made it clear to her that LAWMA "does not dictate personnel policies" and that Frank should discontinue the RETA audit and move on to other assignments. Instead, upon returning to LAWMA, Frank shared her findings with her immediate supervisor, Gary Gunderson.

Gunderson had long held concerns about how Pomeroy ran her agency and the preferential treatment RETA seemed to receive from Montague and LAWMA. He contacted U.S. Department of Labor (DOL) oversight officials, who in turn demanded an explanation from Montague. At that point, Montague changed her perspective on investigating personnel policies and told the DOL official that LAWMA was already conducting a review of compensation levels at RETA and should be allowed to complete that project prior to any intervention by DOL.

Montague was livid with Gunderson for blowing the whistle and made sure he and his staff had no further involvement with RETA. She accused him of having a personal vendetta against her and Pomeroy. Meanwhile, Gunderson also shared Frank's findings with the state auditor's office.

Montague's attempt to keep the issue under her control ultimately failed. DOL was not satisfied with LAWMA's investigation and supported Gunderson's request that the state auditor's office perform a detailed review of compensation practices at RETA.

Pomeroy's reaction to the state audit was to order her staff to destroy records that could implicate her in the misuse of government funds. She wanted to shred even more records but was persuaded by Oscar Hirschorn and Geri Tate that most of the material was already in the hands of the auditors from other sources and that she risked being accused of a cover-up if they were suddenly unavailable.

After three months of work, the state's auditor issued a scathing report of RETA and LAWMA. The primary findings focused on the compensation levels of RETA's three top managers, summarized as follows:

Employee	Year One	Year Two	Year Three (5 1/2 Months)	Totals
CEO (Pomeroy)				
Base Salary	$108,748.85	$155,811.27	$85,923.21	$350,483.33
Bonuses	$145,306.45	$212,425.00	$87,170.00	$444,901.45
Total	$254,055.30	$368,236.27	$173,093.21	**$795,384.78**
COO (Hirschorn)				
Base Salary	$102,931.57	$152,931.21	$84,487.99	$340,350.77
Bonuses	$138,561.90	$207,087.00	$81,584.00	$427,232.90
Total	$241,493.47	$360,010.21	$166,071.99	**$767,583.67**
Chief Accountant (Tate)				
Base Salary	$89,137.02	$92,924.46	$43,466.47	$225,527.95
Bonuses	$25,741.00	$36,243.60	$4,714.00	$66,698.60
Total	$114,878.02	$129,168.06	$48,180.47	**$292,226.55**
Grand Total	$610,426.79	$857,414.54	$387,345.67	**$1,855,187.00**

The audit also reported less-than-arm's-length transactions between LAWMA and RETA. It specifically criticized Montague, noting that her friendly relationship with RETA executives might have contributed to LAWMA's inability to objectively monitor the group's spending.

Start Sorting

The auditor's report was greeted with public outrage. Within a couple of days, the governor fired Montague and her boss and called for an internal investigation. The RETA board of directors fired Pomeroy, Hirschorn and Tate; accepted Roger Thurston's resignation from his position as chairman; and opened its own inquiry. Criminal investigations were launched by the FBI and the U.S. Department of Labor, with assistance from state investigators. Records were seized from both RETA and LAWMA.

It was shortly after this that I became involved. As an investigator with the civil division of the U.S. Attorney's Office, I generally did not participate in criminal cases. But the FBI, which had already brought in three financial analysts from other states, needed additional assistance to comb through the massive amounts of digital and documentary evidence.

I was sent to an off-site FBI location to review large quantities of records. It was old and dirty, the high-tech security system being the only recent improvement. I was given a desk in a small, windowless office that was filled with dozens of evidence boxes. On the desk was a pile of shredded paper from a different case that some unfortunate agent had tried to tape back together without much success.

Among the boxes were four or five large plastic garbage bags filled with paper and other trash. This came to us by way of Carolyn Montague's secretary, who was caught at 4:00 a.m. the day after Montague was fired emptying several boxes of documents from her ex-boss's office into a dumpster behind one of the state office buildings. She told police that she couldn't sleep and decided to go to work early and get rid of old files that Montague kept but were no longer needed by LAWMA. Needless to say, it looked quite suspicious.

Unsure of what exactly had been tossed, state police removed everything from the dumpster and placed it in the aforementioned trash bags. As the new guy on the team, I had the privilege of sorting through the debris in search of what surely must be a few smoking-gun documents that would break the case wide open. What I found in the garbage bags was, well, garbage. A couple of days spent wearing those irritating disposable plastic gloves that leave your hands sweaty and wrinkled yielded nothing of value regarding RETA and Montague's role in the scandal. I spent a lot of time wishing that secretary had just stayed in bed until regular working hours.

Too Close and Personal

Meanwhile, federal agents were out interviewing dozens of potential witnesses at RETA and LAWMA. Along with public hearings by the state legislature and an aggressive investigation by the state's largest newspaper, a clear picture began to emerge about a dysfunctional, out-of-control agency and the corrupt officials who were supposed to be overseeing it.

Early investigative findings demonstrated that RETA was rampant with nepotism and cronyism. Roger Thurston, the chairman of the board of directors, got his brother on the RETA payroll years ago and, more recently, had convinced Cindy Pomeroy to hire his stepdaughter. Pomeroy herself had a daughter on staff, and she retained her son-in-law's company to handle the moving when RETA switched offices. Oscar Hirschorn's wife had been hired as a $65-per-hour consultant to help implement a new RETA accounting system. After the three executives were fired, an interim CFO complained that the new system was purposely set up to make it more difficult for auditors to determine the full amount of employee compensation. When board member Jeff Frazier lacked funds at his office to maintain a full-time assistant, Pomeroy obliged by hiring the assistant on a part-time basis at RETA. There was no position actually available, but a RETA employee testified that Pomeroy instructed her to find work for the new part-time employee.

A newspaper commentator observed that to truly understand the political connections of current and former RETA employees, one would need a genealogical chart of the county's political families, cross-referenced with city, county, RETA and LAWMA payrolls.

Pomeroy and other RETA staff socialized occasionally with Carolyn Montague at local bars, and Pomeroy frequently took her favorite employees to a nearby casino for afternoon gambling on company time. A couple of employees reported taking part or all of the day to help build a deck at Pomeroy's residence and to assist with landscaping projects at the home of a RETA board member. Time cards were routinely falsified to cover up these activities.

In addition to blood relations and political alliances, romance and sex played a major role in Pomeroy's manipulations. Rumors of a romantic relationship between Pomeroy and Roger Thurston had first been suggested 20 years earlier by RETA's executive director at that time, who had just been fired. He accused Pomeroy (who was appointed interim executive director) of claiming she was at an out-of-state conference when she actually spent the weekend with Thurston. Both denied it, and an investigation found no evidence of the impropriety.

At the trial, Thurston acknowledged much more recent sexual engagements with Pomeroy but insisted their private relationship had no influence on his role in overseeing her activities as the chairman of the board. True or not, he received no other benefits from the scheme, considering there was never any evidence that he profited financially.

The investigation got even more interesting when we realized that RETA board member Jeff Frazier was also having an intimate affair with Pomeroy at the same time she was sleeping with Thurston. And unlike Thurston, Frazier did receive financial benefits from RETA. Frazier earned $20,000 in two years for loosely defined "consulting services." The services included lobbying for RETA's interests at the state and federal level, which is illegal with federal funds. Apparently, neither Thurston nor anyone else on the board was aware of Frazier's consulting contract and its potential conflict of interest. Shortly after receiving one of his payments, Frazier and Pomeroy purchased a speedboat from Geri Tate, RETA's accountant. They registered the boat under Cindy's name, but with Jeff's home address.

Our review of documents also showed that RETA had received grant money from the board of an area casino, on which Frazier was a director. When we put together a timeline of events, it was interesting to see that the boat purchase occurred within ten days of RETA receiving a $25,000 grant from the casino. Frazier also received a $3,000 consulting payment from RETA within those ten days.

Initially, Roger Thurston denied knowing about the extravagant executive compensation. He contended that he sometimes signed documents without reading them but eventually admitted to knowingly approving at least some of the bonuses. He believed his signature was forged on other bonus letters, and we also found some in the files that were not signed at all.

Excessive Compensation Packages

I spent a considerable amount of time digging into RETA payroll records and working with an FBI analyst to document who received the hundreds of thousands of dollars in bonuses. With or without Thurston's authorization, Pomeroy knew she needed to keep generating funds for RETA if she wanted to maintain her bank balance (and her gambling hobby). Pomeroy once made an urgent plea to the county board of supervisors to help make up a drastic shortfall in funding from the federal government. That earned her a quick $250,000, almost all of which went to staff bonuses.

On another occasion, LAWMA found itself with $225,000 in unspent job training funds at the end of the fiscal year. Pomeroy told Montague that she wanted the funds to pay cost-of-living increases for the RETA staff. However, Gary Gunderson, the analyst who would later blow the whistle on the compensation issues, pointed out that there were many other groups under LAWMA's supervision that might need the funds as well. He sent out a last-minute e-mail alerting the job training network, and a few organizations expressed a need for some extra funds. Nevertheless, Montague gave $200,000 of it to RETA. Gunderson later learned that the money was used for more bonuses, including $66,897 to Pomeroy, Hirschorn and Tate.

During the trial Montague acknowledged that she and Pomeroy had been friends for years and sometimes went out for drinks together. In addition to socializing, Pomeroy often used her after-hours time with Montague to badger her for more LAWMA funds.

Pomeroy attempted to defend her compensation by referencing a survey that she claimed showed comparable executives earned almost $90 an hour. However, those executives turned out to work for large, for-profit corporations with thousands of employees. Pomeroy was indignant when she testified before a state legislative committee, confidently maintaining she deserved every penny of her compensation.

Interviews of RETA board members demonstrated that, except for Roger Thurston, no one knew about the extraordinary executive compensation packages. Board members claimed that topics from their own meeting agendas were rarely discussed. Instead, issues were presented for the board's information, as if the decision had already been made by Pomeroy and Thurston. Board meetings typically consisted of a 30-minute lunch buffet and a 15-minute rundown of business. Pomeroy was actually able to persuade the board to move the monthly sessions out of downtown due to traffic issues and had them meet in a private room at a suburban casino. How convenient!

When Tracy Frank and Gary Gunderson first called attention to the scheme, Pomeroy and Thurston tried covering their tracks at the following RETA board meeting by passing a motion to *reaffirm* Thurston's authority to unilaterally award employee bonuses. In reviewing the agency's personnel policies and board decisions, however, we found no evidence that the chairman had ever been given that authority in the first place. We discovered a not-so-subtle e-mail from Pomeroy to Jeff Frazier the day before the meeting that said, "The motion needs to be stated in these words: to reaffirm the personnel policies and that the Board Chair has the authority to set wages and supplemental pay levels for RETA staff."

Cindy Pomeroy was the ringleader, and Oscar Hirschorn was the mechanic who manipulated the budget and payroll systems to hide the huge compensation packages from outside auditors. Carolyn Montague was essential in funneling government funds to RETA, and Roger Thurston approved applying those funds to executive compensation rather than agency initiatives. Other players benefited from the scheme, but these four were the cornerstones of the corruption.

Justice for All

A federal grand jury indicted Cindy Pomeroy, Roger Thurston, Geri Tate and Carolyn Montague on 27 counts of conspiracy, fraud and obstruction of justice. Oscar Hirschorn would have been indicted, but he pleaded guilty to conspiracy and misapplication of federal funds while agreeing to cooperate with the investigation. Thurston also pleaded guilty prior to trial, and Jeff Frazier joined the group under a superseding indictment.

Tate, Montague and Frazier went to trial. Tate received a two-year prison sentence. Montague received probation and a $10,000 fine. Frazier was acquitted on all counts. He did not testify, but apparently his attorney made a persuasive argument to the jury that, like the other board members, he had no knowledge of or role in determining the exorbitant executive compensation. Frazier was the only person who took the Fifth Amendment and declined to testify at the state legislature hearings.

As for those who pleaded guilty and cooperated with prosecutors, Oscar Hirschorn received 20 months' imprisonment, and Roger Thurston, who never profited financially from the scheme, was given a one-year sentence.

While the investigation was under way, Pomeroy moved into a mobile home in Louisiana owned by Frazier and worked briefly in the housekeeping department of a nursing home. After an alleged suicide attempt, her attorney fought to prevent a trial by telling the court she was not mentally competent to assist with her defense. When that tactic failed, Pomeroy entered a guilty plea. For her role as ringleader and director of the cover-up attempts, Pomeroy received a seven-year prison sentence.

One issue that hung over the investigation since the beginning was calculating the dollar amount of losses. Everyone knew the compensation was extremely excessive, but how excessive? The state's auditor, the attorney general, the new leadership at LAWMA and the reconstituted RETA board of directors all toyed with this problem but ultimately punted it to the feds.

The court eventually ruled that the total loss to the government was just under $1.8 million, based on information submitted by prosecutors and Gunderson's calculations using compensation averages from other job training groups around the state.

Lessons Learned

The primary lesson gleaned from this case was that boards of directors, even for nonprofits, are not always diligent and proactive in monitoring their executives and officers. Organizational leadership should be continuously scrutinized for its conduct, because strict policies cannot prevent problems if the individuals implementing them are not of high character. RETA wasn't the only organization damaged — the public outcry hurt the fundraising efforts of many area nonprofits and provided government critics with fresh ammunition to attack job training programs. The RETA case triggered a nationwide investigation by the DOL's Inspector General to evaluate spending at the 600 other local workforce boards.

Despite the presumed monitoring by federal, state and local government bodies, as well as the outside auditors, this corruption went on a long time without being detected. When it came to light, embarrassed overseers blamed each other for not doing enough. At Pomeroy's sentencing, her attorney argued for less prison time by saying that there were many entities responsible for RETA's finances, which reduced Pomeroy's culpability. Multilevel oversight is good, but only when responsibilities are clearly defined.

RETA lacked a strong policy against nepotism. Neither board members nor their companies should be paid as vendors or contractors for the organization because such relationships tend to create a culture that puts individual needs above the group's mission. Participants who benefit from these arrangements are less likely to notice and challenge someone else's questionable behavior.

Recommendations to Prevent Future Occurrences

There was no shortage of proposals from the community to make sure such abuses of power never occurred again. Some suggested that although the state already had an elected auditor and a criminal investigations unit with a director appointed by the governor, a better system might be to replace or supplement these agencies with an inspector general. A few recommended adopting the federal model, where inspector generals are appointed to indefinite terms and have dual reporting requirements to the chief executive and the legislature. There was also a call for better whistleblower protections for government employees who identify and report misconduct and questionable relationships. As the federal prosecutor noted at Pomeroy's sentencing hearing, "The culture and corruption at RETA, and fear and intimidation that existed at RETA, kept

(continued)

(continued)

an awful lot of people's mouths closed." Our state still has no hotline for reporting waste, fraud and abuse related to government programs.

Many of the suggestions related to the management of nonprofits and quasi-government organizations. Some recommended that directors should pledge to question issues presented at board meetings and spend a certain amount of time outside meetings scrutinizing the policies and actions of their executive staff. They should receive training on their responsibilities, including how to balance the need to challenge staff with the tendency to micromanage. Others believed there should be a limit on the number of board memberships that public officials may hold so they have the time to devote to their duties and term limits for the board to help prevent members and staff from getting too cozy with each other. It was also proposed that a board's chairman should certainly have a term limit, because so much authority rests in that position.

Money is almost always involved in corruption, and this case was no exception. What made this investigation unique was Cindy Pomeroy's ability to use her charms, personal friendships, political connections and sexual favors to obtain financial compensation far above acceptable levels. The investigative and audit community has become increasingly effective in identifying red flags in financial statements, cost reports, bank records and similar documents. However, we also need to recognize and expose individual fraudsters who manipulate the watchdogs along with the financial statements.

About the Author

Rick Hoye is a Certified Fraud Examiner whose federal investigative career began with the U.S. Office of Personnel Management in 1989. In 1997, he transferred to the U.S. Department of Transportation, Office of Inspector General. Since 2001, he has been an investigator with the U.S. Department of Justice, fighting fraud against government programs.

CHAPTER

Kickbacks on Demand

PHILIP LEVI

Mike Blanchard did not look as surprised as he should have been. The police approached him as he pulled into his driveway at home. Two officers brandished their badges and waved a warrant to enter his personal residence while three other strangers, whom he did not know at the time, stood by and watched. I was one of those three non-police participants, and we were there to seize anything deemed relevant to the fraud allegations against Mike.

I realized that he was not surprised but relieved; his ordeal had finally come to an end.

Mike was in his late 20s, married with two grade-school children. He had worked in the plastics industry since leaving high school and felt that he had accomplished a lot with his life. Unfortunately, he hadn't accomplished it all the old-fashioned way.

Food Products Inc. was a Montreal-based manufacturer of plastic dishes, cutlery and cups. Annual sales were approximately $40 million; its sister company in the United States, which manufactured the same products, had annual sales of about the same.

The company employed two full-time purchasing agents responsible for identifying the best supplier and price. They were also responsible for preparing and issuing the purchase order and then matching it with the receiving report (from the receiving department) and the supplier's invoice, which they approved for payment.

The Anonymous Informant

On February 13, Arthur Phixer, a director, officer and shareholder of Food Products Inc., received a telephone call at his home in the late evening. The caller identified himself as Jack Striker, which he said was an assumed name.

Striker stated the following:

1. Food Products Inc. was being defrauded of between $300,000 and $1 million.
2. The fraud was possible due to the collusion of Mike Blanchard, one of two purchasing agents employed by Food Products Inc., and a supplier, Eastern Printing.
3. Mike Blanchard owned a company called Buyart (an Internet search quickly confirmed that allegation).
4. Buyart was an integral part of a kickback-purchasing scheme Blanchard was using to defraud Food Products.

One morning as I was returning to my office from a court hearing for another case, Arthur Phixer called to introduce himself to me. He told me he got my number from his personal accountant, Robert Agnew, whom he first approached with the story that he was about to tell to me. I immediately recognized Arthur's name; our firm was employed as the auditor for his company, and Rob and I knew each other well. We were both partners in local accounting firms. At my firm, I was in charge of the litigation support and dispute resolution department; Rob was an audit partner. We were also both on the same local school board. Phixer asked me to meet him in his office. When I arrived, he explained the "deep throat" phone call. I suggested that it might be a hoax from a disgruntled employee but said that it could be real and the consequences of ignoring the information might be very costly. Therefore, we agreed to commence an investigation into the allegations and await further contact from Striker, should it occur.

The first step in my investigation was to secure an image of the disk from Mike Blanchard's company-owned computer in his office. I made this image the same night I had my first meeting with Phixer.

I also inquired about fidelity insurance for employee theft. Phixer was not sure what Food Products' coverage included, so we examined the company's policy and discovered that it had $1 million coverage plus up to 10 percent of that amount for professional fees necessary to establish the claim. In addition, the policy required that the insurer be notified as soon as it became known that a claim might exist.

We were then faced with a dilemma. We needed to limit the number of people who were aware of the allegations to those who had an absolute need to know. I considered the situation and we consulted with the company's legal counsel. Based on my opinion that at the present time we only had unsubstantiated allegations, it was determined that the insurer need not be notified yet. If we determined that a claim was possible, that would be the earliest we would need to notify the insurer.

On February 18, Striker called again and Phixer asked him to contact me directly. I had prepared Phixer for such a call and told him to explain to Striker that we needed more evidence, which would not exist in Food Products' books because the allegation was a kickback scheme. Striker called me the same day, explaining that he was only calling on behalf of a friend who was afraid of becoming known. I was able to convince Striker that the informant's identity would be protected. The next morning, a man identifying himself only as Paulo came to meet me at my offices.

During this meeting, Paulo told me:

- He had been in the plastic business for 27 years and at Eastern Printing for 8 years. He left Eastern Printing approximately $1\frac{1}{2}$ years ago to start his own company, Paulo-Pack.
- Eastern Printing was owned by John Rama and his brother Gerry Rama.
- The owners of Eastern Printing and Mike Blanchard began a scheme to inflate the prices charged by Eastern Printing on purchases by Food Products Inc.
- The prices were inflated by as much as 20 to 30 percent, of which 5 percent was paid to Buyart as Mike Blanchard's share of the excess billing.
- Paulo began working on the order desk two years before the anonymous call to Phixer. He received instructions directly from the Rama brothers to do the following:
  - Inflate the quantity shipped on invoices to Food Products Inc. by 5 percent.
  - In certain instances, issue invoices to Food Products Inc. when no goods were shipped.
  - Accept returned defective goods and redo the order. Both times invoices were issued, and no credit note was issued to cancel the returned defective items.
  - Personally deliver envelopes to Mike Blanchard, which Paulo said contained checks from Eastern Printing to Buyart. (Paulo was periodically called into John Rama's office and saw him place checks into an envelope, which he gave to Paulo to deliver to Mike Blanchard.)
- Paulo stated that when he left Eastern Printing to start his own company, he was replaced on the order desk by Jake Blanchard, Mike Blanchard's brother.
- Paulo said that the Rama brothers created a new price list consisting of three columns and gave it to Mike Blanchard. Paulo explained that the first column, labeled Old, was the original price before the kickback scheme began; the second column, labeled New, was the price Eastern Printing started charging Food Products to cover Jake Blanchard's salary; and the third column represented the kickback amount to be received by Buyart.

- The investigation later revealed that an identical price list existed on Mike Blanchard's computer, except that the New and Old price columns were not there and some of the Buyart kickback amounts were missing. The remainder of the six-page price list was identical.

I told Paulo that his story was interesting, but without hard evidence to support the allegations, the case would be much more difficult. Paulo left and called me the next day and said he could bring me some documents to support his allegations.

The following day, Paulo returned with a copy of the price list, copies of invoices to Food Products from Paulo-Pack, invoices from Buyart to Paulo-Pack for consulting fees and the canceled checks for two transactions with Buyart totaling $1,102.15. The Paulo-Pack invoices contained handwritten calculations of 5 percent of the invoice amount (sometimes including the sales tax and sometimes not), which produced the "consulting fees." Paulo told me that he was approached by Mike Blanchard to provide the same kickback scheme to Buyart as he was doing while at Eastern Printing. When he was dropped as a supplier by Mike Blanchard, he decided to come forward with the scheme.

Keeping It Quiet

Because the allegations involved third parties, we had to proceed carefully and quietly so as not to trigger a concern that an investigation was under way, which could lead to valuable evidence disappearing or being destroyed.

My analysis of the disk contents captured from Mike's computer revealed a copy of the price list Paulo told me about, giving his story more credibility.

Phixer informed me that when such purchases were made, the actual quantity shipped varied from the quantity ordered by 5 to 8 percent in either direction. However, my analysis of the history for the latest three years from Eastern Printing and its sister company, EastMost, resulted in 30.11 percent and 14.02 percent in overshipments. The investigation later revealed that Eastern Printing was intentionally and regularly inflating the shipping quantities when invoicing Food Products Inc.

Total purchases by Food Products Inc. from Eastern Printing and East-Most during this period amounted to $1,491,432.

From the information obtained from Paulo and other information gathered during the investigation, I developed a relationship chart, which would grow as we continued our investigation.

Time to Get Tough

Paulo was now ready to come forward and testify. With his testimony, the price list from Mike Blanchard's computer and the documents from Paulo showing his invoices and checks to Buyart, I was convinced that the allegations were indicative of a purchasing kickback scheme. I made an appointment with the municipal police commercial crime unit and met with the intake lieutenant in early March, less than one month after first hearing of the anonymous phone call.

We also revisited the need to inform the insurer since we were now convinced that a claim was likely. However, in discussions with the corporate lawyer and a criminal lawyer who had been hired as a consultant to the investigation, we determined that a further delay of a week or so would not affect the policy coverage. Since we were instituting police action, the criminal lawyer strongly advised against any other involvement at this time.

Based on the evidence I had accumulated to date and an interview between the detective assigned to the case and Paulo, we were successful in securing search and seizure warrants for Mike's personal residence (which was also the registered address of Buyart) and the offices of Eastern Printing.

The two locations were approximately ten miles apart and, because we wanted to be sure that no one was alerted to our activity, we coordinated the entrance into both locations.

Four police detectives, two lawyers representing Food Products and eight fraud examiners from my office split into two teams. The Eastern Printing's office was occupied, but no one was at Mike's residence so we waited nearby and watched the house. Not long after, Mike Blanchard pulled into his driveway and we drove up behind him: first the police with the warrant and then the lawyer and two from my team.

We found little additional documentation during the search of Mike's home (e.g., bank statements, canceled checks, deposit books or copies of Buyart invoices to Eastern Printing), but later, Mike admitted that he received a visit from Gerry Rama and Lewis Chamberlain, a friend of Mike's and a sales representative for Eastern Printing. They warned him that a police search was imminent and told him to destroy any relevant documents. However, Mike also said that he never retained such documentation.

Nevertheless, we were able to recover documents relating to Buyart's financial records, including bank deposits that we traced to canceled checks seized at Eastern Printing. In addition, we found deposits to Buyart from three other suppliers of Food Products that were minor players in the grand scheme of the fraud, accounting for an estimated $30,000 of additional overcharges to Food Products. These were all settled quickly with a single visit to their offices, identifying ourselves as fraud examiners in connection with an apparent purchasing kickback scheme in which they were involved. One of the companies involved provided a certificate to Food Products that contained the following details:

1. I, Giuseppe Cataloni, am the sole shareholder of Flat Printing.
2. Earlier this year, I became aware of certain payments made by my company to Buyart, supposedly in payment of invoices for consulting services.

3. These transactions were negotiated by Mr. Rah Ish who was working for my company at that time. Upon learning that these payments were not for consulting services but were in fact kickbacks to Mike Blanchard, owner of Buyart and your purchasing agent, I terminated Mr. Ish's employment with my company.

4. I do not know Mike Blanchard personally nor have I ever met him.

5. The two checks issued to Buyart were dated August 27 and November 14 of the previous year, in the amounts of $1,150.00 and $3,220.70 (including taxes).

6. Mr. Ish was employed by Paper & Scissors, Inc., prior to joining Flat Printing.

7. Mr. Ish advised me that while he was working at Paper & Scissors, he became aware that invoices were being issued by that company to Food Products with no goods being shipped.

8. It is my desire to continue our business relationship and regret that my company was used, without my knowledge, in the manner described above. Furthermore, I am prepared to issue a credit note to Food Products in the amount of $3,800 plus taxes, which will be applied against future orders on a schedule to be agreed upon by us.

9. I agree to provide the original copies of checks and invoices between my company and Buyart to your investigator.

The revelation that another, as-yet unknown, supplier was involved led us to discover an additional $26,000 of overcharges to Food Products, which was recovered as well. Because the Ramas became aware of the pending police search in advance, they had the opportunity to remove or destroy the most relevant documents. However, we found most of the checks issued by Eastern Printing to Buyart and a copy of the price list locked up in John Rama's desk.

Now it was time to notify the insurer. I set up a meeting at the offices of Food Products and told the insurers some very basic details over the phone. As a result, the manager of the fidelity department, the internal legal counsel and an insurance agent all attended the meeting.

After hearing the full details to date, the insurer immediately gave Food Products confirmation that the policy had not been breached by the delays and that it was justified under the circumstances. The insurer also approved of all of the actions taken to date and agreed to have us continue the investigation.

The Confession

At the seizure, I presented Mike with his letter of dismissal for cause and suggested he contact a lawyer immediately. He did and he received good advice: cooperate and minimize the consequences as much as possible. As part of the agreement for Mike Blanchard's cooperation, he agreed to reimburse Food Products $20,000.

Several meetings occurred with Mike Blanchard, during which he described the various schemes used in connection with Eastern Printing, and he assisted in reconstructing the methods used to calculate the various amounts for each scheme.

Mike Blanchard said the kickbacks applied only to printed items and that the charge for the artwork and plates were included in the unit pricing; thus, there was no kickback to Buyart on the initial order. Repeat orders maintained the higher price, which included the cost of the artwork and plates. This inflated amount was kicked back to Buyart.

A handwritten price list was provided to Mike Blanchard by Eastern Printing and identified the kickback rate per 1,000. Mike used the list to calculate the monthly amount he charged Eastern Printing, but he intentionally used an inconsistent calculation method to make it difficult, if not impossible, for someone who did not know how the monthly kickback was calculated to verify the figures. Mike applied the kickback rate to the units shipped, rounding to the nearest dollar and, in some cases, rounding to the nearest 1,000 units shipped before calculating the dollar amount. He then gave the copy to Eastern Printing and prepared an invoice, including sales tax.

During the latter part of the previous year, Mike Blanchard became aware that Eastern Printing was regularly inflating the quantity shipped on certain items. At that time he approached the Ramas and requested — and received — an additional kickback of $3,000 per month related to these inflated quantities, which totaled $6,000. The total amount received by Buyart for these kickbacks amounted to $24,515.36, according to Mike's calculations. After a while a flat 5 percent was added to all the items; Buyart received 3 percent, which amounted to $15,408.72, and Eastern Printing retained 2 percent, which amounted to an additional $10,272.48.

Three years ago, Mike Blanchard's brother Jake Blanchard was employed by Eastern Printing as a salesman. Shortly thereafter, he replaced Paulo on the order desk and assumed responsibility for Food Products sales. At that time, all prices to Food Products were increased by 8 percent to cover Jake's salary, and Mike created the new column on his price list to reflect the 8 percent increase. This amount was estimated to be $77,156.18.

Commencing three years ago, Eastern Printing issued invoices to Food Products for items that were never shipped and Mike would create a purchase order to support the invoice. One of the Rama brothers then created a packing slip and faxed it to Mike, who signed it as proof of receipt and processed the invoice for payment. From the purchasing history between Food Products and Eastern Printing, Mike was able to identify 20 such purchases totaling $95,724.96, of which Buyart received two thirds and Eastern Printing retained one third.

The Second Confession

Mike convinced his brother Jake to meet with us and provide information about his activities at Eastern Printing. Shortly after Mike's employment at Food Products was terminated, so was Jake's at Eastern Printing.

One of Jake Blanchard's responsibilities at Eastern was to manually track the products shipped to Buyart. When he first started at Eastern he noticed the signed tracking sheet that was returned to him always showed a larger quantity than what was actually shipped. When he confronted the controller, he was told, "We'll talk about it later." In a subsequent meeting with Gerry Rama and the controller, Gerry told Jake that "the quantity was changed and don't say anything or you will lose your job." Jake explained that this scheme was done on all bags shipped in rolls since it was difficult to check the quantity received accurately, only the number of rolls.

A Cooperative Supplier

The chairman of the Food Products board decided that he wanted to send a message to all suppliers that this type of behavior was unacceptable and would not be tolerated. I consulted with him and we decided that an initial notice would go out to all suppliers of consequence, advising them that the preliminary results of a forensic audit revealed certain irregularities in our purchasing department. These results were currently under further investigation with the police. However, our preliminary findings indicated that the amounts involved did not appear to be in excess of $50,000. We also announced that Mike Blanchard's employment was terminated. We followed this notice by requiring the CEO or president of each supplier who wanted to continue doing business with Food Products to sign a statement saying:

1. To the best of my knowledge, neither the Company nor any of its employees and/or agents have offered or given gratuities, gifts or favors of any nature to employees and/or agents of Food Products with a view to secure orders and/or contracts from Food Products, with the exception of the following items: [space provided to list common industry gifts, etc.]
2. To the best of my knowledge, the Company has not manufactured and/or sold any products that were known to be for delivery to Food Products but were sold and/or invoiced to another company or individual, with the exception of: [space provided to list existing subcontractor arrangements, etc.]

Eastern Printing used a vendor, Western Printing, to produce the products that Jake Blanchard identified as having inflated quantities. We wanted to determine how many products Western had printed for Eastern and compare these shipments to the quantity on Eastern's invoices. In addition, because Western Printing shipped the items directly to Food Products, the owners of Eastern Printing could not argue that they added items from their inventory.

Western Printing cooperated with us fully. Management supplied us with copies of all relevant documents, and a comparison revealed that the invoices were inflated by 10.52 percent. Without complete access to all of Eastern Printing's records, we calculated the likely amount of overbilling for inflated quantities as follows:

1. Mike and Jake Blanchard identified all invoices on the Food Products purchasing history from Eastern Printing that were subject to inflated quantities.
2. We applied the percentage obtained from the Western Printing sample to the value of the identified invoices.
3. The estimated charges for inflated quantities amounted to $93,428.

Based on our investigation, interviews and documentation obtained from the various individuals who participated in the purchasing kickbacks and other schemes, the following amounts were improperly obtained from Food Products, directly or indirectly, by Eastern Printing:

Type of Irregularity	Amount
Inflated pricing for Buyart kickback	$24,515.36
3 percent of 5 percent pricing kickback to Buyart	$15,408.72
2 percent of 5 percent pricing retained by Eastern Printing	$10,242.78
$3,000 monthly additional kickback	$6,000.00
8 percent pricing for Jake Blanchard's salary	$77,156.18
Fictitious invoices	$95,724.96
Inflated quantities	$93,428.00
Total	$322,476.00

Furthermore, Mike Blanchard informed us that Eastern Printing had hidden charges of more than $100,000 in its invoices to Food Products to cover artwork, negatives and plates. However, Eastern did not inform Food Products of these charges and maintained possession of the artwork. Based on Mike's disclosure, we determined that the printing material had been paid for in full by Food Products and belonged to our client. Consequently, it was seized and returned to Food Products during the police search.

Recovery

The criminal process in Québec involves the investigation phase by the police followed by a complaint by the police to the Crown Prosecutor to file charges against the perpetrator. For undisclosed reasons, the Crown Prosecutor refused to file charges and left the matter in the civil arena. The insurer stepped in to repay the losses, less recoveries through settlements, as well as all of our fees for the investigation. The insurer then took over the litigation against Eastern Printing and its shareholders, resulting in an undisclosed settlement before going to trial.

Lessons Learned

This story has many lessons, both for the fraud examiner and the employer.

The fraud examiner must always keep an open mind and consider all possible scenarios. An allegation is only that — an allegation. It is the fraud examiner's job to prove or disprove the allegation, but it should not be ignored.

Fraud examiners must also know when to consult lawyers and the police. In this case, I knew the insurance policy was a legal contract that should be interpreted by a lawyer, not a fraud examiner.

Fraud examiners must be able to improvise when they meet a dead end. Look for alternative theories and different ways to prove the conclusions. In this case, I followed leads like the deposits to Buyart, which led us to Flat Printing and then Paper & Scissors and the friendly contact at Western Printing who helped us prove inflated quantities.

Fraud examiners also need to be able to forensically analyze computers to identify additional evidence that might ultimately prove invaluable. If this expertise is not available in-house, fraud examiners should align themselves with outside experts to be ready to perform these examinations on short notice. Without the price list on Mike Blanchard's computer, we likely would not have interested the police in connection with Mike Blanchard, and the entire investigation would have ended there. Without the searches, we would not have found the Buyart receipts that led us to other companies involved in the scheme.

Recommendations to Prevent Future Occurrences

Employers should ensure that their systems and controls are such that no one individual can manipulate the records, process documents and authorize payments without a secondary review. Systems do not have to be designed in such a manner that suggests that all employees are dishonest. However, management should not place blind trust in all employees either. An effective and efficient happy medium must be found.

Employers should have their systems tested for identifiable weaknesses and create an environment that is hostile to fraud. The employees must know that fraud will not be tolerated and that the perpetrator will be pursued to the fullest extent of the law.

Food Products made sure that all of its suppliers and employees were aware of the fraud and that action was being taken against the culprits. This response likely made other vendors think twice about perpetrating a fraud against the company.

About the Author

Philip C. Levi, CFE, FCA, CPA/CFF, CA•IFA, is managing partner at Levi & Sinclair, LLP, founding president of the Association of Certified Fraud Examiners (ACFE), Montréal Chapter, and 1997–1998 Vice-Chairman of the Board of Regents of the ACFE. Mr. Levi has been an auditor for more than forty years and specializes in computer systems, auditing standards and techniques and investigative auditing. Mr. Levi is one of 18 CAs in Québec who was grandfathered by the Canadian Institute of Chartered Accountants into the Investigative and Forensic Accountant specialist category in 2000. As a member of the teaching faculty of the ACFE, he has lectured in the United States and Canada extensively to other accountants, fraud examiners and bankers on computers, forensic auditing and other related topics. Mr. Levi has published numerous articles in the United States and Canada on these topics and acts as an expert witness in fraud, auditor negligence and dispute resolution litigation. He has been a member of the Fraud Conference committee of the American Institute of Certified Public Accountants and of its Fraud Advisory Task Force. In 2007, Mr. Levi was selected as the Fraud Examiner of the Year by the ACFE. In 2010, Mr. Levi was appointed by the Québec minister of finance to the board of directors of the Chambre de la Sécurité Financière to represent the public for a three-year term.

CHAPTER

High-Flying Ambition

MANJIT CHODHA

Sean Coultard studied public business administration at the University of Hertfordshire, England, and graduated with honors. At the time of this case, he had been married for 15 years and was the devoted father of three children, age 13, 11 and 3. Coultard was dedicated to meeting his family's needs in any way he could, including providing the best private education for his children.

Coultard began climbing the corporate ladder after joining Smith Williamson LLC directly out of college; after 12 years of service, he had reached the position of senior procurement manager. Smith Williamson was a timber merchant and hardware manufacturing firm that had survived economic downturns and recessions and evolved to provide niche services in the building trade industry. Coultard was ambitious and quietly assertive; the senior management team saw him as a role model in the field of procurement. He had a charismatic personality and developed peer relationships with relative ease.

Coultard was meticulous in every respect, from his excessive care and attention to his appearance and attire to his exacting nature of tracking his daily business routines though timekeeping. He had arranged for the IT staff to provide him full access to Smith Williamson's network and systems, and he was known to work very early and late. Most peculiar was that he had a full social agenda outside of his family life, in which his business and personal connections often overlapped. To this end, he was popular and developed extraordinary professional associations outside work, particularly in aviation. In contrast with Coultard's charismatic persona was his tendency to be short-tempered and dictatorial when circumstances did not go his way. This almost dysfunctional behavior brought out his dark side, and low-ranking staff under him often complained about his tyrannical behavior.

Coultard led a lavish lifestyle. He had several expensive cars, vacation homes and high-interest-earning investment portfolios. He also began

341

developing a hobby in aviation (which he couldn't afford on his salary), and his children attended pricey boarding schools. He was clearly living beyond his means, but no one questioned how he was funding his lifestyle. Coultard excluded himself from training events at work, but most of his peers looked to him as a savvy, business-minded official who wouldn't have needed the training anyway.

Smith Williamson

Smith Williamson LLC had been in existence in one form or another since 1797, when Benjamin Ingram founded a company of joiners and carpenters at 33 Beech Street in London. A series of mergers over the centuries resulted in Smith Williamson. The company provided building services and products to high-end custom tradesmen and was considered the finest in the industry. A few years ago management announced an $850 million takeover of BSS Group, the only serious competition that Smith Williamson had had in past few decades. The company's board quickly agreed to the acquisition. With no serious competitors left in the field, the future looked bright for Smith Williamson.

The Last Person We Suspected

I was one of 12 internal auditors employed by Smith Williamson. In addition to routine risk-based internal audits, I was assigned to lead the few fraud investigations that occasionally cropped up and typically involved operational staff pilfering inventory from warehouse depots or accounting employees misappropriating cash.

The other internal auditors and I prided ourselves on our professionalism and integrity, particularly in internal controls; most of the frauds at Smith Williamson were relatively small and discovered quickly. However, what transpired in this case was a wake-up call to us and to the board of directors about our financial governance arrangements and procurement processes. What unfolded would lead to a paradigm shift in which the company policies, procedures, roles, responsibilities and segregation of duties were to be reengineered.

I recall on one brisk Monday morning in January, I had just logged on to my computer and was enjoying my first cup of coffee when Paul Duncan, the internal audit manager, pulled me into his office, perched himself on the end on his desk and said, "Brace yourself, Manjit, we've been given a case of a potential fraud involving a senior member of the procurement department and we need to act immediately. Top managers have been notified by an external source at the bank that Smith Williamson has incurred losses totaling more than $275,000. The evidence collected thus far is compelling and it seems to be pointing to Sean Coultard, the procurement manager."

"How can that be?" I asked. "Coultard is a role model in this organization." I had gotten to know Sean over the course of two years and found him to be remarkably helpful — perhaps too helpful at times, now that I think about it. But other employees, too, had developed a level of respect and trust for him throughout his tenure. It just didn't make sense at first, but the more I thought about it, the more feasible it seemed.

Unannounced Audit

Paul Duncan and I decided to begin our investigation with a standard, unannounced audit of the procurement function. These were normal activities for the internal auditors at Smith Williamson, and kicking off our examination with one would not arouse the suspicions of Coultard or his associates, if he had any. We announced our intentions to the other internal auditors so they would not raise concerns or share sensitive information with Coultard. Duncan told me that questions about Coultard started cropping up when a board member received a call from the bank. The agent said, "Sean Coultard has made two attempts to transfer $15,000 from the company's central account to a printing supplier, but we were hesitant to make the transactions because the credentials he provided were not on our list of Smith Williamson vendors." The transactions were aborted. We received the supporting documents from the bank and from our finance department and escalated the inquiry immediately.

After a cursory background check into Coultard, Duncan discovered something interesting. "Well, it also looks like Coultard has an interest in a small chartered jet, which he co-owns with a few associates," he observed. "We need to act quickly and make this case our top priority." Even partial interest in a chartered jet was well beyond what Coultard could afford on his salary.

Coultard was a stickler for details, and he knew the financial protocols of the company inside and out. If the case was to be unraveled, we needed records of the transactions that had taken place under his authority and in what mode he conducted them. I thought if anyone had the audacity to defraud the organization, it would have to be someone who knew the systems well. I used our in-house IT audit software to conduct data analysis on financial transactions. I also compared supplier accounts and telephone calls from Coultard's office line. I was able to check on his mobile, landline and fax usage and identified several transactions with aviator suppliers that Smith Williamson would have absolutely no need to do business with.

I searched through our vendor files for companies that matched the names or numbers of the aviation supply companies, and — surprise, surprise — not only were they listed as vendors, they had preferred-supplier status. Digging a little deeper, I noticed that the majority of the invoices from those companies had been approved by Coultard. It could be a coincidence or have a valid explanation, but with a large procurement staff that took turns approving vendor paperwork, it was odd that Coultard signed most of the invoices from suspicious suppliers.

Moreover, Smith Williamson had recently implemented a new e-procurement system that was supposed to speed up the process and ensure an audit trail existed for all the contracts. However, it appeared that Coultard had managed to grant himself full authorization rights within the system, rendering the purchase order life cycle at risk of being accessed and edited at his discretion.

We turned our attention to the document trails created in the e-procurement system. Despite Coultard's ability to delete or edit records at will, we were able to uncover approved, fictitious purchase orders from a printing supplier for a period of two and a half years. They were, without exception, approved by Coultard.

Duncan muttered his regret over internal audit's failure to detect these issues earlier. "How could we have missed this? All the signs were there: Coultard had full access to the e-procurement system, so he could certainly pull it off. We need to check with finance for the management information reports. We also need to conduct more data analysis and then we can start piecing this together."

What we found next was the link we needed to pin down Coultard. Interestingly enough, the connection to the printing vendor was Coultard's wife, who had owned and operated the business for the past four years (Coultard was a shareholder). This meant that our internal controls had either failed to pick up on this conflict of interest during the supplier reviews or Coultard had managed to cleverly hide the fact from us. The implication of this discovery was that the competitive bidding process had been circumvented by Coultard to generate business for his wife's company through high-priced services paid for by Smith Williamson.

Interviewing Made Easy

Once we prepared a synopsis of our analyses and gathered our supporting documents, Duncan and I decided it was time to interview Coultard. We requested a meeting with him but kept our intentions hidden because we wanted him to be relaxed and open; we told him we needed his help deciphering some of the reports we were analyzing for the routine audit.

He met us in a conference room, and we greeted him pleasantly. After some chitchat, I started pulling out the evidence Duncan and I had gathered, piece by piece. I began by asking him why Smith Williamson was conducting business with aviation suppliers, when that was clearly beyond our scope of activities. He stuttered for a moment and said he did not have an explanation. He offered to look into it and get back to us, but we politely pressed on. Next we pulled out the contracts with his wife's printing company and asked him if the charges seemed in line with industry standards. He paused and seemed to be trying to figure out how much we knew. He looked over the contracts and finally said, in a soft voice, that the prices did appear to be a little high. "And what if we told you these printing services were never even rendered? What would you think about that?" Duncan asked him. Coultard was getting pale and looked nervous. He said he wouldn't know. Next we pulled out the incorporation documents for the printing company and asked him if the owner's name was familiar. At that point he gave in. He put his head between his hands for a few seconds and took a deep breath. When he lifted his head, he looked at me and said, "Okay, let's just be honest. You know what I've done, and I'm sorry."

Coultard wrote a full confession in our presence and signed it. After the interview, Duncan and I created a final report and submitted it, along with Coultard's confession and the case files, to our legal department, who reviewed it and passed it along to the U.K. Serious Fraud Office (SFO). After examining the report and evidence, the SFO agreed with our conclusion that Coultard's deviant, dysfunctional and charismatic behavior eventually got the better of him as his pursuit for greater financial gains led him to wrongdoing. Coultard pleaded guilty to charges of fraud, including collusion with a vendor with the intent to systematically defraud the organization for more than $275,000. The full charges included:

- Abuse of power and breach of loyalty by an officer of the organization as a result of unauthorized transactions
- Maladministration by willfully falsifying material facts to process false or fictitious statements
- Dishonesty and improper dealings with respect to the organization's money
- Improper enrichment
- Receipt of improper advantage

Coultard was ordered to pay full restitution, his assets were seized and he was incarcerated for two years.

Lessons Learned

This case revealed serious flaws in our internal controls procedures surrounding IT and procurement. We enhanced our processes (e.g., segregation of duties commensurate to job roles and functions) for each of the strategic business units within the organization, and, more important, we as an internal audit department took greater initiative to learn more about investigating complicated frauds, as this was the most extensive one we had seen to date. One of the most critical lessons we learned was the importance of maintaining the chain of custody over crucial evidence. Our in-house counsel was a great help in that regard.

Recommendations to Prevent Future Occurrences

After Coultard was charged and we were able to wrap up the case, we assembled the following list of recommendations for Smith Williamson:

- Implement enterprise-wide fraud prevention controls and take strict action against all fraudulent activity, including publicizing frauds to heighten awareness in rest of the organization.
- Factor in a better understanding of the behavioral traits and drivers in addition to the rationale, pressures and opportunity for fraud to occur in the workplace.
- Secure support from senior management to enhance anti-fraud protocols across the organization. If employees think their superiors don't care, they won't either.
- Install a whistleblower hotline and implement a formal anti-fraud and ethics policy.
- Establish additional controls over the purchasing department, and randomly test the authenticity of purchases.
- Introduce a risk-based internal audit regime that includes risk of fraud and financial impropriety.
- Formalize a fraud policy that underpins the chain of command and details escalation procedures for fraud cases.
- Conduct a complete review of logical access rights to operating systems for staff commensurate to their level of seniority, roles and responsibilities.
- Improve relationship management with the company and bank officials to proactively investigate potentially suspicious transactions.
- Introduce exception-based reporting that will highlight variances of material significance on a continuous basis.

With an increasingly pressured workforce and the growing tendency to rationalize fraud at all levels, unwelcome and costly "surprises" are bound to occur. Management must emphasize fraud prevention and adopt a proactive anti-fraud approach rather than continue to react after the losses occur.

About the Author

Manjit Chodha earned his master's degree in audit management and consultancy from Birmingham City University. He is a member of the Association of Certified Fraud Examiners and of the Institute of Internal Auditors, UK & Ireland. He is currently a research fellow at the University of Ghana Business School undertaking Ph.D. research into business ethics in developing communities and lecturing on international business strategy and organizational leadership management. He has extensive practical experience in both system- and risk-based internal auditing for major private and public organizations.

37

The Cleaner Who Swept His Way to the Top

SHANE RINGIN

To the holiday makers and retirees relaxing with a walk along the magnificent Gold Coast beach of Queensland, Australia, Peter Felgate appeared to be just another jogger enjoying his retirement from corporate life. Until recently, the 53-year-old had been a member of the Australian Reserve Bank Board and, as chairman and chief executive officer of Reno Ltd., had been one of the most powerful and highly paid businessmen in the country. Only 12 months earlier, he had reached the pinnacle of his career, which began 37 years before as a janitor in a Reno variety store in South Australia. When he retired, Felgate was the CEO of Reno with a salary package of $1.5 million a year, a mansion in an expensive area in northeast Melbourne and six luxury cars, including a Ferrari and a Bentley. After retiring, he rarely used his mansion, preferring to spend much of his time at his $1.9 million luxury apartment, with its uninterrupted views of the Pacific Ocean, close to the heart of Surfers' Paradise.

During his career, Felgate held a series of prestigious posts, including a foundation member of the Business Council of Australia, a board member of Melbourne University's Graduate School and a member of the Federal Government's Advisory Committee on Prices and Incomes. The Australian government even awarded him an Order of Australia for his services to the retail industry.

But life was not all sun and relaxation for Felgate. The Victoria Police Corporate Crime Squad in Melbourne was investigating an estimated $6 million in renovations allegedly carried out on his home in Melbourne by Reno contractors. The police were also investigating a further estimated $3 million of work allegedly completed on a beach house that Felgate used while he was CEO and that he had an option to purchase upon retirement.

The investigation centered on why the work on the homes was billed back to Reno and how much work was actually done.

Felgate's home was central to a conspiracy within Reno, a conspiracy that involved Reno personnel, contractors and suppliers — corrupted by the greed of the CEO. This corrosive tone from the top opened the door for opportunistic dishonesty to cloud the judgment of many, resulting in good people doing bad things.

The Reno Reach

The origins of Reno can be traced to a discount store opened in Collingwood, a working-class suburb of Melbourne, on April 9, 1914. The variety store was founded by George James Bollard, who had studied U.S. and U.K. chain store retailing methods.

In 1919, a much larger store was opened, again in Collingwood, with the slogan "Nothing over 2 cents." During the twentieth century, Reno experienced a series of expansions and mergers and became one of the largest publicly traded companies in Australia. The huge corporate clout that Felgate wielded can be measured by the sheer size of the organization he headed and how it touched every Australian. At his peak, Felgate oversaw annual sales of $15 billion and managed 160,000 staff.

During his reign as the head of Reno, every man, woman and child in the country spent an average of $900 annually in a Reno store. At the time, the company operated a wide range of supermarkets, discount department stores, department stores, women's clothing stores, toy stores, liquor stores, fast-food outlets and office-supply superstores. Reno Ltd. was Australia's leading retailer in terms of number of stores (more than 1,800) and selling area. Such was its size that it was nearly impossible for anyone in Australia to survive without setting foot in a Reno entity.

The Whistleblower

As a detective sergeant and team leader with the Victoria Police Corporate Crime Group, I was selected to undertake a training course in commercial crime control and terrorism in the United Kingdom. While I was at Cambridge University in England, I received a call from my boss in Australia; he told me that I had been appointed to investigate allegations of fraud and corruption within Reno.

I learned that the director of a painting company had contacted a Reno security officer and said he had evidence that his firm performed private contractual work and dishonestly charged it to Reno. The security guard reported his concerns to the police for investigation.

I flew back from England and got to work. Our initial investigation centered on identifying where the private contractual work had been performed, on whose authority and who had authorized payment.

After reviewing a number of invoices from the painting firm, it became evident that a substantial amount of work had been performed at properties not owned or managed by Reno. Next we reviewed all external contractors involved in the building and maintenance of company properties, which identified further fraudulent work, highlighting the extent of the deception and conspiracy.

The Big Picture

When my team and I met and planned the initial stages of the investigation, we had no idea it would consume the next few years of our lives. I was fortunate that my team consisted of investigators, accountants, lawyers and IT experts who, as I soon discovered, were essential to unraveling the tide of deception that had engulfed Reno.

First we assessed the case to date and set our goals. We identified potential outcomes and complainant motives and then formed a sound basis for the investigation plan. Little did we know the extent of the dishonesty meant that we would need to interview hundreds of witnesses and review tens of thousands of documents.

We initially focused on establishing the amount of work that had been undertaken on premises not owned or leased by Reno. We reviewed every invoice the company had received from all the contractors involved in providing building and maintenance services, including painting, building and construction, electrical, landscaping, air conditioning and plumbing. Our research revealed work charged to Reno without supporting purchase orders or maintenance requests. We performed site inspections and interviews with staff members at a number of Reno retail outlets to confirm that work charged for had not performed. We also found invoices that appeared inflated, with discrepancies between the hours charged and those actually worked. The fraudulent invoices were verified and authorized for payment by a number of senior managers within the Reno maintenance department.

Senior management at Reno and contractors themselves owned a number of the properties where work had been performed. From our initial findings, it appeared that those who had been responsible for managing and controlling Reno's maintenance expenditures had been compromised, from the CEO down.

A review of bid documents for maintenance work at Reno revealed many submissions that were doctored. The procurement process was compromised with bogus estimates and inflated quotations, submitted in a calculated and organized process to ensure a systematic sharing of maintenance work among a small band of "preferred" contractors. Furthermore, contracts often displayed a pattern of overruns that required additional payments. Executives used these overruns to pay for maintenance and construction at their private residences. In one case alone, Reno checks totaling $213,000 were traced to the private bank account of David Wilkins, the director of a painting firm called Decoray.

Search Warrants

We executed search warrants on numerous contractors and private businesses that had issued invoices to Reno for work performed on Felgate's and others' private residences, or had submitted bogus bid documents and quotations. We seized and examined hundreds of boxes of documents, computer records and financial accounts.

The evidence exposed a level of extravagance not seen before within Reno. Felgate had agreed to renovations that, according to the prosecutor, "had transformed a modest suburban house into something approaching the Palace of Versailles." The invoices included $151,000 for glass, $72,000 for front gates. $214,000 for marble for the bathroom, and $1.1 million for internal painting by Decoray.

We also discovered that suspicions about Felgate's spending had surfaced years earlier, after an air-conditioning firm complained to police about irregularities on an invoice to Reno for work totaling $243,972. At the time, Felgate backdated a personal check to repay the money because he feared that a police investigation would snowball and uncover further illegitimate accounts and expenditures. Felgate also provided a misleading statement to police to thwart the investigation.

Felgate continued to have renovations done to his house and charged to Reno, instructing subordinates to bury the invoices among legitimate expenditures. Felgate recruited some of his trusted management team to assist in the fraud, including the national maintenance manager. In return for his assistance, the manager was allowed to bill work done at his house to other cost centers within Reno.

As the investigation progressed, the suspects began falling like dominos, one after another implicating others in a vain attempt to mitigate their involvement or hopeful of a favorable review of their conduct by the courts.

Satisfied that we had established the extent of the fraud and how it was committed, the issue of why remained a mystery. The only person who could provide us with that answer was Felgate; we began to plan our interview of him. But before that happened, Felgate's legal team approached me and offered to provide evidence and testimony of criminality by other Reno executives, in return for Felgate not being charged. I declined.

Although Felgate had publicly professed his innocence, when we formally interviewed him, he declined to answer any questions, leaving us no option but to charge him and let the courts decide. Felgate was arrested and charged with 49 counts of theft totaling $4.8 million and conspiracy to defraud. Felgate's arrest was the sixteenth stemming from our three-year investigation; among the others were Reno executives, contractors and suppliers.

We found it difficult to identify the start of this conspiracy, but the catalyst appeared to be the extensive renovations undertaken at Felgate's residences and his direction to subordinates that the costs be disguised as legitimate company expenditures. Our interviews with staff members confirmed that Felgate instructed employees to falsely assign contracts to Reno cost centers. The documents review revealed that Reno had been charged more than $10 million during many years for maintenance work and renovations on Felgate's various properties. We found an additional $3.2 million in invoices for work performed on other executives' and contractors' homes.

The Sixteen Suspects

Now that we had completed the investigation, my team and I began to compile briefs of evidence against all the accused. Initial discussions with Crown Prosecutors at the Department of Public Prosecutions (DPP) established that the most effective and prudent course would be to charge suspects with overarching crimes to encompass all their criminality, as opposed to multiple individual charges that could lengthen any potential trials.

With this is mind, we arrested and charged 16 people with theft, conspiracy to defraud, giving and receiving secret commissions, making and using false documents, obtaining property by deception and false accounting.

During Felgate's trial, a dog-eared blue exhibit album containing 108 pictures of his much-talked-about marble bathrooms and ornate dining parlors was the most popular piece of evidence; everyone wanted to get a glimpse. Marble, granite and wrought iron abounded, along with molded ceilings and wall friezes. There was a different style in every room, and the house would have been a feast for interior design magazines.

Then there was the garage, which was a monument to Felgate's well-documented love of fast and expensive cars. During the renovations, the garage was doubled to fit eight vehicles, and a timber-lined ceiling and a patterned tiled floor were installed.

The building supervisor at Felgate's home, Tony Hart, said in court evidence that he was on site for nearly six years. According to Hart, some work, such as glazing and laying marble in a bathroom, had been done two or three times because Felgate's wife changed her mind so often. At one point she asked contractors to move a recently completed upstairs bathroom five feet to the left, which required a complete refit of all the plumbing.

The prosecutor for the Crown asked the jury, with regard to the spread of corruption through the managers at Reno, "Is it all that surprising that when they saw the boss hog sticking his snout in the trough they put their snouts in alongside him?" He further commented, "It is where fraud began that matters and the man accused here was the father of the fraud."

Felgate's trial alone required more than 12,562 pages of court exhibits. It lasted three months and resulted in conviction. Felgate was sentenced to four years in jail.

In addition to Felgate the following individuals were also charged:

- Arthur Morton, 49: the head of Reno's maintenance department was charged with 93 offenses, including false accounting, obtaining property by deception and receiving secret commissions involving more than $9 million. Morton was convicted and sentenced to two years in prison.
- Harold Barnes, 46: the former Reno employee and regional controller of maintenance pleaded guilty to five charges of receiving a secret commission and charges related to building services carried out on his home. He received a four-month suspended prison sentence and was fined $7,000.
- William Allan, 36: the former Reno maintenance supervisor pleaded guilty to receiving secret commissions for free painting services. He received a two-month suspended prison sentence and was fined $5,000.
- Keith Lane, 42: a former contractor to Reno pleaded guilty to 29 charges of having made and used a false document amounting to $1.3 million. He was convicted and fined.
- Andrew West, 41: a former contractor to Reno pleaded guilty to 12 charges of having made and used a false document; he was fined.
- Harold Platten, 59: a former contractor to Reno pleaded guilty to and was fined for 11 charges relating to false quotes totaling $240,000.
- Michael Clarkson, 52: a former contractor to Reno pleaded guilty and was fined for charges relating to false quotes.
- Gavin Bowles, 57: a former plumbing contractor to Reno faced 19 charges of false accounting, 21 counts of giving a commission to an agent of Reno, 33 counts of receiving a secret commission and 13 counts of making false documents. He received fines.
- David Wilkins, 52: the former director of Decoray, a painting contractor to Reno, was charged with 13 counts of obtaining property by deception, 15 counts of false accounting, 22 counts of theft and 15 counts of giving a secret commission totaling $495,115. He was convicted and fined.
- Sean Catterall, 30: a former plumbing contractor to Reno pleaded guilty to charges of making false documents and was sentenced to community service with no conviction recorded.
- Chris Windsor, 59: a former plumbing contractor to Reno pleaded guilty to charges of making false documents. He was sentenced to community service with no conviction recorded.
- Peter Notman, 53: a former Reno manager of building, construction and maintenance was charged with 58 counts of false accounting worth

$2.16 million and 13 counts of receiving secret commissions in the form of renovations. He was convicted and received a suspended jail term.

- Hamish Tait, 64: a former contractor to Reno faced charges of stealing more than $200,000. He received fines.
- Andrew Knox, 32: a former Reno employee was charged with receiving secret commissions. He received fines.
- Russell Scott, 39: a former Reno employee was charged with receiving secret commissions. He received fines.

Prior to his trial, Peter Felgate sold his house for a little more than $2 million, despite the $6 million spent on what became one of Australia's most controversial refurbishments.

Lessons Learned

The most valuable steps we took in our investigation were maintaining a detailed master chronology and following strict rules for exhibit recording, numbering and handling. These precautions ensured our evidence was admissible in court.

I also learned the value of keeping tight control over a fraud examination and the importance of focusing on objectives. Fraud examinations tend to take on a life of their own. We had to ensure that our investigation did not give birth to multiple investigations or be distracted by others that were outside our objectives.

Setting objectives is crucial in any fraud case. Our investigation was similar to many others in that the majority of perpetrators were internal personnel of the victim company. Therefore, our initial objective was to establish which employees were involved. Then we needed to consider what civil action was available for the business to recover stolen funds or receive compensation for loss. In most jurisdictions, dual civil and criminal prosecutions cannot be run in parallel because there are issues of self-incrimination. If the criminal action takes precedent, then any ill-gotten gains may be dissipated. (This is not the case in the United States.)

Finally, we considered what internal processes needed to be overhauled at Reno to minimize the opportunity for further dishonesty. Most employees are honest and ethical; it is incumbent upon management to make it hard for them to be dishonest.

The underlying problem with Reno was that management had failed to clearly define the ethical behavior it expected from its employees and what was considered dishonest. There was scant regard given to articulating these guidelines in any code of conduct, and a number of internal controls relied on trust, with less emphasis on control.

(continued)

(continued)

In my early police training as a detective, I was taught that "failure to find is failure to search." This investigation taught me that a key to identifying and finding fraud is knowing what it looks like. One method to improve the ability to identify fraud is to use the reticular activating system (RAS). This is the part of the human brain that automatically filters out what is not important to the individual and calls attention to things that are important, based on what he or she has thought about, observed and consciously focused on recently. For example, have you ever thought about buying a new car and then all of the sudden noticed new cars everywhere you go? That is your RAS bringing the new cars to your attention because it is important to you.

To benefit from the RAS in investigations, fraud examiners need to keep themselves informed about schemes across industries. It is equally important to conduct fraud awareness training in organizations to help others identify acceptable and unacceptable behavior.

One tool I use to keep fraud important to my RAS is the Association of Certified Fraud Examiners' Uniform Occupational Fraud Classification System (also known as the Fraud Tree). It is my must-have tool, whether I am setting objectives in investigations, planning new policies or procedures or conducting risk assessments and audits. I use the classification system to identify what the fraud may look like and where I may find it, and has been invaluable. Whatever method you use, you must keep fraud prevention at the front of your mind at all times.

Recommendations to Prevent Future Occurrences

Essential to a successful fraud prevention program is the tone at the top. This case highlights what can happen to the ethical culture of a company when the leader not only undermines the effort but effectively promotes a culture of dishonesty.

As a result of this investigation, Reno immediately initiated a number of significant reforms to minimize future delinquency, including:

- Establishing a corporate loss prevention department headed by a recently retired police chief commissioner
- Instituting a complete review of the organizational code of conduct, with greater emphasis on honesty expectations
- Implementing organization-wide training in fraud awareness
- Installing a whistleblower hotline
- Increasing control and auditing of procurement and maintenance functions
- Expanding internal auditing functions, including the use of computer-aided audit techniques

About the Author

Shane Ringin is the general manager of Pro Active Strategies Pty Ltd and was a member of the Victoria Police Force for 20 years, and a member of the National Crime Authority, investigating organized crime nationally. Shane is a member of the Association of Certified Fraud Examiners and has a Master of Business Administration (Latrobe), Bachelor of Arts (Criminal Justice Administration), Advanced Certification (Accounting), Diploma in Commercial Crime Control & Terrorism (Exeter, UK) and a Certificate in Fraud Investigation (Latrobe).

CHAPTER

38

Sorry, This Fraud Has Been Disconnected

MERIC BLOCH

Dan Jackson was a man going places. There seemed to be no limit to where he would go in the company. He had recently been promoted to corporate vice president in the IT department at NyTel USA. NyTel paid him a good salary with an annual bonus. Dan just completed the company's Senior Leadership Training course, a two-week seminar in Lillehammer, Norway, where NyTel executives are groomed for advancement. The walls of Dan's offices were covered with photos of him with NyTel big shots. The credenza behind his desk was littered with knickknacks from his world travels and Lucite paperweights commemorating his big IT projects.

Dan had come a long way from Beaufort, South Carolina. The son of a career Marine officer, Dan spent his childhood moving from one military base to another. After his father retired from the Marines, the family settled in Beaufort when his father accepted a job teaching military history at a nearby college.

Major Jackson ran his family like a military commander. The kids were expected to obey orders without question. Resistance was futile. "When my father told us to do something, the only option was to salute and carry on," Dan was heard to say more than once. Although Major Jackson thought the application of military discipline built character in his children, it left Dan with a constant insecurity that he would never meet his father's standards.

Dan sought the major's approval, confident that someday he would earn it. But he never got the chance. During Dan's senior year at the University of Maryland, his father was killed in a car accident on a rain-slicked road. Dan would never make peace with his father.

That was 20 long years ago. Now Dan seemed to have it all. Besides the job at NyTel, Dan and his beautiful wife, Sue, were renovating a 1750s farmhouse they bought near Towson, Maryland. Sue thought it would be their dream house. Their children attended private school nearby. Sue enjoyed being a stay-at-home mom, and she felt lucky that her husband's success at NyTel meant she didn't have to work.

Dan had been at NyTel for six years. Believing that being an executive meant looking like one, Dan always wore Brioni suits — at $2,000 each — and a gold Rolex President watch. The company's travel policy required renting only mid-size cars, but Dan personally paid the extra charges and always upgraded to a Cadillac. When people questioned how a VP could afford those things, Dan explained that he shrewdly cashed-out his investments before the dot-com bubble burst in the late 1990s.

Dan took frequent vacations despite all the expenses in his life. Sometimes he took the family to Disney World or the Bahamas. Other times he went for a "boy's weekend" with some of his coworkers. Sue thought it was harmless fun and a way for Dan to decompress. She never knew that "one of the boys" on those trips was actually Melanie, NyTel's head of human resources. Dan had so far managed to keep his affair secret from Sue for the past 18 months.

On the outside, Dan looked like the ideal NyTel employee. But was he? Behind the carefully crafted image lay a troubled person. "How long can I keep this up?" he constantly asked himself. With the promotions came increased responsibilities for the company's IT networks, infrastructure and computer applications. The technology was getting more complicated, and Dan was not sure he could keep up with it. With his natural good looks and charm — he had enjoyed a college social life most men would envy — he was more talented in sales than as a computer geek. If he wasn't leading the IT department, no doubt he could have been a top NyTel salesman.

Enter Jake Marshall. Jake was also a military brat. After high school, Jake joined the Army, where he served for five years as a telecommunications field engineer. Once discharged, Jake used his telecom skills as an entrepreneur. During the next 12 years, Jake ran through a string of companies. All had big-sounding corporate names and used the right marketing buzzwords. But each company had only one employee — Jake. None was particularly successful, and Jake was coming to realize that he would never be a successful entrepreneur. Why not try his hand at consulting?

Dan and Jake met each other at a telecom convention in San Diego, one of those nondescript conferences where the promoters promise "networking" and guidance on "emerging issues." Over drinks at a reception, Dan explained how NyTel was about to begin the largest telecom project in its history. After touting his expertise in network design, Jake offered to help Dan as a project consultant. "Just let me stay in the shadows behind you. I can keep the other vendors honest," Jake promised. "There's no telling where we can go together. The sky is the limit."

The collaboration would have long-term implications for them, their families and NyTel.

NyTel USA

NyTel USA is one of the newer telecommunications companies. NyTel is a division of Nyheter Tekommunikasjons AS, a Norwegian company. Nyheter was started after World War II by Anders Nyheter, and it has since expanded to 50 countries with annual revenues of €70 billion. Nyheter is headquartered in Oslo, and its stock is traded on the major European markets.

Nyheter established a compliance department after its auditors found discrepancies in the way NyTel had been recognizing customer revenue. The announcement that the auditors would not verify the financial results tanked Nyheter's stock and led to an ouster of top management. The resulting investigation, however, showed only weak internal controls and not fraud. Nyheter's board of directors ordered the creation of the compliance department as well as the implementation of a whistleblower hotline, ethics training and mandatory reporting of fraud concerns.

Since then, the current management of NyTel has been stable. Amundsen Bryggeri, sent over from the Oslo headquarters, is the current U.S. CEO. Brooke Nokklekort is the CFO. Chester Plumpton is the chief information officer and Dan's boss. Chet is responsible for all of NyTel's IT needs. Bryggeri is holding Chet responsible for the successful consolidation of the company's computer systems.

The DCC Project

Like most big companies, NyTel looks more like a collection of smaller ones knitted together. NyTel has four business divisions: NyMobile (wireless services), NyHome (fixed-wire or landline services), NyComputer (Internet services) and NySatellite (television services). Each division was the result of a corporate acquisition, so each has its own legacy data system. Some of these data systems are old, and none is sufficiently integrated with the other systems.

Nyheter's board of directors recently approved the data center consolidation project to co-locate the systems and redesign the network in the United States. Because he designed the project timeline, with more than a little help from HAL, Inc., the lead vendor on the project, the leaders in Oslo appointed Dan as the project executive.

Dan's first task was to calculate the project budget. He did this in a few hours without a lot of effort. Curiously, the budget had a chunk of money set aside for consultants, although HAL would be doing 99 percent of the project work. No one questioned Dan's assumptions or calculations, however, and the budget was quickly approved.

Although Dan valued the chance to raise his profile in Oslo, he was worried. "Great. Now I have to pull this off, on budget and on time, and I also have to keep Chet from grabbing all the credit." Dan was still fuming from the fact that, three months earlier, Chet had refused to push for Dan to get a promotion and a raise. "Once again, I am doing senior VP work at a junior VP salary."

True to form, once Chet appointed Dan, Chet turned his back on the project. He rarely asked Dan for information, and he never spoke to anyone else on the project. Even when Bryggeri and Nokklekort asked to be updated, Chet had Dan make the presentation, only to sit and fiddle with his BlackBerry while Dan plowed through the PowerPoint slides.

NyTel had engaged HAL to provide a turnkey solution. This meant that HAL would provide almost all of the project professional services. A few additional vendors would provide the specialized services HAL didn't, usually because some piece of equipment or application had proprietary software that HAL's engineers didn't understand.

Dan needed to get Jake on to the project. After an argument with HAL's enterprise architect, the lead designer of the new network, Dan found his opportunity. Blowing the disagreement way out of proportion, Dan convinced Chet that the architect had to go or the project would fail. Because HAL would likely replace the architect with "another flunky off their bench," as Dan explained, NyTel needed someone from the outside. With some more of Dan's famous salesmanship, Chet — who once again didn't ask too many questions — approved the engagement of Jake Marshall. Jake would be a project consultant, and Dan would supervise him. HAL would just have to deal with Jake as the new enterprise architect.

How It's Supposed to Work

As a NyTel vendor, Jake would submit an invoice for his services to get paid. NyTel used a centrally managed system for processing invoices for its four business divisions. Each vendor would send the invoice to a mail drop box, where it was opened and the invoice was time-stamped to show the date it was received. The invoice would then be digitally scanned and uploaded into BOONIS, the automated accounts-payable system.

BOONIS assigned the invoice to the internal cost center — the ledger account number assigned for a project or department — and the expense was charged against the appropriate account. The invoice then traveled electronically to the cost-center owner for review. Chloe Portela was the financial controller for the DCC project, so BOONIS listed her as the project's cost-center owner.

NyTel had a schedule of authorizations that allowed Chloe, because of her management authority, to approve expenditures up to $5,000. Expenditures above that amount but below $25,000 also had to be approved by Chet. Expenditures worth more than $25,000 also had to be approved by Nokklekort, the CFO.

Once approved in BOONIS, the cost center was charged for the expense and its budget was reduced accordingly. NyTel's accounts payable department then mailed a check directly from the headquarters in Livingston, New Jersey.

The DCC project, however, put a slight wrinkle in this standard company process. Chloe was a financial whiz, but she knew nothing about IT projects. Consequently, she couldn't confirm that an invoice's goods or services were actually provided. To accommodate her lack of knowledge, once BOONIS sent her an invoice, she would e-mail it to Dan for his review. Dan would, or so he told her, validate the invoice and confirm this in a reply e-mail. If the invoice was instead presented to him in hard copy, Dan would scribble "OK to pay" on it and sign his name. Either one was Chloe's assurance from Dan that she could safely approve the invoice.

If Chet or Nokklekort also had to approve an invoice, each first looked for some indication that Dan had validated the invoice. If they saw it, they'd approve the invoice immediately. Their invoice-review process, consequently, became little more than a search for Dan's signature.

Dan's Way

About six months into the DCC project, Chloe was concerned. Her job was to make sure that the project stayed within the budget. Based on the project timeline, only 40 percent of the budget should have been consumed by now. But Chloe calculated that approximately 70 percent had been used, and costs were rising.

Chloe knew that HAL provided virtually all of the vendor services for the project. She saw invoices for other vendors, but Dan always assured her that these vendors were needed for small, specialized tasks. But she noticed that two of the vendors were sending frequent invoices for successively larger dollar amounts. One of the companies was called Information Technology Company, and the other was called Technology Equipment Services.

Chloe picked one of the ITC invoices and sent it to Dan for an explanation. "Who were the consultants who did the work here?" she wrote in the cover note. Dan e-mailed back the same day:

> I just spoke with Kim at ITC. She is responsible for AP and will send me the time sheet associated with the onsite resources that were dispatched to rack, power up, test network equipment/connectivity for the project. I will just re-class Bob and Mike's time once processed. They were unable to finish-out the work performed by them.

That was a lot more information that she had asked for, and Chloe could not understand a word of it. When Chloe got stumped on IT matters, she always turned to Willie Ming. Willie was an old hand in the IT department, and he had been working on the DCC project since the beginning. If anyone could translate Dan's e-mail into plain English, Willie could do it.

"Who the hell is ITC?" were words Chloe would long remember. "I never heard of the company, and they sure didn't do any work on the DCC." Chloe quickly pulled copies of all the ITC invoices from her files to show to Willie. "But isn't that Dan's signature on each of them?" she pleaded. "Sure looks like it," Willie replied.

Trying to conceal her growing panic, Chloe printed off from BOONIS a list of all the project vendors and showed it to Willie. She also showed him one of the TES invoices. Willie knew each of the vendors on the list other than ITC and TES. "I have no idea who TES is," Willie said while perusing the invoices, "but I gotta tell you, the description of provided services is gibberish. Sounds like something you could pull off the Internet in five seconds."

Getting Involved

Brooke Nokklekort called me about 3:00 that afternoon. I was at the airport flying home from wrapping up another case. "I need to talk to you about something important. How soon can you be here?" she asked. I told her I could be in the corporate office first thing the next morning. "Good," she said, and hung up. For the next 15 hours, I did not know whether I had landed a big case or was about to lose my job.

Experience taught me that it is important to manage the expectations of executives and keep them from hyperventilating over their own speculation. Corporate life is rarely exciting, and, even when fraud or serious misconduct occurs, it tends to be less serious than originally feared. Well, not always.

By this time, NyTel had paid 64 invoices from ITC and TES. Brooke explained when we met that, although she had signed off on the invoices over $25,000, she had simply relied on the earlier approvals of Chet and Chloe, as well as seeing Dan's "OK to pay" on the invoice. Brooke told me that her entire department was at my disposal and that she had already told Chet to shut down the project until this was straightened out. For good measure, she said, "I already called Oslo about this, and I am surprised you didn't hear the big shots screaming from across the Atlantic."

A quick call to Ollie Eckmer in procurement confirmed that they had no contracts, statements of work or rate cards for either company. There would be no project-related documentation for ITC or TES other than the invoices.

Nancy Lynn in accounts payable confirmed that, other than the DCC Project, NyTel had not paid either company for any other project. Nancy Lynn accessed BOONIS and got me copies of the ITC and TES invoices. I reviewed the invoices and noticed two things that piqued my curiosity. First, each one of them appeared to have Dan's "OK to pay" and signature on them. The invoices were the PDF images pulled straight from BOONIS. This meant that Dan approved the invoices *before* they were even sent to NyTel for payment.

The second thing was the time stamps on the invoices. The dates on the invoices varied, but most of the time stamps were not contemporaneous with the invoice date. Some of the invoices also shared the same time-stamp date. This meant that the invoices were probably submitted in batches rather than individually.

But why? What vendor sits on his invoices and lets them pile up? By sorting the invoices by time stamp, it appeared that many were submitted near the end of a calendar quarter. I asked Chloe if there was any significance to the calendar quarter. "We do a project review at the end of every quarter to see how we are doing," she explained. "If there is any extra money in the budget, Brooke makes us give it back right away."

Because ITC and TES had Pennsylvania addresses, I checked with the Pennsylvania Secretary of State for corporate filings. It turned out that ITC was a Pennsylvania corporation with offices at 20 Hollow Road, New Park, Pennsylvania. The registered agent for ITC was Jake Marshall. An online White Pages search confirmed the address was Marshall's home address.

A similar search was made for TES. TES was also a Pennsylvania corporation with offices at the same address. TES's president was also Jake Marshall.

NyTel's treasury department retrieved images of the canceled checks mailed to ITC and TES. I compared the checks. The endorsements showed that all the checks had been deposited in the same bank account. The handwriting matched on some of the endorsements for checks sent to both companies indicating, of course, that the same person endorsed checks for both ITC and TES.

I now had objective proof tying ITC and TES to Jake. Jake was implicated directly into the likely fraud scheme. But even if he had some friendship with Dan, could I show that there was collusion?

The next step was to confirm that the invoices were bogus. Besides Dan and Jake, five NyTel USA employees worked full time on the project. I interviewed each of them, and we pored over the ITC and TES invoices. The employees collectively explained how each of the invoices was fictitious. The services described were either not needed for the DCC project, provided by HAL or provided by NyTel's IT staff. Additionally, none of the witnesses recalled knowing or meeting anyone from ITC or TES.

So the investigation was presented with the obvious question: if ITC and TES were "ghost" vendors, and no one ever saw them, how did NyTel end up paying the invoices?

It turns out that Dan and Chloe had a different process for approving the ITC and TES invoices than with the other vendors. "Dan said it would save us both some time," Chloe explained. The two agreed that the placement of Dan's signature on an ITC or TES invoice meant that he had already validated the invoice and determined that payment by NyTel was appropriate. Unfortunately, Chloe never questioned why Dan had a special process for only two vendors but not the others. She also never questioned why Dan was receiving invoices from only these two vendors before BOONIS received them. She saw Dan's signature, and that was it.

Chet also relied blindly on Dan's signature. Chet approved invoices over $2,500 and under $25,000. He consistently assumed that Dan's signature meant Dan had already validated the invoice. Chet never validated an invoice personally or asked other core team members for information; instead he relied exclusively on the information from Dan. Chet and Chloe failed to consider that, as the invoice was referred higher for approval, the next approving manager would view their earlier approval as an indication that the invoice was valid.

I had my evidence against Jake. Now that I had spoken to everyone else, it was time to confront Dan.

Building Blocks

Dan started off the interview in his usual glad-handing way. He expressed shock that NyTel might have been defrauded. "Anything I can do to help you, you just let me know," he promised.

I approached his interview in a building-block style. First Dan admitted that before NyTel should pay any invoice, the following must be true: (1) the services described in the invoice were actually performed, (2) the services were done by the vendor submitting the invoice and (3) the services were not rendered by someone else.

Dan also explained that he was the "go-to guy" for validating project invoices. He acknowledged that each of the signatures on the ITC and TEC invoices were, in fact, his.

I then got Dan to admit that he knew the significance of his signature in the invoice-approval process. He admitted that Brooke and Chet would be relying on his earlier validation if they also had to approve an invoice.

Considering that he had validated the invoices, I asked Dan to justify the use of the ITC consultants described in the invoices. Dan explained that the services from ITC consultants were necessary because there were resource gaps in the delivery of project services. (The investigation had already determined, however, that there was no business need for additional services from ITC.)

Under further questioning, Dan's explanation collapsed. He said that he did not make the decision to engage additional ITC consultants. Although he was the project executive and the person validating the invoices, Dan claimed that he neither knew who made that decision nor why it was necessary. Dan admitted further that no one on the core team had asked for the additional resources, and he never made any inquiries to determine if additional resources were needed.

Moreover, although he validated the ITC invoices, Dan couldn't explain the specific services ITC provided. He never saw a time sheet to substantiate the consulting work, and no invoice identified a consultant. Dan did not set the consultant's hourly rates, and he did not know who set them. Dan admitted that he had no idea whether the time billed and the rates specified in an invoice were accurate. Dan never made any inquiries to find out either.

Despite his damaging admissions, Dan insisted that TES was needed. He claimed that TES provided necessary staff-augmentation, cabling and hardware-rental services because HAL had underresourced the project. Dan said he made the decision to engage TES. But, with some probing, Dan conceded that he neither met nor knew anyone from TES who provided services to the project. TES's fees were not established before the services were purportedly rendered. Dan also never made inquiries to the core team whether or how TES was providing the services.

Dan, the project executive, had effectively conceded that he approved more than $1 million in invoices for two companies he didn't know and for services he couldn't explain. He was savvy enough to know he'd dug himself a hole he couldn't climb out of.

To close the loop, I e-mailed Jake after Dan's interview to request his assistance contacting the management at ITC and TES. The e-mail explained that time sheets and other information were needed to validate certain invoices.

Jake replied quickly with his own e-mail. He wrote that "in regard to ITC & TES, they are both my companies and I handle all the invoices and billing." Jake was unable to provide time sheets for the consultants, however, because "they were lost due to a stolen laptop while traveling abroad."

I replied a few hours later. Because of the "theft," I asked Jake to (1) identify the ITC and TES employees and consultants who provided services to the project, (2) identify the NyTel employees and consultants who might confirm that these services were provided and (3) provide copies of any documents TES created in connection with the extensive services it provided to the project. Not surprisingly, Jake didn't reply to this e-mail.

Although it was outside the scope of the investigation, we had reason to believe that Dan had been defrauding NyTel in other schemes before he met Jake. The red flags were there, but everyone missed them: the lifestyle, the trusted employee who feels underpaid and unappreciated and the one person who controls both all the information and key duties. Because he set the budget and tracked the expenses, Dan even knew when there was sufficient slack to quickly submit some ITC and TES invoices.

NyTel terminated Dan's employment and Jake's "engagement" immediately after the investigation was closed. His career now in tatters, Dan muttered as he left the corporate offices carrying the box of his credenza knickknacks and paperweights, "I'm glad my father is not alive to see all of this."

Referral to the FBI

Once the investigation was complete, I contacted the FBI. Because the company checks were sent by U.S. mail from New Jersey to Pennsylvania, I knew the FBI would have jurisdiction under the mail-fraud statute. I gave them my forensic investigation memo and all the exhibits to prove that this was a fraud scheme and not just bad corporate management. Fortunately, my "gift-wrapping" of the investigation appealed to them — "You did 90 percent of the work for us," the agent told me later over a beer — and a criminal investigation was opened.

The subpoenaed bank records for ITC and TES showed that all deposits in the account were followed almost immediately by a corresponding cash withdrawal. In other words, Jake was laundering the money he received from NyTel. The FBI quickly determined that NyTel's money had paid for home renovations, expensive cars, payments of mortgages and credit card bills, trips to Las Vegas and the Dominican Republic and season's tickets for the Baltimore Ravens. To ensure that Dan was in as much trouble with his wife as with the feds, the FBI showed that Dan's mistress had been ensconced and maintained in an expensive condo near the family home.

Two months later, Dan and Jake were indicted by the Middle District of Pennsylvania on multiple counts of mail fraud and money laundering. The indictment also included one count of criminal forfeiture to allow the seizure of their homes, cars and bank accounts.

Nevertheless, Dan maintained his innocence. His explanations ranged from "Marshall duped me" to "I saved NyTel more money than you think I stole." After multiple continuances, it looked as if Dan and Jake were going to take their chances with the jury, but the internal investigation and the FBI investigation were too airtight. Finally, Dan and Jake accepted the inevitable and negotiated a plea bargain with the U.S. Attorney.

Standing before the judge in one of his Brioni suits, Dan was now a ruined man. Since his firing, his wife had left him and his assets had been seized. He was paying his lawyer with money from his relatives. But Dan claimed only to have "made mistakes" and "cut corners." Even the prosecutor was amazed that Dan still failed to accept responsibility. Jake, to his comparative credit, took responsibility for his role. He did his best to explain to the judge that this was just an unfortunate, unwise step in an otherwise exemplary life.

The judge, however, saw things differently. Jake was sentenced to 30 months in federal prison. Dan received 37 months because he had also abused a position of trust with NyTel. The judge ordered them jointly and severally to pay NyTel restitution of $1.5 million.

It was a bill from the phone company that Dan and Jake will never be able to pay.

Lessons Learned

Based on the lessons we learned from Dan and Jake, NyTel changed a number of its internal policies and procedures:

- Accounts payable staff members now conduct spot-check validations of invoices to raise the perception of detection. The spot check includes contacting the vendor that submitted the invoice.
- Invoice approvers can no longer safely rely on the validation efforts of their subordinates. Each approver is responsible for personally validating each invoice.
- Project duties are segregated so that budgets, purchases, approvals and information do not rest exclusively with one person.
- Financial controllers must understand the projects for which they are providing oversight.
- Company vendors must be prequalified and placed on a master vendor list. Vendors must also have contracts and statements of work on file before any work begins.
- Fraud-awareness training is provided annually to the finance staff to help spot the red flags of fraud.
- The company will promote increased use of the whistleblower line, including mandatory reporting of fraud concerns.

About the Author

Meric Bloch is the North American Compliance Officer for Adecco S.A. He has conducted over 300 fraud and serious misconduct investigations. He is a Certified Compliance and Ethics Professional, a Certified Fraud Examiner, a Professional Certified Investigator and a licensed private investigator. He is an author and frequent speaker on investigation topics.

CHAPTER

39

Bid Rigging and Kickbacks Under the Bridge

EDWARD J. GAIO

Dylan Murphy grew up in the countryside of Ireland. He came from a well-to-do family that owned several mines, but as a young man he aspired to immigrate to the United States and become a successful engineer. While in his senior year of boarding school he met Susan Ross, the daughter of a wealthy exporter who dealt with many of the mines in the area. After graduating, Dylan and Susan were soon married and decided to move to America to pursue their new life together and attend college.

Once the Murphys arrived in their new country, Dylan was accepted to the Rose Hulman Institute of Technology, where he would spend the next four years earning a bachelor's degree in civil engineering. Given that both Dylan and Susan came from families of means, neither one worked while Dylan was in school. In fact, the Murphys tended to come across as possessing a sense of entitlement when around others, which did not make them very many friends. By the time Dylan graduated, the Murphys had one daughter and another one on the way.

After Dylan graduated, the family moved to a small suburb of Denver, where he was offered an entry-level position as a resident engineer for the Regional Transportation District (RTD). Over the next 13 years, Murphy worked at RTD with very little upward mobility to show for it. Dylan thought he was an ambitious person, but he was unwilling to take the necessary steps to make himself more marketable. The Murphys' cultural upbringing contributed to their sense of entitlement, and they believed that they should obtain rewards with little or no personal risk.

To make up for his lack of career success, Dylan and his wife pursued different investment opportunities with the hope that they would be propelled into the social status they so desired. The first was opening an Irish pub in their suburban neighborhood; due to their lack of small-business experience, the pub failed in less than two years. The second was investing in rental property in a neighboring community. After a series of poor financial decisions, the rental property went into foreclosure, prompting the Murphys' need for more cash.

Regional Transportation District

RTD is located in Denver, Colorado, and provides bus and light-rail public transportation to the 2.8 million residents living in the eight-county region that populates the metropolitan area. In 1969, the Colorado General Assembly organized the RTD by combining several bus and trolley services used in Denver and its neighboring communities to form one large public transportation system that would eventually provide service to 40 different municipalities in the area.

Throughout the 1970s, RTD experienced continued growth through a merger with Denver Metro Transit and an expansion of bus service with a series of sales tax increases voted by the public. After 15 years, RTD decided to revive and expand its light-rail train service. In 1994, RTD opened the first of three light-rail corridors, bringing rail transit back to the region. Over the next eight years, RTD continued to expand and rehabilitate its light-rail train service to include the addition of two new corridors. In 2001, RTD broke ground with the Transportation Expansion Project (TREP), a multimodal construction venture combining light rail, highway, bike and pedestrian traffic. The TREP project was meant to alleviate the volume of traffic for one of the busiest interchanges in the United States. As the latest installment of light-rail expansion, the Southeast Corridor would be RTD's crown jewel of the TREP project. It ended up being a success changing the way people commuted in the Metro Denver area, finishing under budget and almost two years ahead of schedule.

FBI Investigation

I was one of six auditors in RTD's internal audit department. Most of our work consisted of contract compliance and operational processes; very seldom did we encounter any significant fraud during the course of our audits. One November afternoon I received a phone call from my boss, Matt Wilhelm. Special agents from the FBI had contacted our general counsel to notify her that Dylan was under investigation and was soon to be indicted. Additionally, our counsel was served with a subpoena requesting the release of contracts and project files that Murphy had been working on. Specifically, it included four major bridge rehabilitation projects and four small construction projects. All of them had been completed within the previous five years, with Murphy as the project manager on four of them. The FBI agents also instructed our counsel not to interview any employees or contractors while their investigation was ongoing.

Knowing my background as a Certified Fraud Examiner, my boss decided to bring me in. To protect the integrity of evidence and to establish a chain of custody, our legal department would be securing all engineering project files and procurement contracts related to the subpoena. After reading through the subpoena and grand jury indictment, I was able to determine that Murphy was being charged for receiving kickbacks from four different contractors on eight different RTD projects.

Once she reviewed the subpoena, RTD's senior counsel contacted the department heads in human resources, procurement and engineering and provided them with a list of documents that were to be pulled and sent to legal. These included Dylan's personnel files, procurement contracts for each of the projects and the project files from the engineering department. After Murphy was arrested, he was placed on administrative leave. My boss and I removed all files from Murphy's desk and office and secured them in our office, which has restricted security access. Additionally, we removed his personal computer and storage devices and delivered them to our IT department to be cloned for data analysis.

I then began the daunting task of inventorying everything received by legal and all the files retrieved from Murphy's office. The documents that appeared to be relevant to the subpoenaed contracts were set aside for further review. Once this had been done, certified copies were made and retained by RTD; all original documents were subsequently released to the FBI.

Charges indicated that Dylan received kickbacks from the contractors through bribery and extortion. It was alleged that his crimes also extended to mail fraud and a conflict of interest violation of RTD's ethics policy. Furthermore, he was suspected of being involved in bid-rigging schemes with two of the contractors. In total, Dylan had been charged with 21 felonies. Once I completed my review, I linked each of the eight projects to their applicable grand jury indictments. This practice allowed me to identify any unnamed conspirators and contractors in the indictment as well as any other possible RTD employees who could be involved. Armed with a better understanding of the FBI's case, I attended the trial along with Anna Chiles, a colleague from RTD's legal department, to learn more specific details about Murphy's crimes.

An Eye-Opening Trial

During the trial I learned that Dylan had conspired with three of the contractors in a bid-rigging scheme to inflate prices on the four small projects and inflate change order proposals on one of the four bridge rehabilitation contracts. Kickbacks from these prices would then be paid to Murphy in cash. He was able to obtain cooperation primarily by withholding his approval for payment on work already done or threatening to discontinue a relationship between RTD and the contractor. Additionally, the U.S.

Attorney demonstrated that Dylan had extracted bribes from one of the contractors by requiring that his wife's cleaning company be used as a sub-contractor to provide cleaning services on three of the four bridge reha-bilitation projects. Dylan's wife, Susan, had formed G&F Cleaning Service only weeks before Dylan made his initial demand from the contractor. Fur-thermore, G&F Cleaning Service had only one other client. Using his wife's company allowed him to receive profit for personal gain while conducting official RTD business, which created a conflict of interest per RTD's code of ethics policy.

During the trial, Scott Drake, president of Athena Painting, testified that his company had been responsible for the rehabilitation of the central viaduct bridge during the expansion of RTD's southwest light-rail corridor. Drake said that Athena contracted with Andros Painting as a silent partner. During the construction, Drake and his silent partner, George Rifkin, the president of Andros, were instructed what scopes and amounts should be included on change orders. Each of them had an inflated amount that Drake and Rifkin used to pay kickbacks to Murphy, totaling $45,000. Drake testified that at the conclusion of construction, Murphy refused to pay Athena's final contract bill of $115,000 without the guarantee of one last kickback of $15,000.

After Drake testified, the prosecution questioned his silent partner, George Rifkin. He corroborated Drake's testimony about having to inflate prices on change orders to pay kickbacks to Murphy. Additionally, Rifkin swore that he formally served as the vice president of North-East Construc-tion, a contractor on two of the small projects. The first was to repave a rapid transit station parking lot and the second was for repairs to a train platform. In each instance Murphy instructed Rifkin on the amounts he should bid and how much would be paid as a kickback. RTD grossly overpaid for these projects, allowing Murphy and North-East Construction to pocket $25,000 in kickbacks. To avoid unwanted suspicion, Murphy conspired with Rifkin on the other two small projects to hire a subcontractor, Campbell Construction, to place inflated bids. Both projects involved subsequent drainage repairs needed for the viaduct bridge that had been rehabilitated by Athena Painting and Andros Painting. Testimony indicated that Rifkin received a 10 percent cut of the contracts awarded to Campbell Construction and an additional $10,000 in cash went to Murphy.

Alec Berg, former president of Salcer Construction, was the final co-conspirator to testify at the trial. Berg said that he had worked as the manager for three separate contracts related to RTD's TREP. Each contract was for the rehabilitation of a light rail bridge. Two of the bridges (Madison Street and Water Street) were part of the southeast corridor, and the third (Center Street) was part of the northwest corridor. When Salcer Construction was awarded the three contracts, Murphy approached Berg and demanded that he hire his wife's cleaning company to clean construction site trailers. Berg initially rejected him, but Murphy implied that he would make things hard for Berg during the course of the contracts and possible future business if he did not do as told. Berg went on to testify that Dylan had mailed all G&F invoices to him throughout the project and he had never actually corresponded with Susan. Invoices presented at trial illustrated that Salcer Construction had paid $80,000 for cleaning service over an 18-month period. Based on market rates and the nature of work required to be performed, it was estimated that $80,000 was twice what an outside cleaning service actually would charge.

Berg also said that he was instructed to power wash the Madison Street and Water Street Bridges rather than sandblasting them as required in the contract's scope of services. In turn, Murphy was to receive kickbacks for the difference in cost between sandblasting and power washing, which was estimated to be $30,000 for each bridge. It was also revealed that during the course of these bridge rehabilitations, Murphy had Berg pull one of his employees off the project during working hours to go to Murphy's personal residence and perform emergency flood damage repair and repaint his porch.

After little deliberation, the jury convicted Dylan Murphy on all counts of conspiracy, bribery, extortion, mail fraud and making false statements. Months later he was sentenced to eight years in prison and ordered to pay RTD $88,000 in restitution. Susan was convicted of making false statements and was sentenced to one year in prison.

Post-Trial Recovery

Once a verdict had been rendered against Murphy, members from the internal audit and legal departments formed a joint task force lead by Anna Chiles and me. The goal was to evaluate testimony and evidence presented at trial as well as RTD documentation to determine how and why Dylan Murphy was able to commit a fraud against RTD and to see if there were any losses we could identify and recover. Findings from our internal investigation would be used to seek further restitution as well as a recommendation for management to improve RTD's internal controls.

During our review, the task force established that RTD had weak and inefficient internal controls in both our procurement and engineering departments, which allowed for Dylan to get away with his schemes. We were able to determine that the chain of custody for dealing with bid submissions was inadequate and had little or no documentation. Particularly, some procurement files had missing or incomplete information pertinent to their contracts. We also concluded that Murphy was not properly overseen by his supervisor, which allowed him to abuse his authority when dealing with the contractors. Last, our review indicated that personnel in both the procurement and engineering departments lacked the latest training for dealing with construction projects, as suggested by industry guidelines.

The task force presented management with our recommendations, which included:

- Evaluating and improving the procurement policies and procedures, especially for bid submissions and the chain of custody for bids
- Reconciling procurement policies and procedures manual to the engineering policies and procedures manual to ensure all parties are in compliance with industry standards
- Establishing a debarment policy, which would allow RTD to "bar" contractors from bidding on RTD projects if they have any criminal convictions or civil judgments against them involving fraudulent acts
- Implementing a watch list to preclude irresponsible companies
- Providing the latest training for contract administrators
- Instituting a fraud hotline for employees, contractors or customers to provide tips for suspicious and fraudulent activities

We also recommended that RTD file a crime claim with our insurance company, Pacific Mountain, to determine if we were owed additional restitution and to ask if it had tips to prevent and investigate fraudulent activities in the future. Once Pacific Mountain received the claim, our insurance agent hired Washington Tax Group (WTG), a forensic accounting firm, to investigate on behalf of Pacific Mountain.

Donald Sanger, a senior associate for WTG and the lead investigator for our case, requested documentation to review, mostly of the same information the FBI agents requested. Sanger also identified a list of current and former employees he wanted to interview.

They included current employees who had worked with Murphy on the eight contracts. Jim Nagy and Erica McDonald were procurement contract administrators who were assigned to Murphy's contracts; Nagy was contract administrator for one of the four large projects, and McDonald was the contract administrator for two of the four small ones. The remaining five contracts were administered by Anthony Fatica, who had since retired from RTD. Murphy's immediate supervisor, Henry Atkins, and Todd Sinclair, the vice president of engineering, were also interviewed.

Sanger and his associates conducted their investigation in similar fashion as the FBI and RTD's task force, by going through all related personnel records, project files and procurement contracts. After reviewing the trial transcripts and evidence, Sanger and his team conducted employee interviews while Anna and I observed. All the interviewees gave descriptions of their job duties as well as the procedures that are in place for working on construction projects. Furthermore, the employees were questioned about any involvement they had with the eight projects that Murphy had worked on. When his investigation was complete, Sanger presented Pacific Mountain and our general counsel with his findings report. WTG quantified the total loss incurred by RTD at about $200,000, calculated on four key variables:

1. Kickbacks Murphy received from inflated bids
2. Funds from change orders and other kickbacks that Murphy collected
3. Payments to G&F Cleaning
4. Repairs to Murphy's home

WTG's report also included a series of recommendations to improve RTD's internal controls, some of which coincided with what my task force had suggested. One was to terminate Murphy's supervisor, Henry Atkins. He had been a well-respected bridge engineer with RTD for 25 years, but records from each of the projects indicated that he had blatantly disregarded the proper performance of his duties in reviewing and overseeing Murphy's work. This same sentiment came across while we interviewed Atkins. After the report was reviewed and accepted, a claims check of $200,000 was issued by Pacific Mountain to reimburse RTD for its incurred losses, and Henry Atkins was terminated.

Lessons Learned

Our findings indicated that it is essential for any business to have strong internal controls. While RTD did have some controls in place to ensure that contracts were properly executed, a lack of training and employee supervision allowed for these controls to be ignored and manipulated. When construction projects are an important part of your business, it is essential to ensure that your policies and procedures are continually updated to meet industry standards and guidelines. It is also essential to ensure that the proper chain of custody is in place to protect the integrity of the project. Businesses need to make sure that the roles of their employees are clearly defined to certify a proper segregation of duties.

It is also important to have controls in place to prevent and detect fraud, waste and abuse, such as watch lists and debarment policies. Having these allows management to know when it is dealing with potentially untrustworthy contractors or clients.

Perhaps the most important lesson to be learned is to make sure a business has both an ethics and a fraud policy to protect the company and the employees. No fraud policy should exist without a fraud hotline and whistleblower protection.

Recommendations to Prevent Future Occurrences

After concluding this investigation, I found that it is essential to have solid controls in place to prevent and detect fraud, waste and abuse. Any organization should at a minimum have an ethics and/or fraud policy in place as well as a hotline that will give individuals the opportunity to comfortably report suspicious activities. Additionally, policies and procedures should be clearly defined throughout an organization.

After an employee has been hired, management should periodically perform background investigations on those who have been placed in a position of trust. It would also be beneficial to enforce a vacation policy and rotate employees who are in a position to work repeatedly with the same vendors or contractors. Each organization should also offer continuous training and education to keep employees sharp and aware of any new standards and guidelines.

In addition to performing employee background checks, do the same with vendors and contractors. When contracting or partnering with another firm on a long-term project, it is important to know with whom you are dealing. By implementing a debarment policy, an organization will be able to set guidelines and standards for ethically and legally conducting business. Any organization contracting work should include a watch list as part of its bid process to exclude contractors that might have been sanctioned or participated in any illegal or unethical activities.

About the Author

Edward J. Gaio, CFE, is a criminal justice and finance graduate of Kent State University with ten years' experience in auditing and compliance review. Mr. Gaio has experience working with corporations and public agencies and has participated in the recovery of more than $2 million in misappropriated assets.

Index

A

Abuse of authority, 315
Accountants, as fraud perpetrators/
    accomplices, 14, 20, 54, 57,
    275–276, 320
Accounting controls, 251
Accounting departments, 116–117
Accounting practices, faulty, 163, 164
Accounts-payable departments, 118,
    184–185, 360–363, 367
Accounts-payable systems, 360
Account statements, 277
Administrative subpoenas, 4
Affidavits, 32
Agency agreements, 99
Alaska, 299–307
Anti-corruption codes, 252
Anti-corruption laws, 251
Anti-fraud policies, 122
Approved vendors, 183
Asbestos-containing materials (ACM),
    266, 268
Asbestos Hazard Emergency Response
    Act (AHERA), 262, 265–267
Asbestos remediation fraud, 261–269
Asset control and inventory, 93
Assistant managers, 177–178
Association of Certified Fraud
    Examiners, 175, 354
ATM withdrawals, 254–255, 257, 258
Attorney-client privilege, 108, 213
Attorneys, 194
Audits, 3, 41, 133, 272, 288, 321, 322,
    343–344
Audit fees, 142
Auditing, 142
Auditing software, 343

Audit trail, 135, 344, 347–354
Authentication tools, 62
Authority, abuse of, 315
Automated alerts, 196, 197
Automobile industry, 209–215
Automobiles, as bribes, 203, 204
Aviation suppliers, 343, 344

B

Background checks, 19, 20, 51, 98–99,
    202, 242, 259, 294, 311, 312, 314,
    316, 376
Bank deposits, 333
Bank fraud, 53–63, 133–139
Bank managers, 133–139
Bank reconciliation statements, 142
Bank records, 61, 366
Bankruptcy, 16–19, 86, 93, 107, 150,
    152, 155, 294, 295, 305
Bank statements, 60, 110, 173, 221,
    240, 249, 257, 273, 277, 333
Bank transfers, 343
Benchmarks, 119
Bid collusion/rigging, 3, 6, 8–10, 45,
    152, 154–155, 157, 159–168, 204,
    206, 231, 233, 237–238, 240, 290,
    291, 295, 311, 344, 371, 372, 375
Bidding on contracts, 11, 152, 162, 170,
    240, 373
Bid documents, 291
Bid rotation, 206
Bid solicitations, 237
Bid tampering, 9
"Bill of rights" (prison inmates), 288
"Blanket purchase order" agreement,
    170
Blgojevich, Rod, xii

Boards of directors, 27, 319, 320, 323–328
Boats, 19–20
Bonuses, 324, 325
Breach of trust, 95
Bribery. *See also* Kickbacks
  bank loan fraud, 135
  cab license fraud, 90–92
  café/restaurant licensing fraud, 123–131
  engineering firm fraud, 48, 49
  film festival bribery case, 65–73
  hotel supply kickback fraud, 179–182
  Japanese bid-rigging case, 167, 168
  jewelry industry fraud, 282
  manufacturing fraud, 229–234
  manufacturing purchase management fraud, 197
  Mexican windmill company fraud, 248–251
  mining contractor kickback case, 174
  multinational manufacturing fraud, 218–219, 221, 223
  Nigerian government employee fraud, 199–207
  Ohio DOT procurement fraud, 7
  outsourcing procurement fraud, 314
  public transportation construction fraud, 371–373
  Tanzanian tax fraud, 145, 146
Briefs of evidence, 351
Budgets, 68, 116–117, 359–361, 363
Building services, 349
Bureau of Indian Affairs (BIA), 261–269
"Buy-bust" arrest, 38
Buyers/buying, 107–113

C
Cab license fraud, 85–94
Café licensing, 123–131
Cameras, surveillance, 122. *See also* Surveillance systems
Canada, 329–338
Capacity (Fraud Triangle element), 289, 290

Career advancement, 167, 168, 174, 213, 214
Cash, 7, 29, 133, 135–136, 173, 218–220, 227–229, 233, 277, 280, 283, 291, 292, 294–296, 366
  tracing of, *see* Tracing of cash
Cash advances, 48
Cash conversion, 220
Certificates of deposit, 136
Certificates of income, 254, 256
Certified Fraud Examiner, 42, 109
Certified Public Accountants (CPAs), 54, 57–59, 62
Chain of custody, 254, 345, 373
Chain of evidence, 277
Charter boat trips, as kickbacks, 2–6
Chartered account, 277
Chauffeur's license, 87, 88, 90–93
Checks, 58, 59, 108, 174, 175, 249, 277, 331–334, 363
Checking accounts, 173
Check stubs, 144
Chief executive officer (CEO), 213–214, 225
Chief financial officer (CFO), 162, 165, 245
Chief information officer (CIO), 160, 164, 359
Circumstantial evidence, 40
Civil claims, 113
Cocaine, 35–42
Codes of conduct/ethics, 13–21, 197, 203, 283, 284
Collateral, 303, 305
Collusion, 144, 168, 228, 258, 280–283, 329–338, 345. *See also* Bid collusion/rigging
Colorado, 369–376
Commercial crime unit, 333
Commissary, prison, 287–296
Commissions, 49, 68–69, 71, 110, 111, 247, 248, 250, 272, 276, 301, 312, 351, 352
Commodities, 109, 111–112
Communication, for fraud prevention, 147–148, 184, 197, 242, 251, 321, 325–326

Competitive bidding, 149, 167, 296
Compliance departments, 359
Compliance standards, 251
Comprehensive Environmental
    Response, Compensation, and
    Liability Act of 1980 (CERCLA),
    266
Computer forensics, 15, 16, 60, 218,
    300, 307, 321, 338
Concert tickets, as bribes/kickbacks,
    290
Confessions, 196, 242, 283
Confidentiality, 242, 255
Conflicts of interest, 9, 29, 81, 95–105,
    120, 180, 213
Conglomerates, 235–243
Consensual overhear (COH), 91,
    92
Conspiracy, 30, 373
Construction, 43–51, 300–301,
    369–376. *See also* Home
    repairs/renovations, as kickbacks
Construction bids, 151
Construction contracts, 202–203
Construction fraud, 115–122,
    149–157
Consulting services/fees, 29, 44, 78, 82,
    84, 194, 195, 220, 227, 233, 324,
    332–334, 358–361, 364, 365
Contacts, development of, 99
Containment, 214
Contracts, awarding of, 201, 229–231,
    236, 238–240, 289
Contract administration, 374
Contract amendments, 228, 233
Contract bids, *see* Bidding on contracts
Contract notes, 272, 276
Contractors, 115–122, 281, 351
Contractor background checks, 376
Contractor fraud, 149–157
Contract steering, 157
Controller, 336
Control logs, 294
Corporate culture, 102–104
Corporate investigations, 188–189
Corporate policies, 180
Corporate tax, 220

Corruption (defined), xi
Cost, budget v., 118
Cost codes, 163
Cost-cutting programs, 226
Cost overruns, 118–120, 149, 349
Councils of government (COGs),
    24–25, 27–29, 31
Counterfeit licenses, 87, 91
Credit cards, 10, 254–259, 281–283
Credit card fraud, 253–259
Culture, risk-based v. incentive-based,
    62
Custodial interviews, 274–275
Customs brokers, 221, 224
Customs fraud, 219, 221, 223

D
Data center consolidations, 359–360
Data extraction/analysis, 15–17, 19–20,
    47, 108–109, 249, 371
Debarment, 374
Deed of trust, 302
Defense witnesses, 248–249
Denver, Colorado, 369–376
Department of Public Prosecutions
    (DPP; Australia), 351
Destruction of records, 321–322
Detectives, 333
Deterrence, 122
Development projects, 242
Disbursements, 311
Discount stores, 348
Discretion, in investigations, 255
District attorney, 295, 296
Division of duties, 121
Divorce, 282
Documents, 107–108, 276, 304
Documentary evidence, 26
Documentation, 242. *See also*
    Supporting documents
Documentation, lack of, 143
Document trails, 344
Downsizing, 196
Draft financial statements, 142
Drug trafficking, 35–42
Due diligence, 42, 50–51, 62, 224,
    251–252, 312, 316

E

Eastern Europe, 47–48

Electronic files, 47, 48, 190, 192, 196

E-mails, 15–16, 48, 191, 237, 239–241, 305, 326, 361, 365

Embezzlement, 199–207, 228

Employee crimes insurance, 111. *See also* Insurance

Employees, trusted, 183

Engineering firm fraud, 43–51, 95–105

Engine parts, 209–215

England, 341–346

Enterprise architects, 360

Environmental fraud, 75–84, 261–269

E-procurement, 344

Escrow management, 299–300

Ethical culture, 197

Ethical governance checklists, 317

Ethics policies, 150, 180, 234, 284, 372, 375, 376

Ethics programs/training, 10, 152, 155, 157, 214, 224, 250, 359

Ethics standards, 215, 353

Evidence, 35–42, 171, 345, 353

Exception-based reporting, 346

Expense accounts, 166

Expense reimbursements, 247

Expense reports, 47, 48, 51

External auditors, 210

Extortion, 175, 228–229, 231–232, 291–293, 371, 373

F

Falsified billing documents, 172

Falsified loan applications, 53–63

Fannie Mae Form 1006: Verification of Deposit, 63

Federal Bureau of Investigation (FBI), 69, 70, 110, 169, 170, 322, 366, 370–371

Federal employees, 149–157

Federal Reserve, 63

Federal Sentencing Guidelines, 72, 250

FedEx receipts, 17, 18

Fees, 142

Fictitious vendors, 18

Fidelity insurance, 330, 334. *See also* Insurance

Fieldwork, 147

Fifth Amendment, 7, 326

Film festival corruption case, 65–73

Financial Crimes Enforcement Network (FinCEN), 294, 295

Financial disclosure forms, 152, 157, 203

Financial statements, 142, 148, 276

Finders' fees, 10

501(c)(3) organizations, 27

Fixed-price contracts, 227

Foreign Corrupt Practices Act (FCPA), xii, 45, 49, 67, 69, 72–73, 222, 247–250

Forensic accounting/auditing, 15–16, 112, 170–173, 290–291, 374

Forgery, 82, 135, 136. *See also* Signatures, forged

Formal communication, 102

Fraud-awareness training, 367

Fraud Diamond, 289–290

Fraud hotlines, *see* Whistleblowers/whistleblower hotlines

Fraud Tree, 354

Fraud Triangle, 121

Front company, 18–19

G

Gambling debts, 40–41

Gender discrimination, 293

General ledger, 15

Gift cards, 179, 180, 182

Gifts/Gratuities, 5, 6, 48, 151–157, 168, 193, 196, 247, 248, 251, 290, 324, 336

Gossip, 102

Government contracts, 247–250

Government corruption, 23–33, 149–157, 199–207, 271–278

Government funds, *see* Public funds

Government retirement fund fraud, 271–278

Grand jury, 174

Grant fraud, 75–84, 324

Gratuities, *see* Gifts/Gratuities

Great Britain, 341–346

Green manufacturing, 245–252

H

Hardware-component buyer fraud, 107–113

Hazardous materials, 266–267

"Hip pocket" concept, 26, 28

Hiring procedures, 259

Historical evidence, 26, 32

Home repairs/renovations, as kickbacks, 151, 154–156, 173, 203, 347–351, 373, 375

Hospitality industry, 177–185

Hotels, 177–185

Hotlines, 84, 157, 175, 184, 280, 284, 346, 359, 374, 376

Housing construction fraud, 115–122

Hush money, 295

Hypotheses, for investigation, 188–189

I

Imports, 220

Incentive-based cultures, 62

Incentive compensation, 63

Income statements, 284

Income tax statements, 56

In-country agents, 99

Independent contractors, 281

India, 235–243, 271–278

Industrial conglomerates, 235–243

Inflated invoices, 331

Inflation, 310

Informal communication, 102

Information technology (IT), 345

Information technology (IT) audit software, 343

Information technology (IT) consultants, 227

Information technology (IT) departments/staff, 160, 161, 164, 222, 357–367

Inmate commissary fraud, 287–296

Inmates' "bill of rights," 288

Inspector general, 327

Insurance, 108, 111–113, 299–307, 330, 333, 334, 338, 374

Integrity, qualifications *vs.*, 242

Integrity rules, 316

Intermediary companies, 220–223

Internal auditors, 210, 307, 345, 373

Internal audits, 82, 83, 108, 118, 122, 175, 179, 188, 190, 211, 224, 227, 237, 313 314, 344

Internal controls, 14, 49, 83, 133, 167, 175, 187, 196, 207, 233, 248, 256, 257, 259, 282, 291, 316, 338, 345, 353, 359, 373, 375, 376

Internal controls department, 311, 312

Internal controls review, 247

Internal controls supervisor, 253, 258

Internal cost center, 360

Internal legal department, 215

Internal promotions, 179

Internal Revenue Service (IRS), 69–71, 172, 195

Internal Revenue Service Form 4506-T, 56, 58, 63

Inventory tracking, 3

Invested funds, 271–278

Investigative interviewing, 168

Investment certificates, 278

Invoices, 6, 15, 17, 19, 25–26, 49, 174, 180, 185, 188, 189, 192, 220–222, 227, 281–284, 331, 332, 334, 335, 337, 343–345, 349, 360–364, 372, 373

Invoice-review process, 361–365, 367

IRS, *see* Internal Revenue Service (IRS)

Islam, 103

J

Jail commissary fraud, 287–296

Japan, 159–168

Jewelry industry fraud, 279–285

Job cost code, 118

Job rotation, 317

Joint ventures, 159–168

K

Kickbacks. *See also* Bribery

automobile industry fraud, 212, 213

bank loan fraud, 133, 135–137

coffee company procurement fraud, 18, 19

drug evidence diversion case, 39–40, 42

engineering firm fraud, 48, 49

film festival bribery case, 65–73

Kickbacks. *See also* Bribery (*Continued*)
  Florida loan fraud, 53–63
  government contractor fraud, 157
  hardware-component buyer fraud, 108–111
  hotel supply kickback fraud, 177–185
  Indian manufacturing fraud, 235–243
  Indian retirement fund fraud, 271–278
  jail commissary fraud, 288, 290, 292, 294
  Japanese bid-rigging case, 168
  jewelry industry fraud, 282–284
  manufacturing fraud, 228
  manufacturing purchase management fraud, 194–197
  Mexican windmill company fraud, 248
  multinational manufacturing fraud, 219, 222–223
  Nigerian government employee fraud, 201, 204–205
  Ohio DOT procurement fraud, 5, 8–9
  Oklahoma environmental grant fraud, 81–82
  outsourcing procurement fraud, 312
  plastics industry fraud, 329–338
  public transportation construction fraud, 371–373, 375
  Romanian credit card fraud, 258
  state senate corruption case, 29, 32

L
Laptop computers, 241–242
Large Tax Payer (India), 143, 146
Leadership failures, 234
Ledgers, reconciliation problems with, 164
Legacy data systems, 359
Legal department, internal, 215
Licensing fraud, 85–94, 123–131
Lifestyle checks, 133, 242
Lines of credit, 256–258
Loan fraud, 31, 53–63, 134–136, 301–303
Loan officers, 54

Loan payments, 174
Lobbying, 324
Lumber sales, 116–120

M
Mail fraud, 174, 175, 366, 371, 373
Maintenance contracts/services, 1–11, 349
Management, 83, 84, 104–105, 112, 113, 120, 161, 177–178, 217–224, 351, 354
Management consulting, 160
Management information systems (MISs), 159–168
Managerial oversight, 196, 197, 289
Manufacturing, 159–168, 187–197, 217–234
Marketing directors, 209, 211
Markups, pass-through invoicing, 189, 190
Master chronology, 353
Materiality, 296
Mergers, 50–51
Mexico, 245–252
Middle Eastern engineering fraud case, 95–105
Mind-map template, 143
Mining, 169–176
Misappropriation of public funds, 23–33, 75–84, 275, 319–328
Money laundering, 40, 68, 69, 72, 206, 227, 366
Money orders, 39
Money trail, following, 201–203
Motive, 103, 121, 172, 289
Multicultural ethics, 97, 102–104, 167–168
Multidisciplinary teams (MDTs), 124–126, 129, 130
Multinational corporations, 43–51, 159–168, 217–224
Muslim cultures, 103

N
Native Americans, 261–269
Negative evidence, 273
Negligence, 306

Nepotism, 327
Nigeria, 199–207
No-bid contracts, 289
No-knock search warrants, 7
Noncompete clauses, 213
Nonprofit organizations, 26–29, 31, 319–328
Nonverbal communication, 168

O
Objectives, setting, 353
Obstruction of justice, 28
Occupational fraud, 183
Occupational Fraud Classification System, 354
Occupational Safety and Health Administration (OSHA), 265
Office supplies, 179–180
Official misconduct, 295
Off-market transactions, 273–274
Ohio Department of Transportation procurement case, 1–11
Oklahoma environmental grant fraud, 75–84
Operating budgets, 211
Operating systems, access to, 346
Opportunity (Fraud Triangle element), 103, 121, 289, 290
Organization of Economic Co-operation and Development (OECD), 51
Outsourcing, 309–317
Overbillings/overcharges, 170–174, 330–338
Overpayment, 111–112
Overtime fraud, 291–296

P
Padding, 212
Painting companies, 348–350, 372
Paper files, 190
Parallel imports, 219
Partnerships, 116, 117
Pass-through invoicing, 189
Payroll departments, 296
Plastics industry, 329–338
Plea bargaining, 30–33, 366

Police corruption, 35–42
Police detectives, 333
Political corruption, 23–33, 319–324
    See also Government corruption
Pollution remediation grants, 75–84
Ponzi schemes, 58–59, 61–62, 276
Postal money orders, 39
Preferred contractors, 349
Preferred suppliers, 343
Pressure (Fraud Triangle factor), 121
Price inflation, 331
Price lists, 331–332, 334, 335, 338
Pricing strategies, 212
Printing companies, 330–338, 343–345
Prison commissary fraud, 287–296
Private investigators, 108, 109, 255
Private lenders, 301–303
Process governance checklists, 317
Procurement contracts, 371
Procurement departments, 362
Procurement fraud, 1–11, 160, 167, 206–207, 236, 291, 309–317, 341–346, 349, 373–374
Procurement managers, 165
Procurement policies, 316
Professional accounting body (PAB), 146
Profit margins, 13, 282
Project costs, 118
Project executives, 359–360
Project management/managers, 166, 236–237, 370
Promissory notes, 136
Proof of performance, 224
Proxy accounts, 201
Public assistance organizations, 319–328
Public funds, 23–33, 75–84, 319–328
Public relations officer, 135
Public transportation construction fraud, 369–376
Punitive termination warning, 102
Purchase orders, 121–122, 170, 183, 268, 290, 291, 344
Purchase tickets, 119
Purchasing, 1–11, 25–26, 122, 226, 237
Purchasing controls, 346

Purchasing cycle, 196
Purchasing departments, 184–185
Purchasing directors, 190
Purchasing fraud, 1–11, 13–21, 23–33
Purchasing kickbacks, 329–338
Purchasing managers, 187–197, 237, 238

Q
Qualifications, integrity v., 242
Quid pro quo, 32, 195
Quotes, 5, 6, 9, 11, 82

R
Rationalization (Fraud Triangle element), 121, 289
Real estate, 24, 201–202, 299–307
Rebate programs, 75–84
Receipts, 153, 222, 338
Receiving departments, 17, 18, 122
Receiving logs, 18
Reconciliation, 142, 164
Records, destruction of, 321–322
Records reviews, 99, 268
Reference checks, 242
Regional Transportation District (RTD; Denver, Colorado), 369–376
Reimbursements, 247, 250, 335
Relationship management, 346
Relatives, as vendors, 315
Repair orders, 280–284
Repeat orders, 335
Reporting mechanisms, 284
Reserve Bank of India (RBI), 273–274
Restaurant licensing, 123–131
Restitution, 72, 175, 296, 345, 373, 374
Retailers, 347–354
Reticular activating system (RAS), 354
Retirement fund fraud, 271–278
Rewards, for reporting fraud, 284
Rigging of bids, *see* Bid collusion/rigging
Risk assessments, 296
Risk-based cultures, 62
Romania, 253–259
Rotation of employees/executives, 215

S
Safe Harbor provision (Bank Secrecy Act), 295
Sales agents, 116, 246, 247, 279–285, 335
Sales taxes, 143, 145
Sarbanes-Oxley Act (SOX), 45, 46
School asbestos remediation fraud, 261–269
Scope of investigation, limiting, 175
S corporations, 68
Search warrants, 7, 29–30, 32, 38, 39, 69, 273, 305, 333, 350
Securities and Exchange Commission (SEC), xii
Securities certificates, 272, 274
Securities fraud, 271–278
Security guards, 122
Segregation of duties, 10
Self-motivation, 214–215
Sentencing, 174
Serious Fraud Office, U.K. (SFO), 345
Sharia, 103
Shell companies, 29, 67, 125, 201, 205, 220, 276
Siemens bribery scandal, xii–xiii
Signatures, forged, 81, 135, 136
Silent partners, 372
Site supervision, 116
Skepticism, 20, 147
Slush funds, 305
Socializing with vendors, 166, 211
Social media websites, 284
Social networks, 211
Social services, 319–328
Software, 300, 307, 321
Sole-source construction contracts, 149, 151
Source (loan referrals), 57
Special auditors, 133–134
"Special payments," 219
Specialty materials, 159–168
Sports tickets, 290
Spot checks, 124
Spreadsheets, 218–219
Staff reductions, 177, 190, 196
State funds, 25–26

Statutory auditors, 142, 147
Steering of contracts, 152
Stock investments, 240, 242
Stock market, 237
Subcontracting, 9, 10, 67, 169, 189, 227, 372
Subsidiaries, 209–215, 220
Subsuppliers, 193
Succession planning, 178
Summary cost reports, 117
Supervisors, 177, 288
Supervisory fraud, 209–215
Suppliers, *see* Vendors
Supporting documents, 25, 47, 48, 58, 63, 148, 188, 192–193, 196, 221
Surveillance systems, 14–15, 122

T
Tally sheets, 38
Tanzania, 141–148
Taxes, on withdrawals for bribes, 172
Tax evasion, 69, 72, 143, 218
Tax fraud, 141–148, 218–220, 223
Tax ID numbers, 3, 11
Taxi license fraud, 85–94
Tax officials, 144–145
Tax returns, 55–57, 59, 61, 63, 71, 110
Teamwork, 147–148
Telecommunications company fraud, 357–367
Temporary chauffeur's license, 87, 88, 90–93
Theft allowances, 117–118
Third-party contractors, 281, 284, 332
Third-party sales agents, 245–252
Third-party vendors, 220, 222
Tickets, as bribes, 290
Timber/hardware procurement fraud case, 341–346
Time sheets, 365
Time stamps, 363
Title history examinations, 301, 305
Title insurance fraud, 299–307
Town-hall meetings, 105

Tracing of cash, 249
Tracking sheets, 336
Transfer vouchers, 277
Transparency, 97
Travel costs, reimbursements of, 247, 250
Trial balance, 142

U
Unannounced audits, 343–344
Underwriting, 57–58, 301, 303
U.S. Department of Labor, 321, 327
U.S. Department of Treasury, 294
U.S. Postal Inspection Service, 39

V
Value added tax (VAT), 144, 220
Vendors, 3, 4, 6–7, 47, 97–98, 110, 166, 169, 170, 179–182, 185, 190, 192, 209–215, 226, 228, 233, 236, 237, 242, 284, 288, 290, 291, 294, 296, 311–312, 314, 315, 336, 343, 360, 361
Vendor audit, 212, 215, 314
Vendor background checks, 376
Vendor contracts, reviewing, 215
Vendor lists, 367
Vendor management systems, 113
"Vendor-providers," 97–99
Video surveillance, 294

W
Warehouses, 202
Watch lists, 374, 376
Weapons possession, 41
Web design, 67
Whistleblowers/whistleblower hotlines, 50, 113, 131, 175, 197, 207, 251, 284, 325, 327, 346, 359, 67, 374, 375
Windmills, 245–252
Wire transfers, 32, 68, 69, 71, 110, 249
Witnesses, development of,
Witness evidence, 26
Witness intimidation, 7